Also by Jane Stern
TRUCKER: A Portrait of the Last American Cowboy

Also by Jane and Michael Stern
AMAZING AMERICA

ROADFOOD

ROAD

Random House / David Obst Books
New York

FOOD

JANE AND MICHAEL
STERN

Copyright © 1977, 1978 by Jane and Michael Stern
All rights reserved under International and Pan-American Copyright
Conventions.
Published in the United States by Random House, Inc., New York, and
simultaneously
in Canada by Random House of Canada Limited, Toronto.

Library of Congress Cataloging in Publication Data

Stern, Jane.
Roadfood.

Includes index.
1. Restaurants, lunch rooms, etc.—United States—
Directories. I. Stern, Michael, 1946– joint
author. II. Title.
TX907.S73   1978   647′.9573   77–90314
ISBN 0–394–73508–0

Manufactured in the United States of America
4 6 8 9 7 5

TO NORMA AND DICKIE
Wish you were here

ACKNOWLEDGMENTS

It was somewhere in the vast Nevada desert that the enormousness of this project struck us. We looked at the map, which placed the distance between one tiny town and the next at around a hundred miles, and we looked back to our car's odometer, which was threatening to spin its way back around to zero. America is one huge expanse of land, and because of the time it takes to cross it traveling on backroads, we depended on some friends to help point the way. Bruce Margolius, part-time cowboy and gonzo journalist, habitué of Montana's best greasy spoons and all-night truckstops, provided us with highway-honed wit and his recommendations in the mountain states. John Stamets an old friend, and veteran hitchhiker, staked out some of the best cafés in the Pacific Northwest. Harry and Florence Stern, experienced travelers and passionate eaters in their own right, helped us plan our routes, and between trips provided real home cooking to balance the kind served on the road. We offer a special thanks to Michael Rudell for his counsel and support when the going got tough, and to David Obst for his confidence in and enthusiasm for the book. Kathy Matthews, our editor, who mentally hit the road with us during *Trucker,* vicariously lent us her taste buds and appetite for *Roadfood,* and consistently provided sure relief for periodic fits of mental indigestion. We thank her for her wit and guidance over the long haul.

CONTENTS

ROADFOOD

INTRODUCTION

Roadfood is the story of our love affair with American food. It started while riding cross country for three years with truck drivers, the mythical culture heros whose lives we documented in *Trucker: A Portrait of the Last American Cowboy.* These gearjammers were supposed to know all the good places to eat; and, in fact, some of them did. Veteran wildcatters led us away from portion-controlled truckstops on the interstates and introduced us to small-town catfish fries, backwoods chili parlors, seaside lobster pounds, and their favorite stops for biscuits and "red-eye" gravy. It became clear that travelers *do* have an alternative. It *is* possible to escape the homogenized cuisine that lines the highways and makes eating in Arizona indistinguishable from eating in Maine. After *Trucker* we fine-tooth-combed the country for the best food around; food easily accessible to the traveler; inexpensive food; food cooked by and eaten alongside a region's people.

Roadfood is the name we gave to the cooking we found in the small cafés, truckstops, roadside stands, and tearooms of America. Chain restaurants and convenience foods have weighed the odds against it. It takes time to cook good food; and it takes skill, sometimes skills that are passed on from generation to generation. The varieties of edible national treasures are as diverse as the country itself: Johnny cakes from New England, Tigua Indian chili from El Paso, sticky-sweet shoo-fly pie from Pennsylvania Dutch country—even the all-American hamburger from the lunch counter where it was invented in New Haven, Connecticut.

Roadfood is geared to the pockets of the workingman, the farmer, and the rural family who wouldn't eat in a fancy continental restaurant. A full meal at any restaurant in this book costs under $5, usually much less than that. A few exceptions to this rule go over our $5 limit, but are still much less expensive than most eateries, and are roadfood landmarks that no traveler ought to miss. In each of the few cases where you can expect to spend more than $5 for a meal, we've indicated the higher price range in the text for that restaurant. For the sake of travelers, our choices are convenient to major highways. We hope that you will find our choices to be as we describe them, although it is inevitable that some restaurants will change in style, decor, quality of food, and prices. We hope that any changes you encounter will be for the better.

The use of stars is an attempt to rate the relative excellence of the food. But sometimes we take into consideration other attributes like unusual decor or irresistible charm. Local eccentricities can be noteworthy too. Food is of course the focus of our attention, and a "four star restaurant" is always one that serves the best possible meals around.

★

One star indicates unusual atmosphere
or a few good specialties on an otherwise mediocre menu.

★★

Two stars means good food; a nice, reliable place to stop.

★★★

Three stars means very good food;
a great place to stop; some superlative specialties.

★★★★

A four-star restaurant is a roadfood landmark,
a singular experience worth a trip for its very special food.

Some disparage the notion of "American cuisine." It is often thought that the best American food hasn't the breeding or sophistication to rival its *haute* European competition. It does however have a heritage and a character all its own. Often it is an expression of regional pride or a reflection of the ethnic melting pot. In Texas it might be the hidden-away bar b que pit in the back room of a general store where an elderly "pitmaster" smokes the best hot links in the state; in the Louisiana bayous, a roadside restaurant where the specialty is cajun crawfish; or in Colorado, a sale barn café where cattlemen gather for sizzling steaks after a livestock auction.

Roadfood is a mirror of our country's soul and a celebration of its character. What makes this book possible is that the very best American cooking is often the cheapest in town, readily enjoyed without a reservation or tie and jacket. Finding and eating this food is a way to see and taste the essence of America. Roadfooding, which began as a sideline while traveling, has become for us the only way to go.

A NOTE ON THE FAIRS AND FESTIVALS

Following each state's roadfood eateries, there is a list of festivals that celebrate American food. Most are held around harvest times, when the fruit, vegetables, berries, fish, or whatever is at full glory. Many of the festivals offer food that is nearly impossible to find anywhere else. The ramp, for instance, billed as "the world's sweetest tasting, worst smelling plant," is too odoriferous to be served in restaurants. But ramp lovers congregate every April in Cosby, Tennessee, to savor their offensive and delicious favorite. Similarly, rattlesnake bar b ques and wild burro roasts are opportunities to sample oddities that are native to a particular region, but never appear on restaurant menus. Of course, not all festivals are so exotic. Raspberry celebrations, peach or peanut gatherings, or the chitlin strut can be simply enthusiastic ways for folks to fill up on their personal favorites—usually at the lowest possible prices. Before heading for one of these festivals, you should confirm the exact date and location by contacting the state department of tourism or local chamber of commerce.

New England

MAINE

Skowhegan
Errol • Farmington •
Rumford • Sandy Point • Ellsworth
• Trenton
Lunenburg • Bar Harbor
St. Johnsbury • Shelburne
Marshfield • Sugar Hill Waldoboro
Damariscota • Thomaston
VERMONT Woodstock Freeport • New Harbor
Fairlee • Conway
Rutland • Plymouth • Moultonboro Portland
Bridgewater
NEW Cape Porpoise
Weston • HAMPSHIRE Ogunquit
Portsmouth •

Rowley
Ipswich •
Essex

MASSACHUSETTS
Granby • Worcester

Plymouth
Storrs • Wareham Buzzards Bay
CONNECTICUT Providence • Swansea
New Haven • New Bedford
Milford • Mystic • Narragansett
West Haven Madison RHODE
Norwalk Guilford ISLAND
Rowayton

Rehoboth •

CONNECTICUT

GUILFORD

★★ THE PLACE

891 Boston Post Road
MID–MAY–SEPT: MON–FRI 5 PM–11 PM / SAT & SUN 1 PM–11 PM,
WEATHER PERMITTING

When we first ate at The Place it was called Whitey's and it was located on sleepy, rural Route 1 in the bucolic New England town of Guilford. Since that time Guilford has been gradually transformed into a bedroom suburb of New Haven, sprouting the commuter traffic, shopping centers, and fast-food restaurants that accompany planned country living. While Whitey's used to look out upon an untamed green meadow, The Place now offers a view of families loading up their station wagons at the Finast or Mammoth Mart.

Undaunted in the midst of progress, The Place, except for the name change, has remained the same. Whitey himself is gone—a fact bemoaned by regular customers who miss his steady stream of wisecracks and ethnic jokes. At The Place, Whitey's colorful presence has been succeeded by a sober and efficient team of young men and women in sneakers and aprons who hustle back and forth between the open wood pit and the outdoor tables. There has been no remodeling or renovation in the last ten years; The Place is still a small shack by the side of the road. The eating area is still a cleared meadow out back, with tree stumps for chairs, construction spools for tables, and millions of chipped clam shells for a floor. Most of the stumps are situated so that you can face away from the highway and the shopping center, peruse the menu—which is a wood plank hung on a nearby tree—and watch your seafood cook over the long wood pit.

Many customers bring their own wine and salad. The Place usually has a radio playing softly. Between the radio, the sound of the crackling wood, the other picnickers, and your wine, you can just about forget about the progress that runs riot across the highway.

The menu at The Place is limited and rather expensive for an eat-in-the-rough style restaurant. The roast clam special is the most popular dish. It's a dozen littlenecks cooked in the shell, then split open and broiled for a few minutes more with hot sauce on top. Steamers, broiled in their own juices with plenty of butter, are reasonably priced. But a dozen small broiled shrimp seem hardly worth The Place's price. Last time we looked, The Place's lobster was cheap by sit-down restaurant standards—rather small, but deliciously charged with the wood smoke flavor from below. Whatever seafood you choose, do not miss the corn. It's roasted in the husk, stripped, and brushed with butter.

In spite of the energetic waiters and waitresses here, the service is slow, as everything is put on the fire when you order it. But The Place is a good spot to linger as you watch your clams slowly roast. The smoke from the pit keeps the bugs away, and if you forget to bring enough wine, you can always emerge from the smoky oasis and dash to the liquor store in the shopping center across the street.

MADISON

★★ CLAM CASTLE
1324 Boston Post Road
MAY–OCT: DAILY 10 AM–2 AM

Clam Castle was once a four-star clam emporium, where, under the sign of a glamourous crab wearing Hollywood-style sunglasses, the yacht and dingy crowd in Madison gathered for the plumpest-bellied fried clams around.

Clam Castle, much to our dismay, has changed management over the last year, and while the ugly white shack has not changed a hair, the famous clam chowder has been massacred. It's no use to lament what was, but the tired white soup in a Dixie cup is a pale memory of the clam-clotted oregano-scented stew of yesteryear. Now, for this blasphemy alone it would seem imperative to cross Clam Castle off the list, but we found that there were a number of items that have maintained the high standards of the past.

The saying around the Connecticut shoreline is "Guilford for Class, and Madison for Clams," and indeed the clams served fried with or without bellies at Clam Castle are outstanding. The bellied clams are prepared with only the freshest of oils and the best crumbs. The clam strips are for those who don't relish the goo. They still retain a real ocean flavor, and bear no resemblance to the galvanized strings dredged out of the deep freeze and served elsewhere in the name of "clam." Johnny, of Johnny's Miniature Golf across the street, was eating a double order at the table next to us. "Dis guy knows what he's doin'," Johnny confided about the new owner. "He's a jerk to ruin the soup, but the clams are still good." Johnny told us about the poor-boy heroes that the new owner started serving. As he talked, one appeared at the take-out counter. It was a length of French bread, scooped out, sprinkled with olive oil and loaded with rare roast beef, peppers, and onions. Clam Castle will sell you a "poor-boy" stuffed with clams, crabmeat, shrimp, or scallops. We can't figure out how a yard of seafood can sell for so little, but we won't dispute the bargain.

"Did ya taste the langostino?" Johnny asked as he neared the end of his double order of clams and belched mightily. We hadn't, nor were we sure what langostino was. We ordered a "lango" on a roll and found it to be a lot like lobster. The flesh was pink like shrimp but with a subtler taste.

Clam Castle, like all the outdoor seafood joints on the shoreline, is seasonal. It's the only place that lets you sit outside under a patch of lovely trees, with a scenic view of the back of an ancient mobile home. There are six wooden picnic benches, a scrawly menu written in a psychopathic script, and as we mentioned, the Jayne Mansfield of seafood logos: the glamorous crab in sunglasses. Chances are good that Johnny will be there to aid and advise you in your selection. You will know him by his bumper sticker: "Miniature Golfers do it better."

MILFORD

★THE MAYFLOWER DINER
Exit 40 off I-95 (203) 878-7345
ALWAYS OPEN

At mealtimes the parking lot of the Mayflower Diner is packed with trucks. For years this place has been a favorite of gearjammers, who come for the strong coffee and the two-fisted cooking that can keep a person well fueled all the way back to "the clean side." The clean side is a trucker's term for any place south or west of "the dirty side," which is the New York–New Jersey–Connecticut bottleneck. Once on the dirty side, most truckers spend their time bitching and griping about how much better life is back in Selma, Little Rock, or Biloxi.

The counters and booths at Mayflower are prime territory for bitching and pining away. Unlike the big oil company truckstops that separate the professional truckers from the "four wheelers," Mayflower allows the two to mix, affording one a great opportunity to eavesdrop on conversations about what life is like on the long, endless road. Recently the diner underwent renovation, changing from an archetypal chrome-and-Formica beanery into what looks like a cross between a railroad car and a greenhouse. There are stylistic *hommages* to diners of old in the applied chrome facade and the rounded roof, but the inside is airy and hardly conjures up memories of the traditional roadside hash house.

The food at Mayflower has remained the same, and for truckstop food, it's pretty good. There are about nine daily specials, and if it's delicate cooking you're after, don't come here. What you get are "blue plates" overflowing with link sausages, mashed spuds and gravy, whole half chickens, or chops that cost you little more than a couple or three gallons of diesel fuel. Mayflower is famous for its soups that seem more like stews, a bowl selling for less than a dollar. The menu is illustrated with drawings of trucks, apparently intended to stimulate the gearjammer's appetite.

The diner is adjacent to the Mayflower Truck Complex. After you eat, take a leisurely stroll through the truckers' store and you can choose from a vast array of Mack bulldog pendants, banners, ash trays, and beach towels. There is also a barbershop on the premises with one of the few barbers in the east who can still sculpt a decent ducktail, a flattop with fenders or boxcar sides, and a Vitalis wave that molds perfectly to the interior dimensions of a cowboy hat.

★★THE OLYMPIC DINER
1440 Boston Post Road (203) 878–6192
ALWAYS OPEN

We appreciate The Olympic's enthusiasm. It is a flagship among the new fleet of Hellenic diners. Their sixteen-by-twenty inch menu and listing of at least twenty-five specials every day is a welcome relief from the "Meat and Vegetables" listed anonymously on the old breed of diners' menus. But we suggest to the ambitious proprietors of The Olympic that they take a lesson from the Bauhaus—that "less is more." To offer well over fifty entrées every day is asking for trouble. The miracle of The Olympic is that so much of what they offer is good.

Avoid the Four Seasons-style exotica like eggs a la russe and poached sole in oyster wine sauce. These dishes are like going to a

Georgia roadhouse and hearing Jerry Lee Lewis attempt a Mozart sonata. The best dishes here are the basic ones. The roast beef sandwich is an exquisite piece of rare meat drenched with gravy, elevated by two silly pieces of Wonder bread, sharing space with the world's best pickled beets and velvety mashed potatoes, running with butter. Likewise, the raisin-studded creamy rice pudding might not make Chef Stockli cry into his Tornedos de boeuf, but these two dishes make us very happy.

The Olympic heads its daily menu with several authentic Greek dishes—usually half the price and twice as large as what you get in all but the very best Greek restaurants. The moussaka is an Olympian dish, layered over four inches high with ground lamb, noodles, and a finely spiced sauce. Some of our other favorites are the pan-ethnic offerings of blintzes (which come with at least a half-pint of sour cream), thick Irish stew with glazed carrots, avgolomeno soup (a tart Greek lemon and egg mixture), and, of course, the Dionysian breakfasts of corned beef hash, eggs, toast, and potatoes.

Warning: Avoid the pastries. Like pop artist Wayne Thiebaud's paintings of baked goods, The Olympic's pies and cakes look great. Giant swirls of stuccolike frosting, layed on with a trowl; pies with goop six inches thick on top, and cakes twice that. If looking were eating, these beauties would rate A-plus for their new dimensions in hautest cuisine. But better leave these conceptual sweets to the uninformed. THEY ARE HORRENDOUS. The banana cream could double as hardened rapid shave; the layer cake tasted of acrid chemicals; another pastry, thankfully, had no taste.

The exuberant overreach that makes breakfast and lunch at The Olympic so exhilarating turns dinner here into a histrionic letdown. A liquor license and velveteen curtains only remind you that The Olympic is a mere diner gone berserk, a place that in the past would have been called "Joe's" or "Acme" now way out of its league. What's tolerable—even impressive—during daylight hours turns tacky when the sun goes down.

MYSTIC

★★THE COVE
Route 1 (203) 536–0061
MAY–LABOR DAY: DAILY 11 AM–8 PM

All rites and rituals connected with fishing and ships have been properly enshrined in the Sea Coast Museum at Mystic Seaport one mile from The Cove. For anyone who wants to wallow in sea lore, Mystic is the place, but for those who only have to look at a masted schooner to think of fried fish, the Mystic port is a disappointment. Since sightseers are a captive audience once they pay their admission to the exhibits, the folks who run the Seaport take too many shortcuts with the overpriced food served within. We suggest that when you are finished with the scrimshaw exhibits and whaling ships, you save your appetite and head for The Cove, perched a mile away on a grassy hill.

There are a few other seafood stands and sitdown places nearby, but their limpid meals have kept us coming back to The Cove. It is a pretty blue and white building with beach umbrellas to sit under outside. Orders are placed at a window leading to the kitchen, and your number is called when the fish is ready. The choices are limited to the more common varieties of seafood. Fish and chips, scallops, shrimp, sole, and clams all come sided with French fries and cole slaw.

For an appetizer, try the bucket of steamer clams, fragrant and buttery, swimming in a rich broth that can be drunk after the clams are eaten. While you wait for your order, walk to the attached fish store and browse at the extensive assortment of fish for sale. It is hard to resist buying an assortment of some of the more unusual seafoods to take home. Unfortunately, no amount of cajoling and wheedling will get the fish store man to walk next door and toss one of his fileted exotics into the deep fryer for you. The store and the restaurant operate independently.

The Cove is a bustling place during the summer months, so expect to wait twenty minutes for your order to be cooked. The wait at the Mystic Seaport restaurant is only five minutes less, and the food nowhere as good as that served at The Cove.

NEW HAVEN

★★★ LOUIS LUNCH

261 Crown Street (203) 562–5507
MON–FRI 9 AM–5:30 PM

Call it Fun on a Bun, or Whopper, or Big Boy, or Triple Decker Monster Burger; the hamburger has no contenders as the most popular food in America. It is a common denominator between the Navajos of Tuba City, the denizens of "21," and the old salts of Bar Harbor. Louis Lunch is where it was invented.

Seventy-seven years ago, Louis Lassen, in the best tradition of New England thriftiness, ground up leftover steak, and shaped the ground meat into little square patties, grilled them and served them on toast. People loved Louis' improvisation so much that the "hamburger" eventually took over his lunchtime menu. His original lunch wagon parked in downtown New Haven was exchanged for a small brick building with a counter and stools. The dish actually had no name until some rowdy sailors from Hamburg named the meat on a bun after themselves years later.

In 1967, New Haven declared Louis Lunch a landmark, and although the tiny brick restaurant has been moved by the hamburger-conscious historical society to make room for a parking lot, the hamburgers are still exactly as they were served 77 years ago. The original hamburger "a la Louis" is a patty of coarsely ground steak, broiled vertically in the ancient stoves ("So the grease drips away," Louis III explains), and served on toast, with options of cheese, bermuda onion or tomato. We will leave it to Popeye's friend Wimpy to determine the world's best variation of this basic formula. Our personal hall of fame would include Winstead's of Kansas City, the earnest, unforgettable "College Educated" burger from Prexy's, Steak in Shake's hamburgers all over the Midwest, and of course the elemental burger served at Louis Lunch.

The worst thing about Louis is the seats. They resemble old-fashioned school desk seats—the type that had an inkwell to dip braids into. They are cramped, and hardly leave room on their little "tables" for more than one burger. These seats line the walls, and there is still an ancient initial-carved counter to eat at. Louis has even added some space—but it is still miniscule, jammed to the rafters at lunchtime.

Dining at Louis Lunch is one of the best ways we know of appreciating history. Louis' small brick building most resembles a working museum, for our money far more interesting than the Smithsonian. Of course, we're partial to edible exhibits.

★★★PEPE'S PIZZA
157 Wooster Street (203) 865–5762
MON, WED, THURS 4 PM–11 PM / FRI & SAT 11:30 AM–1 PM
SUN 2:30 PM–11 PM / CLOSED TUES

Pizza was a dish we hesitated to include in *Roadfood*. For one thing, there is nothing near a consensus on what a good one ought to be—dry, greasy, tomato-topped, 'round the world, cooked in a pan or on a tin, sliced like a pie or pound cake. The permutations are infinite, from the stewlike Chicago variety to the majestic yardwide pies sold by the slice all over New York. Pizza deserves its own book, and since we wanted to focus more here on foods that reflect regional taste and tradition, we intended to pass by pizza. But Connecticut roadfood without Wooster Square is like New Orleans without the gumbo. Nightmare visions of friends doomed to a life of pasteboard crusts and sour tomato toppings would haunt us if we left out the rare and wonderful pizzas prepared at Pepe's and two other parlors along a single block on Wooster Street.

Our apologia for this place is historical—Pepe invented the Wooster Square pizza. While there is no documented proof of this landmark event in roadfood history in the city archives, it is a fact that everything after a Pepe pie seems a pale imitation of the grand and original design. There is a magnificent depiction of what we assume is THE moment of inspiration up on the walls of Pepe's parlor. It is an oil painting of Pepe overlooking the bay of Naples, painted in a primitive style that makes The Creator of Pizza loom as large as the S.S. *Michelangelo.*

We know this painting well, because we have passed hours in Pepe's booths contemplating it. It's usually crowded at Pepe's, but even when the place is empty, the service is unbearably slow. Perhaps it is a deliberate effort to encourage the patrons to drink a second or third quart of coke, or another pitcher of beer; perhaps Pepe's is weary after thirty years of quoting pizza prices to Yalies; some of the slowness is surely due to Pepe's unique method of preparing the pizza.

While you wait, we recommend watching the men in the kitchen perform the rites of the stone oven pie. First they pound the dough into an oval and slide it onto their long-handled wood shovels for the application of your chosen ingredients. Ready for the oven, the shovel is lifted mightily, the cast-iron door opens, and the pizza is placed deep inside the brick inferno to cook slowly over the coals. What emerges twenty to thirty minutes later is a huge, oily affair, served on wax paper in a pan. The crust is thin and ashy from the coals, and the ingredients have merged into something that really looks like a pie. (An urgent note of warning—every ingredient on a Pepe pie is extra, *including* the cheese. So be sure to order mozzarella as an ingredient, or you'll get merely tomato and crust.) The greasiness of this mighty pie is not to be underestimated. When you are through with it, you will notice that there is a pool of oil at the bottom of the pan, and the wax paper that once sat under the pie has simply disintegrated.

For the committed carboholic, Pepe's pizza pie is an experience not to be duplicated anywhere beyond Wooster Street. Even a medium pie will leave two veteran pizza-philiacs in a satisfied stupor.

NORWALK

★★THE FAMILY DINER
71 Main Street (203) 838–6864
ALWAYS OPEN EXCEPT 7 PM SAT–7 AM SUN

As roadfood "experts" we shamefacedly admit to having lived near the Family Diner for years and to having passed it dozens of times while searching for some decent food. It looks like the most typical silver diner you could find. It's clean-looking, but here in downtown Norwalk we figured it for a sure greasy spoon.

We got our comeuppance when the local paper printed a little article about the Family Diner that told all about its proprietors, the Blums, and the real Jewish food (like mama used to make) they serve here. They have had a diner in this same spot for twenty-six years, since they came to America from Czechoslovakia.

The diner presents a standard American menu on which is clipped a mimeographed sheet listing the Jewish specialties—all at low, low diner prices. What the Blums don't make here in the diner kitchen is made at home in Mrs. Blum's own kosher kitchen. The matzoh balls are made there, as is the apple cake (with apples from their own trees). The specialties often include homemade gefüllte fish, cheese blintzes wrapped in a crispy dough and fried almost greaselessly, fresh chopped liver, cold borscht served with boiled potato and sour cream, and a pastrami special worthy of the best New York deli.

There are usually "surprises" on the Blums's menu. As in the most posh exclusive restaurants, "regulars" are treated to little extras from the kitchen—perhaps a piece of noodle kugel or honey cake. If you call in advance, Mrs. Blum will go out of her way to prepare a favorite cake, or matzoh brei (a scrambled-egg dish made with bits of matzoh), or kasha varneshka (a barley and mushroom casserole with bow-tie noodles).

But even if you are not a regular, you will be treated like one once you order a kitchen specialty. Mrs. Blum admits to being a real "Yiddishe mama," who likes nothing better than to see people enjoy her food. Order the blintzes or potato pancakes, and it's likely she will soon appear at your table to make sure the food is to your liking. Eat well, and you will become one of her pets and a recipient of a special treat. Now that we have found the Family Diner, we plan to become two of the most familiar faces at the table.

ROWAYTON

★CAPTAIN HENRY'S OYSTER BAR
Rowayton Avenue (Logan Place)
MON–FRI 7 AM–8 PM, SAT–SUN 8 AM–8 PM

As we sat at Captain Henry's munching his delicious fried clams, two captains of industry discussed high finance at the table to our right. It was their day for an afternoon cruise on the yacht one of them had anchored in Rowayton Harbor. At the table to our left sat two other captains, the kind whose weathered looks identify them with the sea, discussing how the bluefish were running. Rowayton, situated as it is amidst both the commuting gold coast and the working seacoast, is a nautical melting pot for both worlds. Captain Henry's Oyster Bar is at the end of Rowayton's main street, a place often compared for its visual charms to Cape Cod. The restaurant is a tiny one-room affair, up a wooden flight of steps. Through the windows you look out on the harbor, at yachts and fishing boats.

Aside from the good fried clams we recommend Henry's lobster salad, surprisingly long on lobster and low in price. There are also fried scallops, filet of fish, tuna, shrimp and oysters. Dinners come with French fries and cole slaw, and there is a refrigerator case along one wall that offers cold cans of soda on a "help yourself" basis.

Captain Henry's has been part of the Rowayton Harbor scene for a long time. It is a colorful, informal place for a quick lunch or a leisurely look over the harbor. It is only a short detour off the highway.

STORRS

★★ THE ALTNAVEIGH RESTAURANT
Route 195 (203) 429–4490
TUES–FRI 11:30 AM–3 PM, 5 PM–9 PM, SAT & SUN 11:30 AM–8 PM

The Altnaveigh restaurant is a pleasant exception to the rule of college-town food. Storrs is the home of the University of Connecticut, and its basic cuisine consists of college cafeteria muck, a few pizza parlors, fast-food stands, and an expensive steak house for visiting parents. And then there is the Altnaveigh, a true country restaurant that reflects the basic farmy character of the huge Storrs School of Agriculture.

It is easy to miss the Altnaveigh, because there are no Golden Arches or neon arrows on this still country-pure strip of Route 195. It looks very much like a farmer's home. The inside is divided into small dining rooms, all wallpapered with old Sears Roebuck-style patterns. Each room has a fireplace to reinforce the comfy charm of the restaurant.

"Altnaveigh" is Gaelic for "high on the hill," and the Irish touch is well-represented in the cuisine. There is always corned beef on the menu, for lunch or dinner. On Saint Patrick's Day it is hard to get a table here. The beef is cooked New England style—boiled, and accompanied by boiled potatoes, brussel sprouts, and carrots. The vegetables, when seasonably possible, are fresh.

Corned beef is a New England tradition, a reminder of the days when the transatlantic ferry steamed regularly from Cape Elizabeth, Maine, to Galway Bay, Ireland. Some even say that eating the beef accounts for the traditionally remote character of some Northerners. It was christened "corned beef" in Pilgrim days, because it was soaked in saltpeter, obtained from "corns" or rifle shells. The Altnaveigh beef, while spared the saltpeter, still has the vibrant salty flavor of its historical ancestors.

The other good choice here is turkey, a full meal consisting of thick gumbo soup, fresh rolls, salad, and a choice of pie in addition to the turkey, potatoes, and stuffing. The pies are made in the Altnaveigh's kitchen and they are locally famous for a wonderful deep-dish apple.

Connecticut is apple country, and during the fall harvest, the pies are worth a special trip. Other pies are seasonal too. Fruit in summer, squash and pumpkin in the cooler months. In the late fall, after apple season, the suet-rich mince pie is a perfect complement to the snow-covered barns outside and the toasty fireplace near your table.

WEST HAVEN

★★ JIMMIE'S OF SAVIN ROCK
5 Rock Drive (203) 934–3213
SUN–THURS 11 AM–11 PM / FRI & SAT 11 AM–1 PM

On this spot the split weiner was invented and the lobster roll first took shape. Savin Rock has seen a remarkable evolution over the years. In the 1930s it was Connecticut's Palisades Park, a resort-amusement area filled with fun houses, rides and candy stands. The neighborhood has changed from all white to black, to integrated, to all white again. Boxy condominiums have replaced the house of horrors, and the hot-dog stands have been converted to seaside dining establishments. But the ghost of "the famous Savin Rock split wiener" still haunts the Jimmie's of today, and can be found on the menu of this sanitary restaurant as a "famous platter."

As we remembered it in the 1960s, Jimmie's was strictly a takeout place. Sure, there was a dining room inside for the weirdos who preferred to eat off of plates with utensils, but the sensible way to do Jimmie's went something like this: drive in, wait in line, memorize your order, then when it's your turn, blurt it out as fast as humanly possible. In a flash it is ready and the man is screaming at you for your money. You fumble with your change, get pushed out of line, and hustle back to the car with your pints of shrimp, onion rings, clams, oysters, buttered lobster rolls, and, of course, split wieners. As you eat, you throw your garbage out your car window—either by the piece or in a final single huge toss. Everybody used to do it this way, from teen-agers to Yale professors. Use of a garbage can would have been shockingly effete. Part of the floor show here were the seagulls—thousands of them hopping between and on top of cars, flying away with the remnants of peoples' dinners. Believe it or not, what with the gulls and the sweeping patrol, Jimmie's was never an eyesore.

But Savin Rock in the late 1960s was an upwardly mobile place. Town officials decided that new condominium owners would not want to live near a seafood sludge heap, so laws were passed, and the wrecking ball came, and the old Jimmie's was no more. The bullet-fast cooks were fired or relegated to unseen kitchens; the ground is clean; the seagulls thin and deprived.

The atmosphere has been wiped clean, but the good food remains. Jimmie's wieners are still the original article, split and grilled and served on a hot bun—but for our money, they're still not quite up to Nathan's. What is sublime here is the lobster roll, which serves as an object lesson in how to distinguish between a lobster *salad* roll and a true lobster roll. Jimmie's lobster roll is a lot of buttery lobster meat— nothing more—stuffed into a grilled, butter-sopped bun. It's not nestled in sauce, heaped with lettuce, suspended in mayonnaise, or stretched with some sort of "lobster helper." It's sublimely pure: lobster meat, butter, and a roll—served warm, with a side order of onion rings, it is the undisputed top-of-the-line of carry-out seafood. Unfortunately, you don't carry it out anymore. Nor do you watch its creation. Nor do you smell the salt water and grilling wieners. But if you have a vivid imagination and are willing to sacrifice purity of ambiance for purity of lobster roll, Jimmie's deserves a visit.

FAIRS AND FESTIVALS

MILFORD
Milford Oyster Festival / LATE SEPT

WINDSOR
Shad Derby Festival / EARLY MAY

MAINE

BAR HARBOR

★ THE FISHERMAN'S LANDING
West Street (207) 288–4632
END OF MAY–SEPT (WEATHER PERMITTING) TUES–SUN 11:30 AM–
7:30 PM

We have little to offer in the way of undiscovered nooks or hideaways in the Bar Harbor area. This is a well-traveled tourist town during the summer, and we have seen some of our favorite "little" lobster shacks turn into feed-'em-fast traps for the unwary traveler. The area overflows with high-priced, overly atmospheric monstrosities that may as well be in Kansas as on the Maine seacoast for all the *genuine* downeast atmosphere they offer. The Fisherman's Landing has been around for a long time, and while it was never the most charming of lobster huts, neither has it succumbed to fancy-dress pretension.

Architecturally, it is a messy-looking place, designed to serve both take-out and eat-here customers. "Eat here" means on the pier, where there are tables set out to provide you with gulls and fishermen for atmosphere while you eat your lobster. Prices change with the catch, but you can be sure they'll be less than the nearby restaurant whose specialty is "lazy lobster," already extracted from the shell, to save monsieur or madame the trouble. Aside from boiled lobster, the Landing specializes in lobster rolls and haddock dinners both sided by French fries. It is the most informal of restaurants, and you can expect a wait on a nice summer day due to a small, overtaxed staff. But nobody seems to mind waiting here on the pier. After all, in Bar Harbor that's where one is supposed to be.

CAPE PORPOISE

★★★★NUNAN'S LOBSTER HUT
Route 9, 200 ft. from Texaco Station in Cape Porpoise (207) 967–4362
JUNE 5 PM–8:30 PM, JULY–LABOR DAY 5 PM–9 PM, DAILY

Our notes about Nunan's are written on butter-stained paper towels. Just as you save the ticket stub from a great play or a petal from a sentimental corsage, you want to keep something of Nunan's. There is no place outside the State of Maine that can compare to it.

Nunan's is a shack perched over the water. Its interior is all wood, with windows that open in warm weather and close like shutters when it's cold. There is a row of small tables along each wall and down the center aisle. A few bits of nautical decor hang from the rafters. The lighting consists of neon tubes overhead and a utility candle stuck into a piece of cork at each table. In each of the hut's three segments there is a sink with a roll of towels—to which customers frequently repair during their meals.

The menu lists lobsters, steamers, lobster stew, and tuna. There are no frills, and the prices are the cheapest around. The lobster comes inelegantly in a pizza pan, along with a bag of potato chips and a forgettable roll. You bring your own wine or beer. As you eat you notice that the tables all have ribbed edges to keep the shell, butter, stray chips and towels from cascading onto the shipshape navy-gray floor.

Satiated with a delicious lobster boiled in sea water, you choose from an equally simple dessert menu. There are homemade brownies —dense, chewy, but not overly rich or chocolatey—and blueberry pie. The berries are smooth and just barely tart. Surrounding the dark filling is a thin, slightly soft—but not in the least soggy—sugar crust. Either dessert can be had with a scoop of vanilla ice cream.

Nunan's is as simple a restaurant as can be—an eating hut that needs no atmospheric additives to make dining here a pleasure. The rough decor and informal tone perfectly complement the rare and special experience of eating a Maine lobster just pulled from the nearby ocean.

DAMARISCOTTA

★★★ ROUND TOP ICE CREAM

Business Route 1, N. of town
MAY–OCT: DAILY NOON–10 PM

Ask Maggie Gaeth for peach ice cream out of peach season and she will regard you with astonishment and dutifully inform you "There are no peaches." Canned? Frozen? Such fruits may exist, but they'll never find their way into ice cream made by Maggie and Dick Gaeth, the owners and operators of The Round Top. Ten years ago Maggie and Dick were an average married couple in a bedroom suburb of New York. Maggie did the housework, and Dick caught the 8:38 every morning for the ride to Wall Street. But they gave it all up for Maine and for ice cream.

Lest you think that The Round Top is one of those "Newfangled oldefangled ice creame parlours" run by city entrepreneurs, consider this: The Round Top recipe has been in existence for fifty-two years. When Maggie and Dick moved up to Damariscotta, they bought the secret recipe from the farmer who was famous for it, and have changed nothing. Dick still makes the ice cream in only ten-gallon batches— "Any more than that, and you'd lose control of the flavor," he warned.

We have sampled lots of ice cream advertised as homemade, homade, or ho maid. Most of it is inferior; and some virtually inedible. The fact is, you could stuff a sweatsock into a cone, advertise it as "homemade," and it would sell. Few home brews approach the perfect blend of sweetness and cream in Ho Jo's coffee. Certainly none attain the fatty richness of Häagen-Dazs, the Super Wate-on of the ice cream world. None are as loud as the high-intensity quality brands like Sara Lee Double Dutch, Valla's of Chicago, or Wil Wright's in L.A. The pinnacle of ice cream taste, we can say without equivocation and with some measure of agreement among well-known junket junkies and hyperhedoniacs, is the rich bitter chocolate served at The Indian Trail in Winnetka, Illinois. Most local ice cream is either too easy on the cream and therefore airless and overflavored, or it is overaerated and without flavor. It is difficult to attain balance—as anyone who has tried to make their own will attest.

The Round Top blend is a striking combination of strength and delicacy—a perfect reflection in cream of the Maine temperament. When you take a bit of, let's say, Maple Walnut, you do not keel over with your tubes clogged from butterfat, as with Häagen-Dazs; nor are you lulled into a mellow thoughtless bliss as with Ho Jo's. Slowly, steadily the maple walnut flavors emerge. The two are distinct and complementary. Both are much stronger than in any other commercial ice cream; yet both maintain a creamy dignity. This latter quality is vital to first-rate ice cream. It is Baskin Robbins' fatal flaw, almost all the thirty-one flavors calling shrilly with their dazzling promise of immediate gratification. By this overbearing insistence on what are basically low-quality flavorings, Baskin Robbins always winds up as only a vengeful aftertaste and a half-eaten sugar cone. Even jamoca almond fudge aficionados admit to this propensity for thirty-one-fold overkill, the ultimate hideous extension of which is the black tarry concentrate known as mandarin chocolate sherbet.

Tasting Round Top is an organic, progressive experience. The flavor grows and enriches, held in check by the creamy base, never flashy or overbearing, yet always prominent and assertive. It is dense and hard-packed, and leaves an afterglow, not an aftertaste.

The Round Top also serves a dark, grainy cocoa fudge for sundaes, but it seems like gilding the lily. Some of their flavors are blueberry, black raspberry, pistachio, peanut brittle, and a breathtaking ginger, as well as an assortment of the usuals. The only other thing they serve is Seward family cheese, a sharp cheddar, one small slice of which is strong enough to overpower two Ritz crackers and a Triscuit.

You can get your ice cream to go, or there are a couple of pleasant wood tables outside, under awnings, where you can not only enjoy the ice cream, but the Damariscotta woods as well. A few other restaurants in the Damariscotta area do serve Round Top ice cream, but for your first immersion, we recommend the source.

ELLSWORTH

★★ DICK'S DINER
81 High Street (Route 1A) (207) 667–8987
MON–THURS 5 AM–8 PM, FRI & SAT 5 AM–9 PM, SUN 6 AM–8 PM

Dick Anderson runs his diner like a chuckwagon chef. He is up at dawn feeding the hungry workmen who pour in, and creating an amazing number of variations using a small number of basic seafood ingredients.

Scallops, lobsters, shrimp, and fish are the bases of his menu. They appear in different forms from chowders to fries. The Ellsworth natives love chowders, especially in the freezing Maine winters, so Dick has become a master at blending smooth butter and cream-laced soups from pink, local lobster meat, tiny bay scallops, and shrimp. The fish chowder with diced potatoes and celery is the least expensive on the menu. It was too milky for our tastes, but a chowder connoisseur with whom we shared a booth proclaimed it perfect.

Our "expert" told us that creaminess is desirable only for chowders with lobster in them. Fish soup is always thin. The lobster chowder indeed proved richer, a beautiful heavy bisque chocked with lobster meat. Extra butter is served on the side along with oyster crackers. The Maine natives add both to the already succulent soup.

Native fried or broiled fish dinners come with homemade cole slaw, cottage cheese, and freshly baked yeast rolls. The flounder we ordered overhung the plate.

Dick Anderson runs his kitchen with the energy of a Bionic man. He whips up five stews a day, countless fillets of fish and fresh blueberry pancakes. For breakfast the counters are filled with homemade molasses doughnuts and there are always four pies on the counter. Our favorite pie was an ivory-colored vanilla custard in a graham cracker crust.

Dick's is a gem of a diner from the freshly painted, dark-gray shutters to the petunia-filled window boxes outside. We don't know how Dick keeps up his pace; he's reluctant to talk about his cooking. We didn't see any telltale gray hairpins on the floor: a sign that he might have a team of grannies shackled together at the ankle, slaving away for him, so we award him the one-man-band award for superlative Maine cooking.

FARMINGTON

★★FARMINGTON LOBSTER HOUSE
Junction of Route 2 & 27 (Intervale Rd.) (207) 778-4235
END OF APRIL–LABOR DAY (APPROX.) MON–THURS 9 AM–6 PM, FRI & SAT 9 AM–8 PM, SUN 10 AM–8 PM

You get spoiled driving around Maine. Even as plain a roadside restaurant as the Farmington Lobster House serves a top-quality lobster dinner beginning with homemade fish chowder, accompanied by warm baking-powder biscuits, and topped off with a slice of fresh blueberry pie. It is the simplest of take-out places, and yet the inside is bright and clean, tinged slightly with the salty smell of lobsters, decorated with crisp curtains, trimmed with varnished Maine pine. There are a few tables inside, and some outside, but much of the business here is take-home, or eat-in-the-car. It is an ideal stop for the roadfooder on the go.

If a full lobster dinner is too much, there are lesser offerings of scallops and clams, clam cakes, crabmeat rolls and lobster rolls. Every dinner comes with the biscuits, and the chowder is made each day. Shirley Bailey cooks the pies—usually apple, blueberry, and strawberry-rhubarb.

One of the strangest items on display in the refrigerated case was an array of lobster bodies—stripped of claws, legs and tails (which were used for lobster salad). They are sold for 15¢ each, tomalley (lobster liver) included, for the bargain hunter, explorer or gourmet who likes to discover veins of edible substance within.

FREEPORT

⋆ LOLA'S LUNCH
Lower Main Street (Route 95 & 1)
MAY–OCT: THURS–TUES 7 AM–9:30 PM / CLOSED WED

Freeport is the home of L. L. Bean, which after so many years outfitting the woodsman, was given the 1976 Coty fashion award. Fred Downing, the owner and cook at Lola's, just snorts at the mention of it. Fashion? Ridiculous. Fred works at Bean during the busy holiday season and, in fact, when we first spotted his little lunch house, it was like a vision out of the celebrated Bean catalogue. Inside, we could imagine all those Bean models, dressed in down and khaki, drinking coffee and hot chocolate after their backwoods adventures.

But all we found was Fred. He is a reincarnated Maine coon cat who declares with a snarl that he's not interested in "traveling trade," and prefers to serve only locals. We probed, and discovered past his gruff exterior a lukewarm personality who, with the application of some pressure, admitted that he does have homemade bread here. It is kept under the counter, "fòr those who know to ask for it." The happy-go-lucky traveler who wanders in here gets the Wonder bread. For the regulars, Fred also provides homemade doughnuts, which he did reluctantly serve to us after a little coaxing. The bread and doughnuts are made by another local gruffneck—an oldster who Fred says learned to cook as a KP sargeant during World War I. In spite of this background, the bread was delicate and airy. The doughnut was heavier, but nicely sugared on the outside and flavored with cinnamon.

As for Fred, he does the short-order work. That's all, says he. Oh, yea, well he does make a crackermeal breading into which he will twice dip a large piece of fresh whitefish for his $2.50 seafood dinner.

Fred's modest specialties are worth noting because the town of Freeport is sorely lacking in rustic food to provide a suitable complement to a visit to Bean's. There is an all-night pizza parlor just down the road, for those 3 a.m. visits to Bean's (always open), but Mario's just won't do for those in need of a good shot of backwoods ambiance. In fact, we find Beans itself disappointing in this respect. The catalogue is magic, instilling visions in our urban minds of we two city slickers slogging through the swamps in Bean's thigh-high rubber boots, or wrapped in our down bags—good to 90 below. In reality; it is only a store, and instead of chamois-shirted hunters stealthing through the bullrushes, all you see are racks of pork pie hats and clothing displays.

Like Bean's, Lola's Lunch is a little disappointing at first, not being as invitingly rustic as a visitor to Freeport might desire. But it is the best place in town—especially if you know how to deal with Downeasters like Fred Downing. If you don't let his crabbiness get to you, and if you ask what he may be hiding under the counter, you'll get him to turn out a damn good meal. And the next time we're in Freeport, we're going to eat at Lola's, whether Fred Downing likes it or not.

NEW HARBOR

★★THE INSOUCIANT LOBSTER

Route 32 (on Small Bros. Wharf) (207) 677–2791
MEMORIAL DAY–LABOR DAY DAILY 11 AM–8 PM, LABOR DAY–OCT
TUES–SUN 11 AM–7 PM

It is hard for a lobster to be insouciant these days, given its status as the most expensive seafood around. Linen napkin establishments do everything short of listing it as "Homarus americanus," its Latin name, to let you know you are eating a rich man's meal. Fortunately, folks in Maine have managed to keep their heads about lobsters. They refuse to serve them on surf-and-turf platters (usually consisting of two tiny tails of the inferior Homarus south africanus), nor do they stuff them and freeze them and defrost them until the once succulent meat takes on the consistency of a snow tire. Downeasters are content to throw a cage in the water, haul up a lobster, boil it, and eat it without fuss or fanfare.

The Insouciant Lobster is part of the New Harbor Fisherman's Co-op. You make your way here through three somewhat confusing wharf signs, following your nose to the steam pots where the lobsters are cooked. It is an eat-in-the-rough style place, with picnic tables outside that afford a great view of the New Harbor fishing fleet.

The fishermen and their families who staff the Insouciant Lobster do not fry anything. They insist that frying ruins the flavor of good seafood—a finicky philosophy designed to separate lovers of good seafood from eaters of breadcrumbs. Here you can get lobsters at prices far less than the Inns nearby that strangle you with their quilted lobster bibs. In addition, there are mussels, crab and lobster rolls, and tuna for those who get scared by the sight of crustaceans cooked in the raw. The seafood is impeccably fresh, and of course the setting overlooking the water doesn't hurt a bit.

The Insouciant Lobster occasionally gets local ladies to supply cole slaw or homemade donuts and cookies, but the schedule for this is erratic. They do suggest that diners bring their own wine or salads to round out their limited—though flawless—offerings.

OGUNQUIT

★★THE OGUNQUIT LOBSTER POUND
Route 1 (¼ mi. North of Ogunquit Center) (207) 646–2516
MAY MON–FRI 5 PM–9 PM, SAT & SUN NOON–9:30 PM, JUNE–AUG
DAILY NOON–9:30 PM

Be prepared, as you walk through the door at The Ogunquit Lobster Pound, to be greeted by a hostess. Often a hostess signals a pretentious meal and high prices. Here a hostess just means a pleasant middle-aged lady who greets you and shows you to a table. There are two places to eat at The Pound. One is in the interior dining room, a rough hewn rustic surrounding; the other is our favorite . . . under the shade of the sheltering pines, seated at picnic tables.

The Lobster Pound is set back from the road in a pine grove. The sun filters through the trees and onto the lacquered pine tables and swings sized for grown-ups, the kind that sweethearts would sit and sway on in Andy Hardy movies. The lobsters are cooked outside in enormous hot pits, absorbing the wood and seaweed flavor as they cook in the rough style first originated by New England Indians centuries ago.

The menu here is extensive, and includes many nonlobster dishes

like Maine salmon. Salmon is the traditional July 4th meal in Maine, and
if you are lucky enough to be in Ogunquit for the festivities, go to The
Pound. Lobster prices are competitive with other southern-coast restaurants. The lobster stew is cheaper than a whole lobster and could
easily be a meal. It is a thick creamy broth laced with large pieces of
pink claw and tail meat. The salmon dish is beautifully prepared with
a color like that of a 1957 Eldorado.

Desserts at the Lobster Pound are wonderfully simple, yet rich.
The fruit pies use seasonal fruit. Maine is the blueberry state, which
accounts for the abundance of blueberry pies. There are also raspberry
tarts in sugar crusts. At the cash register are trays of delicate sugar
cookies. They are four inches across and feather light.

PORTLAND

★★ SKIPPER DAVID'S
Route 1 in Deering Oaks Park
MARCH–OCT: DAILY 9:30 AM–10 PM

We admit to having a low resistance to small-town charm. The lure
of a village green or town square, the auction barn and corner café are
irresistible. With wonderment we pull into a town with a population of
fifty and one general store. "What do they do for fun?" "Everybody
must know everyone else's business." We guess with fright and fascina-
tion what it must be like to live without the metropolitan cloak of
anonymity. Given this inclination, our roadfood travels with few excep-
tions bypass the big cities.

Portland is an exception. As cities go in Maine, Portland is large.
It has a Holiday Inn and a movie theater or two and enough industry
to keep money flowing in and out. What is charming, aside from the
smell of the ocean everywhere, is that it is laid out around a verdant
public park—much like Central Park . . . without the muggers. At the
foot of this park is Skipper David's. It is a small brick building that looks
like a Park Custodian's cottage. The park across from Skipper David's
has a pond complete with gliding swans and one of the most charming
fountains this side of Amsterdam.

All the seafood at this one-man stand tasted freshly prepared.
Clams are dipped, breaded, and fried fresh, and while this requires a
longer wait than if they were precooked and merely heated, the lovely
surroundings occupy the time.

We watched as Skipper David made clam cakes, the stand's best dish. They are similar to potato pancakes but finely laced with small bits of chopped clam. The second best dish is the fried clams. They seem double-sized and are dipped in batter and rolled in bread crumbs until a thick crust is achieved and then fried quickly in clear oil. Likewise, the scallops are dumpling-sized and crisply cooked.

Only the shrimp made us sad. It is difficult to tamp down the envy and greed that bubbles up when your scallop- and clam-eating friends walk away from the counter loaded down with more goodies than they can eat, while you must savor every tiny shrimp like a pauper his gold. Skipper David's unfortunately was true to form: The plate consisted of a meager handful of comma-shaped prawns.

Desserts are disappointingly city-parkish—candy bars, dairy freeze, or ice milk is the selection. We recommend an extra clam cake or two for the road.

RUMFORD

★★THE RUMFORD LOBSTER HOUSE
Route 2 (Prospect Avenue) W. of town (207) 369–9098
SUMMER DAILY 10 AM–6 PM

People in the rockbound and almost cropless state of Maine take their lobster eating seriously. This intense appreciation for the Maine bounty is best expressed in the small sign over the order window at The Rumford Lobster House . . . "We give discounts on more than 50 pounds of lobster."

Rumford is in inland Maine, but the heavy business done at this combination seafood market and takeout lobster pound attests to the local appreciation of the crustacean. Except for Rumford being the home of politician Ed Muskie there is virtually no tourist traffic here, and the price of shellfish is $1 lower than at the coast.

There is a small order window as you enter the Rumford, and one man does all the cooking and preparation of your meal. Service was fast, only fifteen minutes from selection of the still live lobster to delivery of it cooked and ready to eat. There is a small selection of seafood sandwiches as well as lobster and beer to go. There are picnic tables outside.

Because of the lack of tourist trade here, the Rumfordites seem more friendly than their dour coastal cousins. The lobsterman got a kick out of the family of Tennesseans who wandered in shortly after us for their first lobster. Their children had never seen a live lobster, much less eaten one, and when the lobsterman plunged the wriggling black creature into boiling water and it instantly turned red, the kids let out screams of horror. The Rumford's owners were amused and patient with these novice lobster eaters, taking time to explain the intricacies of eating their order. They must have realized that a first lobster, like a first love, is not soon forgotten.

SANDY POINT

★★★★ THE DOWNEASTER

Route 1, 2 mi. N. of Stockton Springs (207) 567–3655
MID-JUNE–LABOR DAY DAILY 11:30 AM–8 PM

The Downeaster is a beautiful restaurant—beautiful in a way that expresses the special quality of Maine. It is clear and spacious inside, dining tables are arranged symmetrically around a clearing in the center in which there are two serving tables. Placed on a table along the back wall are water pitchers and vases with wildflowers. The walls are a soft cream color, highlighted with blue, red, beige and gray; the chairs are bright red wood. The floor is wood, as clean and highly polished as a bowling alley. A small case with handmade pillow cases and Afghans rests against one wall. There is no Muzak; the tone is set by low conversations and the sound of cooking in the kitchen. You realize as you sit here that there is nothing haphazard in the room. It is a design that is strong and delicate, tasteful without pretense.

The food at the Downeaster completes the picture. The woman who owns it, Lois Hall, is a chef who allows herself no shortcuts. The food here is not merely homemade—it is made with consummate skill. We have eaten here half a dozen times, branching out from the obvious lobster and seafood dishes into steaks, chicken and sautéed foods. Nothing has been less than perfect.

Let us begin with the specialties. No one should eat here without getting a side order of corn fritters. They are airy pastries dotted with kernels of corn, wrapped in a dark brown crust, served in a bowl of warm maple syrup. The lobster stew, better than any served elsewhere, looks meager when it comes to your table—a mere soup-bowlful—but dip into it with your spoon and you'll find a bounty of tender meat. The broth is mild, rich, and very buttery. The fried clams are among the best in an area where every restaurant serves good fried clams. The Downeaster's are full-bellied, firm, and fried in a crisp, greaseless batter. Broiled chicken comes with tart cranberry preserves. Steaks are seared and tender.

Desserts are baked here every day. For a long time our usual selection was chocolate cake. A modest slice is served. It is pitch dark, moist, and topped with a thin mocha icing. On our last visit we were considering the apple pie. "It's made from that tree," the waitress explained, pointing out the window to an apple tree in the back. We received a classic wedge of pie—firm chunks of apple, not too sweet, topped with a layer of flaky pastry crust.

A word must be said about the Downeaster waitresses. A part of what makes dining here special, they are professional waitresses; gentle, almost motherly. They are concerned about your meal—around when you need them, inobtrusive when you want to talk or eat. We guess that Lois Hall runs a very tight ship and makes certain that the demeanor of these ladies is in keeping with the overall design and tone she has established in this great restaurant.

SKOWHEGAN

★★SHIRLEY'S DINING ROOM
37 Greenwood Avenue (off Route 201) (207)474–2470
DAILY 5 AM–7 PM

Shirley's is like a lumber camp dining hall. It is noisy, boisterous, and crowded—especially in the early morning—with big strapping workmen eating immense breakfasts. It is a perfect set piece, like a rehearsal for *Seven Brides for Seven Brothers*. But these six-footers are real. And so is the lumberjack-style food.

We recommend that you arrive at dawn if it's breakfast you're after at Shirley's. The homemade muffins (blueberry, corn, oatmeal), doughnuts (sugar, molasses, cinnamon), and biscuits are gone by 7:30 A.M. What is left—because Shirley makes vast pans full—is heavy homemade bread—white, oatmeal, and raisin. Two slices of the thick-cut bread, toasted and buttered, and a cup of coffee make a filling and delicious breakfast. Two two-inch slabs of the bread are dipped in egg batter and fried in butter for French toast, served with warm 100 percent maple syrup. Also on the breakfast menu at Shirley's are fresh fruit bowls. You get a large cereal bowl filled with raspberries or blueberries awash in a sea of ivory cream. It is luxurious and rich, the kind of breakfast dish you'd expect to order in a hotel dining room, and have served in a silver bowl. None of these meals are designed for weight watchers.

Sandwiches at lunch and dinner are made on Shirley's crusty thick-sliced bread, and many of the workers breakfasting here get their lunch pails filled before they leave—a good idea for roadfooders as well. The lunch menu is a refreshing change from the "olive philosophy" of labeling, which starts at "colossal" and works its way up to "triple titanic." Here, all lunches come in four sizes—large, medium, small, and baby: The choices are basic "worker" food, blue-collar specials of roast beef, meat loaf, pork roast, and turkey. We went all the way and ordered two large chicken croquette dinners, which were brought to us in three fully-laden trips by the waitress. There were two tubs of clam chowder, baseball-sized croquettes that had been freshly made from chopped poultry and crumbs from yesterday's bread, peas, carrots, cole slaw, raisin bread (still hot), two baked potatoes, and two slices of walnut pie. The two meals were enough for four.

Aside from the gargantuan food, Shirley's is worth patronizing for a healthy lift in spirits. You might feel wizened at first compared to the rest of the customers, but if you give them half a chance, they'll slap you on the back and include you in their conversation. You'll walk out into the brisk Maine air reinforced by several thousand delicious calories, and a meal spent rubbing elbows with Skowhegan's best pictures of health.

THOMASTON

★★IFEMEY'S DINER
Route 1
TUES–SAT 11 AM–8 PM / SUN 11 AM–3 PM / CLOSED MON

The best thing about Ifemey's is its proximity to the Maine State Prison. The prison has a store that sells woodwork—items made by prisoners, demonstrated by prisoners, and even sold by prisoners (except for the handling of the money, which is done by the guard with the shotgun). Each prisoner develops his unique style of working with wood, and once he's sprung, that style is made no more—a fact we were bemoaning one day over coffee at Ifemey's after a visit to the store to try and replace a bucking bronc-carved lamp that a friend of ours had sat on and crushed into splinters.

"Sorry, Jim's been gone for a year. We got no broncs left. But Pete's back, and he's making his hearts." Pete is a recidivist con who long ago became famous during his first stretch in the pen for his heart-shaped carvings—lamps, plaques, key chains, even coffee tables —all in the shape of a heart, reminiscent of a tattoo. So we bought one of Pete's lamps, and drove to Ifemey's for fig hermits and coffee.

Even if there were no prison around, we'd love Ifemey's. It is the local eatery in Thomaston—a pretty building surrounded by pansies, and inside permeated with the odor of baking bread and pastries. The bread is white or pumpernickel. All sandwiches, french toast, and even breadcrumbs for the fried seafood are the bread's progeny.

Ifemey's caters to New Englanders' taste for seafood not only with fried versions of shrimp, clams and oysters, but with a delicious bowl of fish chowder, filled with large chunks of haddock circling the buttery broth, mixing with parsley and cream. A lobster plate is filled with chunks of fresh-picked lobster meat, and french fries made from Maine potatoes.

The best things here are the baked goods. The counter is always stacked with cookies, brownies, and hermits. The hermits are remarkably light, chewy, and filled with dates, figs, or raspberries. There are also fresh-baked pies, the best being apple in the autumn, served with a slice of local cheddar on top.

TRENTON

★PENNY'S LUNCH
Route 3
JUNE–SEPT DAILY 10 AM–12 MIDNIGHT

The same apple pie you buy at Penny's Lunch and eat at the picnic table under the Maine moon will be found in Bar Harbor's fanciest restaurant for about a half dollar more per slice—the extra money no doubt going to clean the waiter's cumberbund. We asked Eddie Robbins how and where he finds such good pie, sold here alongside an otherwise undistinguished menu of lunch wagon seafood platters.

"The wife," he said, describing how Theresa Robbins moonlights as a pastry cook for Penny's after she has made the cakes for the more expensive restaurant. It is her apple pie that distinguishes Penny's from other roadside stands along the coast. The rest of Eddie's menu is serviceable, and he is proud of it. "I put a full two ounces of clams into

my clam roll, and I charge you 50 percent less than the other places."
There is a full array of lobster rolls, clams, scallops, and fish fillets.

Penny's is actually a small trailer which Eddie Robbins hooks to
the back of his car every June and pulls to this spot by the side of the
road in Trenton. He named the wheeled eatery after his daughter, who
sometimes takes over for Eddie inside the wagon. There's barely room
for one in there, so Eddie sits outside on his chair and smokes his pipe
when Penny or Theresa is helping out. On a nice summer afternoon he
will be glad to regale you with stories about his days in the Navy and
his three trips around the world.

WALDOBORO

★★★ MOODY'S DINER
Route 1
CLOSED ONLY FRI & SAT MIDNIGHT–5 AM

Moody's Diner is an institution in Waldoboro. In every respect it
is an ideal place to go for an undiluted taste of the Maine temperament,
with all its eccentricities, stubbornness, and endearing homespun nature. It also serves the best food around.

We first discovered this woodsy treasure one night after making
the foolish decision to dine "in style" on a wharf in Damariscotta, where
the specialty of the house is an adolescent lobster not yet grown into
its shell, piled high with a pound and a half of seasoned breadcrumbs.
This plus a tasteless whitefish turned out to be a sawbuck's worth of
education at the extension course called Cuisineous Pretentious 101, for
which we always seem to be reregistering.

We were salving our offended taste buds at the Round Top Ice
Cream stand. As owner Maggie Gaeth ladled on the fudge, she asked,
"Why didn't you just go to Moody's?" Later that night, when the miniature lobster and limp fish were only distant memories, and our emer-
gency ration of cheddar and Triscuits had run out, we took Maggie's
advice and drove the ten miles to Moody's. What we discovered here
was not only good, cheap food, but the most lively place around. When
we got to Moody's it was past midnight, and the crowd consisted of a
few tourists who couldn't get motel reservations, insomniac fishermen,
hunters waiting for dawn, eccentric backpackers, traveling salesmen,
truckers, and a hard core of people who never seem to leave Moody's
—Downeasters for whom Moody's serves as a general store.

"We're open all the time," a waitress explained. "Except Friday and Saturday nights. We close at midnight and open again at five. To shoo out those that'd likely grow roots if we didn't give them the boot. But they're back for coffee and muffins in the morning."

Moody's Diner is the hub of Percy Moody's small empire in Waldoboro, also consisting of Moody's Motel, Moody's Tent and Trailer Park, Moody's Boat Ramp, Moody's Island, and Moody's Christmas Tree Farm. It's been here "since way when." When we tried to find out what that meant, he pointed to some black and white postcards near the cash register. "Since before then." The cards show 1949–vintage Fords parked around the wood diner. Moody's has the feel of a place that has become as much a part of the Maine landscape as an old pine tree.

Some of the food here is as eccentric as the clientele. One warm summer evening seemed as good a time as any for us to try our first cornmeal-dipped fried pig's liver. It was sweeter than a calf's, and just as tender. A dinner of boiled haddock in egg sauce was impeccably fresh, and flavored with what seemed a distant cousin of Chinese lobster sauce. Dessert consisted of a homemade biscuit smothered with fresh whole strawberries and topped simply with about a pint of freshly whipped sweet cream. We also tried a dish of gingerbread with cream —a sort of cross between bread pudding and cream pie with a gingersnap crust.

Our two meals were accompanied by several refills of our coffee cups, and plenty of coaching from the waitress on what dishes were especially good and other topics, such as who the bearded guy in the far booth was, and what we ought to do about the transfer case problem our four-wheel-drive car was having. "Come by at breakfast and talk to Ken. He fixes Jeeps."

Ken wasn't there when we came back for breakfast about 6 a.m., but we were happy to sacrifice the answer to our transmission problems for a bacon, egg, home fries, and fresh biscuit breakfast, two homemade molasses doughnuts, and a fresh apple muffin that tasted like a sweet fritter.

Owning everything in town has not caused Percy Moody to grow lax in his concern for giving people a square meal and a good deal. His diner—although ancient and made entirely from wood—is clean and inviting, with a freshly painted pine tree design across the white-slatted front. Outside, the neon EAT sign burns all but ten hours every week. "Some people get stranded and stay the whole winter," Jackie told us. "They help harvest the Christmas trees." We can't think of a better place to be stranded in Maine than Moody's.

FAIRS AND FESTIVALS

ALBION
   Farm Days   /   LATE AUGUST

BANGOR
   Taste of Maine   /   EARLY AUGUST

BELFAST
   Broiler Week   /   MID-JULY

HOULTON
   Houlton Potato Feast   /   LATE JUNE

MADISON
   Corn Festival   /   LATE AUGUST

OXFORD
   Beanhole Bean Festival   /   LATE JULY

PITTSFIELD
   Central Maine Egg Festival
      Features the world's largest frying pan   /   LATE JULY

ROCKLAND
   Seafood Festival and Shrimp Fry   /   LATE JULY

UNION
   Blueberry Festival   /   MID-AUGUST

WINTER HARBOR
   Lobster Race   /   EARLY AUGUST

YARMOUTH
   Yarmouth Clam Festival   /   MID-JULY

MASSACHUSETTS

BUZZARDS BAY

★★ MARY'S MUFFIN HUT
107 Main Street (Route 6) (617) 759–9990
MON–FRI 5 AM–6 PM, SAT 5 AM–2 PM, CLOSED SUN

The door of Mary's Muffin Hut has a sign on it that inquires "Did you have your muffin today?" What biscuits and grits are any day in Little Rock, what lox and bagels are on a Sunday in New York, so is the muffin in New England. And Mary has been proclaimed "Miss Muffin" by the residents of Buzzards Bay. For a traditional New England muffin, there is no place better.

"What's the matter, Mary, the writers here get you confused?" asked Elmo, a regular patron, referring to our presence and the fact that he had just caught Mary without a fresh cranberry muffin. New Englanders are in general a tradition-bound lot, and Elmo has been having his cranberry muffin every Sunday morning for about as long as he can remember.

"No, darling," Mary answered. "I've just been waiting for you to ask." She disappeared behind the small partition into the back room where she keeps her muffin stoves.

"She gets letters addressed to Mary Muffin, or Miss Muffin, or sometimes just 'Muffin—Buzzards Bay,' " Elmo told us as he offered an informal tour of the tiny hut, no bigger than an oversized clothes closet. He showed us the primitive drawing of Mary with a crown, subtitled "Miss Muffin." "Dave drew that. There's Dave," he said, pointing to one of the hundreds of polaroids and instamatic pictures that line the wall. The pose never changes: one, two, or three customers sitting at the counter eating a muffin.

Mary returned from the back with two heavy cast-iron pans—one filled with blueberry muffins, the other with cranberry. Steam rose from the pan as Mary lifted out three hot cranberry muffins, one each for us and Elmo. Mary's muffins are served with humble dignity. They arrive on a small paper plate, accompanied by a tremendous smear of room temperature butter and a white plastic knife. Hot from the oven and dripping with butter, it is the apotheosis of the New England muffin. We cannot count the bleak mornings we have stared humorlessly into our toasted white bread dreaming of one.

There are always blueberry and corn muffins, made throughout the day. We asked Mary what else she made. "Anything I can get into my pans," she said.

Elmo told us that in his experience this included strawberries, pistachio nuts, bran, pumpkin, mincemeat, chocolate, butterscotch, acorn squash, rhubarb, and apple. "Of course, I always stick to the cranberries," Elmo said. Of course!

ESSEX

★★ WOODMAN'S OF ESSEX
121 Main Street (Route 133) (617) 768–6451
SUMMER DAILY 11 AM–10 PM, WINTER DAILY 11 AM–9 PM

Not many restaurants can claim they invented the food they serve. Louis Lunch asserts that it served the first hamburger, although this claim is disputed by Frank X. Tolbert, who traces the original burger back to the St. Louis World's Fair of 1904. The hamburger's origins are clouded in controversy, but nobody doubts that fried clams were invented in Essex, Massachusetts. In 1916 Lawrence Woodman first breaded and deep-fried the clam (which had previously been eaten only raw or in chowders) and thereby invented a whole new genre of portable seafood.

Today, Woodman's of Essex still sells clams, along with lobsters, flounder and scrod. Aside from the historic fried clams, which are crisp and full-bellied, you can eat clams in chowder, broths, clam cakes, or even clam balls that resemble fritters, nuggeted with clam bits.

Woodman's is an atmospheric place to dine, perched practically on top of a salt marsh, with ruby-red lobsters displayed out in front, ready to be sent inside when ordered. It is a busy, noisy place, with an old-fashioned ambiance and affable service, a great spot to enjoy a delicious taste of history.

GRANBY

★MARFRAN'S TURKEY RANCH AND RESTAURANT
55 Taylor Street (413) 467-7740
WED–SUN 11 AM–9 PM

If farmlike surroundings whet your appetite, you will love Marfran's. To get to the restaurant you pass barns and pens filled with turkeys. The Marfran people raise and kill their own birds, and we are told that the line to eat here on Thanksgiving practically reaches the next town.

The thing to order here is, of course, turkey. It is first-rate, and comes in all imaginable ways. Besides ordinary sliced turkey, you can order the succulent mild bird carved up as a turkey steak (a thick, grilled slab), turkey pie, turkey salad, turkey livers, or turkey pot pie.

The problem with the Marfran kitchen is that they have rested on their gobbling laurels. The turkey is so good that the stuffing, vegetables and bread that come with it look very bad by comparison. The stuffing had the whipped taste of a TV dinner, and the bread was one of those bogus puffed-up miniloaves that comes straight from the oven to your table, but still tastes like cotton.

But the turkey itself cannot be faulted. We suggest sampling the turkey pie, which is all meat (no potatoes or filler) in a flaky crust. The turkey salads, which need none of the inadequate side dishes, are another good choice.

Next to the restaurant you can buy Marfran turkeys ready to cook.

IPSWICH

★★★WHITE CAP SEA FOOD
185 High Street (Route 133) (617) 356-5276
SUMMER THURS–SUN 11 AM–8 PM

If you stop in Ipswich and ask directions for a good place to eat, you're liable to get sent to White Cap. "Go to White Cap," said the man who was trimming his hedge. "That is, if you like to eat in the rough."

"In the rough?" The exact meaning of this expression—describing a way of eating peculiar to the Massachussetts shoreline—has become one of the roadfood brainteasers we debate on otherwise dreary stretches of highway, some of our other favorites being the correct spelling of bar b que, the best variety of chili, or which two restaurants we'd take with us to a desert island.

For a long while we thought that "eat in the rough" meant that the surroundings were rough, i.e. rustic. Eating in the rough was like roughing it in the outdoors. But we soon learned that many eat-in-the-rough places were indoors, and you ate at tables, like in a restaurant. Some people describe the process of eating freshly opened clams as "eating in the raw," but that reminded us too much of a mess hall in a nudist colony. While we've got nothing against either raw clams or nudists, we don't think we'd venture into a restaurant that advertised "eat in the raw" without first scouting for volleyball nets behind the parking lot. Our tenative conclusion is that "eat in the rough" means that the food comes to you properly cooked, that you are required to wear clothes, but that the meal is roughly served. "Rough" seems to be synonymous with aggressively casual. Telltale signs of an eat-in-the-rough restaurant are cardboard food containers, metal trays, and a large dining room separate from the noisy ordering area.

"Place your order and stand back" commands the sign over the counter at White Cap. This is a no-nonsense eat-in-the-rough restaurant, the likes of which proliferate in the summers on the North Shore, and the kind of place we pine for whenever we find ourselves landlocked. For our roadfood dollar, there is no better eat-in-the-rough restaurant.

The only concession toward decor at The White Cap is a small cabinet in the corner of the eating hall which holds oceanic paraphernalia such as shells, stuffed fish, and a couple of fish hooks. But all the atmosphere you want can be soaked up while you're waiting for your fish to fry. Instead of Muzak, listen to the hollers of the serving ladies and the commotion around the order counter. The clipped upper-Massachusetts accents call out for fish and lobsters over the sounds of crabs and lobsters being cracked open, deep fryers boiling, and new customers calling out their orders. For your olfactory pleasure, the management provides the tantalizing aroma of simmering fish chowder and lobsters boiling in seawater.

For taste, The White Cap has no peer in its skillful preparation of eat-in-the-rough-style seafood. The two best items on the menu are the fried shrimp and the fish chowder. The shrimp are fresh, but what is remarkable about them is the brittle-thin batter that reminded us of tempura. There is no doughy bread taste—just shrimp and a sharp spicy crust. The fish chowder was a rich, butter broth with only a hint of cream, seasoned with an extra shade of pepper, and packed with large chunks of fresh, firm whitefish—enough for a small bowl of fish stew. A clam roll was also gigantic, with the brittle-battered full-belly clams spilling out over the roll and onto the French fries and cole slaw. The menu also includes steamers in various combinations with broth, butter, or hot sauce, lobsters, haddock, sole, flounder, and crab.

The White Cap serves great seafood at low prices in large proportions, and gives you plenty of elbowroom to dig in. It has often placed high on the waiting list of restaurants we figure we'd like to take with us to our desert island.

NEW BEDFORD

★THE ORCHID DINER
805 Rockdale Avenue (off Route 6) (617)992–8517
MON–FRI 5 AM–7 PM, SAT 5 AM–3 PM, SUN 5 AM–NOON

The Orchid Diner has been on the corner of Rockdale Avenue since the 1930s and is a model of extravagant diner design. Under owner Gabe Moura's eagle eye, none of the original chrome or smooth, red leather seats have deteriorated, and the lavender and silver enameled interior shines as brightly as if it just rolled off the diner assembly line.

But The Orchid has virtues beyond its showcase looks. The diner serves as a gathering spot for the Portuguese community of New Bedford, and Gabe Moura acknowledges his patrons' ethnic roots by offering a few meals that veer off the track of the All-American food usually associated with a diner.

Portuguese linguica sausage is not only found on the breakfast menu next to eggs, but in the turkey stuffing and pot pies. Linguica is a garlicky, slightly fatty sausage, distinctive in taste, and a good complement to the mild flavor of the turkey. There is a turkey dinner with sausage dressing and a Portuguese meat pie filled with potatoes and sausage.

There are many American dishes on The Orchid's menu, but none sparked our fancy as much as the Portuguese-accented ones. The pies looked leaden, the soups bland, and the hamburgers ... well, hamburgers.

The Orchid should be a mecca for anyone interested in dinerology. Gabe is a self-styled historian and philosopher. He dreams up a different "quote of the day" at the daily revision of his menu, and it appears at the bottom of each sheet. The day we dined on turkey with linguica dressing in the gleaming booths of The Orchid, the words of wisdom read "As long as you have a window seat, life is exciting."

PLYMOUTH

★ WOOD'S FISH MARKET
Town Pier (617) 746–0261
SUMMER DAILY 7:30 AM–9 PM, REST OF YEAR DAILY 8 AM–6 PM

Good food and tourist attractions don't mix. As soon as the folks with the cameras and the souvenir-hunting kiddies show up, the simple food either disappears or triples in price and turns sour. Take, for instance, Plymouth Rock. The rock has been sunk into a glass-walled hole to protect it from graffiti artists, and most of the restaurants in town serve pancakes that taste less like the "Pilgrim Patties" they are supposed to be and more like foam rubber toss pillows.

But only a few hundred yards from the famous rock is a fish store called Wood's. It is scenically located on the town wharf, where you can see the working fishing fleet come and go. Wood's gets its clams and lobsters from these boats, making them into delicious low-priced stuffed quahogs, thick chowders, soups, and fried platters, dinners, and rolls. (Quahog, by the way is not a hybrid quail/hog, but a thick, fleshy type of bivalve, most famous for its use in chowders.) For a take-out snack to eat while you meander around the wharf or drive away from Plymouth, Wood's has always been tops.

We are told that Wood's has plans to open a sit-down fish restaurant upstairs, above the stand and market. They assure us that they will keep the take-out stand as it is. We hope so.

REHOBETH

★★★ THE LIGHTHOUSE SEAFOOD
Route 6 (617) 336–8218
APRIL–DEC: DAILY 11 AM–8 PM

If we ever die from an overdose of carbohydrates, they will put up a sign at The Lighthouse that reads "On this spot in the summer of 1976 Jane and Michael Stern first ate dough boys." It's ironic, because The

Lighthouse is a seafood restaurant, and of course seafood is light. It is possible to come here and enjoy a delectable dinner of clams, oysters, lobster, or shrimp and walk away satisfied, but not in the least bit overstuffed. That is if you don't eat dough boys.

We were intrigued by this item when we saw it pop up on the menus of seafood shacks in coastal Massachusetts and Rhode Island, but had always passed it up to concentrate on the seafood. Doughnuts, fasnachts, funnel cakes, beignets in New Orleans and sopaipillas in New Mexico: we thought we had tried "dough" in just about every possible permutation. Dough boys are one of several dozen items on the Light-house menu, nestled between the clam cakes and the snail salads. We assumed they were a modest side dish, but the name should have given them away. Dough boys. Boys of dough. Something the witch from Hansel and Gretel might concoct. We ordered a half-dozen and re-ceived a brown bag full of six handballs made from the densest dough, first rebreaded, then fried, then rolled in a bed of sugar crystals. Our thoughts ran to the giant compression machine that crushes cars down to the size of a brillo box. Here, each dough boy was an entire bakery rolled into a two inch ball. We took a couple of chaws. They are not everyone's cup of tea. But for those who love the pastries at the San Gennaro festival, and who like the edge crust of a pizza as much as the center, the dough boy is pure pleasure—chewy, sweet, and obscenely filling.

Dough boys are designed as accompaniments to the major offer-ings of The Lighthouse, which are seafoods of cornucopic variety. There are clams in every form, fried, belly-less strips, clam rolls, red chowder, steamed littlenecks with butter, clam cakes, a littleneck cocktail. There is also fish and chips with your choice of haddock or pollock (a slightly cheaper and oilier fish), baked deviled crabs, scallops, oysters, smelts, snails, shrimp, quahogs, and lobsters. Also side dishes like Portuguese bean soup, onion rings, corn-on-the-cob, slaw, bean salad, and desserts of strawberry shortcake, or watermelon.

The menu says "Smile—Good Food Takes Time." The Lighthouse is an eat-in-the-rough type restaurant where you place your order and wait for your absolutely fresh fish to fry, steam, boil, or broil. While you wait, you can get a table in the small red-lacquered dining room, or in the outdoor eating area if the fog isn't too bad. The Lighthouse is an informal place—really an extended shack—and it's pleasant to linger outdoors in the salty air, or indoors where the management provides checker boards and darts and a wall covered with harpoons, nets, and other sea paraphernalia. The tables are converted barrels, and the chairs are black-lacquered kegs. When your food is ready, they call you in, and you tote it back to your spot. It comes in boxes—to facilitate cracking the crabs, dipping clams, and tearing into lobsters.

The menu announces that "all prices are subject to inflation," which seems like an honest-enough way to deal with the vagaries of the seafood industry. They do have specials here, which are great if you are more than one person and if you don't feel as we do that "specials" don't allow for a broad and gluttonous enough selection. The Lighthouse Special is a double order of steamed clams, a dozen clam cakes, a quart of clam chowder, two ears of corn, two slices of watermelon, and a vat of butter. The Lighthouse clam boil which, they claim, is "enough for 1–1½ persons" is an order of steamed clams, corn, a hot dog, french fries, sliced onion, sausage, and butter. We've always felt this to be a reasonable special, since there would be no trouble bullying the half-person out of his share if the quantities weren't big enough for you. If you buy a live lobster from their pond, for a couple of dollars more than the price of the lobster, they will boil it in seawater, and give it to you with a bowl of chowder, half a dozen clam cakes, a slice of watermelon, a salad, and butter.

ROWLEY

★★ McINTYRES CLAM STAND
Route 133 (near Route 1) (617) 948–7798
SUMMER DAILY 11 AM–9 PM, LABOR DAY–NOV
FRI, SAT & SUN 11 AM–8:30 PM

The north shore of Massachusetts is a particularly nice place. Most of the Cape Cod style cottages are covered with salt spray roses in the spring, and plum and cranberry bogs grow wildly down to the water's edge. In the lovely town of Rowley, there are many beautiful vistas, but few decent places to eat. Save your appetite until you are on the outskirts of town and pull into McIntyres.

You will see this drive-in seafood stand on your right as you head east and will know it by the strange neon sign of a cowboy lassoing a chicken. It's anybody's guess as to the meaning of this tired-looking sign, since there is no chicken served here. What is special about McIntyres is that they have provided a pleasant eating place situated outside under tall pine trees. Unlike many fry 'em and buy 'em fish stands you are not forced to eat your meal in the front seat of your Impala where by some unwritten law 50 percent of the crumbs, two lemon wedges, and a half a Tab must land on your carpeting. After you pay for your box of fish fry, stroll over to the piney patch of forest with the picnic tables and eat it outdoors.

We tried a good-sized plate of fried smelts. The batter was light and the smelts; too often greasy little fish, were moist and tender. The Boston scrod plate was a bargain too. There is also a selection of shrimp, lobster roll, clams and scallops.

WAREHAM

★★ BREAKER 19
Route 6
ALWAYS OPEN

The Breaker 19 goes by two names. Townspeople know it by its old name, Cran Hi, but truckers and CBers refer to it as the Breaker 19. It is always open and seems comfortable serving as both the all-night town eatery and a full-time truckstop.

The interior is disheveled but clean, the counters stacked with muffins, doughnuts, and racks for magazines. The phones are always in use. And the walls are covered with slogans, bumper stickers, and Cran Hi listings of daily, weekly, and seasonal specials.

This place serves some of the largest meals anywhere. The breakfast special is called the Philmont. It sounds like a popular 1950s TV set, but is actually several platters containing four eggs, twelve pancakes, ¾ lb. of bacon or sausage, ¾ lb. of home fries, a pint of orange juice, and two cups of coffee. The bill is $5, unless you eat it in under twenty-two minutes (the record time), in which case it's free. There is a dinner special that offers challengers a five-pound steak, a moderate-sized salad and a quart of chili. This is $10 unless eaten in record time. "It's the chili that always gets them," our waitress confided.

Down the line from the championship platters are enough varieties of food to fill up several pages of menu. The basic breakfast is a special called "the spare tank." This is five eggs, bacon, toast, and hash browns. Varieties of lunch include sandwiches served with cole slaw and French fries or beans and brown bread (Boston is not far). There are about ten specials every day. Some of the more peculiar items on the menu are "S.O.S." (that's chipped beef on toast), and a strangely untruckerly asparagus on toast with cream sauce. Asparagus is grown locally, and in season the stalks at The Cran Hi are garden fresh.

If none of the several hundred sandwich specials and platters suit your fancy, there is a Mako shark sandwich, a big seller here since *Jaws* was filmed nearby.

Muffins are baked fresh every morning. Besides the common blueberry, cranberry, and corn, the Cran Hi cooks have been known to produce pumpkin, chocolate chip, and taffy muffins—flecked with salt water taffy. No, they are not aspiring to thirty-one flavors, but we suspect that if inventive Bobby Fugure, the owner of The Cran Hi, thought that transistors tasted good, he'd tear apart a CB radio and produce Citizens Band muffins.

The Cran Hi is a busy, crazy place. It always seems crowded and there is a steady stream of traffic out on Route 6. It's a good place to stop not only for roadside ambiance, but for solid New England food, from muffins and brown beans to shark meat sandwiches.

WORCESTER

★★PUTNAM AND THURSTON'S
27 Mechanic Street (617) PL 3-5427
DAILY 10 AM–11 PM (GRILL ROOM CLOSED SUN)

There was an article published a number of years back by a magazine that loves to revel in the eccentricities of the famous. The question was posed to the world's great chefs: "What do you cook for yourself on your days off?" The nearly unanimous answer was "boiled beef."

It seemed strange to us that men who could create baskets of spun sugar for bon bons or mousse de brochet havraise for restaurants like La Caravelle would choose to eat such an apparently bland dish themselves. We have since learned better. Putnam and Thurston's is a good place to find out how good boiled beef can be.

"Puts," as the locals call it, is an old dowager of a restaurant. There are two places to eat downstairs. One is all dark wood and cut-glass doors and white linen napery. This is the Dining Room, which is as proper as only a one-hundred-year-old New England restaurant can be. Next to the Dining Room is the Grill Room. This is plain and less formal, with paper napkins and Formica tables. But even here, an ancient brass rail runs along the counter, the walls are trimmed with wood, and portraits of three stern Bostonians (Putnam, Thurston and ?) oversee the room and assure a quiet dignified tone. The food is less expensive and the service is less elaborate in the Grill Room, and it is a perfect place to drop in for a classic New England meal.

Boiled beef dinner is the specialty of the house, prepared in the traditional manner. The beef is salty and dark red-hued, accompanied by boiled cabbage, carrots and turnips—all simmered in the beef's natural juices in the boiling pot. The tastes of this dish are basic—an understandable relief from the fanciful subtleties of *haute cuisine*.

The next day the beef is even better. The menu offers what is called "well-browned" corn beef hash, a deliciously crusty plate of the beef chopped up coarsely with potatoes, carrots and onions, and served with a poached egg on top. This is a corned beef hash in which you can still taste the roast. It is mildly spicy, fresh and wonderfully variegated in texture.

If you want something lighter, there are Puts's omelettes. These beauties come to the table looking like soufflés, airy and fluffed up by whipping just before they are made. It is possible to order them "flat," if that is what you like—less airy and more like scrambled eggs.

You can make a meal of the clam chowder, served with good hard rolls, finished off with a piece of Puts' chocolate macaroon cake or a bowl of their homemade ammaretto ice cream. We have also tried a slightly dry walnut cake and a respectable but slightly bland grapenut pudding. Puts also makes strawberry shortcake in season, mounding the strawberries onto a baking powder biscuit, New England-style, and topping it all with a heavy whipped cream.

★MISS WORCESTER DINER
300 Southbridge (617) 752-4348
MON–FRI 5 AM–2 AM, SAT 5 AM–2 PM

A plaque inside the Miss Worcester once read "#1 Diner." One small sign for a noontime chowhound; one giant step for road-food. Miss Worcester is the original diner, and although the historic plaque has been ripped off by a dinerphiliac, there can be no denying its primal place in the story of roadside dining. With every bite of meat loaf or roast beef, with every sip of diesel-dark "java," one partakes of history.

Miss Worcester is one of the few restaurants we would recommend more for its intangible "atmosphere" than for its edible offerings. The smells of meat loaf on a steam table and "western-style" coffee ("It's been on the range all day") blend with the heavy clink of thick china coffee cups and the rumble of trucks driving by outside to make a meal at the Miss Worcester a vivid experience.

Meat loaf, ham, pork roast—your basic diner meats—are served with powdery potatoes and pale, anonymous vegetables. The beef stew is a paradigm—thick, filling, *very* filling. There are hamburgers and BLT's, liver and onions—anything that will fry on a grill in less than two minutes. Breakfasts are the best meals here—fast-cooked eggs, buttery potatoes and strong coffee. Everything is served on plates that look like they've seen a million meals.

The clientele who frequent this tile-and-wood beauty do nothing to break the spell. Central Casting could not have done better in finding denim-clothed workmen, truckers, and roadpeople to sit at the counter sipping coffee and scarfing down stew. An occasional student of popular culture drops in looking for the plaque, but the diner's owners care little for history and remain utterly unspoiled by the primary importance of their hash house.

FAIRS AND FESTIVALS

ESSEX
Essex Clam Festival   /   LATE JUNE
Clam bake

GLOUCESTER
Portuguese Fish Festival   /   60 DAYS AFTER EASTER
Italian Fish Festival   /   LATE JUNE

NEW HAMPSHIRE

CONWAY

★THE CINNAMON TREE
Main Street (Route 16) (603) 447–8974
MON–FRI 5:30 AM–7 PM, SAT 5:30 AM–2 PM, SUN 7 AM–NOON

The Cinnamon Tree is a small-town café that is located in the heart of eastern ski country. Most restaurants in this area are not restaurants, but "Inns" with names like "Bird and Bottle" or "The Cock-Eyed

Grouse"—eating emporia aimed at the wealthy ski crowd. These people all look like wealthy doctors and their wives; sons of wealthy doctors and their wives (they have styled hair and French jeans) or the parents of wealthy doctors and their wives (they have white hair and look like Euell Gibbons in ski pants).

The Cinnamon Tree is frequented by the residents of Conway, people like "Stone the Druggist" next door whose shingle reads like an advertisement for an antipharmacological society, and André, the French Canadian regular who eats every lunch here. "Soup's the best thing you can eat," André told us. "They boil out all the poisons. Try a bowl of that cream of celery there."

We took André's advice, and got a mild and delicate bowl of the day's soup, and a warm corn muffin on the side. We learned that The Cinnamon Tree—although it has a few sandwiches on the menu—specializes in soups and muffins.

Ken Mosher is the owner, a man with a bull-frog voice like Andy Devine, and a mild, ingratiating manner. He is a soup expert, having narrowed his range of endeavor to concentrate on it alone. "Of course, I don't make only vegetable soups," he said. "I love to make cabbage with frankfurters, or corn and barley soup, or beef noodle in the winter. Whatever I make, I always make a special muffin to go with it."

Ken's soups are made on a rotating basis, with so many varieties that he begins repeating only after a forty-five-day cycle. "Of course, I sneak in more of the favorites—the corn chowder at least once a week."

The restaurant is in a gracious old building dating back to the 1800s. Of course, houses built only a hundred years ago are considered practically condominiums in upper New England, put to shame by the prerevolutionary ones. But The Cinnamon Tree offers real small town charm, with lace curtains on the windows and characters like André philosophizing over their soup and muffins. A lunch made by Ken—soup, a hot buttered muffin, and coffee—is under a dollar.

ERROL

★★UMBAGOG RESTAURANT
Junction Routes 16 & 26 (603) 482–7721
DAILY: WINTER 5:30 AM–8 PM / SUMMER 5:30 AM–10 PM

The Umbagog is a simple family-run restaurant in the Androscoggin Valley. We were waited on by three generations of the George Baird Family. Mother took our order; daughter served; and at the cash register we met Mrs. Vickers, who described herself as "an eighty-five-year-old white-haired grandmother, still going strong." There are two rooms here, very clean, simply decorated. The salt and pepper for each table is set on hand-crocheted orange and black doilies. A few strategically placed plants lend a touch of green. And there are spoon and plate collections—small and personalized, just like at home. Oddly, amidst all this pleasant homeyness there are one or two garish beer signs and a few shlocky souvenirs.

Like the decor, the food is mostly homemade, with a few errant touches of convenience. When we ate here there were three choices of fresh-baked bread—white, raisin, oatmeal. Both raisin and white were served along with dinner. The bread was yeasty-fresh, warm enough to melt the butter that came with it. There was a mild fish chowder and a thick-stock vegetable soup, both diced with small, fresh potato cubes. Dinners of ham and roast beef were fresh, mild and moist but, sadly, sided with phony mashed spuds.

The excellence of the bakery was again demonstrated by dessert and a couple of wedges of tart apple pie, served with good coffee. Mrs. Vickers, the "granny," told us that the Umbagog always serves fresh donuts and muffins for breakfast, and that there are always three choices of home-baked bread.

There was a hard rain falling outside when we ate at the Umbagog Restaurant, but the good pie, coffee and quiet family tone of the place made waiting out the rain a delightful hour.

UPDATE: The Umbagog is now under new management, and they have added spaghetti and grinders to the above menu.

MOULTONBORO

★THE HI THERE RESTAURANT
Route 25 (603) 476–8867
MON–THURS 6 AM–7 PM, FRI & SAT 6 AM–9 PM, SUN 8 AM–3 PM

The Hi There is the jauntily named café run by Mr. and Mrs. Lively. The building looks like a camp canteen: green and white painted wood and counters filled with candy bars, bug spray and post-cards. The café also sells some of the lowest-priced fried seafood that we have seen in the state, as well as delicious pumpkin pies.

The booths are filled with Moultonboro residents who seem partial to red-checked hunting caps and long-winded stories. We finished a whole meal in the time it took one old-timer to tell about the deer he shot last season. While most booths have "reserved" signs on them, nobody seems to pay any attention to this odd quirk and groups come and go ignoring them.

Avoid the meat loaf and overcooked stews offered on the daily special, and order fish. We loved the fish stew that started the meal. Large tender chunks of white fish came in a buttery cream broth. The menu also listed the local favorite, corn chowder, but the fish stew was richer than the chowder and seemed fresher. Fried clams come with bellies or as strips. Fried scallops and fried shrimp cost only pennies more than the clams. The shrimp is on the skimpy side, but the clams and scallops are delicious and more than plentiful.

Side dishes are great baked beans, or fried dough, freshly sizzled bits of bread dough that are sprinkled with coarse sugar. We nibbled at the fried dough, trying to leave room for the pumpkin pie that a local farmer had told us was "about the best you could try."

PLYMOUTH

★B.J.'S DINING ROOM
Court Street (off Route 25) (603) 536-1911
TUES–FRI 6 AM–9 PM, MON 6 AM–8 PM, SUN 7 AM–8 PM

B.J.'s is an old-fashioned diner with an added-on dining room that serves Syrian and American food. There is no hint of Eastern decor here. The diner is a classic American beauty, streamlined with chrome, red leather booths and decked out patriotically with small flags on the walls and near the cash register.

The waitress who took our order warmed when we asked for the "Arabic Plate." It was the highest item on the menu, but her enthusiasm was sparked by our adventurous eating rather than the cost. When our eating companion Andy ordered the fried shrimp dinner, her face fell, and we could see her mentally labeling him an unsophisticated rube, on the order of the farmers and college kids seated at other booths lunching on burgers and Cokes.

The Arabic Plate was so bountiful that it arrived in three separate dishes. There was a long skewer of marinated lamb chunks, a stuffed pepper filled with rice pilaf, tahini dip made from crushed chickpeas, sesame seeds, and garlic, and a goat cheese salad with olives. Pita bread was served on the side. This is a soft warm flat bread perfect for dipping into the tahini.

When Andy's shrimp came our enthusiasm for B.J.'s declined slightly. Four frozen mini-shrimp were artfully arranged on a mammoth lettuce leaf. The shrimp platter on the waitress's tray was sitting next to a "Kufta" sandwich for some other lucky diner. It was a pita bread stuffed with sausage, lettuce, and tomato.

While we have eaten better Syrian food (at twice the price), B.J.'s is good, and spiced mildly enough for novices in Middle Eastern cuisine.

PORTSMOUTH

★ TONY'S
49 Lafayette Road (Route 1) (603) 964–8173
MON–SAT 6 AM–7 PM

Tony's doesn't even have a jukebox, but it has one of the best floor shows in New Hampshire. The show is Tony. When we first asked the waitress if Tony was known for anything special—perhaps his soup, or his pies—she replied without a second's hesitation, "His jokes." Then she added, "Well, maybe the paintings, too." Tony is indeed the renaissance man of the diner world. Owner and cook, he is also toastmaster, host, and primitive artiste extraordinaire.

The magnitude of Tony's talents is slowly revealed as you perch on a leather stool in this basic old wood diner. At first it looks simple—an old marble counter, checked floors, four tiny tables squeezed against the wall opposite the grill. But off to the side is an alcove, Tony's gallery of seascape, landscape, and dinerscape paintings. On shelves around the diner are Tony's "claws"—his creative specialty is the art of painting a self-portrait on a lobster claw. The top pincer becomes Tony's nose, the bottom his chin. There is a claw for each of Tony's many moods.

On a shelf next to some of Tony's claws is the gag roll of toilet paper, and near that the sign saying, "When you're in the dog house, you're always welcome here." That's not far from the wall covered with polaroid pictures of Tony's regulars. But the place of honor here—or rather the two places of honor—are occupied by the air-conditioners. The heat cramps Tony's style, so he's got two running all summer and late into the fall. As you enter, he may peep out from the kitchen and inquire sardonically, "Cool enough for you?" Be sure to bring a jacket when you dine at Tony's.

Just after we had walked into Tony's an old-timer entered and sat down. Crystal, the blond, besieged twenty-year-old waitress, called back to Tony, "Freddie's here." Moments later a poached egg emerged, with a side of bacon and a corn muffin. Tony's recommendation for us, called out from his kitchen in back, was "a beefsteak salad, to beat the heat." Tony loves tomatoes, and this was tomato season, so our salad was a large farm-fresh thin-skinned tomato, sliced into wedges and served with sliced cucumbers and onions. It was a real treat after becoming accustomed to the leather-bound red tennis balls that pass as tomatoes in supermarkets.

We also tried the fried haddock—fresh but bland—with chowder, homemade potato salad, and another tomato. The lobster roll was served with slaw and fries, and to our taste would have been better with less mayonnaise, although there was plenty of lobster meat. The chocolate pudding that Crystal recommended was made from real cocoa, not a mix, and it was dense with grainy chocolate flavor.

As we were paying our bill, Crystal was telling us about how nutty Tony was, and didn't hear him call out that an order was ready. We saw him sneak out from the kitchen behind her, deliver the order, then silently pick up a frying pan and lift it in the air as a gesture of mock-anger. "Look out, Crystal!" yelled Freddie, and Crystal ducked and ran out toward the art alcove.

"Jeez, you've got to beat'em three times a day to get any service around here," Tony told us, putting down the pan and retreating to the kitchen. A sign on the wall reads "Cows may come and cows may go, but the bull in here stays forever." Amen.

SHELBURNE

★CABIN TOWN RESTAURANT
U.S. 2 (603) 466–2565
MEMORIAL DAY–COLUMBUS DAY DAILY 7 AM–9 PM

Scoop and Clair Main run the Cabin Town Restaurant, a popular little eatery in the middle of the White Mountain woods. It is a simple place with no manufactured atmosphere, just basic rustic food. Clair Main is the cook. She shies away from convenience items to the extent that she rolls out the dough for her chicken pie, not satisfied with preformed shells. The same attention is given to scalloped potatoes and ham dinners, and a more plebeian meat loaf. The seasonings of these dishes are mild. They are a rib-sticking cuisine.

Cabin Town is known for its soups and chowders. The most popular varieties are clam chowder, chicken soup, and a rich corn chowder. Meals end with Clair's fruit pies, rice pudding or bread pudding.

There are a few items that ought to be avoided at Cabin Town, like "American Chop Suey," a first cousin of Hamburger Helper and bland to the point of being tasteless, and a peach pie that is equally lackluster. But most food served here can be considered elements of a proverbial "square meal" without the frills, and although simple, it's worth a stop.

SUGAR HILL

★★★POLLY'S PANCAKE PARLOR
Route 117 (603) 823–5937
MAY–MID-OCT DAILY 7:30 AM–7:30 PM

We don't know a better place to eat pancakes than Polly's. The Parlor is in an 1830-vintage building on Hildex Farm. From your table you look over the New Hampshire countryside through the clear mountain air. The pancakes served here are made from light cornmeal, whole-wheat, or buckwheat batters, filled with chopped nuts, blueberries, or coconut. And the star of the show is maple, brought to your table as maple sugar, maple syrup and maple spread.

Polly's began serving pancakes in 1938 as a way of getting travelers to try "Sugar Bill" Dexter's maple products. Back then it was 50¢ for all you could eat. Polly's continues the all-you-can-eat policy (for about $4 today), and this is about the only pancake parlor we know where the pancakes are light and good enough to make it a good deal.

Indeed, what veteran of the road is without a pancake horror story? The time you ate three at the oasis over the turnpike and passed out on the way to your car, or the pancakes so thick they stuck, or so porous they soaked up two pitchers of syrup . . . ? Forget about those inferior rubbery roadpancakes when you come to Polly's. What you get here are small, thin "cakes," made from your choice of batter, and with your choice of ingredients, served in batches of three until you tell your waitress (who makes them herself) to stop. You may go a long while before you quit. Not only are the cakes feathery—the maple is divine. The maple crystal sugar and fancy-grade amber syrup taste like mountain air. And the maple spread—a thick, translucent topping that looks like apple butter—is a mainline fix for sugar junkies. These maple products are brought on a serving tray that also contains a dish with a large ball of butter, a pewter pitcher filled with heavy cream, and a hand-painted scoop for dipping into the sugar.

If you come to Polly's for lunch or dinner, you can follow up your meal of pancakes with desserts that also partake of Hildex Farm's maple bounty. Our favorite is ice cream with maple hurricane sauce. This is made by slicing apples into thin slivers and boiling them down with maple. It is ladled warm onto the ice cream.

We suggest you allot plenty of time for your visit to Polly's. Not only will this give you ample opportunity to sample several of the varieties of pancakes and maple, but it will also leave time to walk around outside. The woodsy countryside and farmlands that surround Polly's are a perfect place to enjoy the afterglow of a mapley meal.

WOODSTOCK

★MT. ADAMS INN
Route 3, N. Woodstock (603) 745–2711
DAILY BREAKFAST, LUNCH, DINNER UNTIL 10PM

There are a lot of tourist traps and slick chophouses in the North Woodstock area, which is why the simple, gracious Mt. Adams Inn seems so special. Rooms at the Inn go for $8 a couple, and the kitchen is staffed with women who look like they could make a piroshki stand up and sing. Although there is American food offered on the Mt. Adams menu, the featured items are *golumbki* (stuffed cabbage), *kielbasa*, and meat or potato piroshki. These authentic dishes—or a combination plate of all three—are served for the same price you'd pay for a mass-market pizza or a fancy sandwich nearby. To be sure, the Mt. Adams serves a no-frills meal. These Polish dishes are simply served with potato or kraut and vegetable. Expertly prepared, they need no fanfare.

For dessert, try the Polish pastry. There is a choice of cherry or apple, an open-faced affair with an abundance of fruit layered over a Danish-style yeast crust.

Like the cuisine, the dining room is simple and immaculate. There are polished wood tables, one or two decorative eagles or falcons on the wall, and a jukebox (quiet) that plays Polish music. After dinner you can retire outside to the wide, sheltered porch that circles the Inn. You can sit down in a big, old-fashioned easy chair with a crocheted cushion and gaze out at the road over the many flowering plants that ring the porch —a tasteful end to a tasty meal.

FAIRS AND FESTIVALS

CENTER HARBOR
Chicken Bar B Que / JULY 4

WATERVILLE
Octoberfest / EARLY OCT
German food and beer

Swiss Independence Day / SAT CLOSEST TO AUG 3
Swiss dancing and food

RHODE ISLAND

NARRAGANSETT

★★THE SEAFOOD SHACK
Route 1A (401) 783–1755
SUMMER: FRI & SAT 11 AM–7 PM / CLOSED WEEKDAYS

The Seafood Shack is one of the many little takeout stands along the beautiful sandy beaches of Rhode Island. It is distinctive not only for its freshly prepared seafood, but for the menu which offers combination plates and fish by the piece, making it possible to create your own platters of two shrimps, one scallop, three clams, a stuffed quahog, and a few clams casino.

The Harvest special is a one-pound lobster, boiled in seawater, steamers, corn-on-the-cob, two stuffed quahogs, and cole slaw. Other platters are in the under $2.00 range. Shrimp are sold by the bucket, unpeeled and garnished with several lemon wedges.

One of our favorite dishes here is the marinated snail salad. Jerry Lewis expressed one possible attitude toward snail eating in his film *The Patsy,* where the rubber-faced comedian is approached by a snooty waiter toting a plate of *escargots:*

Waiter: Do you care for snails, sir?

Jerry (looking green): Like on the lawn?

A non-lawn approach to snails, as at The Seafood Shack, calls for them to be chopped up, soaked in olive oil and garlic with oregano, then eaten while sitting on a piece of driftwood watching the Rhode Island surf crash in against the beach.

The day we first ate at The Seafood Shack, the fog was so thick that even the seagulls were grounded. Phantom surf-lovers darted in and out of the grey waves; a foghorn sounded nearby. It was a beautiful day to get platters of the best seafood around, and eat them in the best Rhode Island restaurant we could imagine—the beach near The Seafood Shack.

PROVIDENCE

★HAVEN BROTHERS
next to City Hall
MON–FRI: DINNER ONLY

We take this detour into urban Providence to find not a truckstop,
but a stopped truck. That is Haven Brothers, and every afternoon just
before dinner you'll notice a hush in the air around City Hall. Street
people, minor-league traffic offenders, politicians, eccentric newlyweds, local badasses, cops, and roadfood junkies all congregate in quiet
anticipation.

Downshifting to make the turn, Haven Brothers restaurant rounds
the corner, lurches to a halt, and opens for business. As the back gate
of the semi swings open, a resident looney, "the broom lady," emerges
from the crowd dressed immaculately in white and carrying her wisk.
She starts to sweep the ground—even before the animated customers
begin to discard the waste from their dinners onto the street. As the
broom lady sweeps, the stove inside the semi-trailer heats up, and the
dinnertime Haven Brothers babble begins.

"Reds, cut up two" is the cry most frequently heard. The reds are
not a Nembutal cocktail, but the stand-up version of New England's
staple—franks and beans. It's the dogs that are cut up and tossed into
a thermal cup along with a scoop of sweet red beans. These emerge
from the back of the trailer at least as fast as they're ordered, the
lightning-charged cooks prodding purchasers to "spit it out!" (that's
your order) or "cough it up" (that's your money) to speed things along.
The point seems to be to do everything as fast as is humanly possible,
and if you've obliged the brothers by scarfing down your reds, you may
find you have a brief interlude between the end of your hot dogs and
the beginning of your heartburn. If so, we recommend an immediate
order of "one bird on a raft and a bucket of suds." This will be chicken
salad on toast and root beer, both of which do a good job of tamping
down the gall bladder attacks to which frank and bean fanciers are
subject. We contend that smart diners just start with the chicken salad,
which is loaded with large tender chunks of Rhode Island chicken, and
is made with fresh and abundant mayonnaise.

But if ordering chicken salad at this double-fisted eatery seems a
bit prissy to you, and if you don't want to risk the aftereffects of Haven
Brothers' reds, you can try the third and final Haven offering, which is
burgers. The cook grills them with breathtaking speed, and just watch-

ing him work is worth the price of a patty. If you order it "all the way," you get everything except ketchup. "High and dry" gets you a lonely orphan burger whose minimal moisture is immediately absorbed by the voracious white bun in which it sits. Although these hamburgers are not in the big leagues of burgerdom, their quick-grilling guarantees they do retain a tasty meat flavor.

Haven Brothers is a traveling circus of a restaurant that may not provide haute roadfood cuisine, but does produce the best show in Rhode Island's capitol.

FAIRS AND FESTIVALS

WEST GREENWICH
Chowder and Clambake   /   MID–APRIL, JUNE, SEPT, NOV

WICKFORD
Chicken Bar B Que   /   EARLY JULY

VERMONT

BRIDGEWATER

★HUTT'S DINER
Route 4 (802) 672–3662
MON–SAT 5:45 AM–6 PM, CLOSED SUN

According to the plump little waitress here, Hutt's is a truckstop. We assume she knows her customers, but it is hard to imagine where a huge semi would park or even where a beefy trucker would sit in this dainty roadside café. The inside is merely a counter with about six close-together stools and outside there are two small tables under the trees. Flower baskets of bleeding hearts decorate the walls, and a sign is tacked outside on an ancient maple tree declaring "Three Squares Daily."

French toast in the morning is day-old homemade bread dipped in eggs, fried in butter, and served with a pitcher of pure amber maple syrup. The baked beans in the winter are traditional right down to the strip of scored salt pork.

The regular lunches include Yankee pot roast with carrots and sweet potatoes or roast chicken or turkey with stuffing. Soups are made here too, corn chowder being the most frequent and traditional offering.

We're a little skeptical about the pies, having stopped by during the summer only to see the meringues and custards sitting placidly on an open shelf, weeping their moisture into the hot summer air. We chose an unspoilable blueberry instead, which was homemade but a little gummy.

Otherwise, Hutt's is a good bet, and this place does seem to be one of the few remaining eateries where it does pay to "eat where the truckers go." Hutt's is a good stop for an inexpensive daily special or a breakfast served with Vermont maple syrup.

FAIRLEE

★★★★ THE FAIRLEE DINER
Route 5 (802) 333–9798
SUMMER: MON–SAT 6 AM–9 PM, SUN 8 AM–4 PM; WINTER: MON–SAT
6 AM–8 PM, CLOSED SUN

Many years ago, when we first started looking for roadfood, we had certain ideals in mind. The perfect diner would be simple, immaculate and friendly. Food would be a matter of pride in local traditions. It would feel like a town gathering place, filled with characters who reflected local spirit and presided over by people who loved their work. The food would be delicious and cheap. The Fairlee Diner is that place.

The doorways are ringed with flowers, the wood siding is sharply painted in white and green. Inside there is a small counter and six booths—all made of highly varnished pine, all occupied by Fairlee folks discussing sled dog racing or the weather. This is the home of the "flannel shirt crowd." Fifty percent of the customers could pose for the L.L. Bean catalogue. The service is quick and friendly. The air smells of the apricot and apple pies baking in the back.

The menu changes with the weather. In the summer there are salads and simple cuts of meat; in the winter there are New England boiled dinners and roasts. There are always at least twenty entrees on the menu. When we ate here the offerings included pan-fried honeycomb tripe, home-baked beans, fried chicken, country sausage, lamb chops, steaks and fresh haddock. Dinners came with real mashed potatoes and fresh carrots, boiled cabbage or green salad. The day's special was corned beef and cabbage. The beef was smooth and subtly spiced, the cabbage firm. Our waitress explained that corned beef one day usually meant red flannel hash the next. This is a New England specialty for which the ingredients of a boiled dinner—corned beef, beets and potatoes—are coarsely ground together, seasoned, and fried on the griddle to a crisp crust.

Dessert was a choice of apple tapioca pudding, apricot, pumpkin, apple, blueberry, prune-apricot or custard pie (all homemade), raisin-rice pudding, or ice cream from a local Vermont dairy.

In the morning there are always homemade donuts, muffins and hermit squares. Other specialties depend on what is available at the markets, and the ingenuity of the Roberts family, who run the Fairlee. When they can get peaches, there is a fresh peach shortcake on home-made biscuits. Whatever berries are available find their way into the pies and muffins. Even left-over coffee is transformed into coffee soufflés for dessert.

The coffee served at the Fairlee Diner is strong; not just freshly brewed, but freshly *ground*. It is that kind of attention to quality that makes the Fairlee a superior diner.

LUNENBURG

★COUNTRY KETTLE RESTAURANT
Route 2 (802) 328–4910
MON–SAT 7 AM–8 PM

"Mom and Pop Kettle" are the CB handles used by the proprietors of this restaurant, which is itself a blend of vulgarity and charm reminiscent of that famous hillbilly couple. CB calling cards and bumper stickers cover the walls, and plastic clothes cover the tables. Yet upon those tables are set muffins hot out of the oven every morning, homemade soups and some delicious puddings. When seasonal fruits and vegetables are easily available, Elsie Herrick (Mom) makes them into pies, soups and side dishes. One special is a zucchini dish made with tomatoes, onions and Parmesan cheese. Corn on the cob is served as a side dish with the standard dinners of roasts and assorted seafood.

When vegetables disappear during the winter the Country Kettle offers a variety of homemade pies, including a highly touted sweet potato pie. In the summer, when pies spoil more easily, they are bought from a commercial supplier.

The menu here demands some exploration to separate the home-cooked from the ready-made. The muffins alone make it a top stop for breakfast, and the bread and rice and grapenut puddings are creamy-rich enough to warrant a snack stop any time. There aren't many restaurants in the Lunenburg area in either direction on Route 2, and so we were happy to brave the few disappointments on the menu and the brassy decor for a basically good cuisine and some occasional flights of fancy.

MARSHFIELD

★ NELSON'S, INC.
Route 2
LATE MAY–LABOR DAY: MON–WED 10 AM–9 PM, THURS, FRI 10 AM–
10 PM, SAT 10 AM–11 PM, SUN 11 AM–9 PM
SEPT & OCT: WEEKENDS ONLY

Nelson's is a great place to know about if you are an ice-cream lover. A sign on the outside of this roadside stand says "We do not serve creemees! We use no milk or cream substitutes. Our ice cream is made from 14 percent whole cream." We sampled the maple walnut flavor, which was indeed creamy, and tasted of pure maple as well. In the fall, Nelson's makes fresh apple and blueberry pies, which you can have either à la mode, or served with Vermont Cheddar—or both, if you happen to be an indecisive glutton. The ice cream and pies can be bought at a take-out window and outside eaten on benches by the side of Route 2.

There is a dining room inside with simple Italian dishes and sea-food, and the girl at the counter assured us that Nelsons' roast beef was delicious. You can also get assorted seafood plates, "fresh frozen" to eat here or to go.

We have not branched out here beyond desserts, but we can say that the ice cream and pie are worth a stop.

RUTLAND

★ JONES BAKERY
14 Terrill Street (802) 773–7810
TUES–SAT 6 AM–5 PM / CLOSED SUN & MON

Jones Bakery sells some of the lightest and most delicious dough-nuts east of Pennsylvania Dutch country. They are so special that an only moderately heavy friend of ours (200 pounds) once ate one dozen between 9 A.M. and noon, *after* a full breakfast around the corner at Lindholm's. We don't recommend eating them by the dozen, but one of the nice things about Jones' doughnuts is that you can buy a dozen in the morning, munch on them during the day, take them back to your motel or tent at night, and the few that remain are still delicious. Even the next morning you'll find them a little crisper, but still innocent of the Dunkin-style lard that appears within six hours after inferior dough-nuts are taken out of their plastic incubator trays.

Aside from the cinnamon, sugared, and glazed doughnuts, we recommend sampling the blueberry muffins and the black raspberry doughnuts—filled with real preserves, not purple paste.

Jones Bakery is one of the few eateries in Rutland that has stayed the same, tucked in among the wood houses and alleyways behind the maple trees. It is pleasantly plain and old-fashioned—even to the dusty yeah-yeah-yeah Beatle figurines still offered as a possible decoration for your child's birthday cake. That is, if your kid is old enough to remember who the Beatles were.

★★★ MINARD'S FAMILY RESTAURANT
2 North Main Street (Route 7) (802) 773–3535
WEEKDAYS 6 AM–8 PM, WEEKENDS 6 AM–9 PM

There was once a beautiful building on this spot. Lindholm's Diner was known to roadfooders and pioneering diner afficionados during the 1950s and 1960s as the ultimate silver masterpiece. A huge stainless steel structure, equipped with every imaginable diner embellishment, it was like a '56 Eldorado Biarritz festooned with everything from a signal-seeking Motorola to a brushed chrome continental kit. A long green and gold awning stretched from Lindholm's out to the street. The inside was a burst of green and silver, highlighted with polished fillips of dark wood. All other diners paled by comparison.

But Lindholm's depended on a traveling trade, as well as sports-men from the gun shop next door. And so sometime in the early 1970s, when diners had become symbols of Crisco cuisine, Lindholm's exquisitely streamlined look was replaced by phony brick and wood siding. The awning was torn down and the name was changed to Minard's. When we first saw the transformation, it was like looking at an old friend emerge from plastic surgery. Once a sleek, exotic beauty, she had become a pale imitation of Connie Stevens.

We winced, we cursed, we entered, and we ate. We do not necessarily pride ourselves on being especially "objective" as we evaluate roadfood, but our attitude at Lindholm's was sinful. Yes, we'll continue to call it Lindholm's, as Johnny Cash continues to wear black, until Lindholm's is freed. You see, after we entered we noticed that the old diner has not been destroyed. It's just been covered over. Peeking out of the corners and from behind the Con-Tact paper are glints of chrome, pieces of mirror in sunburst patterns, and, of course, the rounded contours of the roof. The majesty is still here. We have tried to convince our archeologist friend to wrangle a grant to have "Minard's" declared an historic site. We would be the first to volunteer for the dig to unearth this shrine of 1950 civilization.

Well, after all that, we hate to admit it, but the food at Minard's is terrific. Maybe Lindholm's ghost tends the stew pot, or maybe the whole place was covered over just to discourage the customers who used to order one cup of coffee and spend two hours ooing and ahing over the enamel work, because, if anything, the food has improved. The boiled corned beef dinner was served with fresh buttered carrots and tender little potatoes sprinkled with parsley. The pot roast was well browned and tender, immersed in a marrow-flavored gravy. As an appetizer, the corn soup was rich and tasted as if the kernels of corn had been plucked from an already buttered ear. We also noticed chicken and homemade biscuits on the menu, which ought to be worth ordering if they use the same flaky biscuits we found under our strawberries and real whipped cream when we ordered shortcake. The coffee, too, came with a pitcher of heavy cream. Vermont, we were reminded, is a dairy state, and Minard's takes full advantage. We also learned that pure maple syrup is served with pancakes, and that the fig and raspberry cookies are cooked at Jones Bakery, around the corner.

So in spite of the heinous crimes wreaked upon the premises, we do recommend Minard's. The food is better than ever, cheap, and reflects the best regional cuisine.

ST. JOHNSBURY

★★FARM BOY DRIVE IN
Route 5, N. of St. Johnsbury (802) 748–9796
WED–MON 10 AM–8 PM

The food at Farm Boy is much better than the looks of the restaurant lead you to suspect. It is a simple drive-in, with some pleasant outdoor tables under an awning and lots of pretty flowers all around. Food is served eat-in-the-rough style, which means you place your order at a counter and tote it back to your table. It comes on paper plates and is eaten to the sound of basic Muzak. It's all very speedy and informal.

Look behind the counter and you see the Farm Boy workers breading fish filets just before they are tossed into the fryers. The fish emerges crisp and hot and is served alongside slices of homemade bread. If you order a milk shake, you will see them mix it, using ice cream, milk, and syrup—a pleasant change from the prewhipped fast-food variety that oozes ready-made from a machine. The attention to quality at Farm Boy seems incongruous with the plastic look and tone of the place.

The menu offers mostly fish—shrimps, clams, scallops, oysters, filet of sole. These are fried, but you can also get the sole baked, served with a juicy farm tomato and cole slaw. We would also recommend the stuffed shrimp. Since 99 percent of the stuffed shrimp served in America's restaurants come stuffed with breadcrumbs, it is a joy to find Farm Boy's stuffed with lobster. It is the highest priced item on the menu, but still under $5. You can also get chicken, steaks and sandwiches, but it is seafood that is Farm Boy's specialty, and our recommendation.

WESTON

★★THE VERMONT COUNTRY STORE RESTAURANT
Route 100 (802) 824–5432
JUNE–OCT MON–SAT 8:30 AM–4 PM

One comes across so many pseudoquaint eating establishments along the road that there is a risk of passing by a place that is the real thing. The Vermont Country Store is not an untouched relic from bygone days, unaware of progress, but we figure if any eatery has a right to bask in its own quaintness, it is this one. Vrest Orton, the proprietor, is a clever man who knows the value of his genuine antique restaurant and of the culinary traditions he maintains here.

The decor is relentlessly Victorian. The barroom is covered with mahogany paneling, mirrors, gold and chandeliers, and sports an 1885 soda fountain made from Italian marble, ebony and silver. What is, however, genuinely charming about this room is the food that's served. You can order strawberry shortcake served on a fresh-baked biscuit, spicy Indian pudding, apple pie with a wedge of Vermont cheese, or an ice-cream sundae topped with maple syrup. The two front dining rooms are equally "Victorianized," but again the gaudiness is offset by the offerings on the "Bill of Fare."

Sandwiches at the Country Store Restaurant are served on whole-grain bread made from stone-ground wheat. You can get New England clam chowder, or the venerable dish called "crackers and milk," which is simply a bowl of cold, fresh milk, a piece of Cheddar, and a pile of "common crackers." Another traditional dish is red flannel hash, made with beets and served with brown bread. Of course, there are beans, baked in a brick oven, and cob-smoked ham.

Many of the foods served in the Restaurant are available in the Country Store to take home. There is a stone mill on the premises that grinds eighteen varieties of grain for bread and pancakes. And of course there are gifts galore to buy in remembrance of your visit. But no matter how commercial this place might seem, it is Yankee-spirited to the core. The menu announces that the Vermont 5 percent meals tax is "Not our fault!"

FAIRS AND FESTIVALS

BRADFORD
Annual Wild Game Supper / MID-NOV
Elk, Moose, Bear, Caribou, etc.
By reservation only—Box 182, Bradford, Vt.

Lake George •

East Avon •

NEW YORK

• West Winfield

Coeymans •

West Coxsackie •

Silver Creek •

Woodstock •

• Girard

Hyde Park •

Fishkill •

Lock Haven •

Port Chester •

• Clarion

• Loganton

Stroudsburg •

• Kenvil

Clintonville •

South Kearny •

PENNSYLVANIA

Krumsville •

North Brunswick •

• Hightstown

• Washington

Carlisle •

New Holland •

NEW
JERSEY

• Somerset

• Roxbury

Collingswood Heights •

• Hagerstown

• New Castle
Glasgow

MARYLAND

DELAWARE

• Meadows

DELAWARE

GLASGOW

★★ THE GLASS KITCHEN

Route 40, Glasgow exit off 95 (Exit 1) (302) 368–1359
MON–THURS 11 AM–8 PM / FRI–SUN 11 AM–9 PM

The mimeographed menu handed to us by our silver-haired waitress bore witness to a seriously impaired typewriter. "E" 's read as "O" 's and we spent some time trying to figure out what "Pickled Boots" or "Doop Fried Opplant" were.

Under the guidance of our patient waitress-translator we managed to order a full and satisfying meal, and declared The Glass Kitchen to be our favorite nonseafood restaurant in Delaware.

While The Glass Kitchen isn't a fish restaurant, do order the appetizer of eighteen steamer clams in butter broth. This is an appetizer for the ravenously hungry. It could easily be a full meal for anyone else. There are lightly paprikaed deviled eggs called "Eggs à la Russe" to start the meals for a more modest price.

The roast turkey dinner comes with Dutch potato "Filling" instead of potatoes, the filling dotted with kernels of corn and bread chunks. Braised beef pot roast was fork tender and served with buttered noodles and Blue Lake snap beans. There is a large choice of vegetables, including pickled beets, candied yams, and sautéed zucchini.

A close examination of the menu reveals a German touch. There are three Streusel cakes: apple, blueberry, or cherry. All use fresh fruits, and are topped with a raisin crumb crust, sprinkled with brown sugar.

The Glass Kitchen is a large glass-louvered room, with pale green walls and booths. The effect is breezy and calm. The waitresses are mostly older women, who act as if they have been at The Glass Kitchen for years. The only off-note about this otherwise delightful restaurant is the neon sign outside. It is a glaring portrait of a most malevolent-looking chef in a tall cook's hat, scowling down at all the cars that drive by. Don't let his evil-looking visage scare you away; inside all is warm and homey.

NEW CASTLE

★★ HADFIELD'S SEAFOOD
192 North Dupont Highway (Exit 5A off Route 95) (302) 328–6081
FRI AND SAT 9 AM–10 PM / SUN–THURS 10 AM–9 PM

Eating your way across the country's dinner tables raises vexing questions. Which foods are acquired tastes? Which come naturally? Is it environment or heredity that makes every southerner prefer grits to hash browns? In our perplexity we have turned to science for answers, and have accordingly devised an experiment—which needs only a foundation grant to get underway. A newborn baby is placed in a room with a dish of ice cream, a slab of ribs, a beef taco, and a pepperoni pizza. We watch which way the toddler crawls. A variation of the test places our confused infant in a highchair, its tray spread with a single type of food at various stages of sophistication—raw oysters, oysters with ginger horseradish, a fried oyster roll, and Oysters Rockefeller.

The site for our final and most complex experiment is Hadfield's Seafood in Delaware, where the food-crazed baby is set before the most appetizing display of seafood on the East Coast. If the baby is like us, he'll find himself in a land of plenty so distressingly cornucopic, he won't know which way to crawl. Many are the trips back east from the seafood-impoverished Midwest that we set our sights on a three-pound lobster, boiled in seawater and served with butter and pepper hash, only to arrive and suddenly become befuddled in the sea of seafood choices displayed in Hadfield's cases.

There may be better seafood restaurants in the Chesapeake Bay area, but there are none nearer the highway, and none where you can get as much and as many kinds of seafood. Hadfield's is more of a seafood shop than a restaurant; in fact there are no tables at all, no drinks served, and no atmosphere. What they do have is everything that swims in or near the Chesapeake Bay. Several kinds of clams and oysters, crabs (whole, soft-shelled, claws only, knuckles only, crab cakes), lobsters, snapper, hake, fluke, haddock, eel, and dozens of others. Everything is available ready to take home and cook or—after ten minutes' wait—ready to eat. Naturally, we prefer the latter, the modus operandi being to bring beer or soda, order a first course and eat it either in the car or sitting under the fluorescent lights in one of Hadfield's plastic chairs while eyeing your second course.

The place is a marvel—huge, clean, salty but not fishy-smelling. One of the things we love about eating here is watching the food being prepared. It's like being in a friend's kitchen, working up an appetite as you talk and watch them cook dinner.

There is a range of condiments available for whatever fish or crustacean you choose—lemon, hot sauce, horseradish, horseradish blend, spicy crab sauce, and razor-sharp pepper hash—a local specialty for spicing up shrimp. Do not miss the homemade snapper soup, thick with fresh-cubed vegetables and chunks of rich snapper. There are stews, steaks, fillets, and whole fish from bite-size to six-footers (not, to our knowledge, cooked here to order). Bring your beer, and bring your bib, and pull in under the sign of the huge, hovering papier-mâché crab over the doorway.

FAIRS AND FESTIVALS

Delmarva Chicken Festival / LATE JUNE
  Cooking contests (contestants from all over Northeast)
  Location varies: contact Delmarva Poultry Industry, Box 47,
  Georgetown, Del. (302) 856–2971

MARYLAND

HAGERSTOWN

★★THE PARK CIRCLE TAVERN
  325 Virginia Avenue, Route 1 (south of town) (301) 739–5846
  MON–SAT 5:30 AM–MIDNIGHT / SUN NOON–8 PM

The Park Circle Tavern is a workingman's bar and the unlikely but excellent place to sample the Chesapeake Bay aristocrat of fish dishes —terrapin chowder. Terrapin is like no other dish. The soup is gumbo-dark; a complex orchestration of turtle meat, vegetables, and spice sharing space in the bowl but never quite coalescing into a single taste. The effect is potent, and exhilarating, like oysters on the half shell. It is eaten slowly, with deep breaths taken between spoonfuls. The Park Circle serves it in the traditional manner—with a wedge of lemon and a shot glass of dry sherry. Add both to the bowl to join the kaleidoscope of flavors all reaching for hegemony, searingly intense but ultimately mellow.

Terrapin allegedly lured Lafayette to return to the United States in search of the "French" dish that Americans made better. It was the basis of strained continental relationships when terrapin snobs from Europe tittered at Marylanders' versions of the famous soup. For years it has threatened a small-scale civil war as the Louisianians battle it out over the stock pots with the Marylanders to determine which turtle soup is #1.

Today the turtle has been replaced as the king of Chesapeake Bay tables by the crab, and except for a few good hotels and private eating clubs in Maryland, terrapin chowder is as rare as turtle teeth.

Dark yeasty-smelling place that it is, The Park Circle carries the turtle banner high with its Maryland-style chowder (Maryland-style is based on a clear stock, not a cream stock, as in the South). Being in Hagerstown, the headquarters for the annual Hard Crab Festival, The Park Circle is no slouch with steamed crabs, either. Much of their crab business is takeout—and it's wise to bring a bushel basket or large pot if your intention is to picnic. There is an extensive seafood menu, but the deviled crabs we sampled were a disappointment—especially after the spectacular terrapin chowder. They came stuffed into an aluminum "crab," rather than a real shell—a dead giveaway that the meat had been frozen (also obvious by the heavy texture of the meat and bread-crumb mixture).

We usually don't seek roadfood in taverns, since nine out of ten times the patrons' palates are too numb to appreciate the difference between beer nuts and beefsteaks. But some foods go so naturally with beer (like crabs) or sherry (like terrapin chowder) that a bar is the best place to eat. An icy pitcher of beer and a box of crabs is a feast that only Carrie Nation could resist.

MEADOWS

★★CAP'N JIM'S
9207 Old Marlboro Pike (behind Mockabee's Service Station)
(301) 599–9878
APRIL–NOV TUES–FRI 2 PM–10 PM, SAT NOON–10 PM, SUN 11 AM–10 PM

Cap'n Jim has been steaming crabs behind Mockabee's Service Station for more than ten years. Many of his customers are truckdrivers who take this curvy alternative road around the beltway to get cheap diesel fuel, avoid the smokies, and eat some of the best crabs in Maryland.

Like Bar b que, crabs taste better when they are purchased in some out-of-the-way shack or in the back of a service station. Mockabee's looks like a set from an episode of *I Love Lucy*—rounded gas pumps, faded pin-up calendars, oil-stained grease monkeys, air smelling of petrol. The unsophisticated nature of these surroundings lends the food a certain sparkle, a hard-to-get quality that no linen-napkin establishment could hope to match. Even the most generous roadfooder keeps a private cache of such places, revealed to a few, but generally guarded with the silence of the sphinx.

Aside from the satisfaction of knowing the most esoteric place to relish Maryland's finest crabs, there are level-headed reasons for patronizing Cap'n Jim's. First—the price. Cap'n Jim hardly has any overhead beyond what Mockabee charges him for rent and the little electricity he uses to light the blinking eyes in his crab sign (to indicate he's open for business). The second reason is the taste of the crabs.

Cap'n Jim (who is very particular you don't call him "Captain," preferring the slurred maritime version) uses the "ice-cream method" to cook his crabs. "This will only be clear to those who have made ice cream the right way," he explained, "by layering rock salt, heavy cream, berries, or whatever." Cap'n Jim layers his crabs with myriad spices to assure that each crab absorbs the right amount of flavor. "They spice up better that way," he said. "It's better than just throwing 'em in a pot with a handful of spice haphazardly."

After sampling the Cap'n's crabs, we couldn't agree more. They are peppery, succulent, and tender; just fibrous enough; in a word, sensational. They are sold by the dozen, price depending on size. You get them in a paper bag, to go.

Bring your own mallet if you plan to take the crabs back to your car. And please don't wander up front to Mockabee's to borrow their screwdriver or wrench for more scientific crab-probing.

FAIRS AND FESTIVALS

ANNAPOLIS
Maryland Clam Festival   /   EARLY AUG

CRISFIELD
National Hard Crab Derby   /   LATE AUG

HAGERSTOWN
Hagerstown Crab Festival   /   FOR DATE CONTACT DIV. OF TOUR-ISM, 2525 RIVA RD., ANNAPOLIS, MD. 21401

HOMESTEAD
Corn Roast   /   EARLY AUG

LEONARD
St. Mary's Oyster Festival   /   MID-OCT
National Oyster Shucking Contest

OCEAN CITY
Ocean City Seafood Festival   /   MID-JULY

WOODBINE
Apple Butter Festival   /   MID-OCT

NEW JERSEY

COLLINGSWOOD HEIGHTS

★★ BROWN'S STOP-IN

Nicholson Road (Route 130) (609) 456-4535
MON–THURS 11 AM– 10 PM, FRI & SAT 11 AM– 1 AM / CLOSED SUN

Brown's Stop-In is practically in Philadelphia, which among other things has given us American Bandstand, The Mike Douglas Show, and Nosferatu-shaped comedian David Brenner. It has also given us cheese steak, a Philadelphia obsession consisting of a thin cube steak on a hero roll with cheese melted on top.

Brown's has been in Collingswood Heights for a long time. It was first opened in 1948 by Mr. Brown, a soft-spoken man with an eerie resemblance to Will Rogers. He hoisted his sign "taste what pride can do" about that time, and has been standing behind that statement ever since.

The exterior of Brown's is brown and orange, and you might mistake it for an A and W stand. The strip of road it's on is pretty ghastly —lots of peep shows and adult book stands among the used car lots and nightclubs. It's a main road and one frequented by cruising conventioneers. Somehow Brown's has managed to avoid topless waitresses serving cheese steaks.

Cheese steaks come plain or topped with sautéed onions. There is soup made daily in the back kitchen by Mrs. Brown. Pea soup and chicken rice are our favorites. But the heart of Brown's is the milk shake. Taste one, and it is hard to dispute that Mr. Brown is truly the wizard of the soda-fountain, the king of the ice cream shake. The making of the milk shake is a complex operation. We watched our waitress dip a ladle into assorted containers, and work a long spoon into the milk-shake glass in order to achieve the perfect blending of ingredients. The ice cream used at Brown's is handmade by Mr. Brown and the shake is a more-than-rich drink that will hold a straw straight up, yet allows for easy drinking. The chocolate flavor reminded us of our days in Switzerland where we were the obvious Americans, known by our grimy hands and smeared brown lips.

We have taken a dozen or more friends to this modest stand to sample the milk shakes. Even doubting Thomases and self-proclaimed chocolate mavens have come away in awe.

HIGHTSTOWN

★THE GOLDEN COACH DINER
Highway 130 (609) 443–3030
ALWAYS OPEN

New Jersey is dinerland. Few roads in the Garden State are without their venerable old chrome hash houses. But now there is a new wave of diners rolling across the eastern seaboard. It is composed of shiny, jazzed-up incarnations of the old-time eateries, diners that hardly look like a diner any more—all in hopes, no doubt, of shedding the "greasy spoon" image that has befallen the diner in modern times.

The Golden Coach is a prime example of the mod approach to dinerism. Instead of tile and stainless steel, the entrance to the Golden Coach offers a babbling fountain, clusters of plastic vegetables strung along the walls, wood-style Formica, Muzak, and a tinted lighting scheme. The interior is dimly lit, perfumed with the fragrance of Top Job.

Because of this laminated overkill, we approached the Golden Coach with great hesitation. Blue lights and plastic carrots draped on the wall hardly whet our appetites. But past the bubbling foyer, things got better, and we soon realized that the vegetable motif was the owner's way of symbolizing the extravagant amounts of fresh produce that he lists on his menu.

Despite its slick, contemporary appearance, the Golden Coach reaches back to its roots for a menu. Greek food is the specialty of the house, and although you can get burgers and eggs, just like any other diner, we suggest you try Kim Zoumas's (the proprietor) *moussaka, spanokopita,* or *galaktoboriko,* or the stuffed grape leaves, chicken wings with rice pilaf, baklava or *taramasalata.*

We have tried the *spanokopita* and *moussaka,* both of which were made with a deft touch. The former is a multilayered filo pastry alternated with layers of spinach and feta cheese, served warm as an appetizer or side dish. The Coach's *moussaka* is a towering dish—slightly underspiced, but moist and savory. For dessert, we had *galaktoboriko,* a mild, barely sweet custard. Side dishes to the entrées are chosen from an assortment of about two dozen vegetables, varying in quality from a watery zucchini to perfectly buttered lima beans and an inspired dish of eggplant with garlic.

As at so many of the mod diners that try too hard, the Golden Coach falls short on some counts. But if you stick with the daily specials —the vegetables and the Greek dishes—this unlikely roadside dining car will serve you a tasty meal.

★THE NUTRITION CENTER
Route 130 at Dutch Neck Road in Warren Plaza West (609) 448–4885
MON–SAT: LUNCH / STORE OPEN 10 AM–6 PM / CLOSED SUN

"Have you thought of switching to health foods?" asked our slim friend Cabell. Her question filtered into a dim consciousness. The scene was outside Arturo's Restaurant in Greenwich Village—a place that serves such delicious and monumental pepperoni calzone that one of us had fainted while trying to finish a second portion.

The management had graciously provided a cold towel, a chair, and an escort out to the sidewalk "for air," and Cabell's friend Lewis tried to excuse the sidewalk scene to curious passersby, saying alternately "too much to drink" or "it's really hot in there." The fact is that there is simply not enough vital energy in the human body to wage a war on two calzones in the stomach and maintain consciousness as well. But clear vision returned as small platoons of blood were detoured from the major battle in the stomach to the minor skirmish in the skull. Cabell repeated her question about the health food.

Although the debacle at Arturo's was embarrasing enough to call for a resolution of moderation in Italian food, the prospect of a life of carrot juice and plain yogurt seemed too high a price to pay for overindulgence.

But there are times when even the sturdiest gourmand needs a break. One such time is any trip along Route 130 in New Jersey. We had traveled the length of this once-trucker route one morning and had stopped in so many Crisco-encrusted diners that we began to recall the girl in *Goldfinger* whose body had been coated with paint. She was found dead several hours later, having strangulated, her pores fatally clogged with oil. We were chain-chewing Gelusil, and entreating forgiveness from the offended gods who rule over the temples of our bodies. Forgiveness for the double order of slimy scrapple; for the "drumettes"—plastic sticks wrapped with chicken "substance"; for the dark battery-acid masquerading as coffee in all the hundreds of identical oily diners that line both sides of the road. Or were we seeing double??

A billboard appeared before us: "Health foods aren't everything —but they sure beat being sick." We believe! And like converts in a revival tent we stumbled and fell into The Nutrition Center. Two honey-sweetened plain milk shakes, a fresh vegetable salad, and a cream cheese and walnut sandwich on raisin bread were selected with the advice of Mrs. Mangold, in whose rose-cheeked face we recognized seas of sympathy—no doubt cultivated by the other beaten-down road-fooders who had preceded us at this clean little oasis of health on otherwise treacherous Route 130.

Our spirits and bodies rejuvenated, we looked around and saw the Center for what it was—merely a health food store, not too much different from any other, except that there are a few tables and some sandwiches and salads made up in a refrigerator. What we do like about this place—other than the fact that it saved our lives—is the modesty of the simple operation. There were no waiters. You discuss your meal with Mrs. Mangold who, blessedly, does not proselytize for the health food cause. You help yourself to lunch. She will heat up vegetable soup which, unlike regular restaurant soup, is actually a gazpacho-like puree of vegetables. There are sandwiches, and milk shakes. Lunch is 11 A.M. to 2 P.M., after which, you can take sandwiches, salads, and milk shakes out to your car—which is a great idea if you are traveling further south along that greasy skillet of a blacktop known as Route 130.

KENVIL

★★MOM'S COUNTRY KITCHEN
Route 46
ALWAYS OPEN

We have seen places called "Mom's" all over the country, and we have seen the Moms that go with them: Moms with arthritic hands and starched white aprons; Moms that look like longshoremen in drag; Moms that are black mammies; Moms that are hot-blooded mamacitas; and Moms that are men who inherited "Mom's Place."

Maybe it was too much bottle feeding, but it is practically impossible for us to pass a "Mom's" without at least peeking in. And more often than not, we leave disappointed by "Mom's" awful cooking and glad we are grown-up enough to go eat at the local Chinese restaurant.

Occasionally we have hit it right and found a "Mom's" that satisfies. Mom's Country Kitchen is a good example of momism at its best.

Mom's is decorated inside with nursery-pink formica, but coldly covered on the outside with brown wood-grained siding. Despite its tender interior, this is a face only a mother could love. But it might be the only place between the George Washington Bridge and the Delaware Water Gap where, for a miniscule price, you leave feeling satiated and healthy. It's solid home-cooking geared to a small, loyal clientele.

We saw no evidence of Mom. A nubile young waitress, a teenaged dishwasher, and a part-time middle-aged waitress were the cast of characters here; all friendly but none maternal. The older waitress brought our order of soup and corn muffins to the table. The muffin was double-sized, grainy-fresh, and dripping fresh Jersey butter. The chicken soup was second only to the "Jewish Penicillin" made by our Grandma Molly. It was rich with chicken "shmaltz," filled with nuggets of fresh carrots and noodles. Monday at Mom's is pasty day. Pasties are a traditional Cornish dish enjoyed mainly in Michigan's Upper Peninsula. It is a portable meat pie; in its ideal state a heavenly mixture of cubed beef, suet, potatoes, onions, and carrots all wrapped in a pastry crust. The tradition at Mom's is that customers put a dollar in the "kitty" with their name on it, to reserve a Monday pasty. Fortunately Mom usually makes more than enough, and a traveler will have little trouble tasting this Monday treat.

NORTH BRUNSWICK

★★THE MIDDLESEX DINER
Exit 9 off New Jersey Turnpike (junction of Routes 130 and 1)
(201) 247–7095
ALWAYS OPEN

The "Dineraunt" is not a defunct second cousin of the pterodactyl to be found in the La Brea Tar Pits. Dineraunts are very much with us today, alive and stalking the highways of the Northeast. You can spot one by its mottled mirrors, oversized Hellenic medallions, and crystal-like chandeliers. From the outside, a Dineraunt looks like a diner that has been dipped whole into a vat of sticky terrazzo.

Despite the updated look, this new species is still more diner than restaurant. There is still a short-order cook, turning eggs at supersonic speed. The waitress "hi hon" 's you when you sit down. And the clients are still more William Bendix-like than they are of the Marisa Berenson crowd.

The Middlesex is near-maniacal in its efforts to surpass the limits of dinerdom. For diner prices, you are greeted at the door by a maitre d', and escorted with great solemnity to a booth, where your host hands you a gilt-embellished menu entitled "La Cuisine Epic." The nylon-uniformed waitress wiped off and set our table faster than Duke Wayne could draw his pistol, and she waited impatiently as we perused the vast selection on the menu. Our personal selections from La Cuisine Epic, after much umming and ahhing, included the ham and roast beef lunch-eon specials, both of which entitled us to the salad bar. Both came with soup (a thin chicken rice), appetizer (mild and perfectly seasoned chopped liver, with rolls), mashed potatoes running with butter, and a dish of tasteless string beans. In addition we could choose to our heart's content from a much-better-than-average salad bar that included pic-calilli, fresh and garlicky three-bean salad, and hard-boiled egg halves. The ham dinner was bathed in pineapple sauce. The roast beef was rare, moist, and piled high onto two slices of white bread.

If Dineraunts are characterized by good cheap breakfast and lunch specials, fast service and clean—if gaudy—decor, they are also cursed with the world's worst pastries. Here at The Middlesex they are displayed in a spinning case in the center of the restaurant. Multi-colored, a foot tall, and perfectly formed, they are a hypnotic sight—lovely to look at, disastrously awful to eat. With sphagnum-like me-ringue and cryonically preserved fruit, these Dineraunt pastries seem more the work of a vengeful plasterer than a creative chef. Avoid them, and a good meal will be yours at The Middlesex. It may not be La Cuisine Epic, but Dineraunt food can usually be counted on throughout the Northeast to be inexpensive and competently prepared.

SOUTH KEARNY

★THE ARENA DINER

The New Jersey Truck Center (New Jersey Turnpike Exit 15E)
(201) 344–9763
MON–FRI ALWAYS OPEN / CLOSED SAT & SUN

Pity the poor truck driver. Former mysterious knight of the road, he has become a new culture hero. His cloistered culture has been pried open and invaded by media snoops, counterculture recruiters looking for the new messiah, and truckstop groupies hunting up the great stud on eighteen wheels. News and movie crews now record for posterity what muck the hungry gearjammer eats to afford him the energy to make it to the drop-off point.

"Muck" might sound like a slur to what is generally believed to be a cuisine of fundamental wholesomeness. Isn't it true that truckers have a secret black book of places to get the best food along the highway?

It depends on where they are. If they are lucky enough to be in a rural area where the "good eats" are unheralded by big signs or telephone book ads, and it's a word-of-mouth place only, the chances are that the ratchet-jawed trucker will know. If, on the other hand, the place is industrially overwhelmed Eastern New Jersey, then he is as much a prisoner of roadside horror-show restaurants as any of us.

The Arena Diner is the best of the Jersey Turnpike truckstops. For truckdriver afficionados, it is the ultimate experience. Characters out of central casting loiter everywhere. Whores with hearts of gold, and whores with razor blades hidden in their wigs; the fallen-angel waitress with the gum-snapping sugar-pink lips; the black-cuticled steel hauler with forearms like iron cables; the fresh-faced kid from Carolina; trucking families; pill pushers. The Arena Diner is a small island of chrome. It is a microcosm of every hitchhiker's dream; a layout from *Man's Guts* magazine.

Two tight-lipped kitchenmen ("cooks" is stretching the point) spoon out orders. They will, if asked, shake their heads yes or no in response to an inquiry about the freshness of items on the menu. Stuffed cabbage? A yes. Meat loaf? Yes. Fish cakes? A laugh. Oh oh.

The best two items on the rather grim menu are liver and onions and beef stew. The liver was serviceable, and we detected a hint of culinary aspiration in the neat arrangement of a bacon strip across the top, and a sprig of parsley on the side. The stew was mildly seasoned, and unbelievably thick. Both meals were—if not memorable—palatable and digestible, recommended except for the grade-D phony spuds on the side. Like most truckstops, breakfasts star here. Three-egg omelettes are whipped up faster than a front-tire blow out. There are grits for the southern boys, sausage links and Canadian bacon for everyone. And the black coffee flows like Niagara Falls from the Pyrex pots on every counter.

One unique item on The Arena menu is "red pie." When we asked the waitress what it was, she seemed stumped. "Red pie," she answered. She was right. The pie was indeed "red"; a rubbery-crusted triangle stuck together with Hawaiian-punch colored mucilage, without even the pretense of a flavor.

The Arena Diner is the 42nd Street of the trucking world. It's a crossroads where everyone from "Clean-livin' Pete" to the diamond-ring hustler share the space in the shadows of the idling semis. It can be scary at night with Manhattan's lights shining ahead, and the smell of diesel fuel mixing with the hookers' perfume. But we love it for the strange and unique stage it is—where the trucker is still the star.

NEW YORK

COEYMANS

★SY'S FISH FRY
Route 9W
MAY–NOV: DAILY 10 AM–10 PM

Ask any Coeymans high school kid or local redneck or long hauler out of Albany who makes the best clam fry around, and chances are they'll tell you "Uncle Sy." Usually, if we must ask a stranger to recommend a local eatery, we seek out the ladies' auxiliary or the VFW. They may steer you to a café where their friend does the cooking, and where they themselves are likely to stop for a meal. But if it turns out they want to impress you with the cosmopolitan air of their town, and you wind up at The International Room—distinguished usually by its every window being blocked with beige curtains—then a good last resort is to find a cop and tail him. He'll pull in for coffee or lunch, and chances are the place he pulls in will meet survival standards. After all, he eats there—probably every day.

As it happens, a gas jockey clued us in to Sy's, and gas jockeys are a completely unpredictable lot, having sent us to some of the worst hash houses, and to some of the best places in this book. This particular dispenser of petrol was on his summer vacation, and he told us that he and his buddies all go to Uncle Sy's every night after softball.

A peculiar smile on the kid's face led us to half expect that Sy would be a thin and consumptive roadside pied piper, leading the farm boys astray with French postcards and cigarettes. "He's in the woods, across from the high school," we had been told.

Sy's turned out to be a converted ¾ ton truck, surrounded by a hot rod and two pickups. The drivers were clustered around Sy's peep hole window in the back of the truck, from which he dispensed "fannydaddies" (that is, clam fries) and stories about his travels throughout the fifty states. We got our fannydaddies ($1 apiece) and Saratoga Colas and listened to the story about the time he lost his brakes going downhill in West Virginia. Sy loves to talk. He has traveled so much that now he's only comfortable in his "fish fryer"—the truck—talking to customers about life on the road, or discussing his very personal approach to the business of frying clams.

"I always use fresh peanut oil," he told us. "It gives the crusts a tastier snap. The fish are haddock and cod. I feed the pollack to my cat. It's too fishy for people. I make my own horseradish sauce, too. You can put that on your clams, or on the fish, or some of them even put it on the onion rings." Sy's clam fries are crunchy good, and his fish tastes— if not fresh—at least fresh-frozen, and his onion rings and mild horseradish sauce all help to make a good stand-up meal; but what we love about Sy's is Sy. He is a roadside philosopher and raconteur, dispensing fish fry and fifty states' worth of wisdom from the back of his old International truck.

We asked one of the local kids why everybody calls him "Uncle." "Because he gives us real big pieces of fish, and lots of extra clams." Stop at Sy's Fish Fry, and you may wind up calling him Uncle Sy, too.

EAST AVON

★THE CALICO KITCHEN
Route 20 (315) 226–9809
MON–SAT 7 AM–8 PM

The Calico Kitchen is a pleasant little diner by the side of the road in East Avon, an area conspicuously devoid of good eats. Don Merritt manages the Calico, and also serves as pie baker, goulash chef, and bar b que pitmaster. He runs a blue-plate-special type of operation—nothing fancy, but no shortcuts either. He was cutting a piece of strawberry-rhubarb pie when we first met him. "I picked these strawberries Sunday," he said. "Raspberries, apples, whatever's around, I put it into these pies."

Every day Don prepares a daily special that features home-made soup ("Bean with bacon is the one I like," he told us), freshly mashed or fried potatoes, and a main dish like his special goulash or roast beef. Wednesday is chicken day, when a set price buys all you can eat of

Don's bar b qued chicken. That was the day we stopped by, and we found his sauce to be a kind of marinade—no ketchup or tomato paste, just vinegar, oil and spices. The chicken is slowly roasted in the sauce until the meat is saturated and the skin is crisp.

Don't expect any surprises at the Calico Kitchen. The food is far from celestial, but in these parts—where we were once literally poisoned at a nearby "famous" Inn—a square meal made with Don Merritt's workmanlike skills is something to be thankful for.

FISHKILL

★ M'S COFFEE SHOP
Route 9 (north of Route 84)
MON–SAT 6 AM–8 PM / CLOSED SUN

The doctor had just ordered owner Kate to lose weight. This is no easy chore for a woman whose love in life is cooking, and who is known up and down the Thruway for her "Kate Supreme," a whipped cream peaked peach chiffon pie with a graham cracker crust. "No more pastry pudding or double biscuit shortcakes." Kate went on with her sad story as she forked a mound of mayonnaised macaroni salad. "The doctor said I could only eat salads, so today I made macaroni and yesterday, chicken salad."

Kate's "diet" meals will give you some idea of the rich food on M's menu. Main courses will include country sausage with potato salad, or pastrami with mashed potatoes. There is usually a heavy-duty beef stew simmering on the stove, and soups are made with lots of noodles or barley.

Kate prides herself on how much of the food served at M's she makes herself. "Why put one thing in the oven, when there's room for two?" is her philosophy. Unfortunately, Kate's enthusiasm for cooking occasionally overextends her talents and some of the menu is better left untried.

The pastrami here was thin and dry, it was served with two slices of supermarket rye bread and a small scoop of potato salad. The roast beef too was dry and overcooked, although there were good hard rolls on the side. The country sausage is made every other day by a local butcher who is a friend of Kate's. It is savory and rich with a slightly smoked taste and is the best choice for a main course on Kate's menu.

Desserts are the most popular part of the meal at M's. Pastry pudding is a fancy bread pudding made from day-old Danish, and studded with pieces of citron and almonds. Strawberry shortcake is made the way it is preferred by upstate New Yorkers, on a biscuit. Kate pulls trays of powder-topped shortcake biscuits from the oven and heaps them with hulled strawberries and whipped cream. In peach season Kate makes a peach chiffon pie that makes roadfooders screech to a halt in front of M's.

The café is a pretty place. It is a one-room house decorated on the outside with hand-painted wooden dogs, and on the inside with paintings and nicknacks. Kate was last seen seated at a table over lunch. "I call my cooking 'old-fashioned.' I use nothing but fresh eggs, milk, and lots of butter in the recipes, and I don't cook anything that I don't want to eat myself." Poor diet! Poor Kate!

HYDE PARK

★★★THE COFFEE SHOP
The Campus of the Culinary Institute of America, Route 9, 3 mi. S. of Hyde Park (914) 452–9600, ext. 200
DAILY BREAKFAST, LUNCH, DINNER, AND 8 PM–MIDNIGHT FOR SANDWICHES & BEVERAGE

The Coffee Shop is a model diner—literally. It is a training classroom for students of the Culinary Institute of America enrolled in the course "Coffee Shop." In order to get a good grade in their course, they have to keep it immaculate, provide courteous service, and prepare excellent food. As the students hone their skills, the public is invited to take advantage of their conscientiousness.

How many diners do you know that serve fresh-baked rye bread and dinner rolls? How many blue-plate specials feature baked filet of sole Mornay, buttered spinach leaf, and rice pilaf? Is there another diner in the world that offers braised brisket Jewish style, tzimmes and potato kugel? All are available here at The Coffee Shop as part of a fifteen-day cycle menu that requires the class to create a different type of cuisine each day. One day you will find German-style pot roast, red cabbage and potato pancakes; another, Virginia ham and candied sweet potatoes; or moussaka and tomato sauce; Yankee meat loaf and cottage fries; even broiled frankfurters and Boston baked beans.

Items that you long ago gave up ordering in restaurants (because they were inevitably canned, prepackaged, or portion-controlled), you can order here—confident that if the student cook is caught serving bogus or second-rate food, he or she will fail the course.

The Coffee'Shop is constantly being cleaned, dusted and polished (students rotate daily between cooking, cleaning and dishwashing). Service is attentive, at counter or booth. All students are required to maintain a clean-cut appearance and wear freshly laundered clothes.

The Coffee Shop is in fact so trim, and the food is so beyond the aspirations of most diners, that a meal here takes on surreal overtones. One's disorientation is reinforced by stepping out of the red-and-white dining car into the midst of a unique college campus. Students dressed in "whites" and *toques blancs* (chefs' hats) stand about discussing recipes, butchering techniques, or an upcoming lesson in wine-tasting class. As you walk out to your car in the parking lot, you may want to take one last look over your shoulder to assure yourself that this exemplary diner really exists.

LAKE GEORGE

★★PROSPECT MOUNTAIN DINER AND RICKSHAW ANNEX
Route 9 (518) 668–9847
SUMMERS: ALWAYS OPEN
REST OF YEAR CLOSED MON 10 PM–WED MORNING

The Prospect Mountain Diner is like the souvenir-shop portraits whose eyes open and close as you walk in front of them. From the highway, The Prospect Mountain looks just like a diner; from the parking lot it's a Chinese restaurant. It's both of these, attached by an umbilical cord of a corridor that nourishes each cuisine with strength from the other.

We are usually a little skeptical about hyphenated restaurants, figuring that German-American or Italian-American usually means the worst of both worlds; that the weak spots of each country's cuisine have only watered down the strong points of the other. Witness: the German-American restaurants that serve hot dogs as knackwurst; the Italo-American ones that specialize in "pizzaburgers." The Prospect Mountain keeps its facilities separate, and provides the best of both worlds.

Starting at noon, sitting in either the aged wood and mirror beauty of a perfect Worcester dining car or in modest oriental surroundings, you begin your meal with Wonton soup and crispy egg rolls. If you are in the diner, proceed to braised short ribs of beef jardinaire or fried fillet of fresh perch. Specials of the day on the Chinese side were *Cha Siu* (thinly sliced pork tenderloin), fresh cherrystone clams with black beans and hot sauce, *Sieu Pi Kwat* (baby bar b que back ribs), and Maine lobster, Cantonese style.

It's hard enough to choose from one good-looking menu; harder still from a Chinese selection; and downright impossible when you've got to choose between these two. Reminding ourselves "you're always hungry after eating Chinese," we began with Cha Siu, cherrystone clams and baby ribs, on the Chinese side. The pork was dry, as befits Chinese pork, but this is delightfully remedied by application of duck sauce. The clams were breathtaking—literally. The combination of their oceany flavor, a hot mustard sauce, and the beans was a piercing three-way balance.

We left the Chinese restaurant, walked a few steps, and entered the diner. The atmospheric change provided just the psychological dislocation to restimulate our appetites. Sitting in the red leather booths, we began the second stage of our dinner with something we had neglected in the beginning: Wonton soup, only average, with gummy dumplings, followed by egg rolls which were homemade, filled with fragile greens and sprouts, and wrapped in a light, crispy skin. They tasted all the better for their unusual setting in this prime example of roadside Americana, just as a mediocre pagoda might take on a certain luster if it were set in the center of Levittown.

The short ribs of beef jardinaire brought us back to our senses. It was a no-nonsense platter of stick-to-the-ribs meat, potatoes, and vegetables.

Dessert by this time was an impossibility, so we noted for the next visit that there was a fruity-looking fresh strawberry-rhubarb pie behind the counter. The waitress told us that pumpkin pie was made regularly in the cold weather.

In addition to what we sampled, The Prospect Mountain Diner extends its octopus reach into all manner of archetypical diner fare—breakfasts any time, burgers, steaks, chops, and from "the other side," pungent braised duck and harvest vegetable plates. There were three kinds of curry listed on the menu, and more.

We recommend this place for all but those who have a difficult time choosing one meal from a possible hundred.

PORT CHESTER

★ TEXAS LUNCH
24 North Main Street (Route 1) (914) 939–4850
ALWAYS OPEN

"I don't eat chili," says Edna Kaplan as she drops two large dippers full into a china bowl. "It's too hot for me." Edna is a tall, gracious, soft-spoken lady. "Tell me honestly," she asks. "How does this rate? I mean compared to what you find in Texas. On a ten scale, what do you give it?" Now Edna is the last woman in the world you would expect to belong to that small and eccentric group of chefs who spend their time fussing and fretting over the possible preparations of the celebrated state vegetable of New Mexico, the chili pepper. For one thing, she doesn't even like the stuff. All her efforts to brew a perfect chili are purely altruistic. For another, her hole-in-the-wall in downtown Port Chester hardly seems like the magnet for commuting chilihead cowboys from Greenwich and New Rochelle, cajoling Edna on their way to the office to spice it up. Then there's Edna herself—neat as a pin, silver-haired, precise in her movements, birdlike in her sentience of everything happening along the fifty-yard Formica counter. What is she doing in this twenty-four-hour diner called Texas Lunch, speaking softly and mixing great vats of chili? Why is this lovely Jewish mother so concerned that *her* bowl of red compete with the best?

We had just driven past the Life Saver factory and were gawking at the giant pop-art Life Saver packages by the side of Route 1 when we saw the pink neon cowboy hat and the sign that says simply "Texas." We sat at the counter and were happy to hear that Texas serves only chili—in a bowl or on top of hot dogs and hamburgers. Such exclusivity was at least a promise of culinary concentration. We ordered a bowl, which came with a fresh-buttered crusty roll and an anticipatory look from Edna as she watched us take our first taste.

After a few spoonfuls, our sinuses cleared and beads of perspiration appeared on our foreheads. This chili was as hot as any we've had in any restaurant. In the Southwest, chili cooks are always excusing the mild chili they serve in restaurants as "toned down for people who can't stand it the way I make it at home." Not Edna. On a ten scale, relative to all other restaurant chilis (home brews excluded), Edna gets 10 for hotness, and 5 for taste.

The alleged purpose of making food hot, a Szechuan connoisseur once told us, is to "open up" the taste buds, to stretch their abilities to distinguish among a wide variety of flavors. Many burnt-tongued and red-faced eaters would disagree and say that excess hotness is merely numbing, eventually jading the taste buds to the point where only the hottest foods make any impression at all. Being hot food junkies, we prefer the former explanation. Edna's chili proves the rule. It is searingly hot, preparing the palate, but beyond the jolt there is no mystery, no bouquet. There are only minimal seasonings and ground meat and beans.

Edna's chili helps us understand why maniacal chiliheads have banned the bean and outlawed ground meat. The bean is starchy and thick-tasting. The ground meat takes over and flavors everything. There is little room in Edna's chili for adventure beyond these two dominant tastes. We remembered back to Tigua Indian chili, to the kaleidoscope of seasonings and the mystery of the chili pepper itself—all of which emerged after the initial burst of fire.

What Edna makes is an extremely hot version of basic northern chili "stew." We have had hotter in the kitchens of fellow fireeaters, and better-tasting in chili parlors of the Southwest. But many a night we have worked up a chili craving while reading Frank X. Tolbert's inspirational *A Bowl of Red,* or daydreaming about some mad-dog recipe from south of Falfurias. At these times, we are very happy to have found Texas Lunch, and thankful that sweet Edna Kaplan has made it her business in life to provide chili to Port Chester. We sit on a stool in the fluorescent light and filter out the raucous noises of Port Chester, converting the Puerto Rican street talk into Tex-Mex conversations, and transforming Edna's fine chili into that sublime chili that Easterners are condemned to only dream about.

SILVER CREEK

★THE FRONT PAGE
213 Central Avenue (716) 934–4400
MON–SAT 6 AM–9 PM, SUN 9 AM–2 PM

The Front Page is a small-town restaurant, whose theme is newspaper journalism. The menu is several mimeographed pages, designed to vaguely resemble a newspaper, including "Morning," "Afternoon" and "Evening" editions. Foods are listed as "Features," "Headliners" or, for dessert, "Big Scoops." What we like about the restaurant is that it has not succumbed to a case of the cutes. The newspaper motif is here just for decoration. It doesn't supplant the basically good food and quiet, cozy tone of the small dining room.

The highlight of the Morning Edition is homemade bread, served alongside all the usual egg offerings plus what they call here an "Italian breakfast"—eggs, home fries and green peppers all scrambled together. The Omelette column lists nine different ingredients, from which you choose as many as you like. The Afternoon Edition features "beef on kimmelweck," a favorite in this part of New York State, which is roast beef served on a roll made with coarse-grained salt and kimmel seeds. There is also a full list of sandwiches and a few salads, all available with homemade bread. There is nothing exotic in the Evening Edition, although the hand of an aspiring chef is evident—in the roast beef dinner "cooked in wine," and "Bea's special recipe" spaghetti and meatballs. There is turkey, roast pork, a homemade meat loaf and a few seafood offerings.

If you are not interested in The Big Scoop for dessert, we suggest you try the homemade pie. There is at least one variety each day, baked with the same adroit hand as the bread.

The climate of The Front Page is as homey as its basic cuisine. It is a single small storefront, the window filled with cacti. Tables are surrounded by captain's chairs. One or two of the management's children are in evidence, including the baby, who was crawling around under one of the tables. And as befits either a hospitable home or a hard-working newspaper, the coffee served at The Front Page is strong and bracing.

WEST COXSACKIE

★★THE ORIGINAL RED'S SEAFOOD RESTAURANT
Route 9 (Exit 21B, New York Thruway) (518) 731–9905
JUNE–SEPT: TUES–SUN 11:30 AM–9:30 PM, JULY & AUGUST DAILY

Red's "original" claim is for real; it's been in the same spot for thirty-two years and is surrounded by copycats in every direction. Red's is famous for its fish and a secret recipe "pink sauce" that is dolloped onto the fish in lunchtime sandwiches, or served alongside at dinner. It is a pretty restaurant, with geraniums carefully tended in window boxes outside, and the lacquered wood tables inside topped with cloth napkins, little vases with flowers, and baskets of fresh-baked hard rolls.

Lunch sandwiches are served on these rolls—a choice of scallops, clams, oysters, or shrimp. The pink sauce that is served with it is a mild blend of mayonnaise, chili and spice, like thousand island dressing, only smoother.

Dinners begin with salad that comes with a blue cheese dressing that is, like the pink sauce, whipped into an airy consistency. It is spooned onto the salad, tangy smooth and still lumpy with blue cheese.

Dinner soups are made from scratch, a fact attested to by our waitress who told us that her husband refused to believe Red's really went to the trouble of starting from slow-simmering bones. She took him back into the kitchen, where there "wasn't a bouillon cube in sight," he reported. "It's made just like my Magyar mama made it, from the veal bones." The veal was the base for a thick goulash soup.

The top-of-the-line item on the menu (except for lobsters) is shad roe wrapped in bacon, a rich and gelatinous delicacy served here slightly too dry. But the bacon does a fair job of making up for the lost oiliness of the roe. The sole dinner was flakey and so tenderly cooked it seemed poached. We ordered it broiled and it came with a light, smoky paprika crust.

The big disappointment at Red's was our waitress telling us that the pies are store-bought frozen, then baked in Red's ovens. Unscrupulous café owners call this "home cooking," but our waitress kindly said, "If you want something really good, have the rice pudding. Red's is famous for it." We took the advice, and were happy to get a perfect blend of vanilla, eggs, cream, nutmeg, and rice. "They come from fifty miles away, just for the pudding." Rice pudding fanciers will see why.

Famous for pudding and pink sauce, Red's serves good meals and maintains his position as not only the original, but the best seafood restaurant around. Other Reds may come and go, but the original is here to stay.

WEST WINFIELD

★★★ THE STONE HOUSE RESTAURANT
Babcock Hill Road (315) 822–5369
WED–SAT 5 PM–8 PM / SUN NOON–5 PM / CLOSED MON & TUES

If the cuisine of upstate New York is as much a mystery to you as it was to us, try The Stone House Restaurant. "New York" food is usually synonymous with what is eaten in New York City: pizza, gyros, cuchifritos, bagels and lox, and anything else that can be eaten in one hand while rushing for the subway. But what do northern New Yorkers eat? It wasn't until we met Leona and Morton Halle that we found out.

The Halles run The Stone House, with offerings as removed from the style of New York City as raw farm milk is from Orange Julius. Their restaurant is a favorite among the prosperous-looking farmers of the Winfield area, and the popular spot for country ladies and gentlemen to dine.

The most popular meal served at The Stone House is salt pork and milk gravy. Salt pork is usually associated with the lardy white strip of fat used to season baked beans, and if this is your only contact with salt pork you're in for a delightful surprise. After it is blanched, dredged in flour and fried, the salt pork tastes like a giant strip of tender bacon. It has a well-marbled surface, unlike the fatty pork used for cooking beans. The salty flavor of the finished dish is perfectly offset by the mild milk gravy.

Cream gravy is an important dish at The Stone House. Leona Halle uses it on boiled chicken, which has been arranged on top of two baking powder biscuits. Boiled chicken and salt pork are served for dinner on Wednesday, and come with cornmeal "johnnycakes." Johnnycakes are first cousins to cornpone, hoecakes, or ashcakes, as they are called in other parts of the country. In upper New York State they originally got their name from the times when they were carried in wagons over the rural countryside and called "journeycakes."

The cuisine of New York State is one of bland meats, spiced with tart pies and zesty breads. The dinner of creamed codfish and pumpkin muffins is a classic example. The muffins were ginger-sharp and fragrant with cloves in the orange batter, providing a good counterbalance to the milky taste of the fish. Leona is a veteran muffin maker, and when pumpkin muffins aren't on the menu, pie plant (rhubarb) or fresh raspberry are. Desserts use similar ingredients; rhubarb, either tartly plain or sweetened with strawberries is a favorite. We preferred the delicious peanut-butter cake with orange frosting and a sour cream pineapple with a tall egg fluff top.

The restaurant is in a beautiful old house built in the 1800s. If it were closer to New York City it might wind up as "Ye Olde Stone House" complete with colonial-capped busboys and double-digit prices. As it is, situated in New York farm country and trafficked by gentlemen farmers, The Stone House is an authentic introduction to a seldom publicized cuisine.

WOODSTOCK

★ THE WOODSTOCKER CAFÉ
Route 212 (914) 679-9554
MON–FRI 7 AM–10 PM, SAT 7 AM–5 PM, SUN 7 AM–3 PM

One viewing of the film *Woodstock* was about as close as we ever came to participating in the rituals of the love generation, but we found ourselves ten years after the fact driving through upstate New York, and so thought we'd drop in and see what we had missed, and what Mother Nature's raggle-taggle brood had come to over the course of a decade.

A friend of ours who still wears long hair and a glaze over his eyes suggested The Pub was *the* place to go. But The Pub has apparently become the luncheon stop for the Upstate Ladies Tea and Tennis Society, with escargots and eight-dollar entrees. Our next stop was a "Nature's Pantry," which smelled more like Nature's locker room. Next, the Café Espresso, an Italo-beatnik dive that only a starving poet could love.

Finally, The Woodstocker provided the healthful nature's bounty we were looking for. It is in a shopping center, and appears to be the kind of Formica luncheonette in which you consume a hamburger and a milk shake while your clothes are drying next door. But even so basic an institution as The Shopping Center Café is, in Woodstock, garlanded with love. Breakfasts are served, the menu says, "with love." Sandwiches are not sandwiches, but "five ounces of meat and goodies on a bun." Instead of milk shakes, there is orzata (almond) and tamarind essence. The clientele is a strange mixture of health nuts, suburbanites, post-hippies, and vegetarians who look very much like the vegetables they eat.

The menu is an eclectic blend of New York deli, health food, and small-town café. We ordered a bowl of chili, which was a simple ground beef-and-bean mixture, enlivened with crisp green peppers, served in a china coffee cup. The best thing we ate here was the fruit salad, which fulfilled all our Woodstock fantasies by being a very large dish of fresh pineapple, watermelon, oranges, apples, and even a few dark ripe cherries. Homemade yogurt with some of the same fruits and wheat germ was also genuinely fresh-tasting, and made us feel nobly natural. Our five ounces of goodies on a bun was ham and cheese in ample amounts, served on a hard roll. But the cold cuts were uninspired and dry.

There are bagels for breakfast, and a variety of fresh-vegetable omelettes. We sipped our tamarind essence and gazed around the Formica room at walls hung with macrame and local art. A few "free" children were running amok as their parents sipped tea. The Woodstocker is a nice place to visit and get fresh wholesome food. It's on the outskirts of town—about as far into Woodstock as the traveler need go for a taste of what remains of the Woodstock Nation.

FAIRS AND FESTIVALS

FRANKLINVILLE
Western New York Maple Festival / LATE APRIL

JEFFERSON
Maple Festival / LATE APRIL

NAPLES
Grape Festival / LATE SEPT

PENN YAN
Grape Festival / LATE SEPT

PENNSYLVANIA

CARLISLE

★★DOROTHEA'S FORT LOWTHER RESTAURANT
35 West High Street (717) 249-3644
MON–FRI 6 AM–3 PM / SAT 6 AM–2 PM / CLOSED SUN

Dorothea's Fort Lowther Restaurant is a roadfood mecca along Route I-81. Although the noontime crowds here are mostly local people, we have never failed to run into a fellow traveler who has heard through the grapevine about Dorothea Baumbach's chicken corn soup and funeral pie, or about Bob Baumbach's winter fasnachts. These are the highlights of a simple café menu that reflects without pretense or hoopla the best of Pennsylvania Dutch cooking.

None of the fancy dishes are here; no "seven sweets and seven sours" as on traditional Mennonite tables. "I'm a farmer's daughter,"

Dorothea says. She makes the kind of food she remembers from the farm. Meals always begin with soup, preferably the heavy transluscent chicken corn soup, but also ham and bean, beef barley, chicken and homemade noodles, or split pea. Main courses are likely to be one of the Baumbach's "inventions," like the "turketti" casserole, a so-called poor-man's dish consisting of thick chunks of turkey, ham, spaghetti, mush-room sauce, broccoli, and mild cheddar cheese. We are not casserole fanciers by nature, but we can assure Doubting Thomases that turketti bears no resemblance to meal-stretching mixes or housewife helpers. It is a hearty, spiced, poultry-filled stew. Another eccentric lunch is chicken and waffles. It begins with fresh-made waffles, tasting of butter-milk. They are covered with chicken in a thick stock and sided with buttery mashed potatoes and sweet cole slaw.

There are full breakfasts including fresh waffles and hot sweet rolls. But the season to have breakfast here is winter. That is when Bob Baumbach makes fasnachts—exactly the way he learned by watching his mother make them—an arduous process of getting up every few hours throughout the night to "knock down the dough." The result is a cloud of yeasty potato pastry, like a doughnut with a slit in the middle instead of a hole. But we'll fight the first man who says "it sounds like a spudnut." Bob's fasnachts are like nothing on earth.

Their perfection is partly due to the joy Bob puts into them as he cooks. He does all the heavy work—like the fasnachts, and the sauer-kraut, which he laughingly tells you he stomps down with special "kraut-stomping boots."

Bob also had a hand in the pineapple cheesecake recipe—per-fected by him, Dorothea, and one of his cousins over a ten-year period. It is creamy and light for cheesecake, covered with sweet pineapple on top, with a layer of crumbly graham flour and bran underneath. The best dessert here is Dorothea's old-fashioned funeral pie. This is what the Pennsylvania Dutch call raisin pie, customarily served at wakes. Dorothea remembers that when she was a child, her mother's funeral pies were kept down in a cave in the basement because they had no refrigerator on the farm. She was always terrified of the cave but never too afraid to brave the unknown for a slice of funeral pie.

All the roadfooder need do for a piece is to stop in The Fort Lowther. It is a tiny storefront on the main street of Carlisle, with clean white-starched curtains on the windows. The inside is as narrow as the storefront, with a few tables and a counter stretching far back to the post office lot on the next block. It is a simple restaurant—and one of Pennsylvania's best.

CLARION

★★THE CLARION RESTAURANT
One Sixth Street (814) 226–9251
DAILY 6 AM–9 PM

Eating at The Clarion is like eating in a diorama of a Museum of Natural History. The restaurant is subterranean, but the lack of windows is more than compensated for by a wall-to-wall mural covering all surfaces, snaking around doorways and climbing up toward the ceiling. The mural is a Rousseau-like lushly painted verdant-green farm and forest, and although it was painted thirty-five years ago, the lack of natural light in The Clarion has preserved it perfectly.

The restaurant itself has been in the same underground spot since 1895, and is as much a tradition in Clarion as church on Sunday. In fact, the after-church crowd is the reason for the fancy turkey dinners that proved to be the best food here. The meal starts with homemade soup, usually a vegetable broth, and along with sweet cloverleaf rolls, molasses baked beans, candied yams, and a salad, comes moist freshly baked turkey with stuffing. Dessert, also included in the price, is usually a choice between pumpkin pie or pineapple-cream meringue.

If you miss the Sunday after-church feast, similar meals are served seven days of the week. There might be chicken or pot roast instead of turkey and stuffing, but the double-sized cloverleaf rolls and freshly baked pies are a constant source of enjoyment in this encapsulated forestlike restaurant.

CLINTONVILLE

★EDNA'S COFFEE SHOP
Butler Street (814) 385–6628
DAILY 10 AM–11 PM

Edna's is a plain white café, minutes from busy Interstate 80. The town of Clintonville, despite its proximity to the superslab, is as rural and folksy as Dogpatch, U.S.A. Edna knows everyone who eats here, and she is a local celebrity in these parts.

The words "Edna" and "Meat loaf" are synonymous in Clintonville, and Edna's reputation as Queen of the loaf-pan has kept the café thriving in a town that looks like it would have trouble keeping a discount store in business.

Now we are the first to admit that meat loaf is one of those dishes that it would take a Rose Bowl cheerleading section to get us excited about. As kids, the mention of it made us wish we had slept over at a friend's house, but Edna almost changed our mind. The slice of crusty meat has a tender middle. A blend of beef and ground pork, the loaf is light and finely seasoned with a hint of tomato and chopped onion. It magically slips the bounds of commonplace expectations and brings back memories of delicious *piroshkies,* or stuffed Serbian dumplings. Unfortunately, it comes with the most anemic of vegetables and only passable potatos. We suggest a meat-loaf sandwich as an alternative, cheaper and more to the point.

Edna makes her own peach and apple pies, but they failed to impress us. While they had the irregular markings of a made-by-human-hands pie there was a sharply astringent taste to the peach that turned us off.

You will recognize Edna amongst all the other cotton-frocked farm ladies by her resemblance to a female Charles Laughton, and her gravity-defying pompadour, encased in a forehead-hugging hairnet.

GIRARD

★★THE LANDWEHR HOUSE
1133 E. Main (814) 774–8014
MON–SAT 8:30 AM–10 PM, SUN 10 AM–8 PM, DINNER SERVED FROM 4:30 PM

The Erie, Pennsylvania area is not known for its exotic cuisine, nor has it produced to our knowledge any of the world's great gourmets. So Mrs. Julian of the Landwehr House has to be a little sneaky. "The townspeople," she said, "well, they're just not used to anything different." Although her menu looks like any other coffee shop or mid-priced restaurant (steaks, chops, sandwiches, nothing special), her waitresses are informed of the evening's specials. If a customer asks, or if a customer looks potentially interested, the waitresses might impart the information that tonight there is sauerbraten, made from scratch, served with crisp, oniony potato pancakes. Or perhaps there will be *kasseler ripchen mit Kraut* (smoked pork chops, sauerkraut and mashed potatoes); or *Rouladen*—round steak with stuffing and pork sausage. All these unlisted specialties come with homemade soup and rolls. Not all are available every day. But be sure to ask the waitress, lest she mistake you for a culinary stick-in-the-mud.

You will usually find perch listed on the menu. This is a house specialty, served throughout the spring and summer, and frozen then to last through the winter months. It is served deep-fried in a light breading.

The Landwehr House is a lovely old building made of red brick and white wood. The dining areas inside are a rather confusing maze connecting a coffee shop area to dining rooms to a lounge. The entrance is a small door around the side.

KRUMSVILLE

★★THE SKYVIEW RESTAURANT
Jct. I-78 & Rt. 737 (215) 756–6027
DAILY 6 AM–10 PM

Krumsville is a quick buggy ride from Kutztown, the heart of Amish country and the site of the annual Pennsylvania Dutch Folk Life Fair.

When the Fair is on, most restaurants in the area serve Dutch food, but when the last tourist is gone the funeral pies and scrapple are packed away until next year. The Skyview is one of the few places we found that serves the unusual dishes of the region all year round.

This is not to say that The Skyview is untouched by commercialism. It too has its share of souvenir Amish bonnets and Dutch-style hex signs for sale, but the overall tone of the place is more hometown than hokey.

Carl and Linda Wolfinger run The Skyview, and they have chosen to dress their college-girl waitresses in Amish-like bonnets during fair time. We figured Linda felt it added a touch of authority to their serving of dishes like *Schnitz und Knepp* or *Ponhaus und Brodwurst.* The Shnitz und Knepp is an apple and dumpling gravy in which small pieces of ham are simmered. The Ponhaus platter was an assortment of scrapple (a cornmeal and pork sausage shaped and sliced flat), brodwurst, and sliced roasted apples. The meat platters were disappointing, the scrapple so lifeless and dry that the waitress used it as a trivet for the pepperslaw that she brought with the platter to the table.

It was not the meat dishes that impressed us about The Skyview. The side dishes were eye-openers. A bowl of corn fritters was light and yet buttery, made more perfect with a smear of homemade apple butter. Funnel cakes are spiral-coiled pastry dough, sprinkled with powdered sugar. They are still light enough to be eaten with the main course. Potato Filling is a one-half bread one-half potato mixture with kernels of corn added. It is perhaps the single most fattening dish we can think of, a mainline fix straight to the derriere, but aside from the guilt, delicious.

Shoofly pie is the preferred dessert. The Skyview makes "dry-bottomed" shoofly, which is similar to a crumb-topped coffee cake. But even with a dip of ice cream, their version was too dry and pasty.

We left The Skyview full and fat, lulled into contentment by the wonderful side dishes and the lazy Susan filled with chowchow, home-made pickles, and apple butter. If you find yourself at The Skyview, follow the waitress's suggestion and order a tall cold glass of Kutztown Red Birch Beer with your meal; it is a perfect accompaniment to funnel cakes and potato filling.

LOCK HAVEN

★ JANET'S RESTAURANT
Main Street (Route 220) (717) 748–9928
DAILY 6 AM–10 PM

Pennsylvania is meat loaf country, so, to say that Harold Hochen-berg of Janet's makes some of the best in the state is like finding the very best bouillabaisse on the circumference of the Mediterranean. Well, not exactly. But it is good meat loaf. A three-inch-thick slab, crisped and dark brown on the crust, moist and faintly sweet inside, firm and meaty tasting.

But Harold is not the kind of man to rest on the laurels of his loaf alone. He also makes sandwiches—crazy dreamt-up sandwiches that take shape in the fevered brain of a twenty-year meat-loaf-maker who suddenly, while waiting by the oven, is hovered over momentarily by a light bulb. He goes into action. Thin slices of ham get layered onto a double portion of cheese. The ham and cheese are put between two slices of bread. Then—the inspiration—the whole thing is dipped in egg and fried. It is called "The Hock Special" a cross between French toast and ham and cheese. There are sandwiches of less conjectural progeny, such as hamburgers, egg salad, tuna.

Janet's is a beautiful old luncheonette that looks like a small-town dance hall from the 1930s. Its elaborate interior space is broken up with carved-wood arches, dark mouldings, and Art-Deco faceted mirrors. It is a look of bygone elegance that upwardly mobile city restaurants strive for when they want to attract the disco set for dinner or late-night sandwiches.

But Janet's, being an upwardly mobile small-town restaurant, downplays its bygone beauty. In fact, Harold is thinking of covering all "the old-fashioned stuff" with new, modern, wood-grain plastic panels. They're easier to take care of, and will give Janet's an up-to-date look.

Our only consolation when we think of this unfortunate renewal plan is that Harold has been threatening changes here for the last two years. "I'm going to change the name of the place," he told us in 1975. It's still Janet's. "I'm going to modernize," he said early in 1976. It's still the same elegant café. So maybe Harold won't get around to modernizing Janet's. There are too many new sandwiches to invent, Harold, to fiddle with the fixtures. Please, stick with the sandwiches and your perfect meat loaf, and leave the phoney wood siding to the automat luncheonettes that line Route 80. Janet's is too good to spoil.

LOGANTON

★SI'S VALLEY INN
Interstate 80 (Exit 27) (717) 725–3636
DAILY 8 AM–8 PM, SAT 8 AM–2 PM

There is an old stand-up comedy routine about the nightclub act that's doing lousy business. A man calls the club on the phone to ask "What time does the show start?"

"What time can you get here?" the management replies.

At Si's Valley Inn, that's no joke. The last time we were driving along I-80, we stopped near exit 25 to call Si's to see if they'd be open when we got to Loganton. "We'll be closing early tonight," the man said. "There's an auction we're going to."

"Oh, that's too bad," we said.

"Well, what time could you get here?" he graciously asked.

We didn't get to Si's that night, in spite of their willingness to miss the auction for our sakes. What we missed that trip was one of the homiest home-town restaurants we have ever seen. From the outside it looks like many of the Loganton houses. It is white, ramshackle, and has a front porch where teenagers read hot rod magazines and old people read the paper. Inside is a small kitchen-sized room with a counter and some oilcloth tables. There is a much larger room in front, scattered with easy chairs, old copies of National Geographic, and ten thousand comic books. The purpose of the front room is for friends and patrons of Si's to sit and ruminate, to chat, to read, or just to stare into space as one ancient Loganite was doing first time we ate here.

In the back room—the dining room—there were two truckers, two local cops, and a couple whose house had burned down a month ago and were still moving into a new one.

Daily specials are simple things—meat loaf, pork roast, roast beef, salmon croquettes, and a few frozen patties. The best meals are the bowls of chili, here a thick, cumin-flavored bean soup, and the meat loaf, when they have it. Desserts are first-rate homemade pies. The cherry pie in the summer is filled with tart cherries and only minimum cornstarch binder. The crusts are delicate and dry, dusted with sugar.

When you eat here it is likely you will be asked where you're from. We told one of the ladies behind the counter we were from New York and she asked if we wanted to "set in the parlor awhile. Old George would like to talk to you." She motioned at the man we saw staring into space when we had entered. "He grew up in New York. Albany, I think he said."

We walked to the front parlor, but George had fallen asleep. Two eight-year-olds were playing with a Bionic Man doll at George's feet. We thumbed through some old *National Geographics* and relaxed. The truckers finished their lunches and asked us on the way out if we were heading east. If so, they'd be "front door" and keep an eye out for smokies.

Si's is one of a kind. It's like being adopted by a sloppy version of the Waltons; and it's nice to know they will keep the home fires burning, even when they have to miss an auction to do so.

NEW HOLLAND

★★★ PEOPLE'S RESTAURANT
140 West Main Street (Route 23) (717) 354–2276
MON–FRI 8 AM–8 PM / SUN 11 AM–7 PM / CLOSED SAT

People's is plain and pleasant—a tidy sampler of the fabulous food feast found at the Tri County Relief Sale held by the Mennonites every April in nearby Morgantown. But April comes only once a year, and a craving for shoo-fly pie or Lancaster sausage sometimes just won't wait until the spring splurge. So any other time when you start dreaming of funnel cake and fasnachts, scrapple and fresh chow chow, head for People's and you won't be disappointed.

A first trip here, through the communities of Blue Ball, Intercourse, and Bird in Hand, is likely to leave the unprepared traveler weak from an overdose of commercialization. This arcadian land has been turned into "Amishland"; and Pennsylvania Dutch traditions— including the food—are loudly hawked from giant windmills and phony farms. But there is still beautiful country behind the billboards, a simple way of life beyond packaged souvenirs, and honest Pennsylvania Dutch cooking at People's.

From the outside it looks like a ladies' tearoom. Its otherwise dignified tables are topped with "family fun mats," and flexi-straws are served with drinks, but these concessions to the tourist trade do not negate the down-to-earth efforts of the kitchen.

Our dinner of wiener schnitzel was People's weak spot. It is juicy and tender, but too thick for our taste. We prefer thin slivers of meat and a crusty breading. A better choice is the Lancaster sausage plate, sweet and sage-flavored, roasted to a crisp outer skin, but still moist within. Our favorite meal is the fresh roast capon with sausage filling, a perfect combination of buttery bird and spice. All dinners come with a choice from about a dozen vegetables—almost enough to make up the traditional Seven Sweets and Seven Sours. Among the "sours" our choice is pepper cabbage—a highly spiced cole slaw. The best sweets are cranberry relish and a zesty chowchow (pickled corn kernels).

The highlight of any meal at People's is the wet bottom shoo-fly pie—one of the best we have tasted anywhere. It is served hot and topped with a scoop of ice cream ("The only way to eat shoo-fly pie," our waitress said). This shoo-fly pie is lighter than most, with the intense butter and molasses snap of Indian pudding, though, of course, it's ten times as rich.

ROXBURY

★ CROUSE'S
Route 641 (717) 542-7688
MON–THURS 6 AM–7 PM, FRI 6 AM–6 PM, SAT 6 AM–3 PM, CLOSED SUN

Go to Crouse's for the chicken corn soup, for the fluffy lemon meringue pie, and for the small town perfection of a restaurant that appears to be untouched by time. It is one of the four buildings in town, distinguished by its slightly warping leaf-green pillars in front and a small sign signaling "home cooking." Most of the residents of miniscule Roxbury are "eat-at-home" types so Crouse's is more of a gathering place to sit over coffee and catch up on local gossip than it is a full-scale restaurant.

Because most of the main meals are eaten at home, Crouse's menu relies heavily on convenience items, portion-controlled things that have nothing to do with Roxbury, Pennsylvania, like "Captain's Specials" and "Patty Melts." If you do come here for lunch, we recommend the meat loaf. It is made on the premises, and beats alternative pseudofoods. The chicken corn soup, a Pennsylvania favorite, is delicious. It has large pieces of white chicken meat interspersed with several spoonfuls of corn kernels in a rich, salty broth. For dessert, or with coffee, there are good homemade pies and a tray of broad, perfectly browned sticky buns, sprinkled with nuts and cinnamon. Ironically, these beauties are kept on the counter next to a plastic-wrapped selection of Wing Dings, Ding Dongs and other twirling and gonging junk pastries.

Crouse's is only four miles from exit 15 of the turnpike, but in ambiance and small town charm it is a world away. Skip the junk food, have some coffee and a sticky bun, and you'll fondly remember your visit.

SOMERSET

★★THE GREEN MEADOWS TEA ROOM
Route 31 between Jones Mill & Bakersville (814) 445–2210
SPRING–MID-NOV FRI–SUN 11 AM–8 PM

The Green Meadows does not advertise, but it is an immensely popular place. At peak hours you might find a line of people waiting to get in. Only thirty-eight fit into the tiny restaurant at one time, and nobody eats and runs. It is a lovely place, an eccentric homey space trimmed with dark wood and green leather. There is an old-fashioned wood counter and a few low stools.

The menu varies, but the cuisine is very basic. There are usually four entrées from which to choose. We have sampled broiled pork chops, roast beef, and Pennsylvania ham loaf. These are accompanied by vegetables, a good baked potato, salad and rolls. The Green Meadows does all its own baking, and for dessert there are custard and fruit pies. We tried a creamy coconut, packed with strands of coconut above the flaky crust. The lemon pie was tart, topped with a perfectly crisped meringue.

All the food here is prepared by the cook and owner, Mrs. Beckner. We assume that her weekends-only policy is due to the fact that she spends the week preparing the food. It is not "home-style" cooking, it is the real thing—a basic, wholesome cuisine especially rare along the Pennsylvania Turnpike. The only trouble with Mrs. Beckner's operation is its limited hours. If only she could clone herself and work double-time.

STROUDSBURG

★★ MULLER'S TRUCK STOP DINER AND RESTAURANT
Route 209 (7 miles N. of Stroudsburg) (717) 421–3958
DINER: ALWAYS OPEN; RESTAURANT: MON–FRI 7 AM–8:30 PM,
SAT & SUN 8 AM–8:30 PM

Muller's is on the tire-bending stretch of Route 209 known to truckdrivers as "The Ho Chi Minh Trail." Along with Loveland Pass in Colorado and The Grapevine in Southern California, it is a "killer" road, snake twisty, and the true test of a gearjammer's mettle.

Situated mid-point on the "Ho Chi Minh," Muller's is a perfect haven for a nerve-shattered road hauler to smooth himself out with a couple of cups of "bennie chaser" coffee and a giant steak.

Muller's has long been a closely guarded secret watering hole among swinging beef haulers. These men and women bring carcasses of butchered beef and pork across the country in trucks outfitted with meathooks on which the carcasses are hung. Because of the swinging motion of the meat, the trucks are most prone to rollovers if the driver is anything less than steel-nerved and steady-handed. The beef haulers know exactly where the best sides of beef get dropped off, and this is one reason they congregate at Muller's.

There are two sections to the restaurant: a long traditional diner, and a dining room frequented by tourists. The truckers used to sit in the diner, but have been gravitating to the dining room because the prices are the same, the chairs are roomier, and the waitresses much better looking.

The best and most famous food here is steak, from the chopped sirloin to the trucker-sized T-bone. They are aged, double-thick cuts, served with accompaniments including fresh-baked rolls and pies. Of course, there is good, strong coffee.

Recently Muller's has added a few German dishes to its menu—
"from recipes in the family for generations," Mr. Muller told us. There
is schnitzel a la Holstein—a pan-fried cutlet with an egg on top, and
sauerbraten with kartoffel klösse, a marinated roast beef that comes
with potato dumplings and red cabbage. These seem to be a response
to the springing up along Route 209 of several ethnic restaurants, including a Hungarian kitchen across the road and a Vietnamese diner
further west.

But for us, Muller's will always be meat and potatoes and large
mugs of strong coffee. Even if you haul the hairpin curves of the "Ho
Chi Minh" in a Honda Civic, you may find yourself so well-fortified by
a Muller's meal, that you feel ten feet up in the air-cushioned seat of a
semi, swinging the giant wheel, and rebel-yelling your way to the
George Washington Bridge.

WASHINGTON

★★ THE KOZY KOTTAGE
308 East Maiden Street (412) 222–9985
MON–SAT 6 AM–9 PM / SUN 11 AM–9 PM

The day we found The Kozy Kottage was the day our new car had
broken down. Sputtering and fuming, we wandered the streets of
Washington, our automobile a temperamental inmate of the local fix-it
shop. Nothing, nothing, we vowed, could take our minds off the vio-
lence and hideous fate we were planning for the car salesman back in
Connecticut *if* we ever got out of Washington.

Scowling at dogs and small children, we rounded the corner on
East Maiden Street and saw The Kozy Kottage. Its graceful bay-win-
dowed front lured us inside, where we thought a strong cup of coffee
might help sustain our outrage. But the soothing green walls, ochre
tables, and unassuming menu soon dissolved our anger. Suddenly we
were hungry. We hadn't eaten in six hours, as the nuts and bolts pop-
ping from our "under warranty" engine drove all thoughts of food from
our minds. But now, given the speed with which the average car is
repaired, life stretched before us in Washington, and it seemed a good
idea to eat.

We ordered a corned beef omelette. It came with grilled sweet
potatoes—an eccentric coupling. Our other meal was ham and cabbage,
a poor man's New England dinner served with small new boiled
potatoes. It was all tender but a little bland.

The Kozy Kottage serves mostly plate lunches and moderately priced dinners, but an eater at the next table told us they are well-known in Washington for their grilled cheese and hot pepper sandwiches. Our waitress concurred, adding that the peppers were too hot for many of the clients, but among the callousmouthed, they were a mild addiction.

By the time we cleared the last bites from our plates, psychopathic rage had mellowed to brow-furrowing despair. And then our waitress asked if we wanted to try the coconut pie for dessert—a Kozy Kottage favorite. We have had better, and this could have been lighter and sweeter, but the gentle taste of the sticky coconut lulled us back to days when milk and cookie time was more important than automobile engine trouble.

The happy end to the story is that our car's tantrum was milder than we feared. We didn't spend the rest of our lives in Washington, Pa. And best of all, we realized that the secure little Kozy Kottage was only a five-minute detour from I-70, a highway notable for its miles of restaurantless asphalt.

FAIRS AND FESTIVALS

COUDERSPORT
Maple Festival / EARLY MAY
Pancake and syrup breakfast served all weekend

GETTYSBURG
Apple Harvest Holiday / MID-OCTOBER
Everything made from apples

KUTZTOWN
Pennsylvania Dutch Week / LATE JUNE–EARLY JULY
Shoo-fly pie, schnitz und kepp, sweets & sours, etc.

LEBANON
Cherry Fair / LATE JUNE
Everything made from cherries: pie, dumplings, fritters, cookies, doughnuts, ice cream

McMINNVILLE
Turkey-rama / JULY

MEYERSDALE
Pennsylvania Maple Festival / EARLY APRIL

The South

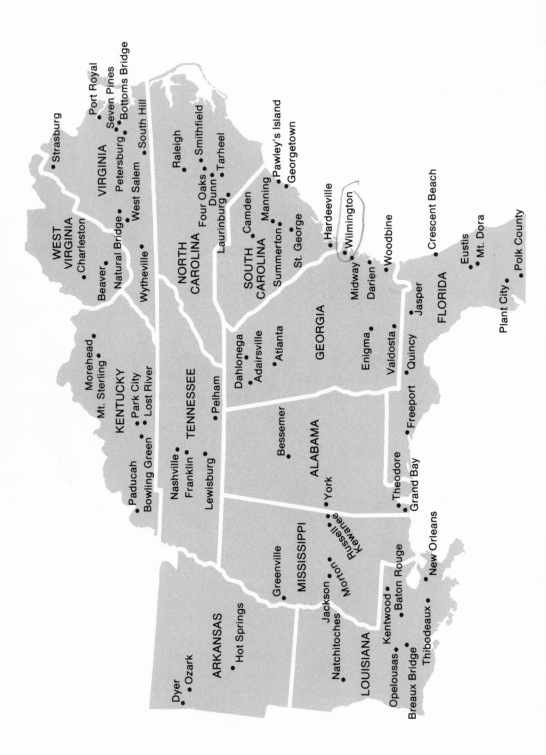

ALABAMA

★★★★ **BOB SYKES**

1810 9th Avenue (Route 11) (205) 426–1400
MON–THURS 10 AM–10 PM, FRI & SAT 10 AM–11 PM, CLOSED SUN

We took notes when roadfooding in order to keep things straight. Sometimes they wound up meaningless cryptograms, but usually, they were helpful in recalling details. What is to be made of two full pages on Bob Sykes that begin with a straightforward listing of what we ordered and how much it cost, proceed to adjectives like "very sweet," "mahogany-colored," and "juicy," and wind up, at the bottom of page two, in a childlike scrawl that reads "THE BEST RIBS AND BEST LEMON PIE IN ALL THE WORLD!!" Bar b que veterans will tell you that good bar b que works that way—progressively. It builds as you eat it, magnifying its taste with logarithmic intensity.

It was just that quality of Bob Sykes' bar b que that nearly caused us to run off the road in gastronomic ecstasy north of Bessemer. We had walked in under the neon sign of the three dancing pigs to investigate what an Alabama roadfooder had told us was the best bar b que in the Birmingham area. It was a clean, tiled place, the air inside heavily smoked with the sweet odor of roasting pork. There are a few formica tables, but most of the business at Sykes is drive-up. On one side of the small building is the drive-through window, and on the other is the pit. Dot Brown, Bill Sykes' pit-mistress for nineteen years, was tending huge, dark hocks and slabs of ribs, lathering them with sauce, rearranging them over the hickory, and removing those that were ready for carving or cutting up.

The menu has a specialty "for five people or two hawgs," which is a pound and a half of bar b que, a pint of cole slaw, a pint of potato salad, and a pint of baked beans. Not feeling particularly hawg-like, we ordered a slab of ribs, a minced pork sandwich, and, on Mrs. Sykes' recommendation, a piece of lemon meringue pie. We hopped in our car and drove on.

We poured sauce over the sandwich and polished it off first. "Good bar b que" our notes read at the top of page two. We moved to the ribs. They looked like they had been smoking since Elvis joined the army. They were the darkest possible red-brown, beautiful to look at and almost varnish-crisp on the outside. They were meaty without being greasy or fat—so clean and crisp that they could be eaten almost daintily. By the time we finished the slab, we were approaching ecstasy. The lemon meringue pie put us over the top. The lemon was creamier than any we have ever tasted: light, airy, yet powerfully rich, like a lemon soufflé. The meringue was a tall, crispy-pure sweet cloud. And the crust was a tangy gingersnap crumb bed of sugar and spice.

We took no more notes after this, our pen having dropped to the floor as we scrambled for rib tips and crumbs of pie that might have fallen onto our laps or the car seat.

GRAND BAY

★★★★ MAMA'S RESTAURANT
Route 90 (205) 865–4859
SUN 8 AM–8 PM / MON–SAT 6 AM–9:30 PM

What is most nostalgic about Mama's is the aroma. We always imagine a displaced Southerner returning to the South after many years absence, driving cooly from the Mobile airport to Mama's, walking in the door, and breaking down in tears at the primal memories that only cooking smells can generate. When we first arrived at Mama's, the odor was a mingling of yeasty buttermilk from her hot biscuits, and toasted nut, sugar, and molasses from her pecan pie. We were hungry as we approached the front door; we were famished five seconds later as we sat down.

The lunch that day was either turkey and cornbread dressing or baked ham. Both came with candied yams in heavy molasses, fresh green peas, and corn O'Brien—a sweet pepper and cracklin-enriched bowl of kernels. We had biscuits on the side, which lived up to their aromatic promise. We finished our meal with pecan pie which was still too hot to eat as it came to our table, but celestially rich once it mellowed to warm. We also tried a wedge of Mama's sweet potato pie which was so light and airy it seemed whipped.

After our meals, we searched behind the scenes for this wonderful Mama. She was busy with a new batch of pies, practically waist-deep inside her ancient black stove. She fiddled and fussed until one of her customers, who no doubt felt it his filial duty to trail us into the kitchen, drawled out, "Mama, there's some folks here looking for you."

"I hear you. I know they're looking," she said, without lifting her head from the oven. "There!" she proclaimed, straightening up after having finished her work with the pies. Mama told us about her Gulf Coast seafood, snapper, gumbo, and her specialty, fried chicken. We stepped outside of the clean and cozy café into the heady salt air of southernmost Alabama, and vowed that we would soon return to this sweet Mama's restaurant in the mossy woods for another perfect country meal.

THEODORE

★★★ THE BOB CAT
Route 90 (just west of Mobile) (205) 661–3590
DAILY 6 AM–10 PM

The worst meal we ever ate was at a "world famous" restaurant in Mobile, to which every hotel clerk sends his customers. We went there to double-check our standards, to see if an endless line of cafés, roadside stands, and diners might be warping our sensibilities. We put on our dining-out clothes and went for some food that we hoped would reestablish new standards of excellence. To say that the food was bad is to be demure. To say that one of us was on the verge of calling the hotel physician that night, and the other stayed locked in the bathroom until morning is more accurate. The next day we gathered our remaining strength and double-timed out of Mobile toward The Bob Cat, one of our favorite truckstops.

Route 90 in Alabama is a golden path to good eating, having three roadfood landmarks within minutes of each other. Heading west, The Bob Cat is the first you'll find, just past Bellingrath Gardens—the showplace of the Old South. Stop in The Bob Cat for a real Old South breakfast. Opal Shanks, the owner, and her short-order man will fry you up a stack of the lightest banana batter pancakes you have ever tasted. Or if you prefer, there are pecan pancakes, coarse with chunks of nutmeat in the batter. Opal makes biscuits, too, but in this roadfood-rich part of the South, that's like saying a duck quacks. Opal's come four to a plate, topped with sausage gravy.

A Louisiana touch is evident at The Bob Cat as early as 7:00 AM when the baker delivers yard-long loaves of fresh French bread for po boy sandwiches. This is a favorite place for Mobile's local truckdrivers and workmen, who order the giant po boys filled with crab, ham, oysters, or shrimp. On Mondays they come here for traditional red beans and rice, a ritual observed throughout southern Louisiana and Alabama. It is unusual to see a po boy at lunch any Monday in this territory, when the red beans are simmering on the stove and sending the sweet odor of hambones and onions into the air. On other days, The Bob Cat makes wonderful gumbo top—a grand stew thick with crabmeat and shrimp.

Opal Shanks doesn't have much time to talk. She is usually too busy feeding her regulars. She told us that if we wanted to stay around for lunch, she was in the middle of preparing her famous upside-down pineapple cake. When we heard this, we seriously considered commandeering a booth under one of the silly duck etchings that hang on The Bob Cat walls, and not leaving until we smelled the juices of pineapple and brown sugar bubbling from the cast-iron pans. But two truckers eyed our booth as the breakfast dishes were being cleared away, and we were too weak from the previous night's culinary fiasco to fight them for squatter's rights.

★★★★ THE RED BALL RESTAURANT
Route 90
DAILY 4:30 AM–9 PM

The Red Ball Restaurant is haute cuisine of the highway. June and Barney Estes run this place for two-fisted eaters who won't settle for small portions of anything, and who'd just as soon make the *cook* eat a plate of poorly prepared food. They make "X-rated chili" and something called "a man's breakfast," which is like many huge truckstop breakfasts, except for the fact that each item is a model of southern culinary art. The country ham is a thick, highly salty slab, six inches across; the red-eye gravy is sharp and bracing like a cup of hot chicory; the grits are laced with melted butter; and the biscuits are double-sized and air-light.

The Red Ball isn't exactly a truckstop, although it has the hunting-lodge feel of some of the smaller roadside cafés in the South. The men that do eat here regularly told us about June Estes' diary of menus, which guarantees that no day will be a repeat of any other.

We first learned about The Red Ball sitting next to a driver who had ordered the "chef's salad" in a Pennsylvania truckstop and was so disheartened by the wilted lettuce he looked ready to cry. "I'd give anything right now to be at The Red Ball," he sighed, "with a plate of June and Barney's mustard greens, hominy, buttered beans and biscuits." When we got to The Red Ball we pinchhit for our friend. The hominy here is big, golden puffs, buttery and flavored with large chips of bacon. The speckled butter beans, the fried okra, and the black-eyed peas were each delicious.

June also makes fritters that are as light as her biscuits, but sweetened and dotted with corn. Her seafood gumbo would sell for three times as much in any modest Miami restaurant. And her apple turnovers come fresh from the oven every morning. You get a gourmet meal at The Red Ball, and you eat it to the sound of a country-western jukebox in a wood-paneled lodge room in the company of good old boys whose everyday cuisine could serve as a photographic model for a cookbook. And we used to think that all those guys knew how to eat was chicken-fried steak!

YORK

★★MARTHA'S TOURESTA
Route 11 (205) 392–4592
ALWAYS OPEN

Martha's Touresta is about as down-home and funky as Alabama can be. Martha is a chubby white girl who, with her two chubby black girlfriends, runs this twenty-four-hour restaurant as if it were her back porch. For Alabama ambiance, it can't be beat. The inside of this wood-panelled room seems as overgrown and as dark as the Oakmulgee woods. Customers plant themselves in booths for entire afternoons or evenings, passing time with Martha and her friends, or just reading the paper. The large space is littered with jars of candy, old maps, dusty toys, year-old magazines, and hundreds of other items looking like they were set down months ago and forgotten. Martha and the two other girls sit at a table nearest the steam table, and whenever a customer enters, the three of them nod a hospitable greeting, and get up to help the newcomer select his food.

The food at Martha's is a perfect rendition of simple deep South cooking. Dinner includes a choice of meat and two vegetables. The potential choices are country-fried steak, chicken and dumplings, rice and chicken jubilee, black-eyed peas, vegetable stew simmered with cracklin, candied yams, white beans and ham hocks, or collard greens.

Biscuits or corn dodgers come on the side. Desserts include peach and apple cobblers, sweet potato pie, and upside-down cakes. Everything is cooked by Martha and her two friends, and the quality varies directly with how well a food survives when it is kept warm on a steam table for several hours.

Martha's Touresta is not a place for a quick snack or an anonymous meal. The sign on the door says "Martha's Touresta Welcomes You," and it's for real. It's not that anybody would bother you if you wanted to sit and eat in privacy. But it would be a shame to come to Martha's Touresta without enjoying the specialty of the house—Southern hospitality.

FAIRS AND FESTIVALS

DOTHAN
National Peanut Festival / THIRD WEEK IN OCTOBER
Houston County Farm Center

OPP
South Alabama Annual Rattlesnake Rodeo / LATE FEBRUARY

ARKANSAS

DYER

★CATFISH GROVE
Route 64 (at 14-mile marker off Route 40)
MON–SAT 11 AM–8 PM / CLOSED SUN

If you like catfish, you'll love the Catfish Grove. Here you can eat them, certainly, but you can also expound upon their many wonders. That's what the fiddler fishermen who hang around here do, and there's nothing these men like better than telling the tale of a particularly ornery "Leadpencil catfish" that they had to coax from its lair. The wood-panelled walls of this tiny restaurant are covered with Polaroid and Instamatic pictures of famous catfish—forty and fifty pounders that had to be cajoled from the muddy bottoms of nearby streams. There is a local ordinance that forbids the serving of home-caught fish in public restaurants, but it wouldn't surprise us a bit if some of the beauties whose ugly faces line the walls here like a rogues' gallery found their way into the specialty of the house—the catfish basket.

The fried catfish fillet takes center stage in this basket; even the hush puppies seem to have been made especially to complement it. Hush puppies elsewhere tend to be served as a side dish to chicken or salty ham. Here they are drier than most and almost powdery, accenting the sweetness of the catfish. All that is lacking to make this basket perfect is a good cole slaw. Instead, the Grove gives you limp French fries and a blah bun. For those interested in local cuisine beyond the catfish, there is also a fillet chicken basket, known in these parts as an Ozark Fry.

Catfish Grove is a redwood shack, and they've been meaning to put up a sign on the highway "for years," but they have never gotten around to it. We have a feeling that they're not really interested in a lot of people coming around who don't appreciate the beauty of a fiddler-head the size of a baby moon hubcap. But if you do like catfish, stop here. There's none better in the state of Arkansas.

HOT SPRINGS

★★ED'S EAT SHOP
Old Little Rock Highway (junction of Interstate 7 and 5)
(501) 623–0195
TUES–SUN 9 AM–9 PM / CLOSED MON

Ed's is in a beautiful part of Arkansas, nestled in a grove of trees on the side of the road just outside Hot Springs. The first thing you notice inside are giant bottles of mineral water on every table. Our Daisy Mae of a waitress explained that the bottles contained only plain tap water, but the clientele of Ed's like to use the famous mineral water bottles "same as they do in town." Hot Springs restaurants charge high prices, because mineral water devotees can usually afford to pay them. But at Ed's the clientele are mountain people, local residents, and travelers, and so the food is simple fare, geared for the pocketbooks of the hoi polloi.

What we like about this place is the hospitable character of the people who work and eat here, and the basic goodness of the food. The favorite meal is Mrs. Arnold's chicken pot pies, served with hot biscuits and honey on the side and a mess of greens. The pie ingredients are bland and smooth, in a good lard crust, accented by the heady greens that accompany it. There is also a country ham dinner with red eye gravy and honey biscuits. The ham is very salty, and this dinner comes with Mrs. Arnold's vinegary cole slaw. It is a much spicier dinner than the chicken.

Mrs. Arnold's best pies are light egg custard and strawberry-rhubarb with a powdery biscuitlike crust. Judging by our fellow diners, the way to finish off a meal at Ed's is with a large glass of raw buttermilk. Ed's won't provide you with superlative food, but it's a good place to rub elbows with mountain people on their own turf.

★★★★STUBBY'S HIK-RY PIT BAR-B-Q

1000 Park Street (Route 7) (501) 623–0323
TUES–SAT 9 AM–8 PM / CLOSED SUN & MON

Stubby's is unique among the great pits of the world in that it's located right next to a Hot Springs health food store. But leave any hopes of balanced and well-moderated eating at the door before you line up at Stubby's cafeteria-style counter for the juiciest, most lucious feast of meat and potatoes in all of Arkansas. The ribs at Stubby's are a little disappointing—too dry and not smoky enough. What they lack in juice could be compensated for by a generous dipping into Stubby's sauce.

We recommend you skip the pork and stick with Stubby's sublime beef which is served either sliced on a cardboard basket or minced in a sandwich. Crispy around the edges, moist and meaty inside, the brisket has absorbed a maximum smokiness from the pit without ever drying out like the too-glazed ribs. Only a dab of sauce on the beef adds just the right balance to the hickory flavor to make this the finest sliced brisket outside of Texas. The sandwich is virtually all "brownies"—those morsels of smoked meat that are cut from the edges are trimmed of excess fat and then piled onto a bun.

Stubby's also serves a hickory-pit baked potato, smoked until it develops a thick, woody skin and an inside like the creamiest mashed potatoes. If you wish, they'll cut it open, and as the steam escapes, put in ice-cream scoop-sized dollops of butter and sour cream. As if this weren't enough, right next to the potatoes are the ham and beans—a thick, molasses-rich vat of spicy ham cubes and long-simmered baked beans.

Stubby's "feast for two"—which we recommend for one hearty eater—consists of a half-pound of beef, a half-pint of ham and beans, a half-pint of forgettable cole slaw, and a baked potato.

You can buy the sauce "to go" and become the instant bar b que champion of your block with this mixture whose ingredients are listed as "tomato, vinegar, and heavy spices." We were once carrying a trunkful of Stubby's sauce, as well as Arthur Bryant's, and other prize-winners we had collected on a cross-country trip when we were tail-ended by a gravel truck in North Carolina. The sauces spilled out onto the road and co-mingled, and after assuring onlookers that it wasn't blood, and explaining to the cops what we were doing with gallons of the bootleg brew, we wept and wondered if there wasn't some way to hickory smoke the sauce-drenched asphalt.

OZARK

★★★★SMITH'S CAFÉ
106 South Second Street (501) 667–2359
MON–SAT 5:30 AM–7 PM / CLOSED SUN

Smith's Café has been in Ozark for over thirty-five years, and although it is now run by Tom Edgin, he still calls it Smith's, because that's tradition and tradition is the soul of the Southern kitchen. Tom, an ex-farmer, and three older-lady kitchen helpers work like plowhorses to put golden hominy, homemade relishes, and wild blackberry cobblers on the café table at down-home prices.

"Damn! We got us a couple of Yankees here," Tom whooped when we introduced ourselves to him after a first-rate meal. "I bet you don't even know what that hominy you liked so much is." Enthusiastically he started telling us about how the corn kernels are soaked in a weak lye solution until they "blow up" to their final puff-ball size, ready for butter. Tom is more than a little proud of his kitchen. No sooner had we introduced ourselves than he had us sampling a bit of everything. He showed us bushels of beautiful tomatoes and peas that had just arrived that morning, and as we chatted, a farmer with his eleven-year-old son knocked on the door and toted in a large bushel of turnip greens. "They're Yankees," he proudly told the farmer. "Never tasted hominy!"

The farmer smiled, revealing a stretch of toothless gums and just whispered a matching "Damn! . . ."

The lunches we had just eaten had sent us snooping into Tom's kitchen. They were centered around fried chicken, dipped in a thick batter and fried in an oil so pure that it left no residue on the bird at all. Each dinner came with a choice of three vegetables. We chose four between us and started with two bowls of vegetable soup. The soup was almost a gumbo texture. We counted ten different vegetables, with okra predominating. The vegetables included hominy in butter—a pure corn taste with none of the tough jackets of small kernels; pinto beans in a ham hock gravy; mixed turnip greens with a rich and spicy pot likker; and candied yams with a crust of brown sugar. Along with the meals came a small basket of rolls warm from the oven, a fresh wild-berry muffin, and two breakapart slabs of white corn bread. We could hardly believe the low price and the consistent high quality of the food coming from that kitchen.

When we were finished, the waitress told us that Smith's was famous for their pies. How could we refuse? We were brought two selections: wild blackberry, made from the same fruit used in the muffin, and a pecan pie with a gleaming nutmeat crust over a warm grainy center. It was the pie that finally sent us back to the kitchen to see who was responsible for these wonders.

Tom Edgin was a jovial man, as amused by our Northern roots as we were by his Southern charms. After we had tasted a little of everything, he finally calmed down enough to tell us bluntly, "I don't like to brag, but I think we have the best food in the whole state of Arkansas." The kitchen trio of ladies giggled and nodded their net-covered heads in agreement. We think Tom's right. You won't find anything on the menu at Smith's that is exotic, but the traditional food is cooked to perfection with the freshest produce the Arkansas soil can yield.

FAIRS AND FESTIVALS

SPRINGDALE
Northwest Arkansas Poultry Festival / MID–APRIL
Cooking contests, bar b que, chicken dinners

TONITOWN
Annual Tonitown Grape Festival / MID–AUGUST
Grape judging & dance

WARREN
Pink Tomato Festival / MID–JUNE
All-tomato lunch, exhibits

FLORIDA

CRESCENT BEACH

★★THE SANDPIPER SNACK BAR
Routes A1A and 206
DAILY: BREAKFAST, LUNCH, DINNER

Like stunned, naked rednecks they hover about The Sandpiper, Frisbee in hand and zinc oxide on nose. These are the natives of the Florida beaches. They arrive at The Sandpiper in their dune buggies, on dirt bikes, or on surfboards. You'll know them by the color of their skin: the young ones like well-worn saddles; the old ones like skinny shell-less turtles who have wandered in from the water and forgotten how to return. None wears more than one article of clothing.

The Sandpiper is their beachside general store, providing the sun-sand-surf worshippers with everything that they need so they never have to leave their natural habitat. Here you can buy suntan lotion, balls for playing catch, postcards to keep in touch, sunglasses, beach clogs, food, and drink. While the patrons seem slightly groggy from baking in the sun all their lives, the staff of The Sandpiper is on its toes—perhaps to keep the beach people moving. From behind the racks of supplies they scan the customers, yelling, "You! You next? You been served yet?"

The crab dinner we ordered took twenty minutes and three chefs to prepare. One teen-age girl deep-fried the hush puppies. One sliced the beefsteak tomato and spooned out the cole slaw. The third stuffed the crab shells with the deviled-crab mixture and spooned out the beans onto the plate. This platter featured deviled crabs as good and as plentiful as we have had at three times the price. The real crab shells were stuffed with lots of fresh crabmeat, bits of crisp celery, hot mustard, peppers, and a touch of garlic. They were crisped on top, moist and spicy inside. The hush puppies were light and thin-skinned. The French fries were good. The cole slaw was fresh. And the tomato was nearly an entire meaty beefsteak—bright red, not too firm, thick sliced.

There is no place to eat in The Sandpiper, although the surfers do seem to mill around inside, waiting for their food or loitering like sunstroke victims. Tourists like ourselves, to whom the sun is a special treat, can sit outside the shack on wooden benches and observe the comings and goings of the local populace who, if a bit parboiled, are always friendly.

EUSTIS

★★THE LAKE SHORE
936 North Shore Highway 19 (904) 357–9938
DAILY 6 AM–8 PM

Etta Arwood, the mullet princess of Mount Dora, told us about The Lake Shore, and if it weren't for her recommendation and a tornado alert that was announced as we drove by, we might never have stopped. The outside of The Lake Shore is phony wood siding, about as charming as the lobby of a remodeled service station. But the 50 m.p.h. winds, indigo sky, and bent-double trees told us we better take cover or wind up in Oz, so we found shelter in The Lake Shore.

We also found great home cooked meals for very reasonable prices. Lola Woods has been running The Lake Shore for the last seventeen years on a sort of barter system. Local farmers and fishermen trade her their goods cheaply, and she provides them with terrific food. This isn't to say you have to be toting a bale of avocados to get into The Lake Shore and have a low-cost meal. Anyone is welcome, and the Southern charm is laid on as thick as cake frosting.

Meals begin with Lola's table of salads. We saw an avocado and onion salad garnished with tomato quarters, carrot slaw with raisins, potato salad with hard boiled eggs, and two types of macaroni salad. The menu lists fresh catfish and oysters with eggplant fingers and collard greens, and dessert of three-layer coconut cake.

Most customers ignore the menu. A local conch-pea grower sat near us at the counter. "Lola, honey, what's good today?" She brought him the oysters and a piece of coconut cake. "I've been coming here for three years now," he told us. "I give her conchs, Bill gives her key limes from his trees. Everybody sells her stuff as cheap as we can afford to. She sure treats us all right, wouldn't you say?" He motioned to his overfilled plate. "She makes the best sweet potato pie, and turkey with corn-bread dressing on Sunday. Lord, berries in the pies all summer, pumpkin pies in the winter, and okra, greens, chicken, and dumplings all year around. My wife gets jealous 'cause I eat all my lunches here."

Like the farmer, we had the oysters, which were crisply fried quickly enough so that the body of the oyster retained a slightly chewy consistency and a salty taste. The coconut cake with boiled frosting was rough with shreds of coconut and scented with fresh lemons. Lola thanked us for coming, and told us not to worry about the tornado as we left. We walked out the door into the sweeping winds, took one look at the dark foreboding sky, and turned around back into The Lake Shore for two pieces of key lime pie. Lola smiled the smile of a satisfied cook.

FREEPORT

★★BURNHAM'S SEAFOOD RESTAURANT
Route 1 at junction of Route 331 (904) 835–2458
MON, TUES, THURS, FRI 3:30 PM–9 PM, SAT 10 AM–10 PM, SUN
11 AM–9 PM

The seafood appetizers served at Burnham's are larger and better than main courses in most high-priced fish restaurants. Diners used to four meager shrimps arranged around the rim of an oversized bowl loaded with lettuce and red sauce, calling itself "shrimp cocktail," will find Burnham's a radically generous alternative. At least a dozen big beauties go into a shrimp cocktail here, which costs no more than a fast-food burger and fries. Oysters—another stingily doled-out rich-man's dish almost everywhere else—are equally bountiful here. There is some red sauce to go with these appetizers, but there's no need for it to give them a sparkle. They are so snapping fresh that a few grains of pepper and a drop of lemon are all that's required.

Among the seafood dinners, a house specialty is gumbo—thick with shrimp, crabmeat, onions, okra and a rainbow of seasonings. It is an excellent version of the classic opaque, green-gray soup.

Burnham's is the plainest kind of Formica and Naugahyde café, its major bit of decor being the country-western-stocked jukebox in the corner. Patrons are apt to wear Florida-style western straw hats, and appear to be slightly sunbaked. It's an easy-going place, where you can lazily wile away the afternoon over a procession of fresh shrimp or oysters and refills of presweetened ice tea.

JASPER

★★★ THE JASPER CAFETERIA
Route 41 (Main Street) (904) 792–1532
MON–FRI 5 AM–8:30 PM, SAT 5 AM–6 PM, SUN 5 AM–2:30 PM

There is a certain scent in the air of a small town on a hot Sunday in the South; a smell of cologne-dabbed cotton dresses, and molasses-baked hams. It was that kind of a day when we first ate at the Jasper Cafeteria. It was just before noon, and we arrived to find the buffet tables loaded but, strangely, not a customer in sight. We ambled down the long row of trays containing fried chicken, roast beef, chicken and dumplings, yams, squash, mararoni salad, corn-bread sticks, pork chops, buttermilk biscuits, okra, congealed salads, bread pudding, rice pudding, and more. By the time we paid the *prix fixe,* the doors to the Jasper flew open and the buffet line was soon crowded. There are few people in the town of Jasper who don't go to church on Sunday morning, and fewer still who don't come here afterward for the best food in town. Within an hour, there was hardly a scrap left to be eaten.

The Jasper-style buffet is rivaled in abundance only by a Jewish wedding, except here, instead of chopped liver and smoked salmon, the menu is made up of rich, buttery dishes and the ubiquitous southern greens and vegetables.

When we first ate here The Jasper was run by a bachelor named Mr. Douglas, who said he never could find a woman who cooked as well as he did, and whose local newspaper ads declared the Cafeteria to be "under old management." The management is now new (could Mr. Douglas have found his match?), but we are happy to report that the food is as good as ever. Mr. Musgrove, the new owner, has added a bakery but hasn't changed the pleasant blue and white interior a bit. The Jasper Cafeteria is still an outstanding place to sample the full variety of traditional southern dishes.

MT. DORA

★★★THE OAK GROVE MARKET
Route 441
DAILY: BREAKFAST, LUNCH, DINNER

The Oak Grove Market is a general store-grocery next to a fish store. There are dogs sleeping half-sunken into the dusty soil out front. Even the flies seem to buzz lazily in circles in the still air. Ernest and Etta Arwood are the owners of The Oak Grove, a grocery store that we include for one very special reason—Uncle Suggs's mullet.

Uncle Suggs was a black man who lived in the woods near the Oak Grove Market. Blacks, and a few whites, used to walk through the woods to Uncle Suggs' whenever they could smell the smoke from the bar b que. That meant that he was making mullet. Uncle Suggs kept his recipe all to himself, and became a Mt. Dora legend.

Ernest Arwood was one of the white men who used to trek through the woods for Uncle Suggs' mullet and when he opened The Oak Grove Market twenty-seven years ago, he tried to convince the grand old man of the woods to come and cook mullet at The Oak Grove. But Uncle Suggs preferred the secrecy and mystery of the woods. Etta tells the story of how, ten years ago, "One of the colored boys came by and told Ernest to go into the woods. Uncle Suggs wanted to see him. Ernest came back late afternoon and said, 'Uncle Suggs is dying. He told me how he does the mullet.' "

The condition of Uncle Suggs passing on the secret was that Ernest not tell anyone, and Etta swears that even she doesn't know what goes into the sauce. It is a pale red liquid, slightly clouded, and grainy with spices and peppers. It is lightly brushed on as the mullet cooks.

First, the large heavy fish is scaled, split open, eviscerated, and smoked over smoldering wood. It absorbs the barky smoke flavor, but never loses its dense mullet taste. You get your fish on a piece of butcher paper, and can apply extra sauce if you wish before you walk to the shade of an oak tree. Sit down and enjoy the smoked mullet in the most beautiful Spanish-moss decorated restaurant there is—Uncle Suggs's woods.

PLANT CITY

★★ THE BRANCH RANCH
Route 2 (813) 752–1957
SUN 12 PM–7:30 PM / TUES–SAT 4 PM–9:30 PM / CLOSED MON

It's hard to believe, but the food served at the sprawling Branch Ranch is still simple farm food made from the same recipes that made Mary Branch the most sought-after cook in Plant City over a decade ago. Her reputation started almost by accident. She was a Sunday School teacher who invited her class home to eat after lessons. When word of her culinary talents spread from children to parents, families started calling her on the phone offering her money to be invited over to her house for a meal. Mary set the tab at $1.50 and started serving in her own dining room.

The Branch Ranch now seats 400 people. Waitresses dress in matching calico. The gift shop sells jars full of Mary's jams and jellies. Amazingly, for all the aggrandizement of the premises, the food is near perfect, and Mary herself is still very much here—cooking, supervising, and greeting guests.

The Branch Ranch is best known for two things: chicken pot pie and fresh vegetables. The pot pie is a butterflaked wonder of pastry crust lightly topping a creamy sauce, laced with tender white chicken meat. The pot pie comes with a salad that, in Mary's words, "is too good for any dressing except a sprinkle of salt." It is a simple salad of lettuce, cucumbers, and sliced tomatoes—all tasting as if they have been rushed in directly from the garden. Buttermilk biscuits come with the salad, and vegetables are served "family style" in deep help-yourself bowls.

The vegetables—as perfectly fresh as the salad greens—are the basis of the other famous dish, the vegetable plate. This is a potpourri of whatever is available from the Ranch's own gardens and from local farmers. The vegetables are cooked to leave a crunch in the carrots, and a snap to the corn or zucchini squash. They are bathed lightly in butter and sprinkled with salt.

Desserts are simple and rich. The favorite is coconut cake, three layers high, filled between the layers with tangy lemon cream, and topped with grated coconut meat from Florida trees.

There is still something charming and down-home about this place, and about its schoolmarmish owner, Mary Branch. But it is for the fresh food that we recommend The Branch Ranch.

LAKE WALES

★★SHORTY'S BBQ
Highway 60, W. of Lake Wales (813) 676–4300
TUES, WED 6 AM–7 PM, THURS–SUN 6 AM–9 PM, CLOSED SUN

Shorty's is the happy end of a love story. It was founded by "Shorty" Reynolds, who had dreamt since his boyhood of running his own bar b que pit. But fate led Shorty down into the mines, until one day the mine workers went on strike. "It's now or never," said Mrs. Shorty, and so when the strike broke Shorty stayed above ground and opened one of the best bar b que and catfish houses in central Florida. He and his wife tended the ribs and fried the catfish in what they called "The World's Smallest Shopping Center," which looked to us like a conglomeration of oddball junk, antiques, and miscellanea. Shorty and Mrs. Shorty have now retired, leaving their beloved business in the hands of a former employee, Francis Willis. The ribs, catfish, and "Smallest Shopping Center" are just as they left it—the best for miles around.

The bar b que is slow-cooked, southern-style, over hickory, turned with a long-handled pitchfork. You can get either beef, pork, ribs, or a combination plate. These come with baked beans, slaw, and a choice of grits, potato salad, fries, or hushpups. Each table at Shorty's has two salad bottles filled with sauce—one sweet, the other medium-hot. If you like catfish, this is a fine place to get it, fried up in big crusty hunks, as sweet a fish as it is ugly. There are also gallons of sauce to take back to your own bar b que pit at home.

QUINCY

★KITTRELL'S CAFE
Main Street (Route 90) (904) 627–8903
MON–SAT 6 AM–MIDNIGHT / SUN 6 AM–8 PM

Kittrell's is Norman Rockwell South. It is the South of clean white-washed porches, of lavender-scented ladies moving slowly in the summer heat, and of neatly pomaded boys in pastel suits coming to the front door for their date. Kittrell's is where they might go for soda after the dance, and where families table hop to greet friends after church.

If you are fortunate enough to eat here on Sunday, as we did, try the Sunday special of stuffed pork chops. The chop itself was rather bland, but the stuffing was dark and moist. It is served with jello salad topped with an odd mayonnaise dressing, oven-browned potatoes, and buttered squash. The specialties of the house are fresh oysters and shrimps. We ordered the latter with an order of mashed potatoes instead of the oven browns. The spuds were disappointingly bogus, as were the rolls.

It had been a while since we had seen cottony buns. We were spoiled after feasting our way through the southland on corn bread, pecan nut breads, and biscuits. We were shocked by Kittrell's roll basket, and surprised that one of the talcum-powdered local ladies hasn't taken them to task.

Our flagging spirits soared a little when the waitress brought us two helpings of "bread and butter pudding" with raisin sauce. We hadn't ordered them, but she told us, "We ran out of Boston Cream pie, and I thought I better take these to your table before we run out of everything." We tasted the strangely-named pudding: cinnamon and clove, with channels of cooled butter piercing through the sweetened bread pudding. Delicious!

Over the pudding we surveyed the Kittrell scene for a last booster shot of Americana before we hit the highway. We committed to memory the aluminum foil-wrapped milk bottles, heavy with freshly picked blue hydrangeas. There were calendars from the local merchants on the wall, and fresh-set hairdos on the women in every booth. Kittrell's is a great tableau, and a good restaurant at its best on Sundays.

FAIRS AND FESTIVALS

APALICHICOLA
Seafood Festival   /   EARLY NOV
Crab races

DAVIE
Orange Festival and Rodeo   /   EARLY MARCH
Western breakfast & bar b que

FT. MEYERS BEACH
Island Shrimp Festival   /   LATE FEB—EARLY MARCH

GRANT
Seafood Festival   /   MID-FEB

LA BELLE
Swamp Cabbage Festival & Bar B Que   /   LATE FEB

MONTICELLO
Jefferson County Watermelon Festival
Eating and seed-spitting contests   /   LATE JUNE

PLANT CITY
Strawberry Festival   /   EARLY MARCH

SAN ANTONIO
Rattlesnake Bar B Que and Milking   /   MID-OCT

STARKE
Strawberry Festival   /   EARLY APRIL

ZELLWOOD
Zellwood Corn Boil   /   LATE MAY OR EARLY JUNE

GEORGIA

ADAIRSVILLE

★PATTY'S TRUCK STOP
just off Route 75 (404) 773–3779
ALWAYS OPEN

We include Patty's for its menu at least as much as for its cuisine. Any traveler who has eaten in motel dining rooms knows how quickly you become disgusted by the cloying hyperbolic descriptions of bland and banal food. Whether it's "nestled," "honey-dipt," or "krispy-fried," it's still the same tired old bird that died many months ago after its short but brutal barnyard life. A steak touted as "char-broiled," "flaked and formed" or "flame-kissed" will probably be shot through with enough pulverizing enzymes to tenderize a piece of mahogany.

But at Patty's, what you read is what you get. One look at the menu, and you know your dinner money is going to the cook.

The "Menu for Today" at Patty's goes like this: Meat and three vegetables, meat and two vegetables, meat and one vegetable, four vegetables, three vegetables, two vegetables. Above this are two lists, one of meat, and one of vegetables. The meats are baked ham, meat loaf, country steak. The vegetables are mashed potatoes, lima beans, field peas, corn, cole slaw, apple sauce, and peach salad.

There is one extraneous adjective on the mimeographed menu. That is "fresh" before pies. It is not needed because everything at Patty's is fresh. We had the baked ham and meat loaf, both of which were good if not exceptional, and straight from the shank and loaf, respectively. Our two vegetables with the ham were crisply-grated cole slaw and firm peas. With the meat loaf, we chose mashed potatoes (genuine) and lima beans, also for real.

Breakfasts at Patty's are more elaborate than lunch and dinner although they are described just as plainly on the menu. Our favorite is two pork chops, two eggs, two biscuits, two pats of butter, one container of jelly, one bowl of grits, and coffee (unspecified amount).

There is one item on the menu that we have yet to see described anywhere with the purple prose of the Menu Writer. If Patty would only have us, we'd be happy to tackle this item, and offer her our description of "Sharp-witted and tender medula oblongata scrambled into oeufs a la coq, producing a sensitive, noble omelette." Patty calls it brains and eggs. It is a perfect rendition of the rich and spicy dish.

ATLANTA

★★★★ MARY MAC'S TEA ROOM
228 Ponce de Leon Avenue, N.E. (404) 876–6604
MON–FRI 11:30 AM–2 PM / 5 PM–8 PM / CLOSED SAT & SUN

It wasn't until we actually tasted pot likker at Mary Mac's that it dawned on us that pot likker, which we thought had something to do with licking the pot, was actually liquor of the pot. It *is* inebriating. At Mary Mac's you can get it by the bowl or cup with hot corn muffins. It is the heady, tonic-strong liquid remaining at the bottom of the bowl after the greens are cooked with cubes of fatback or ham hock. The intense and penetrating flavor is a revelation to those unaccustomed to the prominence of vegetables on southern plates. It is easy to fall in love with this likker, and with Mary Mac's Tea Room as well. Because the turnip green pot likker is only the beginning—or side dish—to a perfect Georgia dinner.

Our last two dinners at Mary Mac's were Jamestown Country Ham and red-eye gravy and a plate of four enormous pieces of crisp fried chicken—succulent, tender, with as much meat as half a small turkey. Our choice of vegetables included a sweet potato soufflé, white lima beans cooked with ham hock, oven-browned potatoes and onions, Lyonnaise squash, turnip greens, and a congealed fruit salad.

The available vegetables we did not choose included steamed green cabbage, creamed cottage cheese, macaroni and cheese, pickled beets, rice and gravy, green salad, stewed fresh corn, sauteed fresh mushrooms orientale, cole slaw, green beans, sliced chilled cucumber salad, apple sauce, chicken dressing with gravy, and vegetable soup. Among the desserts is a creamy peanut butter confection called "presidential pudding" in honor of the Georgian in the White House.

Other entrees on the Mary Mac menu include chicken pan pie jambalaya, broiled or fried snapper, baked chicken and dressing and about ten others. Dinner here is a leisurely experience with all the civilized grace of the old South. But lest you think the "Tea Room" label or the dainty pastel menus mean that Mary Mac's is in any way stuffy, there is a bar, and the bar guarantees that all drinks contain at least one and a quarter ounces of booze.

If dinner at Mary Mac's is played at 33⅓, lunch has been moved up to 78 r.p.m. The menu says about the noontime meal: "Mary Mac's is the place for good food—for fast service—for value given. Mary Mac's is NOT the place for a leisurely luncheon—for a business meeting—for customers who are not in a hurry." The food is the same as that served at dinner minus those dishes that must be individually prepared. Lunch includes country steak, baked chicken, jambalaya, tenderloin tips, and roast beef. There is still a choice from among fifteen or twenty vegetables. And there is of course pot likker. After 1:00 P.M., they'll serve drinks from the bar, but don't plan to linger over a mint julep. The atmosphere at Mary Mac's between eleven and two is the atmosphere of the new South. It's the look of Houston and modern Atlanta—secretaries, businesspeople, folks on the go—talking fast, eating fast, and getting back to work before the lunch hour's over. We think this is a less than ideal way to savor the southern bounty of Mary Mac's kitchen. But we have yet to find ourselves in Atlanta at lunchtime without making a visit to the Tea Room.

DAHLONEGA

★★THE SMITH HOUSE DINING ROOM

Chestatee Street (404) 864–3566
TUES–SUN 11 AM–7 PM / CLOSED MON

If anyone doubts that the American Family has weathered the cultural upheavals of the last twenty years they have only to head south and look around. Every Sunday, families pour out of tiny churches and gather four generations deep in cafés, dining rooms, or picnic spots under the trees.

The Smith House Dining Room serves true family-style meals, six days a week. It is in the basement of the Hotel Smith. You pay a set price per person and sit twelve per table—either families or perfect strangers —and help yourself from great communal platters and bowls.

It is virtually impossible to leave The Smith House hungry. There is no "end" to a meal. Platters keep coming and being passed around, and you are free to keep helping yourself to the several meats, vegetables, potatoes, dressing, and biscuits. Meals change according to season and the whims of the kitchen staff. Among the most popular items are country fried chicken with a pepper crust, pork ribs—bar b qued and roasted—country fried steak and cream gravy, and fillets of freshwater fish, fried in crackermeal. Around the meats revolve constellations of country vegetables. Two days a week corn-bread dressing is made, to go with roasted chicken. Other times there are candied yams in a bath of thick molasses; turnip greens simmered with ham hocks, beans, corn, yellow squash, hominy, potatoes. . . .

If you can possibly resist just one more helping of sweet potatoes or buttered corn niblets, you are rewarded by having enough room to taste the fresh cobbler served at every meal. Apple in the fall and peach in the summer, both are topped with a light crumbly brown-sugar crust. The coffee is freshly ground in the kitchen. It is a necessary jolt to the eater who is not lucky enough to be staying in a room upstairs in the hotel. There are a number of stunned-looking people in Smith's lobby chairs. They seem to have managed to hoist themselves just that far from the tables in the dining room.

But even for the traveler who must move on, Smith's is an ideal stop. It is a perfect cure for the blues of impersonal dining, and the best way for a single traveler to avoid becoming part of the sad tableau of the lone diner hunched over his plate reading a magazine. The communal tables at Smith's are a social occasion as well as a satiating meal.

DARIEN

★★ ARCHIE'S RESTAURANT
U.S. Route 17 (912) 437-4363
MON–SAT 6 AM–10 PM, CLOSED SUN

The scale model shrimp boat in the lobby of Archie's is a replica of the big one he keeps a mile away on the Butler River. The members of Archie's family have been shrimp fishermen for forty-five years, exactly how long Archie's Restaurant has been in business. Meals cooked here are family affairs. His mother bakes pies when Archie is at the restaurant; when he is on the shrimp boat, she stays behind the cash register.

Archie's is a large, bright, modern-looking restaurant with a mixed clientele. Since it is close to an Interstate exit, a few tourists always seem to be seated among the larger groups of locals. Archie's, while not the only place to eat shrimp in Darien, is by far the most popular. The reason is that nowhere in town are the shrimp fresher.

A plate of Archies "famous shrimp" with the works is the most popular. There are close to twenty-five fried shrimp and liberal helpings of Archie's mother's homemade potato salad, cole slaw, warm rolls, French fries and hush puppies. Between the rolls, the shrimp's breading, the fries, and the hush puppies, the one fault of this meal is the overkill of starch. If you use a little discretion and avoid the rolls, which are commercial, and the greasy fries, the remainder is a filling, delicious meal.

The menu offers shrimp stuffed with crabmeat too but there are far fewer shrimp than on the "Archie's Famous" plate, and the crab stuffing is soggy and unappealing. We have yet to find a dish where one food is stuffed inside another that is as appetizing as the two foods would be if served singly. But cooks throughout history have been fascinated by this concept, and in France a century ago the height of this genre was when a chef, known throughout Paris for his gastronomic genius, created a dish that started with a hummingbird stuffed into a lark, the lark stuffed into a thrush, the thrush stuffed into a quail and onwards and upwards until the whole menagerie was stuffed into a turkey and baked.

There are dinners of catfish, deviled crab, and fried oysters on the menu too, all heaped with hush puppies, cole slaw and the rest.

Make sure you finish your meal with a slice of Archie's mother's pie. Her recipes are well known in Darien, and she is included in a hand-stapled cookbook sold at the cash register, a compendeum of the best Southern dishes prepared by the ladies of this area. We especially liked her rich pecan pie and a tall lemon meringue.

You might leave Archie's singing, "Shrimp Boats Are A Comin'," and smiling contentedly. We did, and the next time we are near Darien we know where to find the freshest shrimp in town.

ENIGMA

★★JACK DEMPSEY'S PIT BAR B QUE
Route 82 E. of Enigma
HOURS VARY

In order to penetrate the interior of this "Enigmatic" roadside restaurant, there are stages through which you must pass. First, outside, you have to get through the lawn displays. These range from lawn ornaments to live rabbits in a cage to put-up peppers on a shelf to old Downey bottles mounted on posts as nonbiodegradable flags. Past the lawn, you mount the porch. Smoke from the troughs below the bar b que ovens is so thick that it's difficult to see. There is a darkened doorway, barely six feet tall. The door looks like it hasn't been opened in ten or fifteen years. But you give it a push and it gives—suddenly you're inside. Could there possibly be anyone here?

"Yes sir! What'll it be?" Jack Dempsey was on his toes. As if he had been laying in wait for a decade, he bounced up at our entrance, shaken from his hibernation. His bar b que is just one offering at this operation, which is a sort of general store for local Enigmites. There is no place to eat here, so you get sandwiches or platters to take out. The choices include ham, ribs, Boston butts, chicken and kid. As delicious as it is, kid is hard to find at all but the most esoteric bar b que pits, so we chose a kid sandwich. It was falling-apart tender, rich with the taste of smoke, just dabbed with sauce. Dempsey told us that he doesn't always make kid. The day's offerings are listed on a small piece of cardboard box he tacks to the door. "Goat sandwich" had horns and whiskers drawn on the letter "G."

MIDWAY

★★ THE CHEROKEE RESTAURANT
Route 17 ¼ mile S. of Midway (912) 884–3318
DAILY: 11 AM–10 PM

If Southern Hospitality is essential to you, drive on. If you can stand slitty-eyed stares in return for fantastic seafood, stop at The Cherokee.

We hit upon the border-theory of *roadfood* during a drive along Route 17 in Georgia. The better a state's food, the nastier the people who live at that state's border. Georgia food is usually excellent, and therefore the natives want to keep it to themselves. So they interview and recruit the meanest sons-of-bitches in the state to take up residence along all state lines to discourage tourists from traveling deeper into the heart of the state and stealing all the best biscuits and peach pies.

The Cherokee is a little further inland than a notorious truck-stop, also on Route 17. At this other place you are taking your life into your hands if you don't pull up in a semi with a Saturday night special in your pocket. The Cherokee is a few miles west, and while slightly more civilized, still nasty. It's a large green café decorated with an assortment of bowling trophies and illuminated beer-company paintings. The large lunch crowd is a mix of rednecks in white collars (used-car salesmen) and guys from the local army base. There is hardly a vehicle in the parking lot that isn't a pickup truck, and one gets the impression that the large picture window looking out into the lot is there to afford the clientele a view of what to them must be the most beautiful panorama in the world—wheel-to-wheel GMC's, Dodges, and Fords.

Our skinny waitress in a metal-flake bouffant took our order quickly, but as customers who arrived long after us were finishing their desserts, we still waited to begin. A few subtle reminders, like following our waitress into the kitchen, finally brought our meal. The appetizers were uneven. An oyster cocktail ($1.85) was a bowl of already shucked briney beauties. There were at least a dozen and a half. They were delicious and impeccably fresh-tasting. The shrimp cocktail was disappointing by comparison. They were warm, indicating that they were boiled to order, but the tiny shrimps were practically tasteless and looked more like "sea-monkeys," those microscopic creatures that kids used to order from the back of comic books.

The entrees were worth the wait, the hassle with our waitress, and the drive across the treacherous border of Georgia. An order of deviled crab was a perfectly prepared meal of spiced and restuffed crabmeat served in the crab's original shell. Three good-sized crabs were placed alongside first-rate hush puppies and small dishes of peppery cole slaw and tartar sauce. We tried a platter of catfish fillets. Three well-seasoned, lightly fried pieces of sweet fish were sided as the crab.

The menu is extensive: fried trout, fried oysters, oyster stew, shrimp, and more. Judging from the waitress' tray bringing meals to other patrons, everything looked wonderfully tempting.

While the waitress may not be thrilled to see you, and the service might be painfully slow compared to that given the regulars, we highly recommend Cherokee to thick-skinned *roadfooders* who appreciate great deviled crab more than charm.

VALDOSTA

★★★ C.H. MITCHELL THE BAR B QUE KING
515 S. Ashley (912) 244–2684
MON–SAT 8:30 AM–MIDNIGHT, SUN 3 PM–MIDNIGHT

"Mitchell's" was the unanimous answer we got from a redneck gas jockey, a postal worker, and a soul musician to the question "Where is the best bar b que in town?" C.H. Mitchell is in a poor, black neighborhood but, like Arthur Bryant's of Kansas City, its lure is strong enough to attract black and white customers from all over Valdosta.

We came on a Saturday night. It was an especially steamy Georgia evening, a night filled with the sounds of funky music and whoops of neighborhood parties. Into Mitchell's came every type of Valdostan: well-dressed couples, black and white, college kids, barefoot farm boys from the outskirts, and flashy street people. There is a small dining area, but most of the business is take-out. Behind the counter, presiding over the crowded cacaphony is Mrs. Mitchell. She is small, soft-spoken, charming. She occasionally has to wake up the sleeping pitmaster in the next room. Mrs. Mitchell is assisted by two girls. One could be Hattie McDaniel at age 16. The other is gaunt and angular, with a gold star imbedded in her front tooth.

For all the commotion, Mitchell's is a relaxing place. Customers share a camaradarie, born of the knowledge that they've all found their way to the best bar b que in Georgia. The food is Deep-South soul food

—rich, plentiful, and cheap. Dinners of ham, beef, pork, ribs, or fried chicken come with creamed corn, pungent greens and rice covered with a peppery Brunswick stew. There is sweet potato pie for dessert. Mitchell's bar b que sauce is among The Greats. It is thick, slightly sweet and mysterious, an opaque red dotted with pepper and spice, rich enough to leave that long, rare bar b que afterglow. If you want some to take home, Mrs. Mitchell will put it into an old juice or wine bottle and set an appropriate price.

Dinner at Mitchell's is exhilarating. The taste of the food and the tone of the meal are vivid expressions of the definitive soulful spirit of Valdosta.

★★★★ **MA GROOVER'S PIG AND PLATE**
1132 South Patterson (Route 41, north)
DAILY 5 AM–10 PM

Ma Groover is so corny that if you saw her in a movie you might throw a handful of popcorn at the screen, and blow rude noises through your empty box of Jujyfruits. A lot of people feel that way about John Wayne movies, but anybody who has ever met The Duke in person will tell you it's impossible to feel anything but awe in his legendary presence. Like a face-to-face encounter with the 6'4" hulk of John Wayne, a visit to Ma Groover's Pig and Plate instantly dissolves cynical irreverence.

When we first met Ma she was surrounded by a circle of Osmond look-alikes—well-scrubbed Carter-toothed Georgia boys who had stopped in to show her their new Sunday church suits.

"Left church a little early just to show you, Ma."

"Oh, you boys look so nice," she drawled. After some banter about their new pastel-colored outfits, the boys sat down for dinner. Ma turned to us. "Boys have been comin' in here for forty-one years. Those were Jesse Ferris's boys, but I get a lot of older ones from Moody Field." Ma was sitting at one of the lunch tables in her starched calico apron, shelling peas with her arthritically gnarled hands. "During the war they would send notes to me, and tell their friends to drop in and say hello. I still have most of their letters, although my eyes are bad now and I can't even read my menus too well."

Ma's menu is a misspelled, typed little page that is, in her words, "food like we used to eat on the farm." Fresh rutabaga greens, steamed squash, fresh pole beans, sweet potato soufflé, green peas, fresh buttered corn-on-the-cob. . . . Lunch always includes a choice of three vegetables.

"This is not the kind of food you pour out of a can, so I can say that all of it is good," Ma asserted when we asked for her recommendation. She sized us up through her thick glasses. "You look like the kind who would like my smoked mullet, and you"—the bent finger poked the air —"you look like a baked chicken and dumplings."

We agreed to her suggestions, and while she fussed out of sight in the kitchen, we nibbled on homemade cracklin bread made from tiny bits of pig skin added to the cornmeal. Later we asked Ma about it. "Oh, I've been making that for years. I once got talked into giving the recipe to some local kids here. They published it in their yearbook." We considered a trip to the Valdosta High School Library after lunch.

The chicken was a tender baked breast with a buttery crust. Ma had made a mistake—it came with homemade dressing instead of the dumplings. Fine. The dressing was made from the cracklin corn bread. The mullet was heavy, smoky, and greasily delicious, surrounded by greens, corn, and sweet potato soufflé. Other customers were eating red snapper, channel catfish, and stuffed pork chops—all tempting enough to make us want to initiate a game of musical chairs.

Our fellow eaters were reaching for bottles of vinegared hot peppers stationed at each table. Ma had been watching us from afar to make sure we liked the food. She came toward us and suggested we use the pepper for the greens. "I grow those in my garden and put them up at home. Just sprinkle on the juice. That's right," she approved as we spiced up the already pungent green leaves.

Ma has been serving "the boys" (and girls) of Valdosta since 1935. If you have any unsatisfied Granny dreams or just a hankering for some great homemade food, head straight for Valdosta and the Pig and Plate. Casual attire is just fine, but if you want to make a hit with Ma, wear your Sunday best.

WILMINGTON

★★ WATSON'S CRAB HOUSE
80 Wilmington Island Road (912) 897–2611
DAILY NOON–9:30 PM

You'll know the kind of place Watson's is as soon as you see the tablecloths. They are daily newspapers, picked up after each customer, and set down fresh for the next meal. Utensils consist of mallets, nutcrackers, and picks. And there are plenty of paper napkins to go around. It is a no-nonsense crab house. There is some tacky wood paneling and a few bright beer signs hung about. It looks like they have expanded their business without much concern for decor or atmosphere. You don't need either when you serve crabs like Watson's.

The best times to visit Watson's are Wednesdays and Sundays, when they offer the traditional all-you-can-eat crab feast. They use their own spice to give the crabs a sparkle, although on our last visit we found the meat a bit too dense, not moist and fiberous enough. There are baskets of saltines set out on the table and a large vat of creamy cole slaw to which you can help yourself as a breather from the crabs. Watson's menu is limited to crustaceans. Aside from the steamed crabs, there are crab legs, dungeness crabs, snow claws, Alaskan claws and stone claws.

There are crab statues, pictures and other memorabilia set out in the eating room, but for the complete immersion into crabology, we recommend you stroll outside to Watson's soft-shell crab shell-shedding facilities and have a look at the crop of crabs on their way to the kitchen.

WOODBINE

★ THE PLAZA RESTAURANT
Route 17 (912) 576-5646
MON-SAT: 6 AM-8:30 PM / SUN 7 AM-8:30 PM

The menu cover at The Plaza invites patrons to "Have your dining pleasures renewed where the food is outstanding and the service attentive." The supplication appears over a line drawing of a soigné couple sipping champagne as a tuxedo'd waiter attends to them.

But look around. Not a tuxedo in sight. In fact, not a single soigné couple, nor a crystal champagne glass. What you see are hex signs for sale, antique farm implements, froufrou dolls in nylon net skirts, car deodorant and tic-tac displays. Instead of the cultivated couple, there sits the town sheriff and his crowd, a couple of local families, and some tourists.

A sharp menu detective will note a certain coming apart at the overly cultured seams as he scans under "Cereals" to find listed between Frosted Flakes and Sugar Smacks the couth breakfaster's choice, "Fruit of Loops."

The incongruity between the florid menu and the Formica café might be explained by our guess that Eudell and James Gooding, who run The Plaza, have a brother-in-law studying at the Famous Menu Writer's School, and so they try to give him a chance. Fortunately, they cook better than he writes, and The Plaza is a good stop in southern Georgia on the I-95 route to Florida.

Dinners are of variable quality, the best bets being local trout, bass, catfish, or whiting. Some of the other food, like the shrimp patties and hamburger steaks, looks suspiciously portion-controlled.

We had a late breakfast one morning, a typically Southern mountain of eggs, sausage, grits, hash browns and biscuits. We also ordered hotcakes, which were too spongy and had the capacity to absorb endless gallons of syrup. Having finished the breakfast (except for the hotcakes), we decided to indulge in one of Mrs. Gooding's specialities. She had made a cherry-filled chocolate cake which proved a perfect balance of tart and sweet.

We recommend The Plaza for its pies and cakes, its giant breakfasts, the fresh local fish, and for its hilarious menu. By relative standards of goodness, it's the best place around.

FAIRS AND FESTIVALS

OCILLA
Sweet Potato Festival / MID-NOVEMBER
Cooking contests

KENTUCKY

BOWLING GREEN

★★ THE SMOKEY PIG

Route 31 (Louisville Road) (502) 781–1712
TUES–THURS 10 AM–8 PM / FRI–SAT 10 AM–9 PM / SUN 11 AM–8 PM

There is a primitive painting of a distant cousin of Walt Disney's Porky outside The Smokey Pig, telling all who enter or pass this way that the bar b que inside is "Guar-an-teed." And since it's his relatives you'll be eating inside, you can assume that the pig isn't kidding.

That painted porker outside would wrinkle his snout and squeal in anger if he heard us say that Kentucky produced anything short of haute bar b que cuisine—because as far as The Smokey Pig is concerned, "cooking" means only one thing, and that's turning oinkers like himself into bar b que. We knew we had hit on a prime source even before we walked in the door. There is an aura that surrounds genuine pits—a combination of the smell of burning hickory and the slightly hazy atmosphere. Once you've become a bar b que addict, this smell and this haze work to immediately release adrenalin into the bloodstream, sending you headlong toward the source. So we careened beneath the metal awnings outside, past the bowling trophies in the window, and into the dark, smoky den that assured us the pig's guar-an-tee was 100 percent.

The distinguishing sound of a great bar b que pit is the silence. People do not speak when they eat bar b que. What you hear are gentle animal sounds: the licking of lips and fingers, the clearing of the throat of hot sauce, the guttural moan of pleasure at first bite, a sigh of satisfaction after the last. Here in the dark pit the men sat, sleeves rolled high around their biceps, partaking of the pig.

We ordered two platters, which included lots of pork, white beans, and slaw. The slaw was only serviceable, and the beans were dull, but the sliced pork was among the best. It was fatty, with a citrus-orange tinge to the sauce cutting the greasy taste and reminding us of the finest Carolina bar b ques. The funny thing about the sliced pork was that it wasn't nearly as smoky-tasting as the thick atmosphere of the dining room had led us to believe. It was smooth and still sweet, the smoke having lent it only an accent of hickory flavor. A minced pork sandwich that we took with us and ate a half hour later tasted extremely smoky. We assume that mincing the pork somehow coaxes more smoke taste from it. Or perhaps once in the clear atmosphere of our air-conditioned car, we could taste the deep smoke that had only seemed to be lacking by comparison to the funky haze in the air at The Smokey Pig.

One quibble with The Smokey Pig is that there is no Coke. The men here drink RC Cola, which is an acquired taste. We have tried every substitute for the real thing, from Moxie to Iron Brew to Nehi, and conclude that there is nothing like Coca-Cola to wash down any hot food—from a Szechuan pepper pod to hot bar b que. Beer drinkers be damned.

LOST RIVER

★THE LOST RIVER TRUCKSTOP
31W S. of Bowling Green (502) 842–9710
MON–SAT ALWAYS OPEN / CLOSED SUN

"This man 'bout to git up an leave if his hoecakes and coffee ain't ready yet." The waitress was yelling into the kitchen at the cook, and referring to the grinning truckdriver who was playfully giving her a hard time. He was no more about to leave those corn cakes and coffee than a dog his favorite bone.

Some native Kentucky food like persimmon pudding or parboiled possum is impossible to get in restaurants. But less exotic Kentucky treats like skillet hoecakes, cornmeal mush, and white beans cooked with hog meat are served every day at The Lost River Truckstop.

The Lost River is about as informal a truckstop as we have seen anywhere, with the possible exception of Naked City in Roselawn, Indiana. Truckers walk behind the counter and refill their coffee cups, or wander into the kitchen to see what's keeping the cook from making their hoecakes fast enough. The inside of The Lost River is real wood and the window has a fading "home cooking" sign hand-painted across the dusty glass. The waitresses are backwoods girls with pigtails and a twang as country as a moonshine still.

We ordered a dinner of baked chicken and white beans with a side order of hoecakes. The hoecakes tasted like fresh ground cornmeal and mountain air, but the chicken had been frozen and/or baked into anonymity. The beans had a fatback kick to them, but were less than inspired as a side dish for the white chicken. A better choice was baked country ham, which was delicious with the hoecakes and a bowl of red-eye gravy. Truckers near us were eating fried local catfish that looked so good we considered leaving our chicken dinner, leaving the restaurant, then returning five minutes later wearing putty noses and ordering again. The catfish came with a combination jello salad and deep-orange buttered squash.

Dessert was a sweet and sticky chess pie, not as good as Mrs. Sykes' pie at Neville's, but still a tasty shot of nearly pure sugar, and a good end to a meal. Chess pie is so rich that it is impossible to eat anything else afterwards.

Lost River, Kentucky, is not the rolling green of the tobacco farms or the raw malevolence of bloody Harlan, but a smoky middleground. Few tourists stop here at The Lost River Truckstop. But travelers seem welcome, and the hoecakes are not to be missed.

MOREHEAD

★THE OLD SMOKEHOUSE
Interstate 64 Interchange (606) 784–9960
MON–SAT 10 AM–10 PM / SUN NOON–10 PM

Our broadmindedness at including The Old Smokehouse is liable to get us into a lot of trouble with serious roadfooders. It is a small touristy building next to a gas station by the side of the highway. Amidst its hokey corn-cob pipes and postcards and Kentucky bourbon candy towers a mountain man with a voice like dripping molasses. He stands there with a large smoked Kentucky ham and makes sandwiches. You pay him a dollar, take the sandwich out to your car and drive on. You realize a little further down I–64 that the alleged mountain man in the theatrically funky shack just sold you a terrific and genuine Kentucky ham sandwich. Delicious roadfood.

But we have a recurring nightmare that goes like this: We are sitting in a small out-of-the-way chili parlor in the back of a bar in Diddy Wa Diddy, Texas. In walks another denizen of the road—one of those hardened, professional roadfooders who prides himself on the ultimate esotericness and exoticness of "his" out-of-the-way restaurants. He nods to us, acknowledging our good taste and fellow-connoisseurship at having found the best chili in Diddy Wa Diddy. But then . . . "Pedro," he says to the man behind the bar, "Bring these good people a bowl of your special rattlesnake chili. You know, the stuff that's not on the menu. My usual." Pedro obliges, bringing us a *cordon bleu* bowl of red that costs 25¢. The stranger sits down and begins to tell us about the gullible Sterns who included The Old Smokehouse in their book about good regional food. . . .

We always wake up from the nightmare and reassure ourselves that even though the Kentucky bourbon candy tasted like gasoline, and the mountain man was probably from Central Casting, the ham *was* from a good Kentucky pig via a real smokehouse. Roadfood is where you find it, even if it happens to be in a bogus wood shack that sells souvenirs.

MT. STERLING

★ THE CORNER RESTAURANT
Main Street (606) 498–4596
DAILY 6 AM–7 PM

A plaque near The Corner Restaurant announces that it was the scene of the last successful raid into Kentucky by the notorious Morgan's raiders. The Corner Restaurant today looks like the least rowdy and least-likely-to-be-raided place in town. We peeked into at least four other local restaurants, most of which prominently featured pool tables in the center of the room, and boiled eggs in brine next to the beer nuts on the bar. We looked into The Corner Restaurant and saw the town priest sitting with the town mailman. We entered, and saw that both men were eating the Kentucky specialty—beans, bread, and onions.

The heaviness of this daily special was monumental. The beans and onions are piled into a large bowl, and corn bread comes on the side. The local way to eat it is to crumble the bread into the bowl and spoon in the mighty mixture until full—which won't be long. We also tried an order of fried chicken which was deliciously thick-crusted with sweet, fresh meat, but unfortunately accompanied by tasteless vegetables. Our pumpkin and apple pies for dessert were nice homemade wedges, but like the beans and corn bread, could have doubled as ballast.

The decor of The Corner Restaurant is more genteel and delicate than the cuisine. There are white curtains on the windows and neat checked oilcloth-covered tables. The natives are friendly, and we found ourselves ordering second cups of coffee and pieces of coarse corn bread as we waited, like the priest and mailman, for the mid-afternoon sun to angle off toward evening.

PADUCAH

★★★SKINHEAD'S
1021 South Twenty-first Street (502) 442–6471
MON–SAT 5 AM–3 PM, SUN 6 AM–2 PM

Long before we ever stopped at Skinhead's, truckers sang praises about this place as the best breakfast stop in the Southern Illinois–Kentucky delta. We hesitated to come here, mostly because of the name. "Skinheads." What could they be? We pictured great hulking mountain boys in overalls, wearing rabbit-stomping boots; bald-nog-gined guys who spend their days making home brew and their nights driving their hot rods to the baddest drinking and fighting bars in the evilest part of town. We have since learned better, although have yet to discover the origin of the name. Skinhead's now stands as a beacon for us whenever we trudge south down the bleak road from Chicago. The breakfasts we get here in P-town are a reminder that we are finally entering the South, and a land of brothers who like to eat as much as we do.

The red-eye gravy and milk gravy that accompany the hot biscuits and grits at Skinhead's are the pride of Paducah. The ratio of milk to gravy to flour to black pepper in the milk gravy strikes a perfect balance between creamy texture and sharp spice. The pitcher is placed along-side the hot biscuits—made fresh all morning by Skinhead's cook—and is used to pour onto them if you choose to eat with a fork, or to dunk them if you eat with your hands. Also on the breakfast platter is a lone egg, two slices of coral-red country ham, a bowl of grits, and the red eye, a gravy made from coffee and ham drippings, used to spike the grits or spice the biscuits. This breakfast is a Paducah institution; Skinhead's has been here for decades.

The young girls who waitress here look like farmers' daughters, or possibly coal miners' daughters. They are so accustomed to the local lingo, that one was astonished when we didn't know what a "fiddler" was. Fiddler had been her response when we asked for a lunch recom-mendation. We imagined Jack Benny or Isaac Stern appearing on a plate, but once our waitress realized we were non-Paducans, she managed to explain that a fiddler was a catfish.

"Is it fresh?" we asked. Another astonished look. It was like asking a veteran trucker if he can drive. Of course! Paducah natives demand fresh catfish. The fiddler served here is not a filet. The cook simply whomps off the head and fins of the fish, cleans it, fries it, and serves it with biscuits on the side. Once the deliciously oily beheaded behemoth appeared on our plate, we realized the naiveté of our question.

Skinhead's also serves a country ham lunch, which is the same cured Kentucky ham that comes with breakfast, only sliced thicker into an eight- or ten-ounce piece. Although it will leave you drinking water for the rest of the day due to its extreme saltiness, it will also leave you wistful for Kentucky and for Skinhead's of Paducah long after you've slaked your thirst.

PARK CITY

★★ NEVILLE'S RESTAURANT
Route 31W & Route 225
DAILY 7 AM–7 PM

Most tourists who get off the interstate at the Route 225 exit wind up at the Highway "rest area" just beyond the exit ramp. Neville's is only a few hundred yards past the microwave ovens and portion-controlled food, and it serves some of the best country cooking in the state.

Mrs. Sykes has run the kitchen of Neville's for over twenty years, since long before the interstate was built. She is an elderly black lady, with a frail hairnet, well-manicured nails, a soft-spoken manner, and a recipe for terrific chess pie. "Chess" is a Kentucky specialty, a simple pie made from cream, sugar, eggs, and a little cornmeal. We pressed Mrs. Sykes for her secret, and she modestly informed us, "I always use three eggs and no pecans." Chess pie tastes like hard sauce, the kind that tops plum pudding at Christmas. Mrs. Sykes' is slightly grainy with sugar. She also makes a locally renowned peach cobbler, but only during the summer because, she says "I am very fussy and prefer not to cook with canned peaches. The rest of the year I try to use my imagination and not repeat myself too often. I mash up bananas for pudding or make a nice pineapple upside-down cake, but of course there is always chess pie. The gentlemen love that."

The gentlemen who eat here are Kentucky's tobacco farmers and some local workers. They come here to "talk shop" and spend long afternoons enjoying Mrs. Sykes' inexpensive lunch specials, coffee and pie. Meals here are simple. "I make a homemade soup every day," Mrs.

Sykes told us, "and my customers always like a small piece of corn bread on the side. For my main course I like to have a roast with vegetables. We serve hamburgers, but a nice sit-down lunch is better for you."

The lunch we enjoyed here began with a murky bean soup, aromatic but mild, sided with a large square of white corn bread. The hot meal of the day was meat loaf, moist with ground pork. It came with strong ham-tinged turnip greens and a small salad. For dessert, of course, we chose chess pie.

Nontobacco farmers might feel slightly uncomfortable at first walking into Neville's. Conversation stops momentarily as the men look you over. But there's nothing intimidating about the once-over. These Kentucky folks just like to know who's here. Conversation resumes again as soon as the "outsider" gets comfortable, and we eventually found some of the farmers to be very friendly, especially when it comes to discussing Mrs. Sykes' pies, and what good care she takes of her gentlemen customers.

FAIRS AND FESTIVALS

ADAIRVILLE
Logan County Strawberry Festival / EARLY MAY

BENTON
Tater Day / EARLY APRIL

CARLISLE
Annual Blackberry Festival / EARLY JULY

HARLAN
Poke Sallet Festival / LAST WEEK IN JUNE

LEBANON
Kentucky Ham Days / LATE SEPTEMBER

PAINTSVILLE
Johnson County Apple Festival / EARLY OCTOBER

LOUISIANA

BATON ROUGE

★★★★ **DIDEE'S**
   115 S. 12th Street (504) 344–7578
   TUES–SUN, LUNCH & DINNER

Louisianians living in Bayou country speak in superlatives. Flowers are called white-whites or red-reds because this "double talk" gives life an intensity that pleases hurricane country people. It could be said that what Didee's serves is duck-duck, because one word is hardly sufficient to describe the powerful flavor of this special dish.

"People always ask me how I do it," Herman Perrodin, Didee's owner and chef, told us. " 'What's the recipe?' they ask. You know what I tell them?" He paused to fan the fires burning in his temperamental chef's eyes. *"I* am the recipe!" *Le duck, c'est Didee.*

His restaurant is inconspicuously located just off the highway on a drab street in Baton Rouge. Yet the reputation of his food is powerful enough to attract gourmets who regularly patronize Galatoire's and Le Ruth's. The restaurant is a soothing, peach-colored room. Cloth napery is on the dozen or so tables. The tone is informal.

The specialty of the house is duck and "dirty rice." Dirty rice is rice boiled with duck giblets. During the boiling, the giblets fall apart, giving the rice a "dirty" look. The flavor and aroma imparted to the white grains is more intense than the duck itself. Even a side dish of vegetables sparkled with a kaleidoscopic array of intense seasonings—the hallmark of Creole cuisine.

But it is not the dirty rice or side dishes that lure gourmets from all over the country to Didee's. Duck is the main attraction, duck basted in oil and cooked for hours until its own runny fats bathe it to break-apart perfection. The duck's skin is a bronzed chestnut red, with rivulets of juice running at the slightest pressure of your fork. It is as juicy as can be, yet utterly grease-free.

Didee also makes duck gumbo, voodoo-dark and muddy looking, spiced with andouille, cayenne, thyme, pepper and the oil of the duck.

Didee's is word-of-mouth famous (say "dead-ē"), a find to be permanently engraved in the roadfooder's little black book.

BREAUX BRIDGE

★★★★ THELMA'S

Highway 94—Exit 167 South; Highway 328—Exit 109 (318) 332–1231
TUES–SUN 11 AM–10 PM / CLOSED MON & IN JUNE "WHEN THE
CRAWFISH GET TOO SMALL"

We had tasted crawfish a few times before we finally came to
Thelma's to see what all the fuss was about. Thelma's had always been
mentioned when we discussed roadfood with hungry fellow-travelers,
and was usually described as "the perfect place," or "exactly what
you're looking for." We once sat uncomfortably for at least fifteen minutes listening to an otherwise mild-mannered traveling man regale us
insistently about Thelma's wonders. "You haven't been to Thelma's!?
My God! You *must* go." We agreed that we must go, but the enthusiast
persisted. We began to feel not a little obstinate. After having been
ordered to go to Thelma's for crawfish, we began to think that we really
didn't like crawfish all that much. We liked either lobster or shrimp, but
not that in-between crustacean called the crawfish. Finally though,
duty-bound, we dragged ourselves by our ears to Thelma's.

We only thought we had tasted crawfish. At Thelma's, for the first
time, we really did.

We began with crawfish bisque, which was designed as a full meal.
The base was a thick, well-browned, smoky roux, and the crawfish were
nothing like the rather rubbery things we always thought them to be.
They were delicate—far more delicate than either shrimp or lobster.
The subtle piquancy of the bisque was a flashed reminder of the close
relationship between Louisiana and French cuisines.

We moved on to crawfish étouffée, another stewlike dish, but here
thicker and highly spiced with cayenne peppers, as befits Louisiana—
the home of Tabasco sauce. But the sharp edge of the cayenne pepper
in the étouffée is considerably moderated by the thickness of what
Thelma told us was crawfish fat, added to the stew.

We were slowing down a little at this point, but infatuated with
the crawfish, we bravely moved on to the fried crawfish. Thelma's
frying process is closer to a tempura than the tasteless smothering
process to which fried shrimp are so often subject. Here, the batter
lends texture and a hint of seasoning to the dominant flavor of the
crawfish. The frying brings out, rather than disguises, the sweet
crawfish meat.

Finally, we regretfully ground to a halt. Well, maybe, just to fix the
taste of crawfish onto our buds until next year, and next crawfish season,

we ordered a grand finale—boiled crawfish. This was the pure, perfect, ultimate dish—the real thing, flavored only by cayenne pepper and perhaps salt that had been added to the boiling pot. We twisted off the tails, crushed the shells between our fingers, and peeled six or ten, eating these sweet little beauties with the last of our Jax beer. At this point, with a pile of boiled crawfish still on the plate, we realized we had eaten almost enough for four people.

We rationalize that it's necessary to fill up like a camel at Thelma's, because crawfish season is short—from April through June—and Thelma does not serve frozen crawfish. The restaurant is open the rest of the year, serving shrimps, oysters, steaks, and even a chicken étouffée, and they say that even in the off-crawfish season, members of the French consulate in New Orleans regularly come to Thelma's for the gumbo, the chicken, and the mirilton casserole (a squashlike vegetable).

From the road, it looks like any other roadside eatery—a low-set brick rectangle. Inside, the walls are wood-paneled, and the tables are clean Formica. Only the tingle of cayenne pepper in the air and the faintly sweet smell of crawfish boiling tell you that when you walk into Thelma's, you are walking into one of the world's great restaurants.

KENTWOOD

★ SKINNEY'S
Route 51 (north)
DAILY 9 AM–12 PM

Skinney's is the kind of country-western café that lies dormant until the weekend when the country-western crooners set up the bandstand and the pop-top set shake their tailfeathers to the music. The rest of the week, the cavernous dining room dwarfs the few diners who wander in, and what little action there is will be found in the Tavern end of Skinney's.

We sat at a table admiring the leather-bound menu covers—lush, thickly padded designs of classico-tropical columns and palm trees—an idealized vision of Skinney's twenty-five years ago. Like the menu, Skinney's today is a little faded, but still clean.

The mimeographed sheet inside the leather listed bar b que, oysters and "wop salad." Scootsie, sitting at a nearby table, suggested we try the oysters. He ought to know. When Scootsie isn't sipping Jax beer here at Skinney's, he's down the road at his own grocery store, selling ground meat and shucking oysters for under a dollar a dozen. In this part of the country, oysters aren't any more a delicacy than peanuts. They are eaten and served with the same casual aplomb.

The oysters at Skinney's are fried. Fried is far from an ideal way to serve an oyster, but what we got were still in good shape, slightly salty, with some body left under the breading. The Italian salad was heavily vinegared, with a handful of green olives, anchovy strips, and lots of oregano.

Since Skinney's is primarily a tavern, there is a good selection of beers and drinks to go with meals.

NATCHITOCHES

★★★ LASYONE'S MEAT PIE KITCHEN
622 Second Street (318) 352–3353
MON–SAT 7 AM–7 PM/CLOSED SUN

Lasyone's serves the only Louisiana meat pies we have found in a roadfood restaurant, so to claim they're the very best we have ever tasted may smack of hyperbole. But it's true. We can't imagine a better-tasting meat pie. A Lasyone (say Laz-i-ôn) meat pie is the Acadian (Louisiana countryside) version of that most pan-ethnic dish, the pocket of dough stuffed with meat, known as ravioli, kreplach, won ton, pirogen, dumplings, etc. Lasyone's is most like the Cornish pasty you'll find in northern Michigan, but much spicier. It is a peppery mixture of ground beef and minced pork, highly seasoned and packed into a flaky tender crust, which is then deep fried.

One of Lasyone's pies is a full meal, but it would be a shame to leave without also having a Lasyone plate lunch. The thing to get is the red beans and rice. If that sounds a bit starchy, just wait until you taste what Lasyone's does to the simple red bean. They use the old Acadian trick of simmering the beans with a cracked ham bone, the marrow of which is gradually absorbed into the bean. This not only enriches the red beans' flavor, but somehow lightens them into small silky pillows.

We have never tried Lasyone's chicken and dumplings with mustard greens or black-eyed peas. We have sampled the hot, dense corn bread and powdery biscuits, always with reserve, saving room for the hot pecan pie.

We recommend sightseeing in Natchitoches before you eat, because the musty atmosphere of this ancient bayou town is a perfect appetizer. You'll know Lasyone's as you drive through town by the giant papier mâché meat pie hanging in the window, looking like a mock-up for the crab in *Attack of the Crab Monsters.* Cutout letters below spell Lasyone's. Other than the letters and the huge half-circle pie and some randomly displayed Louisiana bric-a-brac, the window is oddly empty-looking.

Elise Cloutier, our resident expert on Natchitoches, tells us that meat pies are nearly as old and venerable as the town itself, which happens to be the oldest settlement in the entire Louisiana Purchase, dating back to 1714. The drive in from the north is particularly exotic. We drove down Route 71–84 one night past some of the darkest bars and through the most ominous bayous we have ever seen. Bats sailed across the road between the overhanging mossy trees. The air was so heavy that when we finally got out of the car in Natchitoches, our camera lenses fogged up and the starch wilted out of our shirts. Natchitoches is in the heart of Acadian Louisiana; and Lasyone's is the center of its culinary soul.

NEW ORLEANS

★★★★ BUSTER HOLMES
721 Burgundy Street
DAILY 9 AM–7:30 PM

We seldom suspend our roadfood standards to make way for an eating place that is located in a hard-to-park-near, urban area. But like Tolbert's of Dallas and Arthur Bryant's of Kansas City, Buster Holmes is a landmark, and no book about great, cheap American food can be without it.

Buster Holmes is in the French Quarter, only a bean's throw away from Preservation Hall. Buster calls his cuisine "soul food," which is like Sam Ervin calling himself "just a country lawyer." Indeed, his clients are mostly black working people, and the decor is pretty café-functional. Water is served in empty whiskey bottles. Background music is supplied by a soul jukebox. A somewhat decrepit columned bar is set alongside the back wall. But in this funky beanery you can get the best fried chicken in town, po' boys that will knock you out, and the world's best red beans and rice.

The chicken comes with a thick, dark-gold crust that lifts itself from the bird's tender skin just enough to capture a small cloud of sweet, cooked perfume that is released at first bite. The red beans and rice is the classic Louisiana Monday dish, but at Buster's the rice and length of sausage that come with it are so headily garlicked that one must plan a day of celibacy after indulging. Buster holds his thick arms a yard apart to describe his po' boy sandwiches. "I got po' boys dis long," he intones. "Everybody loves Buster's po' boys."

One of the nicest things about dining at Buster Holmes' is paying the bill. The cost of a full meal (full and then some) is seldom not much more than a dollar.

THIBODAUX

★★★★ JUTZ' CAFÉ
609 Jackson Street (504) 447–3525
MON–FRI 10 AM–8 PM / CLOSED SAT & SUN

We were especially frustrated when we drove through the countryside west of New Orleans and could find nothing to eat. The Brittany-like landscape, the small white houses, the peculiar French accents all suggested that the residents of probably every house we passed were great cajun cooks. We were ready to knock on a door and implore the lady of the house to feed us as we approached Thibodaux and found Jutz', the answer to our stomach's hungry growls.

When we at last found Jutz' we made peace with our angry stomachs with *la mediatrice*—the peacemaker—the food named for its use by wayward Louisiana husbands who brought it home to their wives in hopes of forgiveness. It is known here as the po boy. Lesser versions of this "mediatrice" can be found all over the country as grinders, subs, hoagies, horgies, heros, missles, torpedos, wedges, and blimps. Call them what you will, none come close to the original and the best—the Louisiana po' boy, here at Jutz' a loaf of French bread eighteen inches long, hollowed out and stuffed with fresh-fried huge-bellied oysters. As we waited for ours to emerge from the kitchen, we watched two Thibodaux workers each ingest one sandwich. It was like watching the reverse of a snake eating a goat.

We split our po' boy and meanwhile ordered a "wop salad," gumbo, and the special of the day, turtle piquante. A wop salad is an Italian salad, called "wop" on every menu in the New Orleans area, with the disregard for ethnic sensitivities that perhaps only a gracefully multi-ethnic town could display. Anyway, this "wop salad" was one of the best—piled high with pungent green olives, peppers, anchovies, capers, tomatoes, lettuce, and drenched with a garlicky olive oil dressing.

By this time we were ready to get down to serious eating. First, a smoky bowl of filé gumbo that was as mysterious and murky as the Kisatchie Bayou. Gumbo, specifically, and cajun food in general, can come as a surprise to the uninitiated eater who is accustomed to thinking of all exotic foods as being characterized by bizarre tastes or explosive seasonings. The gumbo at Jutz', like all good cajun gumbo, is extremely subtle. It demands a lot from the eater—concentration, persistence, careful savoring of the flavors. All these pay off in a bouquet of sensual pleasure, an orgy for your taste buds. Every gumbo has its unique qualities, and at Jutz' you can choose from shrimp, shrimp–okra, oyster, or combination gumbo. For full appreciation, you must first position your face over the bowl and inhale, imbibing the seasonings and flavors suggested by the steam. Here at Jutz' we looked into the dark, cloudy brew and detected fresh shrimp, luscious oysters, and a faraway sparkle of red pepper. Our normally voracious eating styles slowed to a measured ceremony, as we savored the gumbo the way wine snobs play with their vintage burgundy.

The gumbo finished, we turned to the turtle piquante. This too was subtle, the large pieces of turtle meat tasting like chicken with a gamy edge. The other accompanying tastes were a kaleidoscope of herbs, pepper, okra, tomato, and the racy accent of sherry. The turtle was served with thick white beans. Other items on the Jutz menu include fried catfish, two stuffed crabs, crawfish bisque, a dozen oysters, fried.

Jutz' is an absolutely simple restaurant. Here, simplicity is a virtue, not an excuse. Workers, local students, and townspeople dine from tablecloths, use real napkins, and expect graceful service.

FAIRS AND FESTIVALS

BREAUX BRIDGE
Crawfish Festival / LATE APRIL (EVEN NUMBERED YEARS)

BRIDGE CITY
Gumbo Festival / LATE OCTOBER
4,000-gallon gumbo pot, eating & cooking contests

COLFAX
Louisiana Pecan Festival / EARLY NOVEMBER

CROWLEY
International Rice Festival / EARLY OCTOBER
Creole cooking contests

DELCAMBRE
Delcambre Shrimp Festival / MID-AUGUST

GALLIANO
Oyster Festival / MID-JULY

GONZALES
Jambalaya Festival / EARLY JUNE
Cooking and eating contests

MANSURA
Suckling Pig Festival / LATE APRIL

MORGAN CITY
Shrimp and Petroleum Festival / LATE AUGUST

OPELOUSAS
Yambilee / LAST WEEKEND IN OCT.

PEARL RIVER
Pearl River Catfish Festival / MID-JUNE

RUSTAN
Louisiana Peach Festival / MID-JUNE

MISSISSIPPI

GREENVILLE

★★★★ DOE'S EAT PLACE
502 Nelson (601) 334-3315
DAILY 6 PM–11 PM

Doe's is a converted run-down grocery store in a shabby section of Greenville. There are two small dining rooms, with tables covered with oilcloth and walls decorated with Pepsi signs. There are also some tables in the central kitchen, where you can watch while salads are made and potatoes fried. Despite its common appearance and casual air, Doe's is among the royalty of roadfood eateries. It has long been a haven for traveling gourmets, roadfood pilgrims, and editors of travel magazines. Despite the frothy press it has received about being one of the best restaurants in the world, Doe's has kept its head. It is still dilapidated. And it still serves the best steaks in America.

When you sit down at Doe's, you tell the waitress the approximate poundage and cut of steak you're looking for. She brings out a tray of raw steaks from which you make your selection. We enjoy sitting in the kitchen which is spacious enough so it's never crowded. From here you get to see the steaks toted back and forth on butcher paper—the four- and six-pound T-bones, the small sirloins, the whole parade of beautifully marbled steaks of all sizes. You also get to see the potatoes, freshly cut into strips, thrown into cast-iron pans and fried to a meaty, crisp perfection. The salads are made here too—great bowls, mixed by whichever waitress has time, using the best heavy olive oil and fresh-squeezed lemon juice.

The steaks are cooked in the front room, which you pass through on your way in and out. We chose a couple of medium-sized T-bones (about two pounds each). They are cooked so that they are almost black on the outside, charred to seal in the juices. A knife slices easily into the center. The steak is tender but still fibrous enough to provide all the succulent pleasure of prime beef.

Other items on Doe's limited menu include tamales, rolled here, which are often served as an appetizer, or which you can buy by the dozen, packed in old coffee cans, to take home; and there are some Italian dishes, too, apparently for local regulars who need a respite from steak. Most of the customers at Doe's seem known to the management. A woman who who introduced herself as "Doe's aunt" sits at the entrance to the kitchen and suggests an appropriate table, if you aren't a regular.

Doe's is not a typically inexpensive roadfood restaurant. Our two steak dinners, complete with several beers, were around $30. We have been to New York steak houses that cost three times as much and that try very hard to affect Doe's virile but casual air. No place can compete with Doe's natural excellence. Whether you are a cognoscente of out-of-the-way heavens or just a traveler looking for a great steak, Doe's will not only satisfy you, but may reward you with one of the great meals of your life.

JACKSON

★★★ THE WHITE HOUSE
848 North Main Street (601) 354–9229
MON–FRI 5:30–8, 11–1, 4–6 SAT 5:30–8, 11–12 / CLOSED SUN

We learned of The White House from a folklorist friend named Bill Ferris. Bill specializes in all things southern, and on his personal recommendation of The White House as a perfect example of family-style Dixie dining, we include it. Bill is well known among his friends for his virtually insatiable appetite, an ability to keep eating as long as the food keeps coming—a talent we attribute to his upbringing at southern dinner tables like The White House.

In the center of each White House table is a "lazy Susan" laid out with food. It rotates to give each of the sixteen people at the table access to some of everything, and the lazy Susan's contents are replenished as needed throughout the meal. You eat your meal with boarders living here, students from the nearby university, and perhaps even a folklorist like Bill who knows a traditional Mississippi meal when he eats one.

Fried chicken is usually on the lazy Susan, and next to it a bowl of cream gravy. Vegetables are always plentiful—collards, turnip greens, butter beans, peas, and hominy. Sweet yams or macaroni and cheese are served as side dishes. And of course there are endless pans of rounded golden biscuits. For dessert you can choose fruit cobbler, layer cakes, or a banana pudding or, if you like, all three.

The bountiful meal is eaten in a genuine old-South atmosphere that is quaint without any artificial efforts to create charm. There are pictures on the wall that look like family portraits, and an old cast-iron stove that holds the biscuit pans. The sign outside declares, "Outside meals," and describes this old white house as "A Home Away From Home."

KEWANEE

★THE KEWANEE CAFÉ
Route 80
ALWAYS OPEN

We might never have stopped in The Kewanee Café had there not been a torrential downpour as we drove by. It looked like any other small, white truckstop café near the highway—the kind that makes you wonder "Who'd ever eat there?" As we pulled up to get out of the rain, we saw the funny, primitive drawing of a grey-faced chef on the window, and the words "Home cooking" drawn with flames coming from the letters. As we entered, Ray Charles' classic "Hit the Road, Jack" was blasting from the jukebox, and Catherine Holifield, chief cook and bottle washer at The Kewanee, was tapping out the soulful beat with a spoon on the counter.

We had walked into a roadfood stageset and Catherine was the star of the show. She is the essence of a country girl—easy going, unsuspecting, and quick to laugh. The Kewanee Café is her world, twenty-four hours a day, and it reveals in its every detail a facet of her personality. There are steerhorns over the doorway, and some spurs on the wall. Indian blankets are hung in deference to the Indian origins of the name "Kewanee." Corny religious paintings of trucks being saved from storms hang on one wall. There is a mileage chart, telling you how far you are from Tupelo or Biloxi. And there is always the rhythm and soul jukebox.

Aside from the truckers who know Catherine, a lot of local kids make it their business to "hang out" here, since a soda purchased from Catherine can be an experience. While we were there two boys sashayed up to the counter and ordered "two suicides." Catherine mixed half Dr. Pepper and half Mr. Pibb, and slid the drinks down the counter to the two boys who said, "Thanks, Catherine," in their deepest voices.

Aside from "mixed drinks," Catherine specializes in buttermilk biscuits every morning, chicken and homemade dumplings, and fried local catfish. We had a bowl of her thick vegetable soup and homemade chili, which was extremely spicy, and heavy on the beans. Catherine's food is not delicate, nor is it subtle. It is heavy truckstop food, designed to keep you fueled up for a long drive. Her favorite specialty is biscuits with "Hoover gravy" (flour and drippings) and sausage crumpled on top. For dessert, we tried her sweet-potato pie. The "suicide drinkers" spoke highly of her bread pudding, which she said is topped with a special lemon sauce. Whenever she gets a bushel of fresh peaches, she makes cobblers.

But it is not so much for the down-home cuisine that we remember The Kewanee. It is for Catherine; for her Ray Charles jukebox; for her breezy country face; for the friendly sheltering tone she gives to The Kewanee. Even if rib-sticking food isn't your dish, we recommend a trip to The Kewanee for a cup of coffee and a counter chat with Catherine.

MORTON

★THE GULF CAFÉ
Route 80 (601) 732–8878
MON–SAT 5 AM–9 PM

On the wall at The Gulf Café is a portrait of Mississippi's Governor Finch with the caption "Mississippi's State Bird—The Red Neck Finch." The Gulf is a bird-conscious café in a bird-conscious town. But it is not the Red Neck Finch that dominates Morton, Mississippi, life. It is the chicken. The Gulf lies in the shadow of the enormous B. C. Rogers chicken processing plant—so dominant an industry in Morton life that nonchicken workers are immediately pegged as outsiders when they walk into the café.

But walk in anyway. The Gulf Café is one of the few places to find a square meal between Jackson and Birmingham, and the only place in town where you can escape the 18 billion flies that buzz around the mammoth "tower of chicken" that lords over Morton.

We ordered—what else?—a chicken dinner. The chicken was fresh and nicely battered, and came with delicious silver-dollar-size biscuits, and good sweet hush puppies. A catfish dinner was not as good. The filet was in good shape, but it was slightly greasy in the way that less-than-sparkling-fresh catfish can be. Coffee and tea at the end of a meal are served in cute and dainty orange pots.

Morton is not a beautiful, lush, and scenic town like the gracious

Southland, but it is a fascinating one. If you do plan to sightsee, bring a fly swatter.

RUSSELL

★★KELLY'S TRUCK PLAZA RESTAURANT
junction of Routes 20 & 59 (601) 485–5141
ALWAYS OPEN

Kelly's is a three-dimensional incarnation of an architect's rendering of a perfect modern truckstop. It is nestled high above the noise of the highway in a grove of trees and, as you eat, you look out on verdant Mississippi woods. Not a truck in sight. Best of all, in spite of Kelly's being part of the Union 76 chain, the food here is distinctive, and the familiar face and homogenized cuisine of 76's mythical "Chef John" are nowhere to be seen.

We sat in the well-scrubbed Formica and Naugahyde interior of Kelly's listening to a terrific "white soul" jukebox. We tried the dinner of bar b qued beef tips. They were tender without tasting tenderized, spiced with a sweet, thick topping that tasted exactly like Chicago's renowned Mumbo bar b que sauce. We also got a stuffed pork chop dinner. The chop was a little dry, and the stuffing uninspired, but it was the side dishes with this and the beef tips that gave this truckstop meal its appeal. Both dishes came with seasoned red beans and rice and crowder peas. There was also a basket of cracklin corn bread and biscuits. The coconut pie we had for dessert was thick with shredded coconut, but the chocolate pie was somewhat bland. None of the food here was superlative. But there was a real cook in the kitchen, not a network of computerized machines.

Route 20 in Mississippi is roadfood-poor territory, and we would happily return to Kelly's should we come this way again. The service was extremely friendly, and the atmosphere was far from trucky and seemed touched by the tone of family decency that pervades so many Deep South restaurants. This was most evident in the series of "American Essays" provided at each table to be read while awaiting service (and later purchased). They are essays about typical Americans—teachers, doctors, truck drivers, pig farmers, policemen, etc. Each essay is identical, beginning with the question "What is a [blank]?" and then proceeding to answer the question, "He is short, he is tall; he is thin, he is fat; he is black, he is white; he is young, he is old"—the point being that he is typical, and average, and nonspecific—an American. When people ask us, "What is roadfood?" we have often thought of answering, "It is steak, it is fish, it is hearty, it is light; it is bland, it is spicy; it is served in tearooms, it is served in truckstops." For that variety of road-food served in truckstops, Kelly's is hard to beat.

FAIRS AND FESTIVALS

BILOXI
Shrimp Festival   /   EARLY JUNE
The blessing of the fleet

NORTH CAROLINA

DUNN

★ J.C. AND MARTHA'S
Route 301 (919) 892–7567
MON–SAT 8 AM–8 PM / SUN 1 PM–8 PM

J.C. and Martha's is a pool hall and a restaurant, right across from Madame Swanee, the Palm Reader. But before you form a mental picture of it, remember that in the South things are rarely as they seem. This pool hall and restaurant is as clean and wholesome a place as there is in the state of North Carolina. The alternative to playing pool after supper is to pick up a piece of the church litera-ture on the counter to read, or to have a pleasant chat with J.C., Martha, or their daughter, who run the place as a family operation seven days a week.

Dinners include collards, butter beans, turnips, or whatever vege-tables can be had fresh. Martha makes the pies, her specialties being apple and chocolate. The breaded and fried rib-eye steak we ordered was meaty and suffered from none of the grease-shock that chicken fries are prone to. The pork chops were simply breaded and pan fried. It was a simple, tasty southern meal. If it lacked anything, it was excitement.

Everything was fresh and nicely prepared, but like the restaurant itself, the food seemed too reserved. It is a friendly place, and a good stop for a meal or a game of pool. All it needs is funk and a bouquet of adventure —which is something we never thought we would be saying about a restaurant that is also a pool hall.

★★ RHODES POND SEAFOOD RESTAURANT
Route 301, 6 mi. S. of Dunn (919) 892–1146
TUES, WED 5 PM–9:30 PM, THURS–SAT 11 AM–9:30 PM, SUN NOON–2 PM

When we first discovered Rhodes Pond it was a fish camp of primordial beauty, set in a cypress grove, serving locally-caught fish and expertly-made pies at the lowest prices. It was a casual place, selling bait and fishing supplies in one room, serving its great food in another. It was only a few miles from a bleak and foodless interstate highway. It was a restaurant with all the qualities of great roadfood.

Rhodes Pond has since changed hands, and the new owner, Mrs. Powers, has "freshened it up a bit" by adding new curtains and replacing the bait buckets and lures with antiques. Fortunately, the rustic charm of the setting is intact, the tone of the place is still casual, and the food is good enough to keep the old cook, Bea, coming back now as a regular diner.

The menu is still mostly fish: shrimp, oysters, deviled crab, and a lone offering of bar b qued chicken. The shrimp and oysters come fresh from the Carolina seashore. The fish is served fried, family-style so that you help yourself from large serving trays. Desserts here are still outstanding. The specialty is apple jubilee, a mélange of apples, pineapple, nuts and whipped cream. A good alternative is the peach fluff, a frothy peach and cream offering that is a little less rich than the jubilee.

It is best to get to Rhodes Pond at sunset, when you can enjoy the cranes and egrets perching on the mossy cypress trees in the pond. It is easy to forget that the highway is only a few miles away.

FOUR OAKS

★THORNTON'S GOOD EATS
Route 301 (919) 963-2289
DAILY 6 AM–11 PM

There can be no question that the South is a land where grease is a central feature of the cuisine, but Thornton's pushes this characteristic to an unheard-of extreme. The lady who wields the spatula makes two things—hamburgers and hot dogs. We're not certain of her name, because even though she told it to us three times, her words were muffled in the sounds of bubbling oil that echo off the walls of this tiny lunch shack. This small speedy-spatula'd cook, who seemed to be wearing a full four ounces of pancake makeup on her face, perhaps as a shield from the oil fumes from the cauldrons below, has taken the two most basic all-American foods and boiled them in oil. Her grill has sides on it to contain the deep-frying meats which, when done, are placed onto buns, then topped with chili sauce slick enough to underslide a studded steel radial. To the dismay of the cholesterol-conscious, and to the delight of our beneficiaries, we love these little burgers.

We have realized that our love arises from a childhood deprivation of White Castle burgers, those twelve-for-a-dollar dime-sized squares of meat served on a steamed bun that we somehow preferred to the two-inch thick patties of ground sirloin that were served on the family dinner table and proclaimed "good for you." We doubt if Thornton's are "good for you," but they do serve a purpose. Somewhere on the family tree of the American hamburger, there is a link between White Tower circa 1955 and Thornton's. Thornton's uses better meat, and a lot more oil. It's certainly not for everyone, but for those nostalgic devil-may-care hamburgophiles with a teflon gut, Thornton's is an experience not to be missed.

LAURINBURG

★★★MRS. FORDE'S COFFEE SHOP
S. Main Street & Bus. Route 74
DAILY BREAKFAST, LUNCH & DINNER

Mrs. Forde greets you at the door of her restaurant and hands you a stubby pencil and a 2′×3″ scrap of paper. On the paper are mimeographed the choices of the day—two entrées and five or six vegetables. You check which entrée and which three vegetables you want, and Mrs. Forde whisks the menu back to the kitchen. Pretty soon, your food is brought to you from the back. Or, if it isn't you can go back yourself and get it. When you're through eating, bring your plate and ice-tea glass to the back and pay Mrs. Forde or one of her helpers. The cost of breakfast, lunch or dinner—75¢.

Mrs. Forde is dressed for action. Her stockings are rolled down below the knee, and her apron is full of pencils and menus. Her manner is brusque. She scolds and cajoles her customers like a medieval maid in a bawdy dining hall. She knows all of them and they know her, and so there is a lot of dialogue across the long family-style table with its irregular chairs and bench seats.

The food is elemental. Entrées are things like meat loaf, chicken, chicken salad, or weiners. Vegetables include mashed potatoes, beets, carrots, rice and gravy, or peas. All are fresh and homemade, served in modest portions in portioned plates. There is no choice for breakfast. You get what Mrs. Forde makes. Sunday dinners are more elaborate and twice as big. They cost $1.50.

Although the tone of repartee in Mrs. Forde's dining hall is rough-hewn and the outside walls are raw brick (it used to be a car showroom), the decor is almost delicate. The central dining table and the smaller tables on its outskirts are covered with soft blue-and-white checkered cloths. The floors are a sharp black-and-white tile pattern. The air is cool and bright in the main dining hall, even sunnier in the vestibule, where a few auxiliary tables are kept for overflow on Sundays.

Mrs. Forde has been in the same place, serving the same meals to the same people and their sons and daughters since World War II. They don't need a sign to tell them where Mrs. Forde's is, and so there is none; but for the traveler, it can be a tricky place to find. There is nothing to mark the plain brick building, but look for the First United Methodist Church. It's right across the street.

RALEIGH

★★ THE PORK PALACE

1421 South Wilmington Street (Route 70) (919) 834–9322
MON–SAT 5 AM–10 PM, SUN 7 AM–9 PM

Our most specific memory of The Pork Palace would have to be our porcine waitress in her too-tight pink shift holding aloft the most enormous piece of fried pigskin we have ever seen. We had tasted fried pigskin once before, as cuchifritos, and thought it to be bland and unpleasant, leaving a film on our tongues that no amount of liquid could seem to dissolve. We were not anxious to accept this crisp offering from our waitress, despite her cajoling and promising that pigskin dipped in Pork Palace sauce was the best eating in all of North Carolina.

We negotiated with her, to a small audience of Pork Palace regulars who had gathered around, amused by her coaxing and our grimaces. We would try the skin, but after a plate of oak-smoked pig bar b que and a side of hush pups. We declined the all-you-could-eat pig-feast in favor of a modest bar b que sandwich with hot sauce. We poured on a few drops of Texas Red, only one of the assortment of hot sauces that are stationed at each table. The pork was moist and only mildly smoked. The hush puppies that came on the side were too homogenized in taste, hinting at a cornmeal mix instead of individually blended ingredients.

Although the backbone of The Pork Palace is bar b que, workers from the nearby factories ordered at least as many daily specials, choosing the fried chicken served with candied yams and butter beans.

As we neared the end of our bar b que we noticed that our waitress had not forgotten our obligation to taste the pigskin. She solemnly approached us, holding the crispy skin aloft. We felt the way missionaries in a strange land must feel when, as a peace offering, the natives bring them a bowl of cowblood and unspeakables to taste. We stalled, ordering two large glasses of orange juice, the most grease-cutting solvent we could think of. The juice came in chilled glasses, a nice touch for a workman's lunch place. Again the puffy crisp came to our table accompanied by a bowl of hot sauce. We broke off a piece—it had the texture of a giant potato chip—and dipped it in the thin sauce. It was delicious, not at all greasy, with a mild taste. Our waitress squealed with delight as we broke off bigger and bigger pieces from the free-form skin.

The Pork Palace appeared to be the only "skin" joint around. The rest? Perhaps it's made into Brunswick stew or footballs. After tasting the skin we can't imagine why its popularity hasn't spread. Eating pigskin is not, as we squeamishly thought, an acquired taste. Make sure that you ask for the special hot sauce, the only kind that isn't placed on the table when you arrive. It comes in three different grades of hot, a marvelous homebrew that adds the right zing to the mild taste of the pig.

SMITHFIELD

★★★ THE WHITE SWAN RESTAURANT
Route 301 (Holt's Lake exit off Route 95) (919) 934–4597
DAILY 9:30 AM–3 PM, 6 PM–10 PM / TAKE OUT 9:30 AM–10 PM

Whenever Dewar's Scotch is ready to do a profile of the Sterns, we are ready for them. Among our "accomplishments," "thoughts," and "last book read," we would like to add "The Sterns' pet peeve." Few things in life raise our dander more than the women stationed at the borders of states in "tourist information bureaus." It is the job of these "Welcome Ladies" to divert tourists from good local restaurants like The White Swan and send them to the most anonymous, plasticene eateries in the state. We asked one such blue-suited Miss Sardonicus at the Carolina border if she could direct us to The White Swan, which we had been told by a North Carolina native serves the best hush puppies in the South. It was bad enough when this smiling Miss had never heard of The White Swan. What was worse was her suggestion that we go to Calabash, North Carolina, instead, where, she told us, we would find the best food in the state. What we found was the most expensive food in the state, and the most grossly hawked. Muzak, blobby miniature golf courses, blaring papier mâché dinosaurs, and mechanized first mates beckoned us to enter various "captain's tables," to "climb aboard the salad deck," and to "walk the planked steak." We headed north, away from this phony Carolinaland, and found The White Swan.

The Swan is a Carolina restaurant and bar b que pit. The restaurant half is clean, hospitable, and frequented mostly by Carolinians. The tables are covered with patterned tablecloths, the waitresses address you civilly as ma'am or sir, and full meals are in the low-priced range. The kitchen is staffed with country-lady cooks, with nets on their hair and flour up to their elbows. The White Swan does not offer "His Majestye's Salade Bar," but they do have an authentic selection of traditional colonial-rooted "salets"—dishes like turnip greens and stewed onions, or candied yams, or rice and gravy. These come with the roast pork or Virginia ham dinners or with the fresh fried shrimp.

When Carolinians aren't sitting down for roasts and "poke salets" or country steaks and yams, they're liable to be found somewhere near a pork bar b que. Right next to the restaurant is The White Swan pit, where we found the celebrated hush puppies. The humble hush puppy, which began as literally a throw-away dish (thrown to dogs to make them "hush") has at The White Swan attained perfection. It is golden brown, crispy without being crusty, just barely sweet. Hush puppies and homemade cole slaw come on both the small platter and the large. The bar b que is spicy to begin with, but if you subscribe to the philosophy that "a little too much is just enough," there is a powerful peppery sauce to add at your discretion.

The one anomaly at The White Swan is that their bar b que sandwiches are prepared West Virginia style. That is, the bar b que is automatically topped with cole slaw. This was a shock to us at first, but we actually found that the gardeny green slaw was a nice balance to the woody taste of the meat. Other than this pleasant peculiarity, and the unfortunate use of prebaked pies, The White Swan is a perfect place to sample North Carolina's favorite foods.

TARHEEL

★★HUGGINS RESTAURANT
Route 87
MON–SAT 5:30 AM–5 PM / CLOSED SUN

Phoebe and Nan are the two sisters who cook at Huggins. They are pink-faced hairnetted country girls of such queenly dimensions that the Huggins kitchen—small by any standards—seems a very tight fit. These ladies are Larry Huggins' sisters and along with Larry and Larry's wife, they make this restaurant into a delightful lunch stop in the Tarheel State. What Nan and Phoebe can't make during the day in Huggins' kitchen, they supplement with their own cannings and pies from home.

The restaurant is a tiny log cabin in the middle of Tarheel. Its patrons are farmers and car salesmen and businessmen from the town. There are a few shameful items on the menu—awful bread from plastic supermarket bags, pale pink frankfurters, and a few patties of dubious origins. But set your sights above these shortcomings, and notice that each table in Huggins is graced with a jar of Phoebe and Nan's put-up banana peppers, and shaker jars of homemade birds-eye pepper marinating in vinegar. The peppers are from the sisters' garden, as are most of the greens served here.

We sprinkled the birds-eye onto the greens and they came to life the way only southern vegetables can do. Phoebe told us that Nan's favorite dish is mustard greens simmered for hours with bits of ham and served with pork chops and glazed yams. The chops were crusty on the outside, juicy and sweet within. The yams and greens sparkled. Our only complaint about this Huggins meal was the dainty portions which seemed odd considering the monumental size of the cooks.

Pineapple cake is a Phoebe specialty, described to us with loving detail by Nan, who said the Huggins' secret was Phoebe's use of her special cast-iron skillet, seasoned with sugar, and used only for upside-down cakes. The day we ate here, Phoebe had made a peach pie instead, which was good but not up to Nan's description of the dark scent of the pineapple and sugar sizzling in the upside-down skillet.

After we had finished our meals and presweetened iced tea, we poked our heads into the kitchen to say good-bye to Phoebe and Nan. Their slightly damp pink faces and spirited giggling as they cut pieces of pie and served up the yams stayed in our minds as one of the sweetest memories of the Tarheel State. If these girls had little wings and pineapple cakes in their hands, Nan and Phoebe might resemble overgrown cherubs.

FAIRS AND FESTIVALS

AYDEN
Collard Festival   /   EARLY SEPT

BANNER ELK
The Roasting of the Hog   /   JULY 4

BARNARDSVILLE
Ramp Festival   /   1ST SAT IN MAY

GRIFTON
Shad Fry   /   LATE APRIL

MOREHEAD CITY
Crab Derby Fish Fry / MID-AUG

ROSE HILL
Fried Chicken Poultry Jubilee / LATE SEPT

SNEAD'S FERRY
Shrimp Festival / MID-AUG

SURF CITY
Fried Spot Festival / EARLY OCT

WAYNESVILLE
Ramp Festival / LATE MAY

SOUTH CAROLINA

CAMDEN

★★REYNOLDS BAR B QUE
129 E. DeKalb Street (803) 432–9521
MON–SAT 11 AM–9 PM

There is nothing charming or decorative about Reynolds Bar B Que. Its atmosphere is smoke from the pit, occasionally laced with music from a white soul jukebox. It is a plain, clean restaurant, divided into two sections by a partition. For serious, no-nonsense bar b que eating, it is a fully satisfying space, with nothing to divert attention from the matter at hand, which is Mrs. Fannie Reynolds' first-rate bar b que.

Platters of pork come with finely chopped fresh cole slaw, sweet, porky beans, crisp hush puppies flavored with bits of onion, and rice drenched in a pungent hash. The bar b que itself is greasy, grainy and mild. If you like it hot, there are jars of peppers and hot sauce on the table. Your beverage is presweetened iced tea, refilled as often as necessary.

GEORGETOWN

★★LAMARR'S FISH AND CHIP
Church Street (Route 17) (803) 546–5634
MON–SAT 9 AM–6 PM / CLOSED SUN

Lamarr's has its name and the legend "welcome to fish and chip" scratched in spidery handwriting into the concrete in front of the door. On the wall, across from the take-out window is another hand-lettered sign stating emphatically with many exclamation marks, "NO DANCIN', NO DRINKING, NO MESSIN' AROUND." The two signs give a strong feel for Lamarr's. It is friendly but proper, a place for serious fish and chips eating, not for carousing.

Lamarr's is in the center of Georgetown's black district, yet as far as we could tell it was accessible and friendly to white patrons. We placed our orders for fried shrimp, and fish and chips, and strolled next door to Iszard's Fish Market to examine the fresh fish that supplies Lamarr's. At Iszard's we noted the beautiful large catfish fillets, plump pieces of cod, and oysters still in the shell.

Ten minutes later, our order was ready at Lamarr's, and to the beat of a soul jukebox we enjoyed the shrimp, which were moderately generous with fourteen to an order, and good large pieces of fried fish that came with hangdog-looking fries as "chips."

While Lamarr's is set up for takeout orders, all tables inside were filled, and Lamarr's, despite its strict signs on the wall, is obviously a popular hangout.

HARDEEVILLE

★SERGEANT SMITH'S CHICKEN-A-PLENTY
Highway 17 (803) 784-2250
MON–THURS 9 AM–10 PM, FRI & SAT 9 AM–11 PM, SUN 1 PM–10 PM

Sergeant Smith was only six when he learned to cook a chicken. He learned because his family was very poor, and his mother was off at work all day. His kitchen skills followed him into the marines, where he became a mess-hall cook. Then the sergeant met Pauline. "Can't anybody cook a chicken like I can," Pauline said, and they fell in love, and opened Sergeant Smith's Chicken-a-Plenty in Hardeeville.

It's an easy place to drive right by, lodged as it is among a long string of fast-food restaurants on Highway 17. In fact, it doesn't look much different from the others, except for a few hand-painted chickens on the front. It's a small stand, with a walk-up window and a few picnic tables outside. There is a handwritten menu on the wall listing the Sergeant and Pauline's specialties.

The smothered chicken was our favorite. This has been soaked for twenty-four hours in a pepper marinade, fried and topped with gravy, southern style. The aroma of this dish is alluring enough to make the marine bulldog bust his chain. There are also plates of livers and gizzards, marinated, floured, and cooked until they bob up to the top of the oil. The Sergeant, like his well-known competitor, The Colonel, sells chicken family-style, from nine-piece orders to the mighty thirty-piecer. These come, like the platters, with French fries, biscuits, and a buttery corn bread dressing.

If chicken isn't your dish, Sergeant Smith's also has slow-cooked sausage, served smothered in onions, tomatoes, tiny cubes of ham, with a side dish of red rice. There are soulful vegetables every day, such as turnip greens, collards, and peas, and occasional specialties like chicken and dumplings, pork chops, or ribs. These are chalked in on the menu when available.

We love eating at Sergeant Smith's not just because the food is delicious and cheap, but because we know the money we spend here goes to finance more chickens, better chickens, and new recipes from the Sergeant and Pauline—two chicken-lovers who have found a way to share their skills with the world.

MANNING

★★D & H BAR B QUE
412 South Mill (just off Route 301) (803) 435–2189
WED–SAT 10 AM–8 PM / CLOSED SUN–TUES

Roadfooding can be a dangerous business. Take bar b que. We offer to our readers this urgent advice: Do not order bar b qued pork in Texas and do not order bar b qued beef in the Carolinas. The idea of cooking a cow over a Carolina pit isn't just an aberration; it's a sacrilege. We asked "W.H."—that's Mr. Healy, the "H" of D & H—what went into his "hash," the gravy that South Carolinians pour onto the rice next to their bar b que. "Pig!" said he.

"What else?" asked we.

"More parts of the pig."

We tasted the hash over a bed of rice next to our sliced pork sandwich. It was salty, very greasy, and of irregular consistency—not far from natural gravy, but charged with flavors of hickory, sugar, pepper, and spice. The sliced pork itself was typically South Carolinian, that is, greasy and succulent and soulful. It is nothing like the heady smoked flavor of a Texas brisket, since the fatty pigmeat seems to absorb less smoke than spice. W.H.'s sauce, which we poured liberally onto the meat, is extremely hot, and about the color of Georgia clay. When we asked him what went into it he said, "No mustard and a lot of peppers."

When W.H. and his two assistants, Pauline and Mildred, realized we were loving every greasy handful of our sandwich and platter, they came and sat down on one of the adjacent wood benches. W.H. silently watched us eat, and Pauline and Mildred told us something about the D & H, and about real Carolina bar b que. First they told us about the cracklin sold to local folks for adding to their corn-bread batter. What this is is pigskin stripped off after the smoking, then deep fried. It is like Puerto Rican cuchifritos, the great hunks of fried pigskin that are sold at neighborhood street-corner stands; or like a larger and nonkosher version of Jewish *greeven,* the zesty strings of chicken skin that result from rendering the bird's fat. Southerners customarily use cracklin to spice up corn dodgers or, occasionally, hush puppies.

We had just finished our hash and rice when the ladies got around to describing the ingredients therein. It was like one of the scenes in a situation comedy where the hero gobbles up his sandwich, then learns that it's rattlesnake meat. What we learned was that hash consists of every part of the pig that was not put into our sandwich or into the bags of cracklin. We swallowed hard, and convinced ourselves that it really did taste delicious, in spite of its ignominious visceral origins.

There's no question we'll return to the simple wood benches in D & H's plain dining room. And we'll probably get the hash again, right next to D & H's first-rate bar b que. But for the squeamish, our recommendation is to not ask the management how they make the hash.

PAWLEYS ISLAND

★ THE LITCHFIELD RESTAURANT

Route 17 (803) 237–4415
MON–SAT 6:30 AM–2:30 PM / SUN 7 AM–2:30 PM

The Litchfield is a small island of pure souls in the sea of commercialism that is Myrtle Beach. Myrtle Beach is the Coney Island of the South; arcades of nickel and dime fun, weenies to eat on the beach, and more miniature golf-lands than there are homes. Pawleys Island is a short hop from this area, and as different as day is to night.

We didn't spot a single tourist in this breakfast or lunch-only café. The booths were lined with Pawleys Islanders who not only seemed to know everyone else by name, but hopped from table to table asking about "Charley's arthritis" or "Billie-Jean's divorce." Even the rest rooms at The Litchfield are homey. There is a bathtub next to the john and a medicine cabinet (we are chronic snoopers) full of someone's hairpins and aspirins.

We sat enjoying a well-prepared breakfast of biscuits and sausage and ham and hotcakes, when a man at the next booth leaned over in our direction and said point blank, "Eatin' breakfast is like a dog wearing feathers . . . dumb!" We didn't know quite how to react. This Elvis lookalike seemed friendly enough, but the invasion of our privacy caught us offguard. We realized from his grin that we weren't going to have to defend our breakfasts in some back alley, and so we chalked up the episode to Pawleys Island friendliness.

We never did get back here for lunches, but the menu lists a fried chicken platter with hush puppies and a dinner of fried oysters. There are daily specials too, but they sounded drab by comparison, containing standards like roast beef and meat loaf. There are no pies or cakes that could be called homemade here, nor are the rolls especially good. But the cook was mixing up the hush puppy batter and flour-dredging pieces of chicken for lunch. For a basic lunch stop with a touch of humanity we would point to The Litchfield.

ST. GEORGE

★★LOWDER'S RESTAURANT
209 South Parler Street (Route 15) (803) 563–4075
MON–SAT 7 AM–3:30 PM / CLOSED SUN

If we wanted to convert a nonbeliever to the joys of southern café eating, we would take him to Lowder's. It is a wonderful picture of Dixie café life, beginning with the little things: presweetened iced tea or icy, fizzy Cokes; silverware neatly wrapped in a paper napkin; the hot pepper jar next to the napkin dispenser. And then there is the food: rich, crispy sweet southern cooking, from chicken and hush puppies with always-fresh vegetables to luscious pies and shortcakes. Finally, there are the people: those who run the restaurant as if it were a family kitchen, and those who leisurely eat here, as if they were sitting down to a large family dinner.

Lowder's is all these things; and while there may be restaurants that lay claim to crispier chicken or more extravagant desserts, Lowder's is special for its balance. Frances, who served us and owns Lowder's, would be just as horrified by a heaping platter or an over-stuffed sandwich as she would be by the thought of meager portions.

Frances, who looks like Betty Anderson from *Father Knows Best,* explains, "If the soup is too heavy, there'll be no room for supper." About beef stew: "I always watch out that the potatoes and vegetables don't outweigh the meat, which is what they came for." "You take chicken," Frances continued. "Everybody loves it. But too many restaurants just bread it and fry it. The outside is good, but near the bone it's rubbery. We precook our chickens fifteen minutes, then bread them. That way it's good outside and in."

Frances does just about everything herself, even during the crowded lunch hour. The service, therefore, can be slow, as in a bistro where your premeal wait is allotted for conversation, contemplation, and relaxing before the meal. It is a gentle and civilized way to eat lunch. We sometimes think of Frances as we try and push to the bar at midtown Manhattan's Charley O's, or scramble for a hot dog at Nathan's. The hurry-up environment of New York eating would simply wilt this rare and measured lady.

At her little café in St. George, Frances flourishes. "I've been doing it for almost fifteen years," Frances said later as she brought the apple pie and strawberry shortcake.

A lunchtime fried chicken platter came with collard greens diced with country ham and a small mound of rice and gravy. This was served in a portioned plate, a flashback to contented childhood, when mother knew exactly how much you ought to eat. Our other lunch was country ham with a side of orange-scented yams. We also tried a bowl of vegetable soup, a temperate mixture of corn, peas, onions, Irish potatoes, sweet peas, and string beans. We asked Frances about okra, which seemed to be missing, and she informed us that many of the regular customers object to its texture, so they have left it out. We spiced up the greens with home-brewed hot pepper sauce, and cleaned our platters, leaving just enough room for dessert.

The strawberry shortcake came in a bowl. It was demure, dainty, and sweet; a small square of white cake, mounded with strawberries and dabbed with whipped cream. The apple pie proved to be the meal's only extravagance. It looked to be nearly one-fifth of a total pie. The apples were spiced with cinnamon, and the crust was a delicious fall-apart sugar pastry.

We were among the last lunch customers by the time we finished the pie, and when Frances asked how we liked it, we realized that its enormous proportions were tailored especially for us—a giant wedge of southern hospitality. We complimented her on the pie. Frances turned on about 500 watts of Dixie charm, declaring the price of our meals in the longest, thickest South Carolina drawl we have ever heard. "Four twenty-faave" has echoed in our daydreams about the South as the sweetest price we paid for lunch, and for the pleasure of being served by Frances.

SUMMERTON

★★THE SUMMERTON DINER
Highways 15 & 301 South (803) 485–6835
FRI–WED 7 AM–10 PM / CLOSED THURS

Miss Mildred, waitress extraordinaire at The Summerton Diner, says that corn bread is the basis of all the food cooked here. It is served for breakfast with eggs, in bread baskets with lunches of roast beef or ham, in The Summerton's corn-bread turkey dressing. Corn bread is lurking as crusty toasted croutons in the homemade soups, and as a crisp platform beneath the chicken and dumplings.

But man cannot live by corn bread alone. What else does corn-bread-happy cook and owner Lois Files make?

"I guess if I had to say we had one specialty, aside from the corn bread, it would have to be the catfish." Lois is referring to the thick sweet cream of a stew made from Santee catfish. Like the ramp—a southern vegetable generally acknowledged to be the best-tasting and worst-smelling around—the catfish is both odious and appetizing. The sweet meat of a fresh-water bullhead is belied by its hideous kisser. But one taste of The Summerton's Santee stew, and you'll think of the catfish as a beautiful animal. Here it is bathed in a creamy bisque and the luscious meat verges on a nutlike gaminess. The stew is served with yellow squash, black-eyed peas, turnip greens or rice and gravy and, of course, corn bread.

If a lot of this sounds like soul food, it is. White soul food, which in South Carolina is not too different than black; just a little stingier on the grease, and more liberal with the pot likker.

Coconut puddings and apple crisps are the best desserts at The Summerton. The crisp had a crunch of brown sugar on top, and a sweet vein of butter running through the apple-filled cake.

The diner itself is clean and quite plain, one of the few decorations, a sign on the wall announcing the house rules: "No drinking—No profanity."

FAIRS AND FESTIVALS

GILBERT
Lexington County Peach Festival / JULY

HAMPTON
Watermelon Festival / LATE JUNE

IRMO
Okra Strut / EARLY OCT

PAGELAND
Pageland Watermelon Festival / MID-JULY

SALLEY
Chitlin Strut / LATE NOVEMBER
Five tons of chitlins; BBQ

YORK
Grape Festival / MID-AUGUST

TENNESSEE

FRANKLIN

★ DOTSON'S RESTAURANT
114 East Main Street (Route 31) (615) 794–2805
MON–FRI 5 AM–8:30 PM

Dotson's Restaurant looks like it might have been almost elegant. But about ten years ago the white Greek revival pillars began to flake and the building started to list to the right, and a gas station was built next door. Time passed and the gas station aged and mellowed too, and now makes a perfect tableau with the fading Dotson's.

Any charm that the pillared exterior of Dotson's might retain does not carry inside. The interior is plastic booths and haphazardly placed tables. The food in the refrigerated cases looks slightly disheveled after the lunch mob has departed.

Lunchtime is crowded and service rushed. This is not the place for slow southern charm, at least between the hours of eleven and two. Our waitress appeared instantly, pad in hand. We hardly had time to crack open the menu, but she impatiently pencil-tapped her order pad as she waited. We asked her what Dotson's was best known for and she answered with brevity: Catfish!

Catfish is served with pinto beans, biscuits, and cole slaw. It was on three quarters of the tables, definitely the local favorite. Our orders produced a thick cracker-crumb fried fillet, not the sweetest piece we ever ate but seemingly fresh and crisply cooked. Waitresses double-trotted down aisles with trays full of fried chicken and steaks. Neither looked as good as the catfish.

Desserts are rather war-torn pies, baked here but too battered-looking to be appealing. We settled instead for the ubiquitous Tennessee fried pie. The pie was filled with apricots, tart and chewy.

By the time we had finished our dessert and coffee, Dotson's was empty of the noisy lunchers. It was almost a different restaurant. Our formerly fleet-footed waitress was lounging at a back booth and seemed to take an eternity to write out our tab. A calm had descended and the former hecticness had been replaced by a more wilted and quiet air that mirrored the old-South exterior of this small-town restaurant.

LEWISBURG

★★ THE GENTLE RESTAURANT
108 Second Avenue North (Route 431) (615) 359–3461
MON–SAT 6 AM–7 PM / CLOSED SUN

We once had a friend, Joe, from Tennessee. Whenever he walked into a deli or grocery store for lunch or supplies, he invariably emerged eating one of those big, doughy pouches filled with flavored paste that is sold as "pie" to accompany takeout sandwiches or hamburgers. It wasn't until we ate a fried pie at The Gentle Restaurant that we realized Joe had been homesick for his state's unique form of pie, and that the dough pockets sold in grocery stores vaguely resemble the real thing. But a real fried pie as served at The Gentle Restaurant is a light, flaky lard crust, fully enclosing what seems like a full cup of dried, tart peaches. The whole thing is quick-fried in clear oil and served hot. The drying crisps the dough and softens the peaches, turning the filling into something on the order of a tart peach preserve. These are served alongside what cook Rena Branch rightfully claims is the "best coffee for a hundred miles around." A fried pie and coffee at The Gentle Restaurant is a mellow afternoon snack that is likely to keep you in a peaceful reverie until dinnertime.

We were on our third cup of coffee, after two pies, just sitting at a table gazing at the photographs of Tennessee Walking Horses on the wall, listening to the barely audible, easy listenin' country music on the radio, and nonchalantly eavesdropping on the conversations of the gentlemen farmers and businessmen sitting at the surrounding tables. We were gently coaxed from our walking horse daydreams by the tantalizing odors wafting from behind the small steam table. First it was the dark, oniony smell of meat loaf being pulled from the oven in back. Then came the sweet potatoes, their intense sugary aroma somehow softened by the marshmallows that were melting on top. By the time we sniffed the fried squash and onions, we were standing in line with our tray and silverware ready.

The meal was strong and delicious—a spicy jolt out of the dream-like state into which the fried pies and coffee had lulled us. The Gentle Restaurant is on an elevated sidewalk, over the street, and is marked by a large neon horse's head sign. It is a comfortable, quiet world apart that lives up to its name.

NASHVILLE

★ THE MUSIC CITY TRUCKSTOP
Interstate 24 and Old Hickory Boulevard (615) 793–6731
ALWAYS OPEN

The Music City Truckstop is a giant trucker complex that serves one of the best country ham breakfasts in the state. Kentucky and Tennessee have the premium on great ham and biscuits because of the wondrous inclusion of "red-eye" gravy. "Red-eye" is the juices that collect at the bottom of the pan after cooking a country ham. This juice is mixed with a little black coffee and served as a "dunk" for biscuits, or as gravy for the grits.

The special breakfast at Music City centers around country ham and red-eye gravy, accompanied by two large, freshly baked biscuits, a mound of steaming grits, a few eggs, a bowl of cereal, and as many cups of coffee as it takes to get you back on the road. If this mammoth feast is more then you can comfortably face in the morning, there is a scaled-down version; no eggs or cereal but lots of ham, grits and biscuits.

Another popular breakfast item is fried pies. A Tennessee trucker known as Bubba Ray told us about fried pies. "You take a fried pie, it's hot and muggy . . . but the pie's still good. It's cold and rainy . . . but the pie's still good. Any time of the year a fried pie suits your needs like a mud hole to a piggy." We have had fried pies with lighter crusts and better fillings elsewhere in Tennessee, but at The Music City Truckstop they are adequate versions filled with peach or berry fillings.

Breakfast is the favorite meal here. It is served twenty-four hours a day and we recommend it over the lunch and dinner offerings.

PELHAM

★ THE CITY CAFÉ
junction of Routes 50 & 41 (615) 467–9996
MON–SAT 6 AM–6 PM

The City Café is the most basic of roadside restaurants, with the simplest of charms. We recommend it especially as an ideal breakfast stop. Try a double order of ham or sausage biscuits. The biscuits are small, dense, with a compressed texture perfectly accented by the pork. There is homemade cornbread, too, with the same firm richness as the breakfast biscuits. We were told that the cooks here also make pies and cobblers, and that their fried chicken and white beans were rapidly developing a reputation among locals and truckdrivers along this rural route. The coffee we had with breakfast was clear, dark and rich, a rather elegant brew, in fact. (Coincidentally, the Coffee County Line is only a few miles away.)

The restaurant is a plain white block building, with remnants of the previous tenant ("The Country Cupboard") still visible beneath the white paint. Inside there are a few plants, a small selection of unusual bottles lined up in the window, and some tacked-up flower pictures.

A very pleasant place in the middle of nowhere.

FAIRS AND FESTIVALS

BELLES
Okra Festival / LATE AUG

COSBY
Ramp Festival / LATE APRIL
Dedicated to the world's sweetest-tasting, worst-smelling plant

DAYTON
Strawberry Festival / LATE APRIL–EARLY MAY

HUMBOLDT
West Tennessee Strawberry Festival / EARLY MAY

PARIS
Paris Fish Fry / LATE APRIL
Kentucky Lake Catfish

SPARTA
Korn Pone Day / 1ST SAT IN AUG

VIRGINIA

BOTTOMS BRIDGE

★★ THE COLONIAL RESTAURANT
Routes 60 & 33, just off Route 64
DAILY 7 AM–9 PM / SUMMER 7 AM–10 PM

Miss Alice has been the cook at The Colonial for ten years. She has in this time examined, reorganized, researched, and renovated every facet of frying a chicken. She keeps a very private kitchen, preferring to be left alone to commune with the chickens, as the very lively Colonial crowd ebbs and flows.

Lunch is a jam session of state troopers, gas jockeys, the hairdresser from down the road, and housewives who have come over to meet their husbands at lunchbreaks. They stand around the murky tank containing The Colonial mascot, a live alligator, or tack up a new novelty item or sale-card on the communal bulletin board.

When the clientele isn't admiring the two-foot-long reptile, they are ordering or eating plates of Miss Alice's famous chicken. You could never guess from looking at the Colonial's menu that this was special chicken. The menu is a laminated photo-job depicting an anonymous-looking plate of poultry with parsley sprouts and sweetheart tomatoes arranged artistically. Miss Alice's chicken doesn't resemble this glossy image. Hers has character and a golden crust in place of the frills and fancy arrangement.

The chicken comes double-dredged in a mixture tasting of butter, milk, and flour. There is a distinctive nutty taste to the finished product. This bird needs no parsley or lace panties to add to its appeal. We tried to photograph it, but as one of us took a light reading, the other took a huge bite out of the center of the breast.

Miss Alice also pan-fries perch. It comes with corn bread, vegetables and potatoes. She is also a fine dessert cook. Shyly she told us, "Men around here is partial to peach pie, but the womens like puddings. I make a good bread pudding with raisins and also rice which has been a favorite for years." We tried the pie. It was not peach season and canned peaches had been substituted for fresh, leaving us disappointed despite the nice light crust. We imagined the same pie a few months earlier in the summer being a first-rate creation with real peaches simmering in the thinly rolled dough.

The Colonial is like many small roadside cafés in the South. It is a meeting place, a social club, and a kitchen away from home. It also might be called a zoo café, since hardly anyone leaves the tiny place without one last look into the town mascot's tank.

NATURAL BRIDGE

★★★ FANCY HILL RESTAURANT
Route 11, N. of Natural Bridge (703) 291–2143
DAILY 7 AM–9 PM

Natural wonders like Virginia's stone bridge always seem more wondrous in pictures than in real life. Seeing them confirms that they exist; but you can never get as good a view as did the *National Geographic* cameraman; and you can seldom get a decent meal within twenty-five miles. The Fancy Hill, just north of Natural Bridge, is an exception. Their trout—fresh from the James River—is itself a natural wonder, although part womanmade, having been fried in butter by the cook at the Fancy Hill. The chicken and dumplings we ate were a classic version of that southern dish. As we consumed these two excellent meals, the man in the booth across the way spontaneously commented for all to hear "This is the best beef stew I've had in twenty-five years!" It was served with biscuits from which we could see the steam rising. Had our own meals not been so good, we might have suspected the stew-eater to be a shill.

Why so suspicious? The Fancy Hill Restaurant, if the truth be known, is connected to the Fancy Hill Motel. Usually this type of establishment, relying as it does on the captive and weary motel guest, is the worst kind of restaurant, offering only the convenience of being able to return to your room for an Alka-Seltzer. There is nothing about the looks of the Fancy Hill Restaurant that leads you to suspect it will be an exception. It is in a plain blue motel, with plain yellow walls, simple booths, a counter and a typed menu. There is a piano against one wall, which we were told is there for anyone who gets the spirit and wants to play.

A dessert specialty at the Fancy Hill is their chess pie. They make lemon chess and chocolate chess. You may not have heard of chess pie if you haven't traveled through the South. It is simply the most delicious way to combine butter, sugar and egg yokes. It tastes like a pecan pie without the nuts. The Fancy Hill adds lemon or chocolate to this elemental recipe and comes up with one of the richest pieces of pie you'll find anywhere.

NEW MARKET

★★★ THE SOUTHERN KITCHEN
Route 11 (703) 740–3514
MON–SAT 6:30 AM–11 PM, SUN 7 AM–11 PM

We will always remember The Southern Kitchen as the place where we first tasted peanut soup. We had heard about this traditional Southern appetizer, and it seemed in our imaginations more like the eccentric improvisations to which Cub Scout troops are prone, such as peanut butter and marshmallow, or pastrami and grape jelly. But in The Southern Kitchen, the humble peanut is elevated beyond George Washington Carver's wildest dreams. The miracle of the soup is that it is amazingly thick without tasting anything like Skippy-in-a-bowl. It is a smooth and grainy blend, toasty in flavor, lightly seasoned with onion bits, celery, cream, and salt. It is the sweetest, most soothing way to begin a meal this side of fettuccine Alfredo—and not nearly as filling.

But this peanut soup is only a beginning. We proceeded, floating on our peanut cloud, to Virginia ham with raisin sauce, and trout pan-fried in butter. This mellow meal concluded with two slices of blackberry pie—each a pastry-flake wedge overstuffed with tart, ripe blackberries. Even the coffee that accompanied the pie was outstandingly rich. It tasted almost nutty—or perhaps we were having a delicious aftershock from the soup.

There are other restaurants that call themselves The Southern Kitchen, but we have found none to match the natural and unassuming perfection of the one in New Market. The ambiance here is plain and simple. It is a popular restaurant, frequented by businessmen, secretaries, and workers for lunch, and by families for an informal dinner. It is lively without being boisterous, rightfully proud of its unique cuisine, and very friendly. The walls are lined with deers' heads and a couple of beautiful hand-tinted pictures of tourists visiting the nearby Luray Caverns.

PETERSBURG

★★ KING'S BAR B QUE
2629 Boulevard, Route 301, South (Colonial Heights exit off Route 95)
(804) 526–0166
WED–MON 11 AM–9 PM / CLOSED TUES

King's is a large operation compared to the hole-in-the-wall bar b que pits that are the mystical landmarks talked about in whispers by professional eaters. It is a large, bright room seating over fifty people. A chef and his two assistants walk between the kitchen and the smokehouse, rotating the smoking shanks of meat, and bringing back inside the slabs that are ready for carving or mincing, a process carried out in full view of the patrons.

Oddly, this Virginia restaurant serves beef that is unmistakably "western-style." The one quality that distinguishes cowboy cooking is the toughness of the meat. Now this might seem a negative virtue. "Tough" usually means gristly, cheap, or overdone. But good Western beef is tough in another sense. It is chewy and packed with flavor. It is a good tooth workout and a challenge to get the long-smoked slice to give up its intense and saturated flavor. Southerners usually abhor meat served this way, preferring greasy, fall-apart pigmeat, so juicy and tender it melts under the touch of the pitmaster's knife.

One can order minced pork, sliced pork, ribs, or beef at King's. The minced pork is served on a bun. This dish has been the occasion for serious debates between us, and in fact, minced pork might be the only potential homewrecker on our horizon. One of us finds it greasy, obnoxious on its soggy hamburger bun, and too ketchupy-tasting drenched in its pale orange sauce. The other thinks the tender shreds of moist pork are the ideal way to enjoy the spicy tang of bar b qued pig, and the absorbent bun is a perfect conduit for the sauce. For the word "greasy," substitute "soulful." Both of us agreed that the pork ribs at King's are good, if a little too dry, resembling Chinese restaurant-style, rather than Southern. The best dish proved to be a slab of beef brisket. The hickory-perfumed beef came with good tangy cole slaw, a pitcher of smooth sauce, French fries, and a shameful biscuit the consistency of a cooked washcloth.

Most bar b que pits don't bother with dessert, but King's, being more a sit-down restaurant than a backwoods shack, provides such amenities. A slice of King's apple pie was, in fact, so delicious that it rivaled the best we tasted in New England's apple country.

We include King's not only for its bar b que, but for its clean airy atmosphere. It is a bar b que for novice roadfooders who might find the cryptlike darkness of the more exotic pits too ominous. The booths here are filled with a cross section of life in Petersburg, from senior citizens to local secretaries on lunch breaks. King's will put up all meals to go, so if the manicured ladies from town and mannered gentlemen in leisure suits distract from your bar b que pleasures, you can sit in your El Camino outside and eat your pork and beef from the takeout trays provided by the management.

PORT ROYAL

★★ EARL'S RESTAURANT
Route 301 (804) 742-2801
MON–SAT 11 AM–9 PM / CLOSED SUN

Earl's Restaurant is at the foot of the bridge in Port Royal, the birthplace of our shortest president, James Madison.

When we first discovered Earl's, the hand-painted pig sign out front was swinging noisily in the spring breezes. Through the wire mesh door we saw an empty, dark room, and not a sign of life. We pushed open the door, and as we heard it slam behind us, we hoped the noise would alert a waitress, a cook, a customer in the men's room, anybody. Nothing happened, so we sat ourselves at a corner table and anxiously inspected the bleak decor. We saw a sign over the cash register saying "Earl—BBQ King of Port Royal" under a crayoned picture of a man wearing a Nucoa-like crown. Finally, there was a rustling in the kitchen, and through the egg-shell colored doorway came Earl, pants falling below belly line, shocks of gray hair growing miles back on an improbably high forehead, and a ten-quart aluminum pot held in his two white-knuckled hands. "My sauce is at the turning point. I heard y'all come in, but if I leave it the whole mess will be shot. I'll be out in a minute or two if you wait."

Intrigued by this apparition chained to a steaming pot, we waited. Grunts and foot shuffling came from the kitchen, as a man and his sauce were grappling it out alone in that back room. After seven minutes Earl emerged victorious, beads of sweat on his vast brow. "Would you like to see a menu, or a plate of bar b que? The sauce is done." After sitting through the labor and being present at the moment of creation, we could hardly resist a look at the finished product, so we agreed on the bar b que.

By the time our platters came from the kitchen, three people had wandered in and taken seats. It was obvious that the sauce is finished at the same time each day, and none of the regulars would think of interrupting Earl, as we had done, at mid-point.

The bar b que is either beef or pig, but the pig sign creaking outside should tell you right away that the latter is the main attraction. It is minced coarsely for sandwiches or sliced for platters. The sauce has a sharply spiced flavor, is thin in texture, and fairly mild.

We examined the rest of the tiny menu as we left. It was mostly plain sandwiches, and a few steaks and chops, but every person eating at Earl's had chosen bar b que. Earl is a retired bartender, or "mixologist" as he prefers to call himself, now applying his mixology skills to a sauce pot. Be wise and wait until after 11 A.M. to enter his little café, or the fate of the sauce, loved by the whole town, might be in your hands.

SEVEN PINES

★ THE SEVEN PINES
375 East Williamsburg (Route 60) (804) 737–8980
MON–FRI 5 AM–2 PM / SAT 5 AM–11 PM / CLOSED SUN

The Seven Pines is a sardine-can crowded lunch spot near the Byrd airport outside of Richmond. Most of the patrons are army men from the nearby base, and when they eat lunch, they want sandwiches and quick service. The Seven Pines is pretty good compared to most army town cafés, and we include it because of the dearth of better places anywhere nearby.

First, what to avoid: daily hot specials proved to be dreary leftovers ladled with floury gravy. Embalmed vegetables and talcum-powder whipped potatoes came alongside. The thing to eat here is sandwiches. This is the only place outside the major southern cities where we have seen "kosher" anything. A wandering Jew among the seven pines?

We questioned the counterman, a southern version of his chronically annoyed brethren at Katz's in New York. "Is this really kosher meat, like it says on the menu?" we asked.

"That's what the sign says, pal," he fired back. But we could detect his hands trembling momentarily as his brain computed our strange presences among the sea of khaki. "Oh oh," his mind spun. "They sent two real ones from New York to investigate. Maybe they're from the

JDL, come to stick a bomb in my pastrami." We smiled at him, and he whisked the gorgeous pink ham from the same cutting board he was using for his "kosher" pastrami.

We ordered two sandwiches—a pastrami on rye, and a country ham. The ham was excellent: pink, spicy, salty, and sliced razor-thin. The counterman watched us, relieved. We hadn't taken notes, nor had we taken a bit of ham to put between glass slides for microscopic analysis.

The pastrami sandwich was not in the ham's league. It was fatty but nonsucculent, underspiced, and stingily hidden between the two pieces of only-average rye bread. This *is* Virginia, and we suggest that travelers stick with what Virginians do best: ham.

Hollywood screenwriter George Zuckerman, who lived for many years south of the Mason-Dixon line, wrote, "The measure of man's retreat from the centers of civilization is gained by adding the age of the rye bread to the amount of butter to be found on a corned beef sandwich. Corollary: when there is butter, there is also Oklahoma." In this case substitute Virginia. Thus spake Zuckerman.

SOUTH HILL

★ DEBBIE'S DINER
111 North Meck Avenue, just off Route 85 (804) 447–8986
MON–SAT 5:30 AM–9 PM / CLOSED SUN

Debbie's is in the same town as our favorite Horseshoe Restaurant, and it's been a dilemma on our few excursions through South Hill to decide between the two. There are some mornings when even Leonora's hot biscuits at the Horseshoe can't lure us away from Debbie's special breakfast of brains and eggs. Debbie's husband, Earl Clark, will tell you the dish is made even better if you add some of her homemade hot pepper sauce, which leads this farmy dish somewhere into the territory of fiery Southwestern huevos rancheros. The brains make all the difference, giving the eggs not only zest, but a salty richness that makes side orders of bacon or sausage superfluous.

Lunch at Debbie's usually involves the Virginia favorite, fried chicken. It is fall-apart tender and verges on the outer limits of "succulence," not far from "greasy." It comes with fresh black-eyes or collards, fresh potato salad, cole slaw, and rolls. Debbie also fries up gizzards or livers.

Debbie's serves what might be called white man's soul food. It is workingman's cuisine: rich, filling, highly seasoned. The workingmen and women of South Hill come to this pleasant blue and white calico diner for simple food cooked in accordance with Tina Turner's philosophy that "Ain't nothin made better without a little grease."

★ THE HORSESHOE
311 West Danville Street (804) 447–8139
DAILY 5:30 AM–11 PM

"You'd be surprised the number of women who don't make breakfast for their husbands. Not even biscuits!" Leonora is almost shocked by her own words, but she knows they are true. Every morning when she arrives at 5:15 a.m. to open The Horseshoe, the men are lined up at the door or sitting in their cars, waiting for the breakfasts they didn't get at home. The men enter and take their usual seats around the semicircular counter, and Leonora goes in back to put on her apron. The fire under the griddle is turned on, but before the serious cooking begins, Leonora takes out her handmade sign and posts it over the coffee pot—"Breakfast Is Being Served. Please Join Us." Then come hot biscuits from the oven, country ham, eggs, grits, and huge, chunky home-fried potatoes—always right next to the ham on the grill. Breakfast is usually a short shift, because the men have to get to work.

First the signs get taken down. No more breakfast. Then the fresh vegetables are taken from the refrigerator—butter beans, garden peas, snap beans, cabbage, potatoes for salad, cabbage for cole slaw. These prepared, Leonora starts to work on the pecan and coconut pies. Once they're in the oven, it's time to concentrate all energy on the fried chicken, always the lunch special at The Horseshoe. Once that's breaded and ready to fry, Leonora has a few minutes to relax and survey her domain.

"Sometimes I wish I'd get a handyman in here. A lot of things need fixin." It's true, The Horseshoe could use some cosmetic work. It is a small disheveled restaurant, mostly because Leonora does it all herself, and has to keep serving from 5:30 a.m. until 11 p.m., every day of the year. The remaining six-and-a-half hours are Leonora's alone, but we figure that a lot of her private time must be spent in front of the mirror, putting on makeup and getting her hair just so.

After all, she is the queen of The Horseshoe, at least the second most important woman in a lot of South Hill lives; the provider of biscuits and fried chicken, the baker of pies, and frier of pork chops. She works by her grill in the center of the restaurant which was once a circular streetcar terminal. The ceiling is high with open rafters, and you could almost imagine klieg lights being mounted to shine on Leonora as she works, center stage, surrounded by a circumference of biscuit-hungry men. But Leonora isn't a jokester, or the kind of waitress who entertains the men with chitchat or idle flirtations. Her task is of a much higher order. Yes, she provides food, but any southerner will tell you that biscuits in the morning are more than food. They are spiritual sustenance; to some as necessary a way to start the day as a morning prayer.

STRASBURG

★ THE OLD MILL RESTAURANT
Route 11 at the junction of I–81 & 66 (703) 465-5980
MON, WED, THURS 11 AM–8 PM, SAT 11 AM–10 PM, SUN NOON–8 PM

The Old Mill is nestled in the bosom of the magnificently scenic Shenandoah Valley. It was built in the 1700s and now has all the charm of a gracefully fading ruin. Its walls are made of stone, and on one side there is a mossy, overgrown water wheel. The inside of the building has been renovated to be a charming little restaurant.

Light filters through windows, softly illuminating the red and white checkered tablecloths and few antique implements that have been "scattered" about to set the tone. There are wood floors and low-hung ceiling beams, and the walls are made of stone and wood.

The menu is a simple affair, mostly steaks and seafood. Although fresh local trout and oysters are available, we recommend trying the crab cakes. They are well-packed with crab meat, held together with perhaps a few too many breadcrumbs and beaten egg. There is also a fried ham dish, although this seemed a little bland in comparison to some of the great cured ham one finds along this route in Virginia. Meals come sided with homemade rolls, vegetables or a salad, and there are some decent fruit pies for dessert.

The nicest thing about the Old Mill is its setting, and although its menu makes it less than an A #1 roadfood choice, the real antique charm of the building cannot be denied.

WEST SALEM

★★ANDREW LEWIS FAMILY RESTAURANT
2101 Main Street Route 11 (Exit 40 off Interstate 81) (703) 389–3334
MON–THURS 7 AM–9 PM, FRI & SAT 7 AM–9:30 PM, SUN 7 AM–8:30 PM

The Andrew Lewis is one of the best pancake restaurants in the South. Its excellence comes from the use of fillings and batters that echo "Dixie." Cornmeal, coconut, ripe bananas, combine with light sugar syrups and plenty of butter to make memorable breakfasts.

There is an all-you-can-eat pancake breakfast served daily. We recommend it especially for those roadfooders under doctor's orders to ingest the largest amount of calories for the least amount of money. The batter used in the pancakes is so light that at least three trips back for more are guaranteed. This is one pancake place that won't leave you feeling like you have a yeast ball in your stomach.

Our favorite pancakes here are the banana ones. Light buttermilk batter is mixed with mashed banana and skillet-fried in butter. The mountainous stack of thin cakes is then topped and layered with fresh sliced banana and drenched with syrup. Another pancake specialty is coconut pancakes, their batter laced with tiny shreds of coconut, topped with still more coconut meat after cooking, and moistened with a grainy sweet coconut syrup. Less expensive are the corncakes served with or without a side order of pink country ham.

This is a real family restaurant run by the Lewis family. The difference between the pancakes and other meals served here and those produced by pancake chains around the country is substantial. This fact can be gleaned from one glance at the salad bar. It is not a series of predictable ingredients which you try and form into your own salad in a mini-bowl. The salad bar here is an assortment of interesting and unusual relishes and salads—three bean, chow chow, pickled beets, macaroni salad, carrot slaw, congealed salad, and cole slaw. Dinners of fried oysters, fried chicken, or miniature deviled crabs all come with hush puppies and helpings from the salad bar. The only things not included in the price are the homemade fresh-fruit cobblers.

Serious road gourmets usually abstain from starting the day with pancakes. They don't leave enough room for the surprise bar b que or traveling pie wagon to be discovered just down the road. But the Andrew Lewis is in an area chin-deep in fast-food restaurants and little else. We wouldn't hesitate to take up their breakfast offer and fill up enough to sustain us on a long trek to more fruitful parts of the state.

WYTHEVILLE

★★ DURHAM'S RESTAURANT
115 E. Main Street (703) 228–5241
DAILY 6 AM–9 PM (UNTIL 8 PM IN WINTER)

We were first drawn to Durham's by its curiosity as an historical site. Mrs. Edith Bolling Wilson was born in an apartment above the restaurant in 1872. You can't see her birthplace ("An old lady lives there," we were told), but there is a picture of the former first lady and hubby Woodrow in back of the large dining area, and there is a plaque outside noting the restaurant's historical importance.

While it is not the most spectacular tourist attraction, Durham's is a good place to eat. It seems to be Wytheville's main eatery, and there is a large menu of Virginia specialties. Since the front window of this café is piled high with country hams, we ordered the ham dinner. It came with fresh corn bread and real mashed potatoes, canned carrots and a salad. The ham had been cured to a slightly sour taste, which admirably offset the salty nature of the meat. We also tried some bar b qued pork, served with a sauce that was more a marinade than a tomato base—very moist. It was neither too sweet nor smoky; the mild taste of the pork prevailed. We also noted that the menu offered ten different vegetables, three of which you can get on a "Vegetable Plate." There was a standard assortment of home-baked fruit pies, but we chose a sticky-thick chess pie instead—a primal blend of sugar and butter in a baked pastry shell.

Durham's is an airy, large room, a local gathering place that welcomes travelers. The walls are covered with a print paper and trimmed with lovely old wood.

FAIRS AND FESTIVALS

CHINCOTEAGUE ISLAND
Annual Seafood Festival / EARLY MAY
Virginia seafood recipes

COLONIAL BEACH
Chicken Bar B Que / LATE JULY

EMPORIA

Peanut Festival / EARLY SEPTEMBER

HARRISONBURG

Virginia Poultry Festival / MID–MAY

URBANNA

Oyster Festival / LATE NOVEMBER

WEST VIRGINIA

BEAVER

★★ THE CHARLES LEE INN
Route 19–21 (304) 253–5123
DAILY 6 AM–9 PM

Charles Lee Hicks has us worried. When we first met him, he had just come from a restaurateur's convention, and told us how much he had learned about food technology, and the new miracles available to people who feed other people. Hideous visions of robotlike potato slicers elbowing cooks out of the kitchen clouded our minds. We trembled in remembrance of the "egg loaf" we had once seen at a restaurant convention in New York. An egg loaf is a yard-long pseudoegg—a tube of yellow egg yolk substance surrounded by egg white substance. When sliced it looks like a respectable cross-section of a hard-boiled egg.

As it turned out, Charles just likes to be up to date on his profession, but has the good sense to keep most of the menu in his small restaurant cooked "like they have been doing in my family for years." Charles' family are West Virginians of long heritage, with family recipes that shame inventions like the egg loaf. The Charles Lee Inn is one of the cheeriest places in this overindustrialized part of the state. It certainly serves the best food in Beaver, at prices geared toward the low income of the townspeople.

A favorite dish, and one Charles guards the recipe of with the vigilance of a bulldog, is potato pancakes in butter sauce. They are thin pancake-sized circles, lacy brown around the edges, moist and oniony in the center. Butter sauce adds a final extra-rich note to the dish.

Charles' mother taught him *her* mother's way of preparing "honey chicken." The bird is allowed to soak in honey all night before it is broiled the next day. By the time it is cooked, the honey has seeped bone-deep.

Pies have also been a source of pride in the Hicks family for years. The pecan pie, dense with sugared nutmeats, was one of the richest we have ever tasted. And the crust was not at all soggy, like so many rich nut pies. We bet Charles' mother taught him the trick of painting the bottom crust with egg white before baking.

There are, however, demons battling for Charles' soul. The menu is torn between the very good, down-home dishes mentioned above, and a few grotesquely exotic creations like "Beef Stew Polynesian," which tastes like chuck steak and grape jelly. Charles still serves good garden vegetables, although he hinted at a few prefab items he was trying out. We sincerely hope that the muse of roadfood feasting wins out over the devil of ready-made sloth.

CHARLESTON

★★THE SOUTHERN KITCHEN
Route 119 (McCorckle Avenue) (304) 925–3154
ALWAYS OPEN

The first thing you notice once inside The Southern Kitchen is the chicken motif. Chicken statutes, paintings, drawings, and doodads are everywhere, and dangling from the ceiling are the egg baskets filled with what look like fresh brown and white eggs. We sat down in one of the private high-backed booths just as a Gomer Pyle look-and-sound-alike set up a small ladder next to the booth. He climbed to the top with a sponge and water and began washing the eggs. They were plastic. But Mrs. Hersman, the owner, sees to it that her chicken and egg collection is always immaculate.

Any restaurant whose owner is so obviously wild about chickens is saying something to the alert diner: Order the chicken! We did, and got three pieces of spicy-crisp, perfectly prepared chicken: thoroughly cooked, juicy, and tender. It came with a mild, fresh potato salad, undistinguished rolls, a small, plain, green salad and coffee.

"Of course we can't serve only chicken here," Mrs. Hersman told us, pointing to a vast two-page menu offering West Virginia favorites like hot baloney, corn bread and beans, as well as roasts, steaks, sandwiches, and a full array of breakfast selections. "We get people from all over the country here; lots of truckers. They love my chicken and biscuits."

We looked around and, sure enough, The Southern Kitchen did seem to be a cosmopolitan sort of place. West Virginia families, kids out on a date, and plenty of truckers and travelers occupied the comfortable, quiet booths. The Southern Kitchen is a little eccentric in decor, but it's the best twenty-four-hour roadfood restaurant in the state.

FAIRS AND FESTIVALS

ARNOLDBURG
Molasses Festival / LATE SEPT

BERKELEY SPRINGS
Apple Butter Festival / MID-OCT
Strawberry Festival / MID-MAY

BUCKHANNON
Strawberry Festival / EARLY JUNE

FAIRMOUNT
Apple Festival / LATE SEPT

HELVETIA
Fasnacht Carnival / MID-FEB

INDEPENDENCE
Watermelon Days / EARLY AUG

MOREHEAD
Poultry Festival / LATE JULY

RICHWOOD
Ramp Festival / EARLY APRIL

ROWLESBURG
Ox Roast / EARLY SEPT

WILLIAMSBURG
Bear Dinner / MID-JAN

St. Ignace

Charlevoix

Ann Arbor

Sandusky Columbia Station

Youngstown

Reynoldsburg

MICHIGAN

Delta Bryan OHIO Yellow Springs

Menominee Beulah New Era Holland Michigan City Shipshewana Lafayette Spring Valley Cincinnati

Gladstone Roselawn Clarks Hill

Ishpeming Remington Lebanon INDIANA

North Shawano Mauston Baraboo Winnetka Carlinville Carbondale

Osseo WISCONSIN Sauk City Berwyn Beverly

Ellsworth Westby Mineral Point Joliet Normal ILLINOIS Wentzville

Winona McLean Foristell

Cotton Lake City Wabasha Durant Marshall MISSOURI

MINNESOTA Homestead Wilton Kansas City

IOWA Casey Lexington

Comstock Walnut Topeka Wamego Lawrence

Redfield Huron O'Neill Abilene Manhattan

Aberdeen Sioux Falls Seward Wilber Sharon Springs KANSAS

NORTH DAKOTA SOUTH DAKOTA NEBRASKA Cozad Hampton Wilson Lindsborg

Bismarck Napoleon Minden

Elgin Bowman Edgemont

ILLINOIS

BERWYN

★★★ THE PLAZA DINING ROOM
7016 West Cermak Road (312) 795–6555
DAILY 10:30 AM–8:00 PM

Nestled in a west Chicago landscape of shopping centers, The Plaza Dining Room is an isle of ethnic home cooking and a favorite gathering spot for Berwyn's Czech families. When we first ate here three years ago, the Plaza was a tiny place; its eight tables were shared family-style by strangers at crowded mealtimes. Breaking homemade bread with these folks was part of the pleasure of eating at the Plaza —a welcome relief from the nearby anonymous shopping malls, drive-through stores and drive-in restaurants.

The Plaza has since been remodeled, and is now a plain block-shaped brick building not too different from the insurance offices and muffler shops that surround it. Inside, there is a banquet room with enough tables so that one never need sit down with strangers, even at the most popular lunch hour and Sunday dinners. For folksy visual ambiance there is a large color picture of Prague's Voltova River. But listen closely: At least half the conversations carried on at the tables are in Czech. And taste: The food still comes from the simple, ethnic kitchen that always made the old Plaza worth a detour from the nearby interstates.

One thing that has not changed is the extremely friendly service. The waitresses will carefully explain to you in broken English the choice of soups, desserts, and dumplings that accompany each dinner. Among the soups our favorite is the goulash: a robust brew thick with potatoes and chunks of meat. For a more delicate starter, there is beef noodle soup: a light gold broth laced with thin homemade noodles and sprinkled with parsley. Accompanying the soup is a basket of peculiar bread. The slices are shaped exactly like mass-produced Wonder Bread. But this bread is made from a dark rye flour, rough in texture and strongly flavored with caraway seeds. It is delicious and a good portent of the substantial food that follows.

Fruit dumplings is the lowest-priced meal and the Plaza specialty. Two apricot and two prune dumplings are enough to fill a large dinner plate. They come topped with pot cheese and sugar, enriched by rivulets of melting butter. They are heavenly rich. Don't expect to finish a plate unless you are ravenous. An equally succulent but somewhat lighter specialty at the Plaza is the roast duck: perfectly browned, crisp-skinned and moist. The duck and other meat entrees come with faintly sweet sauerkraut and sliced bread dumplings. The dumplings are very heavy and slightly dry until you pour on the gravy provided for them in a silver pitcher. Other Plaza specialties include thick-sliced roast pork, kidney stew, and pot roast with potato pancakes.

Small squares of prune, apricot, or cheese kolachky (a Czech pastry) are served for dessert. They are sweet and airy and, with a cup of the Plaza's good coffee, a fine end to a mighty meal.

BEVERLY

★★SVEA'S RESTAURANT
11160 South Western (just off Route 57) (312) 881-9246
WED–SAT 2 PM–8 PM / SUN 11 AM–7 PM / CLOSED MON & TUES
/ CLOSED MID-DECEMBER–MID-JANUARY

Since the Stockyards moved away, Chicago has been searching for its gastronomic identity in "theme" restaurants where fun's the thing and food is measured not by quality, but by the cleverness of its purveyors. But we would trade all of Chicago's singing waiters, meals of "Deep Trout," and drinks called "Climb Every Mounds Bar" for one good meal at Svea's.

A crisp and flaky trout dinner, served with buttery mashed squash and tiny boiled potatoes goes a long way in making up for Svea's completely plain and fading interior. We don't mind eating on old and weathered Formica tables when the table is topped with a dinner of two crisply broiled, juicy pork chops, or when the choice of appetizers includes delicate yellow pea soup or a coral-pink fruit soup filled with raisins, apple chunks, and small pieces of lemon peel. The drab paintings on the wall blur into the background behind a smooth coconut whipped-cream pie and a slice of tart double-crusted strawberry-rhubarb pie.

Svea's is a family restaurant, patronized mostly by the southerly segment of Chicago's Swedish community. It is a clean and peaceful place to eat. You'll recognize it from the outside as the place that looks like a roadside tavern from a 1930s gangster movie. Inside, the service is simple and direct—no match for the "Lettuce Entertain You" pyrotechnics of the North Side. But for our money, a perfectly prepared Svea's dinner is delectable enough. The "character" which theme restaurants bend over backwards to create in all the wrong places will be found in every bite at Svea's.

CARBONDALE

★ MARY LOU'S
114 S. Illinois (618) 457–5084
MON–SAT 7 AM–3 PM / CLOSED SUN

Anyone who ever went to college has his favorite old greasy spoon. If you return to it years later, it's hard to believe that the oily spuds and grey beef once tasted so good. In the clearer light of adulthood you realize that it was the guys you shared the booth with, or the A you got on the term paper that transformed the food. Mary Lou's is beloved by the students of Southern Illinois University, but despite this fact, it is a place that manages to charm those of us who were never students here, and are well into adulthood.

Mary Lou Trammel rules the griddle of this newly expanded version of her once tiny diner, spatula in hand, doling out her famous omelettes. The omelettes come with hash browns, sausages, and biscuits. When breakfasts are finished, Mary Lou cleans the counter and starts the lunch specials. It's blue plate cooking all the way: ham and beans, pork and potatoes, beef stew, or chili. Its quality is a notch above the diner average, and the portions are big enough to please Mary Lou's workman and student clientele.

Desserts vie with omelettes as Mary Lou's specialty. Her "poor boy pudding" is a wondrous pudding-cake dish made with devil's food chocolate cake. There is also a superior banana cream pie.

Mary Lou's is not open for dinner. By late afternoon she is exhausted from taking orders, cooking, and playing surrogate mother to SIU students down on their luck or unlucky in love. Mary Lou will prepare a special batch of "poor boy" for you if you've got a problem she knows of, or she'll cook up a double-size omelette for graduates who return for one last look. Mary Lou's is today what Mory's has been to Yale and what the beer hall was at Heidelburg U. Mary Lou's is a

Carbondale institution with enough real charm to make it well worth an omelette or poor-boy stop for travelers who are just passing through.

JOLIET

★★THE MARKET PLACE RESTAURANT
the Joliet Livestock Exchange, Arsenal Road (Exit 66) (815) 423–5959
MON–FRI 6 AM–2:30 PM, 5 PM–9:30 PM, SAT 5 PM–11 PM, SUN NOON–8:30 PM

The Market Place is a restaurant designed to serve the cattle buyers and cowboys who work and trade at the Joliet Livestock Exchange. The Exchange is a transfer point for pigs and cattle. They are dropped off by breeders and then trucked to points all over the country for slaughter. The Market Place Restaurant is located in a squat brick building surrounded by holding pens of squealing pigs and shuffling cows.

The clientele at The Market Place observe the proprieties of using the boot scrapers located to the right of the entrance, and if need be, the garden hose too. The odor of cattle on the hoof and cattle in the skillet mingle inside The Market Place's dark interior.

It should come as no surprise that steak is the number one item on the menu. Starting with simple breakfast steak and upwards to the top-of-the-line dinner specialty, the steaks are extra-heavy cuts, well aged and tender. Dinner steaks come with homemade soup, rolls, a green salad, stuffed tomato, and coffee. The complements to the steak are fair, and no one seems to pay much attention to them. Hungry cattlemen save their appetites for the meat.

The room itself is dark and masculine, fancier inside than most other livestock restaurants. There is cloth napery and lighting that casts a rose tone on the weathered faces and muddy boots of its clientele. Service is fast and professional. Waitresses act as if they are used to waiting on men who don't have much time to sit and chat.

As you leave, take a look in the lobby. There is a network of corridors with the cattle buyers' and shippers' offices, and the radios broadcasting hog and beef futures are the building's version of Muzak. Walls are hung with full-color drawings and charts of cattle. Here you will see portraits of the wall-to-wall black angus whose meat costs as much as gold, and pitiful illustrations of the scrawny utility grade cow whose fate is to wind up in a can of Alpo.

There are few places in the Midwest that serve beef as good as The Market Place, and even fewer whose "cattleman" themes are as convincing.

McLEAN

★THE DIXIE TRUCKERS HOME
Route 66 (junction 136) (309) 874–2323
ALWAYS OPEN

John Geske ("Say 'guess-key,' " says he) opened this truckstop in 1928. Although it is in the center of Illinois, it is named "Dixie" in honor of southern friendliness. John has not closed The Dixie since its founding, except the day in 1965 when it burnt down. John quickly moved the cooking facilities to a building next door until workmen were able to restore The Dixie's preflame hospitality.

The food at The Dixie is not great. It's hearty and inexpensive, and mostly cooked fresh in the kitchens, although canned vegetables and instant mashed potatoes are substituted for the real thing. We prefer breakfasts to dinner, and our favorite is the fried mush and eggs. Large slabs of cornmeal are double fried in butter and served with three eggs. A side order of bacon or sausage makes it even better.

Chicken is the specialty of the house. The bird can be bought in sizes from a half-chicken with the works to one and a half sides. There are also gizzards and livers and chicken salads as well as a good home-brewed chicken soup.

The Dixie Truckers Home is a large truckstop but it manages to maintain a friendly atmosphere. Truckers leave messages for each other on cork bulletin boards, and snapshots of regular patrons are tacked up inside glass cases. There is a large store full of trucker magazines and "wide load" signs, as well as a barber shop and showers on the premises. The Dixie is a good coffee and relaxation stop on the seemingly endless Route 66 in Illinois.

NORMAL

★★ STEAK 'N SHAKE
1219 South Main Street (Alternate 66) (309) 829-7515
DAILY 10 AM–1 AM

If any state is entitled to a town called Normal, it would have to be Illinois. "Normal" to some of us means bland and uneventful, but Steak 'n Shake contradicts any dullness or homogenization that normalcy might imply. It is, as its name suggests, a chain restaurant, and it can be found all over the Midwest. We include the branch in Normal not only because it's the best restaurant in town, but because the service at this particular Steak 'n Shake was remarkably personal. The food at every Steak 'n Shake is reliably good; here in Normal, we had a memorable meal. We chose "restaurant style dining" from among the four ways offered (the others being at a counter, in your car, or in a bag— to go). Our waitress suggested her favorite dishes, guided us in our selections, and watched to make sure we were enjoying the meal.

We got a steakburger, ground here and formed into an irregularly shaped patty, then seared to a crispy outside, maintaining a juicy interior. It came served on a good quality bun, with a plate of "Suzy-q" French fries—that is, the thin, long variety, served semicrispy and presalted. We also got a bowl of chili, which takes its cue from Steak 'n Shake's midwestern location and is served Cincinnati-style, "3-way," with beans, cheese, and chili-ground beef. It was a perfect mild-seasoned ratio of meat to sauce, and there are hot peppers on every table to spice it up. We also enjoyed two milk shakes—made from real milk, ice cream, and chocolate syrup; NOT oozed out of a frozen custard machine. Our meal was filling, but the waitress' description of the brownie fudge sundae twisted our respective arms, so we got two and finished off both with the last of our milk shakes.

Aside from the food, Steak 'n Shake is notable for its beautiful design. Unlike other fast-fooderies which look like they are slapped together from prefab walls, fixtures, and personnel in less than a day, Steak 'n Shake's facilities seem solidly built from a classy Art Deco design. All the plates are heavy china, and the glasses are real glass. All are emblazoned with the Steak 'n Shake winged emblem which looks like the logo for a 1930s airline. Most intriguing is their enigmatic motto, "In Sight, it must be Right." We assume this means that if a Steak 'n Shake is within your field of sight, it is the right place to stop and eat. In our experience through much of the Midwest, the motto is correct.

WINNETKA

★★★★ THE INDIAN TRAIL

507 Chestnut Street (312) 446–1703
TUES–SAT: LUNCH, DINNER / SUN NOON–8 PM / CLOSED MON

If old age is a sign of great wisdom, then the sea of blue-white heads at The Indian Trail is no surprise. In the midst of a Chicago restaurant boom which is wreaking havoc with good food, comfortable dining and fair prices all over town, The Indian Trail has maintained its high standards of fine quality food for a reasonable price.

Some may turn up their noses at our enchantment with this restaurant. "Hell," they say, "The Indian Trail is a lace-pantied tearoom for every octogenarian in the suburbs." But fond memories of a little sister selling a red wagon full of home-grown rhubarb to The Indian Trail's owners for their fruit compote and fonder memories of countless unexcelled meals here keep us waiting for a table amidst the walker and cane set.

To begin at the end, The Indian Trail has the best ice cream in America. It is called rich bitter chocolate. One scoop in a silver cup, slathered with fresh blueberries if you wish; there is no food outside the Vienna city limits that is as exquisitely chocolaty. If you ever plan to be marooned on a desert island, it is the one dessert to pack.

Now, back to the beginning: a short selection of some Indian Trail notables. We feel lucky if a restaurant has three outstanding items, but at The Indian Trail a mention of only ten is a disservice to the extraordinary menu. We always begin our meals with either chicken salad appetizer with capers and pecans, or cream of corn soup. These come with a basket of breads that are so distinctively different that it is tempting to make a meal on bread and appetizer alone. There are warm, eggy dinner rolls and semisweet break-aparts laced with berries.

The appetizers are followed by a green salad with a sweet celery seed dressing or Bartlett pears with honey. The salad dressing is an Indian Trail invention, faintly creamy and translucent. It is the sort of stuff one mops up from the plate with a roll to get every drop. It is not to be missed.

Our favorite lunches are corned beef Vermont-style with mustard mayonnaise and filet of wall-eyed pike. There is a famous crab-meat bowl with mounds of fresh meat lightly laced with mayonnaise. Choice dinners include roast young duckling with watermelon preserves, a baked Lake of the Woods whitefish, and a perfectly broiled club steak with gorgonzola cheese. The vegetables that come with these meals are just like "little sis" sold them—fresh from the garden, not an easy task in the platinum suburbs of Chicago's North Shore. We always prefer the baked plums, sugar-glazed carrots and buttery-rich "Noodles Indian Trail."

Every day there are at least a dozen freshly prepared desserts. We can usually narrow our choice down to four, but no lower. Double desserts are necessary here. There is the ice cream. There is also cherry pan dowdy, blitz torte filled with whipped cream, apricot lattice pie, bread custard pudding, Swedish fruit compote, apricot crisp, blueberry tart, and sour cream apple pie. Most are served with mounds of hand-whipped cream. The tarts and pie crusts are crisped and delicate. The fruits and berries are in perfect condition.

It is hard to spend over $5 for lunch here. Dinners are between $5 and $8. It's expensive for roadfood, but not when you consider that it is perfect. Senior citizens and a few lucky local businessmen who sit at a special round table installed just for them are the staunchest supporters of this wonderful grande dame of a restaurant. We hope she never changes.

FAIRS AND FESTIVALS

CARMI
Kiwanis Corn Day / MID-OCT

MORRIS
Grundy County Corn Festival / LATE SEPT

NAUVOO
Grape Festival / LABOR DAY WEEKEND
"The Wedding of Wine and Cheese"

SHANNON
Pork Chop Bar B Que / EARLY SEPT

SYCAMORE
Pumpkin Festival / LATE OCT

THOMPSON
Melon Days / EARLY SEPT
Free Watermelon

WARREN
Pumpkin Festival and Pork Chop Bar B Que / LATE SEPT

INDIANA

CLARKS HILL

★★ THE ROSE HAVEN DINER
junction of Routes 52 & 28 (317) 523–2722
DAILY 5:30 AM–9 PM

The Rose Haven looms up out of the Indiana flatlands like a souvenir of New Jersey. It is a pale pink and chrome beauty that has weathered the sands of time. Its survival may be due to the clean farm air here in the middle of nowhere or, more accurately, on the outskirts of Fickle, Indiana. Not much changes the face of this earthy country, and when our barn-sized waitress handed us menus, we gazed for a long time at the covers before we got around to reading the inside. They were hand-tinted photos of The Rose Haven, circa 1952, the streamlined diner ringed with shiny DeSotos and Hudson Hornets, its zoot-suited patrons dining in chromed elegance. The telephone number of the diner is given in four digits, and we noticed that the jukebox is still a dime a song. It is a collection of classical country-western hits from the era long before country went "pop." One selection is "Happy Birthday." Obviously, The Rose Haven is essential to Fickleites looking for an appropriate place to celebrate.

We were delighted to find The Rose Haven's food better than most diners. Our ham steak was a spicy dark pink, served with ice-cold apple sauce and good, oily American fried potatoes. The roast beef reminded us of a Jewish pot roast—dark, moist, falling apart with tenderness. It bore no resemblance to the pink or red beef you get in hotels or better restaurants, but it was nonetheless delicious—slow-cooked and heavily seasoned. It came with perfect oven-browned potatoes, crisp outside, tender inside, and not at all greasy. The pies looked like they were made from the same substance that had tinted the menu photos, so we passed them up, not wanting to spoil what had turned out to be a topflight meal in Indiana's most debonair diner.

LEBANON

★ THE M & M
junction of Routes 39 & 32
MON–FRI 7 AM–4 PM / SAT 7 AM–1 PM / CLOSED SUN

The M & M is the smallest sit-down restaurant we have ever seen. There are four counter stools and two tiny tables and a five-by-five kitchen in back where Mrs. Maxwell bakes the morning biscuits and afternoon pies. One teen-age waitress does all the order-taking and serving.

The Kentucky influence is evident in all of the small menu. The breakfast special is biscuits and gravy. Lunch is ham and bean soup—a grainy thick brew served with squares of Mrs. Maxwell's corn bread. One available side dish is the Kentucky specialty of fried apples—heavy, sweet, and delicious. We recommend you try the apples unless you plan to have dessert, which is apple pie, or, fried apples in a crust.

The M & M is only a hole in the wall with a limited menu. The prices are right and the food is hearty. It is a good taste of south-midwestern down-home cuisine.

MICHIGAN CITY

★★ PETE'S BAR B QUE PIT
2227 E. U.S. Highway 12 (219) 879–6046
TUES–THURS 10 AM–9 PM, FRI–SUN 10 AM–MIDNIGHT

We found Pete's one day when we had wandered off I-94, trying to escape the monotony of the superhighway. We asked a gas station attendant what road we were on, and he replied "It used to be Route 12." We asked what it was now. He answered "Nothing." We asked what had happened to 12. "They abolished it," he said. All of which will give you an idea of how out-of-the-way Pete's *seems* to be, even though it's actually not far from the highway. It's in a part of Indiana that has been, as the gas jockey said, abolished.

However the times have changed, Pete's Pit has remained intact. Even the management has changed hands more than once in the last several years. But the bar b qued ribs are still as good as ever, as is the sweet-potato pie. Perhaps a great spirit watches over this solitary soul-food shack, a spirit who likes his ribs spicy and his pie mellow.

We have always felt that the beauty of Pete's ribs resides in their long-lasting taste. An hour or two after you've eaten a slab, there is still a "settling in" feeling across your palate, a long afterglow that doesn't quit until you're miles away. We always get our sweet potato pie "to go." As the ribs start to fade into memory, this wonderous pie provides a gentle, sensuous aftershock to cushion the primary experience of the ribs.

The jukebox here is a library of the best Chicago rhythm-and-blues —a perfect accompaniment to a dinner of top-notch soul food. Pete's has a charm that like the taste of the food lingers long after you've left the restaurant.

REMINGTON

★ THE REMINGTON CAFÉ
Ohio Street (219) 261-2357
MON–SAT 6 AM–3 PM / CLOSED SUN

The Remington Café looks a lot quainter from the outside than from within. It is an old, pale-green brick building in a town that looks like it hasn't changed since the turn of the century. Its clientele are leathery-necked farmers and ample-armed corn-fed mamas in print dresses. These good people of Remington come to this café for what is unfortunately mediocre food. The interior has been remodeled, and the plastic-wood walls are covered with signs advertising portion-con-trolled food such as "patty melts" and "whalers." We looked around and saw most of the farm folks eating pies and drinking coffee, so we too skipped the advertised specials and chose a creamy coconut custard pie and a dessert dish with no name (The Remington specialty) that con-sisted of vanilla ice cream laid on a bed of crumbled vanilla wafers, then topped with more cookie crumbs. Mary Lou, our waitress, approved the selection and advised us that the beef Manhattan was good, if we wanted something substantial before dessert. We declined, but Mary Lou told us that beef Manhattan is the midwestern version of a hot roast beef sandwich, drenched with gravy and layered on top with whipped potatoes. She told us that the roast is cooked here, and the bones go into the stockpots for soup and gravy.

The Remington does not serve the best food in the Hoosier state, but the town and townspeople make Remington well worth a visit.

ROSELAWN

★THE ADAM AND EVE
Route 10 (in Naked City) (219) 987–2000
FRI 6 PM–MIDNIGHT, SAT 9 AM–MIDNIGHT, SUN 9 AM–8 PM

The Adam and Eve is a nudist restaurant. Its patrons wander over in the buff from the sauna baths and volleyball courts of Dick Drost's Naked City, and while it isn't necessary to peel down to eat here, you'll definitely feel overdressed wearing anything more than your Timex. The old cook, "Southern Exposure"—named in honor of that region left uncovered by his chef's apron—has moved on to sunnier climes, and now the kitchen is run by "Panda," who keeps the famous Naked City ham steaks frying every night.

The ham steak dinners come "with the works," which in this case means vegetables, apple sauce, cottage cheese, coffee, and Miss Nude America dancing around your table. During the winter months, she puts on a floor show every night in the small café, and since there isn't a stage, she performs among the tables.

The beauty of The Adam and Eve is that the ham dinners are not just throw-aways to keep the patrons' hands off Miss N.A. They are so good in fact that many of the weary truckdrivers who pull into Naked City for a steam bath and a dinner pay much more attention to the ham on their plate than to the hams on the hoof. Our nude waitress told us that The Adam and Eve serves breakfasts too, and for those who aren't fond of ham, they have steaks, hamburgers, and sandwiches.

While we wouldn't suggest that The Adam and Eve is the place to take your Aunt Fannie on her 75th birthday, we were surprised at the relatively decorous atmosphere. No liquor is served, and although the truckers and local gents hoot it up when Miss Nude America gets into her act, they behave well "between the acts." When Miss Nude America isn't actually performing, you might mistake The Adam and Eve for a nude Howard Johnson's. We have seen more flirting with fully-clothed waitresses than we ever did with the in-the-buffers here. We were, however, a little uncomfortable when the bump and grind music started and Miss Nude America came out with a spray can of whipped cream. As there was no chocolate pudding or wet bottom shoo-fly pie in sight, it didn't take us long to realize that dessert would be a heavy dose of the proverbial cheesecake.

SHIPSHEWANA

★★ THE AUCTION RESTAURANT
Route 5 (219) 768–4129
WED 6:30 AM–END OF SALE / FRI 4 AM–END OF SALE

Although this restaurant is only in operation two days of the week, it is almost worth altering your trip plans to fit its hours. The Auction operates from an Amish Sale Barn, one so big and bustling that six auctioneers are on duty during trading hours. The town of Shipshewana is only a few miles from the Indiana toll road, but it seems like a world apart. There are more buggies on the streets than cars, and a majority of the population are the bearded and bonneted descendants of the 18th-century Germans who settled here.

Although the Amish are a severe and old-fashioned people, The Auction Restaurant is as lively as a disco on Friday night. It is not unusual for 130 pies to be sold during a day. "I couldn't even begin to count the number of plates of German sausage we sell," Edith Herschberger told us. She manages The Auction Restaurant, and in spite of a large staff of help, service is erratic.

But it is worth the wait. The bustling tone of the place is an appetizer in itself. And when the potato soup arrives, and the sausage and potatoes shortly thereafter, and then the milk sugar pie or wet bottom shoo-fly pie, you enjoy a dinner that is not only delicious, but unique. The restaurant itself is plainly decorated with simple curtains on the windows, white walls, Formica tables. The black-garbed customers make a striking contrast, but the ambiance here is anything but stark. It is a joyous place to eat.

★★ TROYERS RESTAURANT
Morton Street (219) 768–4444
MON–THURS 5 AM–4 PM, FRI & SAT 5 AM–8 PM, CLOSED SUN

If you are lucky enough to arrive in Shipshewana on a Friday or Saturday, head straight for Troyers. It is on these days that the cooks here go a little crazy and try to outdo each other at producing the best buffet in the area. The staff cooks roast pork, Dutch chicken, potato filling, corn fritters, apple rings and tables full of different relishes and salads.

Troyers is on a small winding street in the farm town of Shipshewana. The road is hardly wide enough for the black buggies to pass through. Because of the large Amish population, the town provides few facilities for auto traffic. Horse and carriage trade is more visible than cars. The interior of Troyers is fairly modern with a small steam table set up in the front room, and about twelve tables. The back room is larger with seating for around thirty.

We felt that the roast pork dinner was the best item on the menu. More than generous portions are served, and one could make a meal just on the delicious potato filling—a mild mix of corn, potato, and bread crumbs. The bread at Troyers is homemade and so popular that loaves are for sale at the cash register. Desserts are all laid out "help yourself" fashion on a circular table in the back room. Puddings are popular and there were five varieties. Fresh banana was by far the best, the butterscotch a disappointment, tasting as if it came from a mix. Jello salad with marshmallow is a good slightly lighter choice for ending the meal.

Service is very polite and fast. Troyers advertises in the town paper, and possibly because of this, we saw a handful of tourists like ourselves enjoying the bountiful Friday meal.

FAIRS AND FESTIVALS

CLINTON
Little Italy Festival / LATE AUGUST, EARLY SEPTEMBER
Cooking demonstrations & tasting

CORY
Cory Apple Festival / LATE SEPTEMBER
All apple cooking

FRENCH LICK
Orange County Pumpkin Festival / LATE SEPTEMBER
Pie-baking contest

LEITERS FORD
Strawberry Festival / EARLY JUNE

MITCHELL
Persimmon Festival / LATE SEPTEMBER

PETERSBURG
White River Catfish Festival / EARLY SEPTEMBER
Fishing derby, catfish dinners

PLYMOUTH
Marshall County Blueberry Festival / LATE AUGUST—EARLY SEPTEMBER

ROCKVILLE
Parke County Maple Fair / LATE FEBRUARY—EARLY MARCH
Pancake-sausage-maple syrup meals, tours of sugar camps

SALEM
Fodder Festival / EARLY OCTOBER
Baking contests

TIPTON
Tipton County Pork Festival / EARLY SEPTEMBER

VERSAILLES
Versailles Pumpkin Show / LATE SEPTEMBER
Pumpkin pie eating contest, cook-off

VEVAY
Swiss Wine Festival / MID-AUGUST
Wine stomps, Bavarian & Swiss food

IOWA

CASEY

★★★ MARY'S CAFÉ
Main Street (515) 746-2721
DAILY 7 AM–8:30 PM / SUN 8 AM–2 PM

In the manner of the haughtiest haute cuisine, Mary and her cook, Velma, are in attendance as you select from this restaurant's menu. They assist in your choices and suggest possible revisions in order to give the meal its correct flow and balance. This may not be unusual at the fanciest restaurants, but it's a surprise for a low-priced café in the middle of Iowa.

Mary's little yellow menus are written in longhand and tacked inside stiff covers. Her customers start arriving at daybreak, and grab the choicer booths of this very old-fashioned café, or sit on the wood counter stools. Breakfasts revolve around Mary's homemade cinnamon rolls, a tradition so firmly rooted in Casey's recent history that a disgruntled farmer was still scolding Mary for failing to bake them one cold morning three weeks before.

Lunch and dinner specials are interchangeable. The people of this picture-perfect farm community like a hot meal twice a day, and they are partial to locally-grown pork or beef. The lunch will be either pork roast or beef, or a more exotic choice like pan fried chicken or catfish filet. Mary and Velma's kitchen skills are seen in the accompaniments. There is a choice of two side dishes, and an average menu here lists such items as "ambrosia salad," "glorified rice," "pea salad with pimentos," scalloped corn, and about a dozen more. Our favorite is Mary's "Watergate salad," a jello combination salad with a pale yellow hue. She explained that the color of the dish was the source of its name.

Desserts are the only thing not included in the meal's price. Like the salad and vegetable selection, the dessert list appeared too long and tempting to allow for an easy decision. It was a hard choice, but we were more than happy with our orders of three-layer chocolate cake and a meltingly rich peanut butter cream pie.

It is difficult to say what dish Mary is most famous for, because as one townsperson starts to describe his personal favorite, another breaks in with "Yes, but you forgot about the . . ."

Mary's cooking is as old fashioned as the giant rotating fans that swing overhead in the dark wood-grained café. Velma scoots from counter to kitchen with her order pad after she helps plan a meal. She and Mary are an odd couple, one thin with a fading flowered apron, the other beefy and white-haired with sensible shoes and rolled nylons. The two of them lavish enough attention on their customers and cuisine to make Mary's unforgettable.

DURANT

★★★★THE WHITE WAY CAFÉ
8th Avenue (Route 6) (319) 785-6202
TUES–SAT 11 AM–8 PM, SUN 11 AM–7 PM, CLOSED MON

The White Way is a great restaurant masquerading as an average one. We might never have stopped at this anonymous box of a building had it not been for a high recommendation by a finicky traveling friend whose reports on journeys through the Midwest are usually curt post cards that read: "Dear M & J; No food from Chicago to K.C.; Love, G." G called us from an Iowa motel room one night, bubbling over with news of a discovery—the great restaurant of the Great Plains. The enthusiasm was hard to believe when we first saw the place, which looks like a new design for prefabricated garages. But a "1975 Excellent Pork Award" plaque on the wall hinted that there was more here than met the eye.

In deference to the pork plaque we ordered smoked pork chops and a country pork sausage. The chops were mild, succulent and subtle. The sausage was more highly spiced, but still temperate enough to let the sweet taste of the pork dominate. Dinners entitle one to help–yourself servings at the salad bar, which at the White Way, is extraordinary. There are about a dozen freshly-made selections, including a potato salad made with lots of eggs, an eggy pea salad speckled with pieces of yellow yolk, celery cubes, sweet pickle chips, and flakes of cheese. For the green salad there is a White Way celery seed dressing —a rich semisweet vinegarette. There were several fruit ambrosias, slaws, and relishes.

Dessert was another dish improved by the use of eggs. A tawny raisin cream pie resembled a rich fruit-studded custard hefted into a thin crust—a luscious, substantial dish. The White Way rhubarb custard pie had been strongly recommended, and we discovered it to be a mighty dessert, in which the tart fruit and bland custard are perfectly balanced.

There aren't many places in the Midwest that reflect the region's rich agricultural bounty as deliciously as the White Way Café. It is a rare restaurant, well worth knowing about if you're traveling along Route 80 west of Des Moines.

HOMESTEAD

★★ THE OLD HOMESTEAD
the Amana Colonies, Route 6 (319) 622–3971
MON–FRI 7 AM–8 PM / SAT & SUN 11 AM–8 PM

The Old Homestead is in the Amana colonies—those tiny communities of German-American immigrants who banded together upon coming to the United States to keep their old-world standards of craftsmanship alive. Today they are as well known for their cured meats and breads as for their refrigerators and appliances. The colonies are big tourist attractions, and The Old Homestead is the only Amana worker café in the area. Even here there is a back room where visitors can sit in an "Amana styled" atmosphere, but the front room is a simple green-walled workman's café where the famous Amana breads and meats are served at low prices.

We ordered two local specialties: Kassler Peppen and a bratwurst plate. The Kassler Peppen was a plate of two large pork chops, smoked and cured to taste like thick slabs of ham. Both platters came with family-style bowls of vegetables, including rough cut, new sauerkraut, apple sauce, fresh peas, mashed potatoes, and slices of Amana-baked white and dark bread. There were also sandwiches of Amana ham and sausage on the menu. Dessert was a German chocolate cake, its pale chocolate body topped with a sugary icing of nutmeats and shredded coconut. The cake seemed to us that it had been left over from the day before.

The Homestead also serves breakfasts called by silly names like "The Hog Callers Delight" or "The Old Amana Standby." Despite the labels, they are all deliciously centered around Amana smoked hams and breakfast sausages, and fresh-baked Amana breads. They are a good way to begin a strenuous day of sightseeing in the Amana colonies.

WALNUT

★★★ THE GARDENS
Pearl and Atlantic Streets
DAILY 5:30–10 PM OR LATER

The Gardens is the kind of place one yearns for after a long day on the road. It is in the small farm community of Walnut, one mile from

I-80 and the two oil-company-operated "restaurants" that straddle the interstate. The night we first ate at The Gardens, we had pulled in late to our motel and were weary but unwilling to settle for a prebreaded defrosted chicken-fried steak. The Yellow Pages in our motel room yielded no clues for finding a decent meal. So we took a chance and asked the Grandma Moses-looking lady who was the desk clerk if there was a nice, pleasant restaurant nearby "that served drinks" (this being our way of eliminating the nearby gasoraunts from consideration). She hesitated, looked us over, then as if imparting a town secret said fraily, "There is such a place."

Dissolve now to The Gardens and two perfect steak dinners. Steak is all that is served here. We were asked only if we wanted small, medium, or large steaks, and whether we wanted our potato baked or hash-browned. Our two "medium" steaks turned out to be over a pound each, their crisply singed outside enclosing a tender red inside, fibrous and dense with natural juices. The steak was presented alone on its plate, without garnish, and with only a trickle of the juices seeping out underneath. On another plate was an eight-inch-diameter pancake of shredded potatoes, crisped and buttery, tasting faintly of onion. With this there was a green salad with cream Roquefort dressing, supplemented by extra hunks of cheese. Also a basket of bread, toasted, buttered, scented with garlic. Two such dinners, two cocktails, two beers, two glasses of wine, and three glasses of club soda came to a total cost of $14.80.

The Gardens is ideal not for its food alone. After a wearisome day on the road, small amenities can mean a lot. Like a sharp waitress: a waitress with a vocabulary extending beyond "huh" and with endless patience for travelers who don't understand that The Gardens is only a steak house; a waitress who, wonderfully, doesn't need a long, gesticulating explanation that club soda is simply seltzer water—fizzy, plain bubbles without flavoring.

The waitress here takes your order and brings everything except the steak. That is cooked by Russ and brought to you by Russ, straight from his grill. He brought us ours and most of the other patrons nodded a greeting to him. Russ is a respected pillar of the community.

Then there is the tiny town of Walnut itself, surrounded by fields of corn and corrals of brown cows and stables of horses, smelling of the richest earth in the world, a town of decades-old houses and lawns with tire swings from the branches of trees, and a family dog on every porch. The Gardens is *the* restaurant of Walnut, and the people here are groups of old ladies, families, couples, young farmers, and young men who just come in for a beer or to meet a friend. As we paid our bill, we noticed that the town doctor paid for his family's steaks with a chit, to be redeemed later, we assumed, when Russ goes for his annual check-up.

The Gardens feels like the very best of America's heartland. It is a place to linger after supper and imbibe the spirit of the place. The restaurant is dark and wood-panelled, almost tavernlike with its strange fur lampshades on the wall and 3-D illuminated dioramas of Iowa life near Russ's kitchen. There are panoramic farmscape paintings on the wall. There is a jukebox, and a small area surrounded by the booths where couples can dance to "Blue Moon" after their steak dinners.

We stepped outside The Gardens and took a deep breath of the night air that smelled of Iowa's black dirt. We first came to this restaurant in hopes of an adequate meal. It has since become, in our minds, a reflection of all that is best about small-town farm life.

WILTON

★THE WILTON CANDY KITCHEN
Cedar Street (319) 732–9278
DAILY 7 AM–11 PM

The Wilton Candy Kitchen is not a place for a meal, or even for candy. Yes, it is an old candy store in a smaller-than-usual Iowa town and it has been on the main street since 1910. The candy is mostly M&Ms and licorice whips, nothing unusual at all. Mr. Napoulous, the owner, is known around these parts for the extraordinary old-fashioned drinks that he whips up behind the aging wood of his soda fountain.

Mr. Napoulous, who keeps the long long hours listed above, likes to keep things as they might have been around the turn of the century. Not that he has made any efforts to keep his place looking like an antique. He just hasn't changed anything since he took it over. We are sure that somewhere behind one of the well-worn counters are postcards showing scenic Wilton circa 1900.

While he tells you about his daughter, a small-town beauty who was a runner-up in the Miss Iowa pageant, he will mix you a "green lizard" (his nickname for a green river), a "hadacol," or perhaps a "New Jersey." If these drinks don't tickle your fancy, he has a foot-long list of others that might. Maybe you came in for a "red river" or an "odd ball." He explained the ingredients of a few of these nostalgic creations to us, but prefers to tease his customers by inferring that the fizzy pastel concoctions have the kick of a Missouri mule.

The "green lizard" we ordered was in fact lime syrup and seltzer mixed with a dash of white vinegar, producing a sweet-sour drink that immediately cut through the worst Iowa heat wave in years.

Mr. Napoulous also makes his own ice cream. He thinks that the maple walnut and cherry nut are the best, and after sampling both, we would agree.

The Wilton Candy Kitchen is a guileless survivor of easier days; or maybe it's just that times haven't changed much in this tiny Iowa town.

KANSAS

ABILENE

★★ CITY CAFÉ
Northwest Third Street (913) 263–3251
MON–SAT 6 AM–8 PM / SUN 7:30 AM–10 AM; NOON–3 PM

Any aficionado of the bizarre will tell you that there is no place like Kansas. Not only does this flat and seemingly uneventful state play host every year to the Annual Pancake Derby, where housewives race across a field flipping flapjacks, it is also the home of the Greyhound Dog Hall of Fame, a giant concrete portrait of Ulysses S. Grant, and the world's largest ball of string. Yes, tourism in Kansas is a booming business, and Abilene, the home of Dwight D. Eisenhower and the town once known as the wickedest in the West, gets its share of tourists just like the rest. In fact, ask Iola Burgraff of the City Café, and she'll tell you that "The dead are rising and coming to Abilene." She's certain she's seen Ike on his way here, coming back home.

Iola's time is divided between having visions and running the City Café which, as her sign says, "offers home cooking and a Christian atmosphere in which to eat." Other than seeing famous dead presidents loitering about Abilene, her visions seem to focus on two things—Nixon and oil. The sign over her booths warns, "Do not talk badly about Richard Nixon in this café," and there are hand-drawn pictures near the cash register showing tricky Dick standing in the palm of the Lord, with an oil well spouting behind him. Our waitress, Zelda, told us that this vision meant that there was oil in Abilene, and that Iola and her flock had dug a well somewhere behind the café and are waiting for it to bring forth the promised oil.

In addition to being the outlet for Iola's religious brochures and for literature about the ex-President, City Café also happens to serve the best inexpensive meals in Kansas. Everything here is designed to make the patron susceptible to religious conversion, and so the food, like that once served in Father Divine's earthly "Heavens," is spectacularly good and ridiculously cheap. Dinners range between entrees of baked ham, pork chops, fried chicken, and roast beef. All come with potatoes, a macaroni salad, corn bread, and "snow slaw." Coffee is inexpensive but weak. And, of course, dessert is angel food cake. Breakfasts can be as simple as fried mush and coffee or as substantial as two wheat-germ pancakes, a fried egg and sausage. All of this is prepared with an angelically light touch and served by the most ingratiating waitress we have ever met—Zelda.

Zelda was rushed the day we dined at the City Café, "Because it's hard to get Christian help," but she was so friendly toward us that it was almost embarrassing. She could not do enough to please us or the other customers. A young mother was having trouble seating her toddler. Zelda ran over with a phone book for the infant to sit on. It was too small. Zelda ran back with another phone book, not satisfied until the customers were comfortable. "How'd you like your meal?" Zelda asked the man in overalls. "Just fine," said he, and Zelda smiled, her eyes magnified behind her rhinestone harlequin glasses. Like the City Café, Zelda is one of a kind.

Iola Burgraff's brochure says, "If you have not been in City Café, you have not seen Abilene." She has been told, "Tell My people in this city of Abilene that they are chosen of God for the greatest work and blessings of any of My people in any age!

> Holy, holy, holy
> Is what the angels sing
> As they fly over Abilene.
> Morning, noon and night
> They are singing:
> O, Abilene; O, Abilene!
> Fair city of renown!"

We must confess we heard no angels singing, but our visit to City Café is one we will long remember for the divine inspiration of its food and prices, and the heavenly tone of its warm Christian atmosphere.

LINDSBORG

★★★SVENSK CONDITORI
107 N. Main Street (913) 227–3525
MON–SAT 6 AM–10 PM / SUNDAY UNTIL NOON

Most of us who grew up in the 1950s were fortunate enough to see Grant Williams, *The Incredible Shrinking Man,* diminish in size from a perfectly normal guy to the point where he is practically crushed under the paw of a tabby cat. Eating at the Svensk Conditori, surrounded by giant blond Kansas Swedes, makes you feel almost half-way to the shrinking man's final fate. The Conditori is the gathering place for the Swedish community of Lindsborg, a town famous for its "ethnic purity"; and while the Svensk isn't the fanciest or most expensive restaurant in town, it is the most informal and the best.

We didn't know quite what to do when we first entered. Diners moved from one table to another; some carried their own food to their booth; some chatted with people who at first seemed to be the waiters and waitresses, but who then sat down over coffee. A young man in clogs came over to our booth and explained that we should look at the menu, then walk over to the bakery counter and order. He'd bring us our food when it was ready. We still don't know if he was actually a waiter, or just a friendly guy who saw us hungrily eyeing the pancakes and rolls. We ordered pancakes at the suggestion of the cook, who said they were "more healthy" than the frosted yeast rolls. We then helped ourselves to the King Oscar coffee and heavy cream that is set out for the patrons.

The pancakes were like light, eggy crepes, moistened with butter, rolled up, then drenched with warm apricot syrup or lingonberries. They practically fell apart to the touch of the fork, and had a meltingly divine flavor, more tender and gentle than the best breakfast griddle cakes. These are eaten as breakfast or lunch, so we chose to make them lunch, and follow the delightful roll-ups with dessert. Our "waiter," seeing we needed advice, suggested the *Ostakaka* which he described as "just an old-fashioned pudding," but which we found to be an amazingly light vanilla-scented custard, sweetened with a topping of lingonberries.

We noticed that a few of the other patrons were eating thin-sliced ham sandwiches on a dark-looking Swedish rye bread, which looked good but not good enough to divert us from pancakes next time around. There are no checks given to patrons at the Svensk Conditori. When finished with our meal, we walked over to the cash register, where the cook asked how we liked the pancakes, and suggested we might want to take home some of her divinity or coffee fudge. We chose a square of each, recited how many cups of coffee we had, and paid up. The fudge turned out to be delicious, and we were relieved as we drove further along Kansas highways to find ourselves once again in the company of skinny farmers and other normal-sized people who don't view anyone under 6'6" as "Shorty."

LAWRENCE

★★ BIGELOW'S BAR B QUE
Route 24–40 (northwest) (913) 842–9456
MON–FRI 10 AM–7 PM, SAT 10 AM–9 PM / CLOSED SUN

Any dreamer who wants to recapture a taste of Hank Williams circa 1953 or Badlands teen-age days à la Charles Starkweather should rush to Bigelow's. There is more brooding and romantic melancholy in one square foot of Bigelow's dusty floor than in the whole state of California. The jukebox alone should be bronzed and put into a time capsule, with its perfect selection of heart-wrenching country-western laments. Sunlight tries to filter in the windows, but the inside haze keeps it from penetrating the sanctum where plaid-shirted cowboys eat their bar b que and barmaids hand out the Coors and hot sauce.

For all its dark mystique, Bigelow's seems as friendly to strangers as it is to its own regulars. You might be expected to drop a coin in the jukebox to keep the tone appropriately dusky, but feel free to moan in your beer with the rest of the boys.

The bar b que at Bigelow's is almost a bonus. It is enough of a treat to find such a well-preserved and accessible piece of dark American romance. Ham bar b que is popular in the Kansas City area. It has a smoky taste that cuts the ham's saltiness, and comes dripping with a not-too-hot sauce. The bar b que is available by the pound in beef or pork ribs, or by the slab.

Chili at Bigelow's is an odd moniker for chunks of ham, beans, and onions brewed in a pot. It is a highly-spiced stew, and goes well with Coors and a country-western lament.

MANHATTAN

★THE SALE BARN CAFÉ
Route 24, E. of Manhattan (913) 776–4815
MON–SAT 8 AM–3 PM

"This is a cattle barn," said Freda Ensley the cook, "and beef's what they like. We buy our own critter and it's processed over at St. Mary's. It's all A-1 meat." Sure enough, the bare menu listed roast beef, Swiss steak, or beef and noodles, with the option of ham for nonbeefeaters. The beef is served with potatoes of dubious authenticity and an assortment of jello, peas, bread and butter, and beverage. These are blueplate lunches. The meat is of good quality, but plain. It is in perfect keeping with the rough-and-tumble tone of this café, which is a small annex to the cattle sale barn.

The first thing we noticed when we walked in was a huge oil painting of Elvis Presley hanging over the counter. He holds the microphone in his hands and appears to be singing into a strong wind. "That's exactly the way he looked that night," Freda told us wistfully. She bought the painting in Wichita after a concert. There's another picture next to Elvis of the Marlboro Man, Wayne Dunafon, whose son happens to be a denizen of this very sale barn. There are other pictures of Roy Rogers and Dale Evans and even Ol' Festus.

There is no need for pictures to create a western atmosphere in this café. Its customers are working cattlemen, and this is the place they visit to relax, sip coffee, shoot the breeze, and have a piece of Freda's fresh blackberry pie.

We would suggest the baked goods over the main courses. The pie had a nice crust, although the filling was on the gummy side. Freda's specialty is "dillybobs." These are the things known as doughboys in certain parts of the Northeast—round balls of dough, deep fried, and rolled in cinnamon sugar.

Although you can get a square meal and some good pastries at this Sale Barn Café, we recommend it especially for its home-grown decor and authentic western atmosphere. After breakfast you can step out and look over a lot of cows or walk into the western clothing store adjacent to the café and buy yourself a new pair of boots.

SHARON SPRINGS

★EMILY'S DAIRY KING RESTAURANT
Main Street (913) 852–4299
MON–SAT 5 AM–9 PM

Emily's Dairy King has nothing to do with similar-sounding places that specialize in dip-tops or "brazier" cooking. Instead of chemically swirled ice cream, Emily's offers a basic midwestern cuisine. She used to be known for her five-inch-diameter cinnamon buns, a favorite of the early morning railroad crews that frequent the place. But Emily told us that she has lost her touch with the delicious buns, and so we had to settle for wheatcakes—which were substantial enough to fuel a railroad worker or a lumberjack for the whole day.

We recommend stopping here for lunch and dinner to try some of Emily's stew or fresh-out-of-the-oven cornbread. It, too, is hearty fare, as simple and rich as the Kansas plains. In fact, if you want to soak up local color, this is the place to do it. And if you get arrested for vagrancy while you're hanging around, don't worry. Emily makes the meals for the town jail.

TOPEKA

★★IRA PRICE CAFÉ
Route 24 (north) (913) 296–9103
ALWAYS OPEN, EXCEPT SAT 9 PM–SUN 7 AM CLOSED

The sign on the roof of Ira Price's declares, "I don't want a million dollars, I just want a million friends." Well, old Ira might have some of the best truckstop cooking in the state of Kansas, but no matter what his sign says, he is the most ornery and unfriendly fellow we've met west of the Mississippi. It might be that he already has a million friends and we were 1,000,001 and 1,000,002 and he wasn't interested, but no two ways about it, Ira wasn't going to have anything to do with us. Whatever his problems, Ira has found the perfect therapy in running a real "home cooking" café, and making delicious food at low prices.

"The meat here is new beef," trucker John Hermann told us as he bit into a filet mignon. New beef tastes different from the aged or prime most of us take for granted. It has a gamier flavor; and at Ira's it was oddly served rolled up and held together with toothpicks. The steaks come with sides of French fries or real whipped potatoes and vegetables. Another Ira Price favorite is pan-fried chicken. This is lightly breaded and fried until crisp—a simply cooked but perfect half bird.

Three women divide up the cooking chores. As we watched one breading and frying chicken, another simmered large pots full of cream gravy and black bean soup. A third was frosting a pink birthday cake with a butter cream icing that tasted like it had a strawberry in each bite.

The tone of Ira Price's café is, like the owner, a little eccentric. On revolving stands there are gag postcards so old that the punchlines have worn off. Truckstop items like razor blades and Kleenex are sold from behind the counter. Faded pictures of cattle and other oddments line the walls. We left Ira down in his basement where we had followed him and hoped to talk. He was mumbling all the time about his "receipts." We tried asking questions about his menu and the café, but he became engrossed in a complicated task of pulling shoeboxes full of papers from shelves, sorting and rearranging the contents, then restacking the boxes in what seemed to us a random order. Was there method to his madness? We didn't stick around to find out; but instead, bid farewell to Ira and went on our way. We wish him all the friends he can stand.

WAMEGO

★ BOB AND LOIS' CAFÉ
Lincoln Street
MON–SAT 6 AM–7 PM / SUN 6 AM–2 PM

"If you wish to put your ashes or cigarette butts in your cup, please tell the waitress and she will serve your coffee in the ashtray." So reads the sign above Bob and Lois' counter. This local watering hole is in a town so small that Lois feels no shame at reprimanding a fellow Wamegoite about his uncouth habits. After all, she goes to the trouble of shaping all her hamburgers from freshly ground meat, and she does make the best chicken-fried steaks in town, so please—use the ashtray!

The pale green walls hung with a small collection of barbed wire do little to hint at the personal touch given to the meals served here. Three women wearing pristine white uniforms work in the kitchen. They mix the batter for the breakfasts of wheatcakes and coffee and blend the homemade beef vegetable soup in the winter. But they put most of their communal energies into the low-priced lunches and dinners.

The menu is not daring. It lists standard favorites like meat loaf, fried chicken, and chicken-fried steaks. These dishes are given the boost of being served, whenever feasible, with vegetables grown at a local farm. Sunday is the best day to patronize Bob and Lois' because chicken with apple dumplings is on the menu, and it is served with fresh slices of beefsteak tomato and good cole slaw.

Bob and Lois' is a simple, small-town café where the personnel and regular customers are extraordinarily hospitable. Travelers will find it hard to feel a stranger for long.

WILSON

★★★HERBEL'S CAFÉ
Main Street (913) 658–9235
MON–FRI 7 AM–3 PM

We were about to walk out of Herbel's upon discovering they served no Czech food. Wilson, Kansas, is a primarily Czech community, a clean town populated by bright people, and also the home of folk artist Ed Root's Sculpture Garden. After spending the morning out at Root's farm, we were ready for a bracing lunch of *debrecinka* or *jirtnice,* or at least a *schnitzel* or creamed rabbit. But no, the menu read "meat loaf, fried chicken . . ." On our way out, however, we caught a whiff of the meat loaf, did an about-face, and sat down at one of the simple tables in the tiny café for one of the nicest meals in Kansas.

The meat loaf was a delightfully seasoned, moist slice, served with delicious creamy mashed potatoes and a peppery gravy. The chicken had a thick, barely chewy crust that fell in great hunks from the tender meat. It came sided by a noddle salad studded with large hunks of hard-boiled egg and pickle. For dessert we had coconut pie, in a light lard crust topped with a rich, eggy custard. It was still warm from the oven when it was set before us.

We asked Mrs. Herbel, who was responsible for this excellent food, why she didn't try her hand at Czech specialties. "That's all done at home," she said. Indeed, we noted the 3 o'clock closing time of the café, and figured that even Mrs. Herbel allows herself time to get home in order to prepare the dill sauce for her dinner.

FAIRS AND FESTIVALS

LIBERAL
Pancake Race / SHROVE TUESDAY

MICHIGAN

ANN ARBOR

★ DRAKE'S SANDWICH SHOP
709 North University (313) NO 8–8853
MON–SAT 10 AM–10:45 PM, SUN 3 PM–10 PM

College food fads come and go, but Drake's Sandwich Shop has been around since before students at Ann Arbor's University of Michigan started swallowing goldfish. There have been two major changes since Mr. Drake opened his ice cream fountain and soda shop in 1924. First, Mr. Drake sold the business to Mr. Tibbals, who had begun his career as a soda jerk in the early '20s. Second, the price of milk toast has more than doubled. Other than that, Drake's is pretty much the same. The favorites here have always been the sweets, specifically the cakes that are baked fresh every morning. Chocolate, lemon, banana, spice—each looks like the cakes that are pictured on mix boxes—tall, moist, dense, yet never heavy. Another favorite is the large pecan roll sticky and rich enough as it is, but preferred by many twice cooked—that is, grilled in butter. Drake's also serves collegiately-named sandwiches like the Harvard or Cornell, milk shakes, sodas, and, for the octogenarian set who remember Mr. Tibbals from when he mixed the malts after school, soft and soothing milktoast.

Aside from the cake and large assortment of candies "to go," the best reason for eating at Drake's is a chance to dine in the upstairs Martian Room. This was remodeled in the 1950s, when outer space was in, and when boomerang shapes symbolized modernity. Every surface up here is covered with different shades and shapes of boomerangs. Although outer space, Mars, and boomerangs might be passé in some circles, they're still thriving at Drake's, as are the traditions of simple sweet-shop food.

BEULAH

★THE CHERRY HUT

Route 31 (616) 882–4431

JUNE–SEPT: 11 AM–8 PM, SAT & SUN, MON–FRI 11 AM–3 PM / CLOSED
TUES

We recommend you visit "Cherry Jerry, the Cheery Cherry Pie
Faced Boy" [sic] for the best cherry pie in this part of Michigan—which
is cherry country. It is a grotesquely cheerful hut by the side of the road,
with happy-faced cherries waving from signs at patrons as they sit inside
or outside at picnic tables and consume cherries. There are other items
on the menu including sandwiches, and even dinners of chicken and
roast beef. But the only sensible reason for stopping at The Cherry Hut
is either a slice of Cherry Hut pie, a cherry sundae, or a pie to take out.
All are delicious, as only desserts made from fresh-picked dark, sweet
cherries can be. For those who prefer not to eat under the happy-faced
boy, and those who like their cherries in the rough, there are stands all
along Route 31 in northern Michigan selling washed cherries, ready to
eat as you drive, from late June through September.

CHARLEVOIX

★★★MURDICK'S CANDY KITCHEN

Bridge Street (616) 547–4213

SUMMER DAILY 9 AM–9 PM / REST OF YEAR MON–SAT 9:30 AM–6 PM /
SUN 10 AM–3 PM

Starting at 9:00 A.M. every morning, Gary Murdick, veteran fudge-
maker of Charlevoix town, goes through the elaborate process of making fudge in an open kitchen that runs the length of Murdick's store.
If the aroma of the fudge doesn't pull you in from the street, then the
loveliness of Murdick's dove-gray interior might. The store is immaculately clean and simply laid out. A few counters in front hold the fudge,
and the sides of the store are lined with marble cooling slabs. The back
area has the enormous copper pots and stoves for brewing the am-
brosial mixture.

You can watch the fudge go through all the cooking stages until
it's finally poured into square forms to cool. Then wait until it's cut, and
pick a piece, still slightly warm, from the marble slab. There is nothing

like it. Murdick's varieties include plain chocolate, plain vanilla, chocolate walnut, chocolate mint pecan, and peanut butter. The creamy intensity of the flavors makes it impossible to eat more than a piece or two at a time. It is made from the best ingredients, and has none of the sugary aftertaste of many inferior fudges.

The Murdick family has been making fudge in Michigan since 1887. Charlevoix is an unusually peaceful vacation spot, reminiscent of gentler days when people strolled along the lake's edge looking at the boats and perhaps nibbling a piece of the best fudge in the Midwest.

GLADSTONE

★★ BRYER'S TAVERN
1011 Main Street (906) 428–9082
DAILY 4:30 PM–10 PM

We were alerted to Bryer's by a traveling salesman whose route includes Michigan's Upper Peninsula. He told us that Gladstone is near many small fishing villages, and that much of the fresh-caught fish winds up on Bryer's tables. For some strange reason it is difficult to get fresh lake fish in these parts, unless you go to a very expensive restaurant, raid a sportsman's catch from his campfire, or stop in at Bryer's.

The specialities here are lake trout, perch and whitefish. They arrive as large filets, simply pan-fried or broiled. Meals begin with homemade soup, usually creamy potato or clam chowder. Entrées are accompanied by baked beans, a relish tray, baked potato and cole slaw. For dessert Bryer's makes strawberry shortcake, served on a biscuit New England-style, mounded with whipped cream.

Sunday is the day for Bryer's chicken dinners, and our traveling-salesman friend swore that they were worth a long detour. The bird is served with sausage stuffing and a good help-yourself salad bar with cheeses, fruits and molded salads.

Bryer's is plain-looking on the outside—just a blank wall and a single window. Inside it's more appealing, with randomly placed white-clothed tables and some moody paintings on the walls. Like most towns up north, Gladstone has more than its share of taverns, but the cars parked outside indicate that Bryer's is one of the favorites.

HOLLAND

★★★ THE SHUTTERS DRESS STORE
280 East Eighth Street (616) 396–3444
MON–FRI: LUNCH ONLY 11:30 AM–2 PM

The Shutters is an elegant old house in the well-manicured town of Holland, Michigan. It is owned by the McIlwains, who divide their time between selling mid-priced ladies' fashions, revamping the lace-curtained loveliness of their home, and serving the best meals in Holland. All of these endeavors take place in the same space, and so one eats at assorted card tables, benches, and dinner tables among racks of dresses and a grand piano laid out with handbags and shoes.

Hattie Hoeve is The Shutter's cook, and the woman responsible for the seemingly endless variety of dishes. Many of the customers come here regularly—especially the East Grand Rapids ladies who stop in during a day of shopping in Holland—and so Hattie is always changing her menu. The day we dined here among the dresses, the meal started with a choice of cold Danish cucumber soup or beef consommé. Zucchini was in season, and Hattie had used it to make zucchini bread. Lunch was an elaborate fruit plate of deliciously farm-fresh native melons, dark bing cherries, peaches, apples, plums, and bananas. There was a hot side dish of green bean casserole. It was also possible to get Danish-style open-face sandwiches served on Hattie's dill-flavored dark bread.

"Hattie is best known for her apple and walnut pie," a McIlwain daughter told us. "But the recipe is her secret." We do know that the pie has bits of apples and walnuts under mounds of heavy whipped cream. On other days Hattie makes almond bars, blueberry cheesecake, or homemade berry ice creams and sherbets.

It is odd indeed to dine in the midst of a dress store, but the good home-cooked food and somewhat eccentric layout of the tables and fashions add up to a comfortable and conversational meal. The Shutters is a lovely, gentle place; the McIlwains manage to maintain their good sense and good humor in the midst of the lunch crowds and the fashion parade; and the whole experience makes a delightful change-of-pace lunch stop along the shores of Eastern Lake Michigan.

ISHPEMING

★★★ MADELYNE'S PASTY SHOP
Route 41 (4 miles west) (906) 485–5531
DAILY 8 AM–7 PM

★★★ MADELYNE'S PASTY FACTORY
800 Greenwood Street
(DRIVE-IN SERVICE ONLY) MON–FRI 10 AM–6 PM / CLOSED SAT & SUN

On the Upper Peninsula of Michigan, pasties have managed the Herculean feat of displacing the hamburger as the primary roadside food. As with burgers, the quality of pasties can vary from the most flabby concoctions to sublime creations. While we are loath to select the nation's best hamburger—fearing reprisals from the Winstead-worshippers of Kansas City or the Louis Lunch-lovers of New Haven—the kingdom of the pasty is small enough, and the choice clear enough to declare Madelyne's the home of America's best.

Madelyne's are simple, pure, and made from clear and heterogeneous ingredients—cubed beef, potatoes, onions, and seasonings. The crust is a rough-formed pocket, drier than most pasty crusts we have eaten on the lower shoreline. In this northernmost part of Michigan, Madelyne's pasties seem closer to their original purpose, which was to provide a hot meal to men who worked in the coldest, dampest climates, or underground in the mines of Cornwall. Madelyne's is at its best in the fall, when the sumac trees of the north begin turning bright red and yellow, the lake waters become steel-gray, and the chill in the air is enough to warrant a wool sweater. That's when we like to pull up to the drive-in window at Madelyne's Pasty Factory in town, get two or three pasties to go, pick up a six pack of Stroh's fire-brewed beer, and drive out to the shore of Lake Superior. Pasties are designed especially to retain their heat; and there are few experiences as elevating as taking the first bite into this meaty pie, and watching the steam escape into the lacquer-blue fall sky above Lake Superior.

MENOMINEE

★★THE HARBOR HOUSE
junction of Routes 41 & 35 (906) 863–9331
MON–THURS 6 AM–10 PM / FRI & SAT 6 AM–3 PM / CLOSED SUN

The teen-ager who was the handyman at our cabin on the lake told us that The Harbor House had the best chicken between Wisconsin and Escanaba. "And the dumpling soup," he practically moaned, "that's out of sight." We took his recommendation and hopped in the car, heading for Harbor House. "Look out for the cheesecake," he called out after us and we made a note to look out for it, whatever that might mean.

As we waited for our food, we began to wonder why we took the kid's advice. The Harbor House was obviously a high school hangout (at least at this time of day—8:00 P.M.). From the window outside, the waitresses were dispensing dip-top ice cream, and inside, the local set played musical booths à la *American Graffiti* to the sound of rock songs on the jukebox. It was all low-keyed and amusing, but hardly the harbinger of a great meal.

The chicken dumpling soup came first and immediately allayed our fears. It was a thick, real chicken stock, made into a virtual stew of chicken meat, light dumplings, firm carrots, celery, and subtle seasonings. The chicken dinner came as three large pieces of delicate, juicy, and greaseless chicken and a side dish of "broasted potatoes" which had been cooked in oil under pressure, like the chicken. The chunks of potato developed a spicy, chewy skin and tender insides, like the jo-jo potatoes one gets in the South. It was a fine dinner. As the menu says, "If the colonel had our recipe, he'd be a general."

We asked the waitress about the pastys that are Tuesday specials here, and she assured us they were delicious. "You never know about the cook," she mused. "He puts all kinds of surprises into the pasties." We didn't know quite how to take her comment, but it reminded us of the cheesecake our friend back at the cabin had told us to watch out for. We ordered a piece to go, to be eaten back in the cabin. We took a bite in the car, and practically swerved into Lake Michigan from the hideous acetose taste. It was like boiled-down coffee whitener. "I told you to watch out for the cheesecake," the kid later told us. "But you should really try the homemade raisin bread the next time you go there. It's delicious." We promised ourselves to take this young gourmet's advice. He had warned us about the cheesecake, and steered us to a delicious bowl of chicken dumpling soup.

NEW ERA

★★★HENRICKSON'S HARVEST TABLE

junction of Routes 31 & 20—"Town Corners" (616) 861–5261
DAILY SUMMER NOON–9 PM

If there is any one experience that most immediately brings to
mind the bountiful riches of midwestern farm land, it is a meal at
Henrickson's. The Harvest Table is a new building, constructed in a
"planned rustic" style, with rough-hewn ceiling beams, quilts and farm
implements on the wall, and waitresses in calico aprons. The farminess
at Henrickson's is real, authenticated beyond reproach by the freshest
salads we have seen in any restaurant, open-faced vegetable sandwiches
on cracked whole wheat bread, and a salad table that takes full advantage of the farmland's yield.

Our first meal here was when we were heading north. It was a
lunch of an open-faced ham-asparagus-melted jack cheese sandwich on
thick-sliced white bread and a "Vegetarian Delight" sandwich, which
was sliced mushrooms, red onions, jack cheese, alfalfa sprouts, horseradish, and a sour cream dressing, served hot on toasted whole wheat
bread. This part of Michigan is asparagus country, and the asparagus
was so sharply fresh that it outshone both the thin-sliced ham and the
cheese. The vegetarian sandwich was a delicate balance of flavors,
bound together by the sour cream and horseradish dressing. Henrickson's is not a "health food" restaurant, but the sandwiches here tasted
as pure and as good-for-us as anything we've had at the celebrated
Source in Los Angeles, and were about half the price.

Our sandwiches were preceded by a "Garden Smorgasbord"
which was a large platter of crudities and salad fixings, all impeccably
fresh, and served with an assortment of seeds, nuts, and dressings for
dipping or sprinkling. We ordered one side dish of cole slaw which was
eccentrically spicy and enlivened by the addition of alfalfa sprouts and
powerful caraway seeds. Town Corners is not only asparagus, cherry,
cheese, and mushroom country, but dill-growing land as well. The pickles that accompany sandwiches are "double sour"—intensely flavorful;
recommended highly if you love dill. We finished our lunch with one
slice of deep-dish apple pie, which came warm, highly spiced, and with
cheese laid across its crumbly crust.

Returning south, we stopped back at Henrickson's, after a famous
vegetable sandwich at the Perry Davis Hotel in Petosky, Michigan. The
Perry Davis sandwich is served on better china by boys in white coats,

but it didn't nearly measure up to the perfection of Henrickson's. On this trip we had dinner—pork chops oceana, which had been baked in a cherry glaze; and beef bordeaux, which was roast beef in a mushroom wine sauce. Both were overambitious and overpriced, failing to live up to our fond memories of lunch. But the strawberry shortcake we had for dessert was perfect—a light biscuit cut open and filled with strawberries and piled high with whipped cream.

Lunch is the time to come to Henrickson's, especially during the summer and early fall, when their sandwich selection and salad bar really is a Harvest Table. The second floor of the restaurant is a large attic filled with handcrafts and antiques—not only the best store we have ever seen affiliated with a restaurant, but the cheapest and most unusual we've seen anywhere outside of the usual picked-over antique routes.

ST. IGNACE

★★★ THE HUNGARIAN KITCHEN
Route 2 (14 miles west)
DAILY 8 AM–7 PM

First, a confession: we love Hungarian food. We believe that the best cooks in the world are from Budapest. We eat Hungarian food whenever we can. So it took a lot of thought, debate, and careful consideration before we decided that this restaurant outside the Hungarian community of St. Ignace serves some of the best Hungarian food we have ever eaten. Take *nockerli,* for instance—those small free-form dumplings that come as a side dish to Hungarian meals, the way pasta or rice accompanies Italian or Chinese foods. Nockerli are usually best for soaking up gravy, or mopping the plate. The Hungarian Kitchen raises this simple dish from the level of utility to a magnificent creation of creamy light pinches of dough, flavored with marrow and enriched with a dash of chicken fat and butter, lightly seasoned with paprika and salt.

But back to the beginning, and the Hungarian Kitchen's two special soups—*Csirke Leves,* a thick chicken soup, or *Bab Leves,* a smoky bean soup. Both are mild and light—even the bean soup. The entrees are a choice of *Csirke Paprikas* (a chicken fricassee with small dumplings and paprika sauce), *Toltott Kaposzata* (a rolled cabbage, filled with a mixture of ground pork), or goulash (traditional Hungarian stew). We tried the chicken paprika, which was fall-apart tender and creamy; and the cabbage rolls, which were topped with sour cream—a perfect complement to the spicy pork and mildly pungent cabbage. The meals came with nockerli and large slices of rough-grained white bread.

Desserts avoided the usual clichés of Bohemian dining. There was no strudel and no *palacinte* (stuffed pancakes). Instead, the menu offered a choice of two filled cakes—*Cseresznyes* (yellow cake with cherry filling) or *Almas Lepany* (the same cake with apples). We chose the cake with cherry filling, which was light and mild-tasting: a delicate end to a rich meal. We also took our waitress' suggestion and tried her favorite dessert, *Madartej,* a very large brandy snifter filled with soft vanilla custard, and topped with fluffs of egg white meringue: a smooth, elusive cloud of flavor.

The Hungarian Kitchen is just across the road from slate-gray Lake Michigan and a sandy beach. It is an informal place. We saw children sitting at some tables with their coloring books. They had been dropped off here while their parents went shopping.

Some of the bric-a-brac inside the restaurant looks like the owner sent a Mouseketeer to Hamtramck to find suitable decor for a Hungarian restaurant. There is a silly-looking suit of armor in one corner, and some Transylvanian doo-dads on the wall, but these few tokens of bogus Hungariana do nothing to belie the truth of a classically delicious and low-priced Hungarian meal.

FAIRS AND FESTIVALS

BAY CITY
Potato Festival / LATE JULY

BOYNE CITY
Mushroom Festival / MID-MAY

KALKASKA
National Trout Festival / LATE APRIL

MANISTEE
Strawberry Festival and Ox Roast / JULY 4TH WEEKEND

MUNGER
Potato Festival / LATE JULY

ROMEO
Michigan Peach Festival / LABOR DAY WEEKEND

SOUTH HAVEN
Blueberry Festival / MID-JULY

TRAVERSE CITY
National Cherry Festival / EARLY JULY

VERMONTVILLE
Maple Syrup Festival / LATE APRIL

MINNESOTA

COMSTOCK

★FARMER'S CAFÉ
Route 75, Comstock (218) 585–4655
MON–FRI 7 AM–7 PM, SAT 7 AM–1 PM

The Farmer's Café is a small block building that long ago was a local grocery store. It is now an isolated café on the road heading towards Fargo. It is run by two sisters, Ruth Richards and Patty Bernier, who do an admirable job of serving good food on this lonely strip of road.

The menu is plain meat and potatoes, but the sisters disdain to use convenience items and try to do as much "home cooking" as they can. Meals begin with soups, made from scratch. The favorites are cream of pea, cream of potato, vegetable beef, and a creamy tomato soup that uses *fresh* tomatoes as the base whenever they are available. The soup precedes hearty portions of roast beef and potatoes, meatballs or meat loaf. The potatoes that side the dinners are the genuine article in all cases but mashed, which are made from potato flakes whenever the women can't get good spuds in Comstock.

For breakfast there are fresh-baked cinnamon rolls; desserts are chocolate or yellow cakes, made on the premises daily.

COTTON

★THE WILBERT CAFÉ
Main Street (218) 482–3237
ALWAYS OPEN

Cotton is a minuscule town in the nonagricultural part of Minnesota. The Wilbert Café has been around for thirty-three years and is a local favorite for pasties and homemade soup.

It seemed that almost all the male population of this seven-building town are construction workers. The steel-helmeted crowd lines up at 8 A.M. at The Wilbert for homemade doughnuts and fresh coffee for their thermoses. They are back again at noon for the lunch specials, and then again at 5 P.M. for a pasty and more coffee.

By all means stick to the pasties and doughnuts here. The lunch specials are eat-at-your-own risk. We sampled some lasagna that had the flavor of wet newspaper, and some Swedish meatballs that looked and tasted as rubbery as the kind that Billie Jean King swats over the net. The pasties, on the other hand, are well prepared. Served on Thursdays, these beef-and-onion pies are richly seasoned and the outer crust is firm, yet light. The doughnuts are made each morning by Wilbert's talented baker, and she doesn't rely on mechanical kitchen aids, preferring to shape each pastry by hand. She also makes sweet caramel rolls.

The Wilbert is not an especially charming place, nor could the food be considered "farm cooking" as we found in other parts of this state, but it is a reasonable enough place to stop for a quick bite and a decent cup of coffee.

LAKE CITY

★★THE BLUE MOON

Lake Shore and Center Streets (612) 345–2123
MON–SAT 6 AM–10 PM / SUN 7 AM–8 PM

A first glance at The Blue Moon might remind you of an Edward Hopper painting. It is simple to the point of austerity, innocent of occasional frills. But as we sat and sipped good coffee at our table, huge glass bowls of brightly-colored food began to appear from the kitchen. The Blue Moon was setting up its salad bar—a smorgasbord assortment of salads that in its variety, freshness, and traditional Scandinavian quality put all other salad bars to shame.

We ordered two roast beef dinners. The beef was fine—pink, moist, and freshly cut from the roast. But it was the salads that made the meal memorable. Jello ambrosias, macaroni, tuna, chicken, potato salads, shredded cabbage salad with raisins, carrot salads, three-bean salads, Waldorf salads, fresh sauerkraut, relishes, chow-chow, and four kinds of pickles were one day's selection. Four Lake City women had spent their morning preparing the feast.

The women of The Blue Moon also make soups—chicken and dumpling, potato cream, ham and bean, fresh vegetable, and hamburger chili—a stewlike concoction for only the heartiest of winter appetites. For dessert there are pies. We were fortunate to be here at the peak of strawberry season, and to get one of the juiciest strawberry pies we've had.

Service at The Blue Moon is efficient, clean, almost hospital-like in its precise care of patrons. When we paid our bill, the waitress handed us two sugar cookies, "for later," and we left The Blue Moon eager to come back another time.

WABASHA

★SAUNDERS CAFÉ

Pembroke Avenue and Main Street (612) 565–3871
DAILY 6 AM–8 PM

The Saunders Café is a work of art, to be admired more for its Scandinavian beauty than its food. It is the subtle elegance of simplicity: an unexpectedly sleek place to eat. First, you'll see that on every table the salt and pepper shakers, the place mat, and a canary-yellow menu are all arranged in perfect symmetry under the indirect chrome light that softly illuminates each booth. Then you'll see that each laquered birch booth is separate from the others and high-backed to create a sense of privacy and quietude. The Formica trim, china, and coffee cups are all matching pink, ringed with lines of gray and off-white. Then there is the counter—pine-green and cream-colored, sleek and im-maculately clean, decorated with vases of fresh wildflowers.

The visual clarity of the Saunders Café translates into an unin-spired cuisine. Our batter-fried red-snapper dinner had been frozen and was virtually tasteless. A fried-chicken dinner was fresher, but rather dull. The fresh peach shortcake and large, yeasty doughnut were the best parts of the meal, along with good, strong coffee. It would seem that more energy goes into Saunders' appearance than its meals. It is, nonetheless, one of the loveliest places we know to have a good dough-nut and a cup of coffee.

WINONA

★ TRUCKERS CAFÉ
Mankato Street
MON–THURS 6 AM–8 PM / FRI–SAT 6 AM–3 PM / SUN 9 AM–8 PM

Truckers Café was named in honor of the drivers who stop here on their way to the Twin Cities. The clientele is a mixed bag of gearjam-mers, local families, workers, and students from Winona State College. What all these people have in common are large appetites and small pocketbooks—a fact to which Truckers Café tries to address itself with daily home-cooked meals. The regular repertoire is goulash, bar b qued short ribs, and fried chicken. All are served in medium-sized portions with plenty of potatoes. For extra-large appetites, the menu offers an extra portion of the main course. We recommend the soups at Truckers Café, all thick with their particular ingredients—chicken, dumplings, vegetable, beans, beef, and chili.

A sign warns the often rushed trucker-patrons that the chicken preparation takes twenty minutes. The wait is taken into account by truckers with CB sets who call ahead to get "the bird in the batter and the spuds on the platter" for their arrival. The handle for the Truckers Café is "Big Whopper," and the radio is always turned on low to channel 19.

It's an extremely neat and clean little place, considering the high volume of business. Like a junior version of a modern truck complex, the tiny Truckers sells razor blades, magazines, candy bars, postcards, and other jimcracks. The grill is run by a wonder-woman of a cook and owner who keeps the trucker-patrons on schedule and the Truckers Café sparkling clean.

FAIRS AND FESTIVALS

ASKOV
Rutabaga Festival and Danish Days / LATE AUGUST

COKATO
Cokato Corn Carnival / EARLY AUGUST
Free corn-on-the-cob

FRAZEE
Frazee Turkey Days / EARLY AUGUST

HOPKINS
Raspberry Festival / LATE JULY

KELLOGG
Watermelon Festival / EARLY SEPTEMBER

LA CRESCENT
Apple Festival / LATE SEPTEMBER

McGREGOR
Wild Rice Festival / EARLY AUGUST
Wild rice and pancake supper

MONTGOMERY
Kolacky Day / EARLY SEPTEMBER
Honoring the "Bohemian bun"

OWATONNA
Pumpkin Festival / LATE OCTOBER

WILLMAR
Kaffe Festival / LATE JUNE
Free coffee, cookies, & milk

MISSOURI

FORISTELL

★THE SKYLINE RESTAURANT
Foristell Exit off I-70 (314) 673–2996
ALWAYS OPEN

We include this cavernous truck stop for its convenience to the highway, and for the lack of great roadfood in this part of the show-me state. The Skyline resembles a World War II airplane hangar from the road and a hunting lodge inside. It caters primarily to truckers from the interstate, and while the food is not the greatest, the folks who run the place try to do a little bit better than the truck stop across the way, and for their efforts we give them a nod.

For starters, breakfasts here are served the way truckers like them. There are good omelettes, lots of ham and bacon, and good homemade rolls. The coffee is the legendary "cup o' mud," usually strong enough to pry open the eyelids of the sleepiest driver. Lunch and dinners are trucker-sized, too: meat loafs, roast beef and pork come with mountains of potatoes and wilted vegetables.

We recommend stoking up on the homemade fruit cobblers and pies. They are thick and sweet, the cobblers topped with a decent crumb crust and filled with a good two inches of cherries, apples or berries. The Skyline will package one to go and fill up your thermos with enough coffee to make it to Chi-town.

LEXINGTON

★★THE VICTORY RESTAURANT
Main Street (Route 224) (816) 259–2031
DAILY 6:30 AM–7:30 PM

The Victory is a pretty restaurant. Ferns, trailing ivys, and flowering plants are hung from the ceiling and placed on counters and tabletops. The plants give The Victory a greenhouse feel, accentuated by the large windows in front.

The menu is centered around cream dishes and, while the food is very good, some might find it on the bland side. We started our meal with cream of potato and cream of celery soups. Both were laced with chunks of vegetable. One of The Victory specials is chicken croquettes —chunks of white meat, bread crumbs, and small pieces of celery and parsley blended together and baked. We also sampled a more boldly seasoned pork roast with stuffing. The highest-priced meals on The Victory menu are Kansas City steaks.

The vegetables that come with the meals are particularly good. We had French-fried zucchini and glazed carrots. Our waitress suggested three-bean salad or potato salad as an alternative to potatoes. "We change vegetables all the time. Some of them get pretty fancy, too," she said. The eggplant fingers were, indeed, exotic for this region.

The Victory is a well-mannered and tasteful place, with the atmosphere of a tearoom. There are vases of lovely snapdragons on the cash-register stand. The only strange element in this tableau is the revolving rack of books next to the doorway. Half are Christian texts, and half are sex books. We chalk this up to The Victory's proximity to the wacky state of Kansas.

KANSAS CITY

★★★★ ARTHUR BRYANT'S
1727 Brooklyn (corner of 18th Street) (816) 231–1123
MON–SAT 10 AM–11 PM / CLOSED SUN

Unlike most of our roadfood choices, Arthur Bryant's "House of Good Eats" is in the heart of a major city. It is not immediately convenient to the interstate and chances are good that you will get lost trying to find it. Why include a rundown-looking bar b que restaurant in Kansas City? Because many—like eater extraordinaire Calvin Trillin—believe that Arthur Bryant's is "THE SINGLE BEST RESTAURANT IN THE WORLD."

From the outside you see a dusty window enclosing three ten-gallon jugs of bar b que sauce. Inside there are institutional-pale-green walls and a floor so slippery that Dorothy Hamill could win gold medals skating on it. Blacks and whites line up at the order window, examining the posted list of selections. Ribs are sold by the pound, as is Brisket of beef and Barbequed Ham. On the side are orders of large soft French fries and stuffed mango pickles.

If you peek into the kitchen behind the order window, you'll see Arthur Bryant, toothpick in his mouth, overseeing his cooks. Although some have been with him twenty-six years, they are still underlings to the master. There was a time long ago when Arthur Bryant apprenticed with a pitmaster too, but so many years have passed since those days that Arthur Bryant needn't bother taking on bar b que challengers. He knows that he is King of the Bar B Que Pit, and accepts all journalistic accolades with the casual disinterest of nobility.

You carry your food and beer (or soda from a machine) and a small pitcher of sauce to one of the thirty Formica tables. A brisket sandwich is countless slices of meat mellowed with hickory and yearning for an application of sauce. The ribs are greasy, fall-apart tender like the brisket, and subtly perfumed with wood smoke. The sauce is what it's all about. It is red-orange and grainy with a unique flavor that has little relation to bar b que sauces tasted elsewhere. Arthur Bryant would probably lay down his life before giving up the recipe for the sauce, so we can only guess at what might be in it. It has no ketchupy taste, although it is red and must include tomatoes somewhere in its heritage. The spices are so kaleidoscopic that we thought we detected everything from cayenne to curry. Judging from the gallons resting in the filtered sunlight in the window, it requires some aging to attain perfection.

Airline officials in Kansas City are used to the number of Arthur Bryant sandwiches that pass through baggage inspection and the jugs of sauce carried on board—too precious to put with the rest of the cargo. If you are provident and cautious, buy a ten-gallon jug. If you have only a small trunk and a full car, at least take a small bottle with you. The sauce is packed in old, cheap wine or vinegar bottles, the contents of which become more valuable as they diminish. It's important to take something with you when you leave Arthur Bryant's because although you may feel full right after eating, the craving for Arthur Bryant's will come sneaking back soon. You may then find yourself hitting bar b que after bar b que trying to scratch the itch, sad to discover that there is only one Arthur Bryant's.

MARSHALL

★★ THE COFFEE SHOP
Arrow Street (Route 154 West) (816) 886–5597
MON–FRI 5:30 AM–7:00 PM / SAT & SUN 6:30 AM–1:30 PM

The Coffee Shop is a homey place, situated on a town square and frequented by the townspeople of Marshall. It's one of the best small-town cafés in the state. "Folks in town come here just for the vegetable plate," one young waitress told us. "They know we get all our stuff fresh from the farm and we cook it the same day." This popular meal is a sampler of five different vegetables. There is also a choice of a chicken dinner served on a bed of buttery homemade noodles with side dishes of hot spiced beets, creamed diced potatoes, and shredded cabbage "German style"—doused with celery seed dressing. Another dinner of tender chicken livers broiled in butter and covered with a light cream gravy was served on the homemade noodles and accompanied by steamed buttered carrots, a square of molded jello, and the diced potatoes. There were ham and roast pork dinners also available.

We were seated at the counter, and throughout the meal, we gazed upon a refrigerated case with deep bowls of bread soufflé pudding. This pudding turned out to be one of the very best ever: a puffy custard, topped, when ordered, with a naturally sweet cherry sauce. One portion seems almost too big for a single person, but the cloudlike consistency of the dish quickly changes one's mind.

The irony of life at The Coffee Shop is that many of its staunchest patrons are workers from the nearby frozen-food packaging plant, where "boiling bags" threaten to obliterate the joys of home cooking.

WENTZVILLE

★★ THORNBERRY'S RESTAURANT
Pearce Boulevard (just off Route 61 north) (314) 327–9618
MON–FRI 5:30 AM–7 PM / SAT 5:30 AM–3 PM / CLOSED SUN

Thornberry's is a pleasant cafeteria-style restaurant with especially inexpensive food. We found it one morning after having passed a combination lounge-and-truck stop to which we had been directed by a well-meaning Wentzvillite, who probably figured us for the lounge-lizard types. A charter bus pulled in ahead of us, so we drove on and, happily, found two delicious breakfasts at Thornberry's. One was eggs, toast, bacon, and potatoes. All was good, except the potatoes, which were excellent. They were reminiscent of the kind that Toddle House restaurants used to serve—well-oiled and cooked as a patty so that the shredded potatoes develop a crisp brown skin and a softened inside. The other breakfast was an unbalanced but irresistible plate of one cinnamon doughnut, one chocolate doughnut, and one sweet roll—all hot and yeasty smelling, fresh from the oven. The sweet roll was a free-form funnel-cake-like spiral, as light as a French cruller. We were tempted to go back for seconds, but desisted, since lunch would soon be set out, and we wanted to leave room to taste the goodies we smelled cooking in the kitchen.

Mr. Thornberry joined us after breakfast, and told us the secret of success. "I do things the old way, the way I learned at Notre Dame." He apprenticed as a short-order cook there in the 1940s and brought with him here to Wentzville the recipes for Irish stew, five-cup salads, raisin pie, and sweet rolls. He also brought with him a seemingly endless supply of stories about his days with the "fightin Irish cooks"—tales of sneaking bacon into the kitchens on meatless Fridays, and of Irish stews so large it took three cooks to hoist them off the stove. Thornberry's experiences served him well, judging by the good-looking trays of food being set out along the cafeteria line for lunch. There was roast pork and roast beef straight from the oven. We sampled a slice of baked ham —mildly scented with clove. It came on a platter with pungent German potato salad and stewed apples. There were eight different salads along the counter, four still-warm fruit pies, and a tall sour-cream raisin pie.

We were sorry when we left not to have room to make one more reconnaissance run along the cafeteria line. We did notice as we got into our car that the Wentzville sheriff, who had been leaving as we entered for breakfast, was now returning for lunch. He is a huge man, and wears a gun no more than three inches long that looks like a Cracker Jack prize. We took this as an indication of the minimal crime rate in the Wentzville area. It's a beautiful part of Missouri, not far from the Mississippi River, worth visiting for the scenery as well as a William Thornberry bargain-priced fightin Irish meal.

FAIRS AND FESTIVALS

HERMANN
Maifest / MID-MAY
Beer gardens, German food

NEBRASKA

COZAD

★ THE RED ROOSTER
128 East Eighth Street (308) 784–2080
MON–SAT 5 AM–9 PM / SUN 7 AM–2 PM

A good bet for locating a decent eatery is to look for one with a large, round table near the window. It is from this table that the town "regulars" survey the scene out on Main Street. Such a setup is usually a guarantee of fresh coffee, and a pretty good promise of decent food. We saw The Red Rooster's round table just behind the two chickens that are painted on the front window, and so combining the roundtable theory with another one about handpainted signs equaling creative cookery, we got out of our car and headed for The Rooster. The first thing we noticed was the heavy odor of the alfalfa mills in the air which smells like 100,000 people smoking marijuana in a small closet.

We pushed through the air, and then along The Red Rooster steam table inside. We got two lunch specials consisting of formula broasted (pressure-fried) chicken, some delicious cole slaw, synthetic dinner rolls, and a meat and macaroni casserole. We also got a thick vegetable soup with homemade noodles, two fresh cinnamon rolls, and two cups of coffee.

What charmed us about The Red Rooster was not the merely adequate meal, but Scrappy and Madeline Milner, who run the place and convinced us that Sunday dinner here was really special—turkey and homemade dressing, candied yams, and baked potatoes. On Sundays, there is also the town favorite "Red Rooster Special," a rib-eye steak with the works. We haven't returned to Cozad to look into those Sunday specials, but if we do ever find ourselves mid-Nebraska on a Sunday, we'll head straight for the red and white café with the chickens painted out front and the round table in the window.

HAMPTON

★HANSEN HOUSE CAFÉ
North Third Street (402) 725–3336
MON–FRI 6:30 AM–6:30 PM / SAT 6:30 AM–4 PM / CLOSED SUN

Hampton is a tiny town in the Nebraska farmlands, and Hansen House is where the Hamptonites gather for coffee and homemade cinnamon rolls in the morning, and for sodas and hamburgers after the high school football games on Saturday. If the team has won, Mrs. Hansen and her daughter Cheryl keep the café open past four o'clock, and chances are good, Cheryl told us, that her mother will bring out a tin of brownies and a jar of sugar cookies for the team members. Even if you're not on the Hampton High team, and don't farm corn or alfalfa nearby, Hansen House is still a nice place to eat when you're passing through on Route 80. Mrs. Hansen's rolls are fresh every morning, and lunches are all good, country cooking. We had pan-fried chicken with a thick and crunchy crust, a fresh potato salad, and an ear of buttered sweet corn. The other entrees included liver and onions, meat loaf, and bar b qued beef ribs. All came with potato salad, and since this was corn season, an ear of Nebraska's finest complemented each meal. Dessert was a fresh peach crisp with a crumbly crust, and a thick raisin cream pie.

In the winter time, Hansen House turns its energies to soups, the specialty being a creamed ham and bean soup that Mrs. Hansen told us was her personal favorite. Cold weather also means turkeys with stuffing and mince pies. There are no menus at Hansen House. "Most customers know what we're serving anyway," Cheryl said. Hansen House sells some of its customers' handcrafted rugs and brooms, and serves as an outlet for the ladies' auxiliary. It's a lovely piece of Americana, and a good place to find a decent meal.

MINDEN

★★THE CITY CAFÉ
Colorado Avenue (308) 832–2660
MON–SAT 5 AM–5 PM / SUN 5 AM–2 PM

Minden, Nebraska, is the home of the Harold Warp Museum. Although not a familiar name to most, Harold Warp was a one-man magnet of a collector. His extensive acquisitions of everything from antique autos to historical manuscripts are now on display in Minden, filling buildings which sprawl for acres across the countryside.

Since Minden is a tourist attraction, there is a restaurant next to Harold's museum. One mile away, in the town of Minden itself, there is another restaurant, The City Café, where the food is better, and about half the price.

The City Café is noteworthy for a third reason. The waitresses are extremely friendly—a quality rare among the taciturn Nebraska café workers. Here at The City they welcome your patronage, and do all they can to get you to come back.

The daily lunch special is usually one of the two plains states' favorites—beef or pork. The day we were here, there was a baked ham plate with side orders of salad mold, mashed potatoes, whole ears of sweet buttered corn, and homemade rolls. When we finished, our waitress asked, "Can I tempt you with a piece of praline pie?" No sooner tempted than eaten, and the pie turned out to be memorable. It was a smooth vanilla custard with a thick bottom crust of crushed pecans and brown sugar. The meringue top was sprinkled with sugar. The pie was accompanied by a fresh and perfect cup of coffee.

"Minden is a big coffee town," our waitress explained when we asked her why the coffee was so good. In fact, there is a help-yourself coffee urn on a back table, from which Mindenites help themselves on the honor system. We like the casual but professional air of The City Café, expressed by our waitress when we asked her about the "Help Wanted" sign in the window. She told us, "We like to hire mature women to serve here. You can't expect a child to do a woman's job. Being a good waitress is not easy."

O'NEILL

★★THE M & M CAFÉ
412 E. Douglas (412) 336–2270
MON–SAT 6 AM–9 PM

We love the M & M Café, and so do many of the people who have eaten here since 1913 when it opened. In fact, some like it so much they want to walk off with the fixtures. The owner's wife told us that people come in all the time wanting to buy the antique walnut booths, cabinets, and marble counter top.

But it's not for bygone beauty that we direct you to the M & M. The food is as special and old-fashioned as the decor. Even the noodles served here are made from scratch. Since most of the customers are regulars, there is a large, changing menu. Among the soups our favorites have been a rich split pea, a silky cream of tomato, and a heavy bean soup. We recommend boiled beef or chicken as a main course. Both are served with broad, irregular, hand-rolled noodles. Hot from the oven come Parker House rolls or hard rolls (there is a bakery on the premises), or plain homemade bread. Ribs with navy beans and meat loaf have been simple, down-home standouts, too.

Among the homemade pies we especially favor the apricot and peach. Topped with a light crust and filled with fruit that has not been oversweetened, these, too, are a product of M & M's expert bakers.

If you come here for breakfast, order sausage. The owners don't like those little store-bought patties, so they hand-grind their own. It's considerations like that that make the M & M a winner, especially in a state where the roadfood pickings can be pretty slim.

WILBER

★★★ ANNIE'S JIDLIKE CAFÉ
3rd & Main Streets (402) 821–2445
MON–SAT 6 AM–6 PM

While much of the Midwest chooses to eat the farmer's favorites, meat and potatoes, there are small ethnic communities that still cook traditional dishes that reflect the heritage of their original homeland. Such a town is Wilber, Nebraska, the "Czech Capital of the United States." Although the best and most elaborate Czech dishes are served at home rather than in the cafés around town, we do know of one place that is more than likely to offer a Czech dish or two on the menu.

Annie's is a small, old-fashioned place with a somewhat faded mural on one wall depicting a harvest scene. Annie herself oversees the cooking and help, and the people who eat here are mostly all on a first-name basis with one another.

Besides the standard American fare, Annie's specializes in Czech food. It is not always available, and specific offerings vary from day to day, but the chances are good that at least one of these great dishes will be found on the café menu: liver and dumpling soup—a dark broth dotted with light pinches of dumpling dough; roast pork accompanied by *kuba,* a mushroom-barley casserole; potato dumplings served with dill sauce, a pale-green pungent mixture of cream, eggs, vinegar and dill weed.

Every morning a lady helps Annie bake the *kolaches*—moist sweet rolls that go perfectly with strong coffee. Annie also turns out a lighter, flaky roll called a "butter horn."

Annie's is a Wilber tradition, and a boon to the traveler passing through the midwestern prairies.

NORTH DAKOTA

BISMARCK

★★THE LITTLE COTTAGE CAFÉ
2513 East Main Street (701) 223-4949
DAILY 6 AM–11 PM

The Little Cottage has some of the best food and friendliest service we came across in this barren land. It is owned by Jim Zoller who allows himself occasional flights of fancy with the Little Cottage's menu.

The soups served here are ethnic ones. *Knefla* soup is a thick stock, filled with light, airy dumplings. There is an egg soup, prepared by dropping a thin stream of egg batter into piping hot soup. A delicate pancake forms and then breaks apart into many small, eggy dumplings.

We tried some delicious stuffed pork chops, and a well-prepared pork tenderloin. For less hearty eaters, the Little Cottage's specialty is something called a "cheddar ground round"—a ten-ounce hamburger wrapped with bacon, Swiss cheese, Cheddar cheese, and Parmesan cheese. If you have never been satisfied by the amount of cheese that comes on the average cheeseburger, this is for you.

There are coconut pies, lemon pies, and heartier custards like sour cream raisin. The Little Cottage gets our accolades for its inviting, friendly atmosphere and good food in an often bleak Badland of Whopperburgers.

BOWMAN

★ GENE'S
Main Street (4 blocks N. of Route 12 & 85 junction) (701) 523–3137
MON–SAT 6 AM–10 PM, SUN 6 AM–2 PM

Gene's is a small place decorated in the modern café style: orange tile up front, paneling in back, and a small dining area with "easy wipe" Formica tables. It is not a place to come for quaintness or for a leisurely afternoon of soaking up local color, but for North Dakota the food is pretty good—it's a clean place, and the price is right.

The best item on the menu is chicken-fried steak, often the butt of jokes about western cooking, but a tasty dish if it is prepared well. Here, it is. Another good choice is the ham dinner. Both come with potatoes, vegetables and a roll.

Gene's makes soups from scratch, and a fine sour-cream raisin pie with a thick cloud of meringue on top. For breakfast there are home-made cinnamon rolls and good coffee.

ELGIN

★★ ZACHER'S CAFÉ
121 North Main (701) 584–2844
MON–SAT 6 AM–9 PM / SUN 8 AM–8 PM

We're happy when we can find decent food and a smiling face anywhere in North Dakota. When we found Zacher's, we were ecstatic. Not only are Harry Zacher and his wife Esther hospitable, but their simple café in Elgin offers a regular selection of good Ukrainian food, prepared by knowing cooks of Ukrainian descent. The day we ate at Zacher's, the menu described the special of the day as "pigs in blankets." With visions of disguised wieners dancing in our heads, we inquired what these pigs might be. Harry enlightened us and our spirits soared. "We've got to call it that, so's the customers understand. If we called it *holubsti,* they'd get scared off."

What makes holubsti different from other versions of stuffed cabbage is the way the Ukrainian version develops a kind of skin as it is baked. The cabbage wrapping becomes almost crispy, and provides a tight envelop that encloses the juicy meat and rice within. The stuffing here at Zacher's is beef, only mildly seasoned so that a pungent cabbage taste is still prominent. These authentic holubsti are unfortunately ac- companied by flaked mashed potatoes and dull canned beans—both put to shame by the beautifully prepared cabbage rolls. We tried the knefla soup, which was a light chicken stock with small dumplings and a chicken dumpling soup which was similar, but with large shreds of chicken meat as well. Both had begun with a long-simmered stock, and were delicious.

Our other meal here was not so exotic as the holubsti, but was as nicely prepared, and as fresh. It was a fine country sausage dinner, similar in taste to the holubsti, but more zesty and richer.

Zacher's has a wide selection of traditional American dishes to please its regular patrons who might be scared off by too much exotica. But next time we're in North Dakota, we'll head for Zacher's hoping that Harry and Esther have made their holubsti and knefla soup again, or some of the other Ukrainian delights they told us about, like *nalys- nyky* (stuffed pancakes) or *varenky* (cabbage dumplings). It's inspiring to find so much hidden character in the food of so barren a land, even if it does have to be disguised as "pigs in blankets."

NAPOLEON

★ THE WENTZ CAFÉ
105 Main Avenue (701) 754–2613
DAILY 6 AM–1 AM

The Wentz is the popular spot for the small town of Napoleon to hold their group activities. There is an extra dining room on the side, and as North Dakota "party rooms" are few and far between, you should not be surprised if brides, graduates, and golden anniversarians stroll by as you eat.

The food at The Wentz is plain, but with a German flair that lifts it out of the boring category and into the appealing. Like many cafés, the meal's strong points are soup and dessert. The mid-section of the Wentz's meals are roast beefs, hams, chickens, and about every other standard item you can think of.

There is a wide and far more interesting selection of soups. A good choice is the cabbage-vegetable soup, which owner Maggie Wentz re- fers to as "the best." Chicken noodle, beef noodle, and bean are all good but not in the same league with a German "egg drop" soup and knefla. The egg drop has a thin egg batter drizzled into the rich stock and the knefla is a dumpling soup.

"All our pies are 100 percent pure," Maggie told us. What we think she meant is that she uses only the best ingredients and doesn't skimp on the butter, cream and eggs. Most of the pies are cream pies. The best was an egg custard with a high meringue top. Cheese pie is topped with cherries, and Maggie makes a good rhubarb in season.

OHIO

BRYAN

★ LESTER'S DINER
S. Main & E. Maple (419) 636–1818
ALWAYS OPEN

Lester's claims to serve the largest cup of coffee in the Midwest. We've certainly found none larger than the 14-ounce china behemoth you get here, brimming to the top with serviceable, if slightly weak, coffee. The "joe" doesn't pack a caffeine wallop, but the cup itself is an eye-opener, heavy enough to give your coffee mitt a good morning workout. As of autumn 1977 the cup sells for 30¢ and includes all the refills you want, as long as you occupy your place.

In fact, you might want to stake out a booth at Lester's some morning. It oozes "character" of the sort that long-lived all-night diners develop after years of serving a regular clientele of truckers and local folks. It's a stainless-steel job, not very pretty inside with its phony wood and lime-green paint. But the morning we sat in a booth and drank about 128 ounces of coffee, the joint was jumping. The waitresses are unbelievably fast and provide the kind of on-their-toes service that diners used to be famous for. They are quick with the coffee refills, one-line comebacks, and even a little house gossip: "The third waitress shift (9:30 PM–6 AM) all used to be huge, this big around," our waitress confided. "Now they're just basically ugly."

Breakfasts (served round the clock) are cheap, fast and as good as a basic midwestern egg cuisine can be. Our waitress used glowing terms to describe Lester's homemade pies and lunch specials of chicken à la king on homemade biscuits. Though we were too coffeed-up to give them a try, there's no doubt we'll return to this animated haven for truckers and coffee hounds.

CINCINNATI

★★ "CINCINNATI CHILI"
—EMPRESS, SKYLINE, & GOLD STAR CHILI PARLORS
all over Cincinnati
MOST PARLORS OPEN MON–FRI 10 AM–12 MIDNIGHT / LATER ON
WEEKENDS

Cincinnati is an olfactory wonderland. It smells of the juniper perfume of its gin factories, of cleanliness from the Ivory soap plant, of tea rings and gugelhupfs from the myriad German bake shops. Best of all are the chili parlors on practically every corner—the Empress, Skyline, and Gold Star chains, each serving Cincinnati's particular form of chili: "5-Way." In every parlor the ritual is the same. A large oval plate is first covered with spaghetti noodles, then ladled with beans, then topped with meat, then with onions, then with grated Cheddar cheese. It is all layered onto a plate, and patted into a mound by the hopefully clean hands of the youthful parlor people. The onions are sweet, the cheese faintly nutty, and the meat seems flavored with nutmeg, all of which results in a mild blend of tastes and an at-first disconcerting variety of textures. The final result costs about a dollar, or slightly less if you get your chili three- or four-way, that is, lacking one or two ingredients.

All the Cincinnati parlors look alike, functional, modern, clean. And to our taste, their product is virtually identical, although Queen City connoisseurs manage to find subtle variations of freshness and flavor from parlor to parlor and from one time of day to another. We just pull into the first one we see, happy to be in Cincinnati, the food mecca of the Midwest, enjoying its unique style of chili.

COLUMBIA STATION

★ THE FOUR KEYS
Route 82 (Strongville exit off Interstate 80) (216) 236–8000
MON–FRI 7 AM–7 PM / SAT 7 AM–3 PM / CLOSED SUN

The shopping center may not have been invented in Ohio, but it has certainly attained its ultimate form in the northern part of the state. We are overjoyed whenever we find a business establishment anywhere near I-80 that stands alone. The Four Keys is such a place—a tiny white restaurant by the side of the road with a hand-painted sign of four skeleton keys on the window. Inside there is a counter, a few tables, lacy, white curtains, and a woman named Pat Anderson. Pat has a stove in the back of The Four Keys, and every morning she makes meat loaf. We are not ones to readily rave about the wonders of a good meat loaf, believing that there is only so much that can be done with the basic breadcrumb and meat configuration that finds its apotheosis in Pennsylvania. But here along Ohio's Route 80, a real meat loaf made by a real person in a real café is like an oasis of water, grass, and trees in a bleached desert. Pat's meat loaf dinner is accompanied by creamy cole slaw shredded from Ohio cabbage, and big crisp hunks of oven-browned potatoes. She is one of three farm ladies who work at The Four Keys. All wear clean white aprons, hair nets, and comfortable shoes. On Saturday the ladies make pork roasts and excellent meringue pies for dessert.

The Four Keys is an ideal place to stop for the traveler who is hungry for human contact, and a modest homey meal besides.

DELTA

★THE BARN RESTAURANT
Route 20A (Exit 3 off Ohio Turnpike) (419) 822–5525
MON–FRI 6 AM–8 PM

The motto of The Barn Restaurant, as announced on a sign above the cash register, is "New pork is second only to sex." Monday, Thursday, and Friday the Delta auction grounds right next to this restaurant hold pig auctions, and on the remaining days they have chicken sales. Between auction lots or after the sales, the farmers sit sipping ice tea or coffee and talking about hogs, crops, tractors, and the weather as a radio drones hog futures in the background.

The restaurant is actually built as an annex to one of the Delta barns. It is a friendly place. The men who relax here are hardworking farmers who might give you a curious glance as you enter, but then resume their conversations with no further ado. The food at The Barn suits its customers—beef and pork, with no frills.

The most popular way to eat the meat is in a "wet beef" sandwich. It's pot roast, very tender, put between white bread slices with heavy gravy and mashed potatoes ladled on top. Pork steak seemed to be one of the local favorites, and being only second to sex in the minds of the hog farmers, we assume it's pretty good. It looked like slices of fresh ham, with a thin, natural gravy.

Pies are bought raw and baked on the premises, so we passed them up for what most of the farmers were eating, rainbow sherbet. What we did eat here was good, but for The Barn to be ideal, a vegetable farmer would have to open a stand next door, and a Mennonite pie place would have to be just down the road. These items—along with The Barn's beef, sherbet, and ambiance—would add up to a perfect meal.

LAFAYETTE

★★THE RED BRICK TAVERN
Route 40 (614) 852–1474
DAILY LUNCH & DINNER / SUN 11 AM–8 PM

The Red Brick Tavern is an ivy-trellised beauty built in 1837, when what is now Route 40 (parallel to Route 70) was the stagecoach route through Indiana and Ohio. Five presidents have slept here, and before or after your meal, you can take a tour upstairs to see the old wood-plank floors and simply displayed antiques. There are no tour guides or roped-off areas. Guests are free to wander informally and linger as long as they wish to soak up a sense of the past. This casual atmosphere is reflected in the meals, which are invitingly inexpensive and classically American.

Lunch at The Red Brick Tavern begins with a bing cherry salad, a wedge of cantaloupe, or tomato soup made from the meat of The Red Brick's home-grown tomatoes. There are hot cinnamon rolls and apple butter, a cucumber salad seasoned with onion, or a dish of pickled beets and onions. From among the main courses we chose creamed chicken in a fresh-baked patty shell, and roast pork with bread stuffing. For desert, we chose key lime pie, a displaced but well-made Florida specialty, and a slice of frosted coconut cake.

There is a certain amount of self-congratulation in The Red Brick's management. They know they have a good thing here, and aren't hesitant to tell you how wonderful it is. That was fine with us, because we were being self-congratulatory too, patting ourselves on the back for finding good food in an historical and beautiful old brick tavern for less money than we would have paid in the all-night rest area only a few miles away on I-70.

REYNOLDSBURG

★JEAN'S COFFEE SHOP
Main Street (Route 40) (614) 866–4080
MON–FRI 6 AM–8 PM / SAT & SUN 6 AM–4 PM

Jean's is a pleasant little café in the town that claims to have invented the tomato. Banners all over town proclaimed this fact the day we were here, and while we didn't stay long enough to find out exactly what famous citizen of Reynoldsburg was the inventor, and on what date the tomato emerged from his laboratory, we did enjoy a very nice meal at Jean's—oddly enough, without tomatoes. Jean's was recommended to us by the woman who runs the health food store next to the café. She said that they used her cheese and produce in their food, and we welcomed the thought of a fresh, light meal.

Our lunch began, unfortunately, with a plate of pygmy chicken parts that were still frozen near what used to be the bird's bone. Fortunately, we had also ordered a chef's salad which was everything the health food lady had promised—lots of good cheese, thick-sliced ham, and fresh garden produce, served with an oil and vinegar dressing made with dill seeds.

Dessert more than made up for the bogus chicken. We had chocolate peanut butter pie—a thick, intensely rich wedge that tasted like a Reese's peanut-butter-cup melted into several Hershey bars. The carrot cake was lighter—chocked with coarsely grated carrots and frosted with a spiced vanilla icing.

Jean's is daintily decorated in blue and white, with tablecloths and flowers on every table. There is a giant wiener painted on the window, and candles on the table in case you're the type who gets romantic over chocolate peanut butter pie.

SANDUSKY

★BETTY'S HOME COOKING
325 West Market Street (419) 625–2876
MON–SAT 5 AM–4 PM / CLOSED SUN

Betty's is a block away from the ferry that shuttles Ohioans to the beach islands or Lake Erie. It is a clean restaurant, and the food is reasonably good—certainly light years ahead of the offerings on nearby

Route 80. Sandusky is a semi-resort town, but Betty's is a workingman's place frequented by locals. There are blue and white cabbage-rose curtains on the window and a waitress with a tattoo on her forearm.

The best item on Betty's menu was the braised shortribs. They were sweet and juicy with a good tangy sauce, but came side-ordered with a plebeian salad, soggy French fries, and too-well-preserved rolls. Down the counter another customer had wisely ordered his ribs with a plate of Betty's special onion rings, and we will too next time around. They were models of what a good onion ring should look like—just barely breaded, rough and oily.

Betty's major shortcoming is dessert. She seemed proud of her pies and cakes, but we found them to be bitter-tasting when fruit-filled and mealy when they were custard.

Betty's is a sure bet for a good breakfast, for her hash browns were delicious. They tasted more of butter than grease, and were a perfect variety of textures, from crispy outside to a soft potato smoothness within. It's a popular café during high noon and between 7 and 8 A.M., and you could find it hard to get a table; so it's best to come here on a slightly off-hour.

SPRING VALLEY

★MOM'S KOUNTRY KITCHEN
Route 42 (513) 862–9140
MON–SAT 6 AM–7 PM / SUN 9 AM–7 PM

The Kountry Kitchen looks like a small truckstop from the outside, and it is located next to a service station, but don't be misled by these outward signs of greasy spoonism. There are two "moms" here who make some of the best home-cooked food north of Cincinnati. First, there's Mrs. Evans, who makes the pan-fried chicken and pork roasts and stuffing on Sunday. She makes homemade noodles to accompany the chicken, and a special cracked black pepper dressing for the salads. Dorothy Smith makes the salads, which are bowls of freshly picked lettuce, radishes, bell peppers, cucumbers, tomatoes, parsley, and dill. Dorothy also makes pies, and her specialty is apple dumplings. These are big, cored and peeled apples baked into a pie crust and served swimming in sweet natural syrup. Her other pies include raisin, peach glaze, pumpkin cream, and peanut butter.

During the week, breakfast is the big meal at Mom's, and the favorite is biscuits and country gravy, although Mrs. Evans complains that the more she makes, the more they eat, and so they usually run out of biscuits by 10 A.M. The clientele is mostly local people who know enough to get there in time for the goodies, and for whom Dixie Shepherd, the manager, has set up a permanent hat rack on one wall. Although traveling people do come to Mom's, especially on Sunday for the chicken and noodle dinner, it has the atmosphere of a local place. You are served at large communal picnic-style tables, and chances are that if it's not busy, one mom or another will sit down and strike up a conversation with you or some of the regulars. Mom's is in a beautiful part of Ohio, near the state's oldest village, now being turned into "Caesar's Creek Pioneer Village." We have no idea what Caesar's Creek will be like in its finished form, but Dixie Shepherd promised us that Mom's Kitchen will stay the way it is, producing simple and delicious food.

YELLOW SPRINGS

★★ YOUNG'S JERSEY MILK FARM
Route 68 (north) (513) 325–0629
ALWAYS OPEN

Young's is an idyllic place outside the town of Yellow Springs. The town is best known for its Antioch College, alma mater to avant-garde carpenters, neorevolutionary potters, and angry young vegetarians. Collegians and townies alike have made Young's into a Yellow Springs institution, coming here for dairy-fresh milk shakes, bakery goods, and sandwiches. Young's is a working farm. Cows moo and wander only yards from the food store, and tree stumps and a few benches are provided for sitting and watching Bossie and Elmer as you drink your milk shake.

Young's is not only for dairy goods. There is a twenty-four-hour deli here, a great service for college students and midnight wanderers on the highway. Dessert can be selected from among the ice creams or an assortment of doughnuts and sweet rolls. The apple fritters are heavy, sweet, and deliciously apple-laden.

Young's also sells unusual native products like sorghum molasses, corn cob honey and Racoon Mountain blueberry syrup. The best thing at Young's—and unfortunately the least easily eaten by travelers—is the slab butter, sold in irregularly shaped packages. It tastes totally unlike anything purchased in a supermarket. Combined with a hot loaf of fresh bread from the bakery, it is the basis of a sublime picnic.

It is the milk shakes for which Young's is most famous—regular or "extra thick." There are twenty different flavors, from black walnut to chocolate revel, but our favorite here is the absolutely pure vanilla— as thick and creamy as any we've tasted. It is somehow even more delicious when sipped outdoors, where on one of Young's benches, you can watch the cows, busy producing more of what you are enjoying.

YOUNGSTOWN

★THE RANCH HOUSE TRUCK STOP
Interstate 80 (Exit 46 South) (216) 544-2244
ALWAYS OPEN

The Ranch House is the name of the dining area at this big Union 76 truckstop. For some strange reason—perhaps in celebration of the trucker-cowboy mystique—this midwestern truckstop is fashioned after an old-west ranch, with rough wood walls, horsehead patterns on the curtains, and displays of barbed wire for decor. All this, and the truckers who eat here, makes for a rough-and-trucky macho decor: tough, but not intimidating.

Most all of the food served here is freshly prepared by truckstop cooks who don't believe in boiling pouches or reconstituted turkey loaves. Roast beef, turkeys, and hams are all oven-cooked, and come as dinners or as hot sandwiches. Even the vegetables here can be good. We have had blue lake beans that still had a snap to them, expertly prepared crispy hash brown potatoes, and molded jello salads with good-quality fruit ingredients. On Friday, *fresh* haddock is offered—almost unheard of in a large truckstop.

The Ranch House is no culinary giant. Nothing served here is exotically seasoned or on the avant garde of culinary experimentation. But on the Pennsylvania-Ohio border, a decent plate of beans, a rare slice of roast beef, or a fluffy breakfast biscuit can be a pleasant oasis for the highway traveler.

FAIRS AND FESTIVALS

BUCKEYE LAKE
Millersport Sweet Corn Festival / LATE AUGUST
Corn-eating contests

BUCYRUS
Bratwurst Festival / MID-AUGUST
All the Bratwurst you can eat

BURTON
Apple Butter Festival / MID-OCTOBER
Cauldrons of apple butter, apple syrup; fritters, bread bake-offs

CHARDON
Maple Festival / MID-APRIL
Rooster-crowing contest, pancake eating

CIRCLEVILLE
Circleville Pumpkin Show / MID-OCTOBER
Pumpkin taffy, waffles, pies, cookies, bread, ice cream, pumpkin burgers

GENEVA
Grape Jamboree / LATE SEPTEMBER
Wine, jellies, jams, juice, preserves, pies

JACKSON
Apple Festival / LATE SEPTEMBER
Apple-butter making, food, cider

LEBANON
Ohio Honey Festival / MID-SEPTEMBER

MIDDLEFIELD
Swiss Cheese Festival / MID-JUNE

MILAN
Milan Melon Festival / LATE AUGUST–EARLY SEPTEMBER

REYNOLDSBURG
Tomato Festival / EARLY SEPTEMBER

RIO GRANDE
International Chicken Flying Meet / MID-OCTOBER
Apple butter, cider; butter churning, chicken cooking

SUGAR CREEK
Ohio Swiss Festival / LATE SEPTEMBER
Yodeling contest, lots of Swiss food

SOUTH DAKOTA

ABERDEEN

★ DEFORREST STARLITE CAFÉ
junction of Routes 12 & 281 West (605) 225–5913
ALWAYS OPEN

The DeForrest Café earns special accolades for trying so hard in a land where there is no competition to keep it on its toes. There is a sense when you stop here that your arrival is an event—like the arrival of a stagecoach at a remote watering hole. The waitresses are enthusiastic, friendly, and used to customers who come in for conversation as well as food. We had just enjoyed two dinners of sweet and sour pork and beef stroganoff, when we asked our waitress about the other specialities of the house. She proudly recited virtually the whole menu, declaring that "At least 75 percent is homemade, and I mean from scratch, and great tasting!"

If our dinners were any indication, she was close to the mark in her figures. Our stroganoff was laced with a rich sauce which seemed to be made from real sour cream—not from a can of soup! The sweet and sour pork, while clearly cut from an actual roast, was a bit too heavy on the "sweet" for our taste. The potatoes that came with these dishes were part of the 25 percent of the Starlite food that is commercially prepared, as were the lifeless vegetables. But dessert of two pieces of white cake was freshly baked, with a coconut-flake vanilla icing.

Our waitress told us about the Wednesday night special, which is all the broasted (pressure-fried) chicken you can eat; and about Friday, when it's all the fish you can eat. We're skeptical about fish in this landlocked state, and assume that it is frozen rather than fresh from Lake Sakakawea. But we'd bet on the other meals served here. They're not for the gourmet, but then any gourmet who finds himself in Aberdeen would be very happy, we suspect, to find that the kitchen here is actually run by a chef, and that the Deforrest does its best to make eating a pleasure beyond simple necessity.

EDGEMONT

★ THE STOCKMAN'S CAFÉ
5062 Edgemont (605) 662–7221
ALWAYS OPEN

If you ask Ada Creighton, waitress at the Stockman's Café, "How's the food here?" be prepared for a meticulous description. She is the opposite of those "secret ceremony" chefs who would rather die than give up a recipe. Ada might laud the Stockman's pork chops, for instance, that come sided with a savory stuffing. They are cooked vertically in the pan, with the stuffing between them, so the juices from the chops flow into the breadcrumb mixture. Another dish Ada touts is the beef sauté, a sort of stroganoff without the sour cream, thick and dark, served with homemade noodles. On winter days Ada pushes the soups —vegetable, noodle, or potato—all rich enough to brace a customer against the frigid South Dakota weather.

The best dish here is the Stockman's banana cake with maple icing. Although it is not on the menu every day, it is almost worth reserving a stool and waiting for it. It is moist and crumbly, perfectly counterpointed by the maple icing. When banana cake is not available, there are homemade puddings and another favorite, custard pie.

HURON

★ HAROLD'S CAFÉ
225 Lincoln (US 14) (605) 352–2301
DAILY 11 AM–10 PM

Harold's is a funny little place, a squat building in the middle of a large parking lot on the outskirts of town. It was once a drive-in restaurant with carhops, which explains the expansive parking lot. It is now a locally popular café that specializes in fast service and home cooking.

Harold's wife and some local ladies work the kitchen. They prepare jello salads with grated carrots and pineapples, other salads with chopped vegetables, and their own potato salad. Dinners come with a choice of salads, jello or cottage cheese. The specialty here is broasted chicken—a bird cooked under pressure, a process that keeps it juicy and gives it a crisp crust. There are also sandwiches, and hot plates of beef, ham or steak. Soups are made here and are hearty, but not inspired.

The best reason to stop at Harold's is the pies. In addition to the common fruit and cream varieties, there is peanut butter pie, sour cream raisin, and a chocolate meringue. South Dakotans take their pie-making seriously, and it shows at Harold's, one of the best pie stops in the state.

REDFIELD

★ MARSH'S 66 CAFÉ
Routes 212 & 281 (605) 492–9953
MON–FRI 6 AM–10 PM, SAT 6 AM–2 PM, SUN 7 AM–10 PM

Marsh's gas station café lists Graveyard Stew on its menu. This is South Dakota slang for milk toast—ghoulishly nicknamed because of its popularity with the old or sick. Graveyard Stew is just one selection on an extensive breakfast menu, whose other listings are more prosaic, from eggs, toast, and coffee to chipped beef, scrambled eggs, hash browns and muffins.

The menu clearly identifies which items are homemade, and which come from a can. The best dish is Marsh Haakinson's chicken and homemade noodles. The noodles are broad and eccentrically shaped, made from eggy dough rolled thin and hand-cut. The dish is oddly enough not often listed on the printed menu. It is a word-of-mouth specialty.

We first learned of Marsh's from an Oklahoma trucker who swears that the cooks at this small café are the only people between Tulsa and South Dakota who can make a decent chicken-fried steak. It is available at Marsh's for breakfast, lunch, and dinner, with hash browns and two cups of coffee for the price of one.

Marsh also makes cookies, rolls, and doughnuts. The delicate Scandinavian-style sugar cookies were our favorite. The chicken-fry fan from Oklahoma told us that he always takes bags of them with him when he fills up his thermos at Marsh's.

SIOUX FALLS

★★STOCKYARDS CAFÉ

808 East Rice (605) 338–6391
MON–SAT 6 AM–10 PM, CLOSED SUN

There is something especially delicious about a first-class steak when it is eaten in the company of cattlemen. It is reassuring. You know these guys aren't going to settle for anything less than the best. So when we sat down in the Stockyards Café, we went all the way and ordered two T-bone steaks, thirty ounces each. The steaks had been cut in the Café's butcher shop, behind the kitchen. They came to our table a full two inches thick, the darkest mahogany-brown on the outside, tender but juicily resistant within. Each steak came with a cup of juice, salad and a baked potato of normal size that looked comically dwarfed by the T-bone. Dessert was a scoop of ice cream. The steak obviously takes center stage here, as well it might—you can practically hear the cattle mooing across the street from the stockyards. Our thirty-ouncers were the top of the line and there was a full selection of more normally proportioned steaks, for more normally apportioned appetites.

We were here for an early dinner, and our company seemed to be a mixed group—all associated with meat. There were the ranchers in jeans and boots who had just sold a lot of livestock across the street; there were a few truckers who had just dropped off a load of cattle; there were casually dressed workers from the nearby meat-packing plant; and there were what our waitress called "the fur coat crowd," who had dressed up and come to this plain cement building for the best steak in town.

Dinners are strictly steaks and chops. "They won't eat chicken," our waitress said of the evening crowd. But at noon, the specials include baked chicken with homemade dressing, along with goulash, bar b qued beef ribs, and braised short ribs with horseradish sauce. The noontime eaters, our waitress said, were mostly workers on lunch hour and cattle-men from across the street with only a short while to spare, so service is fast. Our evening meal was enjoyed on the same Formica tables, but at a leisurely pace, with bottles of beer to accompany the steaks. There was still time afterwards to take a stroll across the street to see the beefy animals that were destined to become Sioux Falls' best steaks in the back of The Stockyards Café.

FAIRS AND FESTIVALS

GARY

Buffalo Supper   /   LATE OCTOBER
Buffalo dinners

HAYTI

Farkleberry Festival
FOR DATE, CONTACT: South Dakota Dept. of Economics and Tourism, 423 El Capitol, Pierre, South Dakota 57501

LEOLA

Rhubarb Festival   /   EARLY JUNE
Cooking contests; all products from rhubarb

MITCHELL

Corn Palace Festival   /   LATE SEPTEMBER

WISCONSIN

BARABOO

★★★THE MAIN CAFÉ

Fourth Avenue and Broadway (608) 356-9911
MON–FRI 5:30 AM–4 PM / SAT 5:30 AM–2 PM

"I can honestly say that all our vegetables and fruits are fresh because we grow them ourselves on our farm," spoke Donald Helmbrecht, retired truckdriver and co-owner of this small café in Baraboo. As he talked, his wife Ann, everyone's dream of a solid midwestern farmwife, came from the kitchen, her steel-gray hair wrapped in neat braids circling her head. "We aren't what you would call a *good* restaurant, and we don't serve fancy food, but it's what we folks like to eat —plain and freshly made."

The owners of The Main have been serving this same good food since 1950, and they operate out of a building that was around for decades before that. It has a historical marker on the outside, but don't get the idea that The Main Café is at all self-conscious about its famous past. It's still a workman's coffee spot; farmers, truckers, and high school kids fill the high-backed battleship-gray wood booths.

Ann does all the cooking with the help of another farm wife who was selected because her cooking was almost identical to Ann's. The daily lunches always start with vegetable soup made from the Helmbrecht's own crops, simmered with a large knucklebone in the stockpot. The entrées are simple beef and pork roasts, always accompanied by Helmbrecht's garden vegetables. Ann favors green beans and kohlrabi, but she reeled off the names of ten others that are regularly served here.

"I love to bake, and we buy forty dozen eggs a week from Jake here." Ann motioned to an overalled farmer straddling a counter stool. Jake, we learned, is the local chicken farmer, and his grade A eggs are the main ingredient in Ann's pies. "I make my own mince meat in the fall and winter, and of course we grow lots of squash and pumpkins so we make those kinds, but I think my best pies are the French apple and raisin, and the raspberry cream." Ann was out of the raspberry cream pie, but she offered us a peanut butter cream and the apple and raisin. The peanut butter pie was fluffy and pungent with good quality peanut butter. The French apple and raisin pie was compact with apples and raisins in a flaky crust. With a cup of good coffee it was perfect.

"I remember when I was still trucking," Don told us. "I would have given anything to stop at a place with cooking as good as we have here." Judging by the number of local and long-haul truckers who stop here in Baraboo to eat at The Main, Ann's cooking is his long-awaited dream come true.

ELLSWORTH

★★THE ELLSWORTH CAFÉ
West Main Street (715) 273–4208
MON–SAT 6 AM–7:30 PM / SUN 7 AM–11 AM

The Ellsworth has a fading black and white sign outside that says either "eat" or "meat." It is too far faded to tell. Either way, it fits. The Ellsworth is the only café in this small town, and the menu is always a choice of beef or pork roasts. The interior is clean and attractive, with tall old-fashioned booths and a black-and-white tile flooring. The kitchen is visible from the counter seats, and we saw two white-aproned women preparing vegetables and putting the frosting on a cake.

We began lunch with a bowl of chicken noodle soup. The noodles had been hand-cut, and the soup's stock was deliciously flecked with tiny giblets. The roast beef platter came with plainly cooked beef, and a farmer-sized order of creamy, scalloped potatoes. There was a side dish of spicy cole slaw, accented with celery seeds. A small side dish of succotash appeared to be straight from the can instead of the garden, and the bread served was a neat but unexciting stack of grocery-store white. A serving of graham cracker pie buoyed our spirits. Sweet and rich with a toasted meringue top, the pie was the work of an experienced cook.

Except for the vegetables and bread, The Ellsworth meal was a good one. We find it difficult to be charmed by plain roast beef; but to midwesterners it seems to be a never-ending source of eating pleasure. We would rather return to The Ellsworth just for the chicken soup and graham cracker pie.

The Ellsworth seems to be the local Sardi's. Patrons who received phone calls as they ate were paged loudly by the cooks. We weren't sure if this is as much a status symbol in Ellsworth as it is in New York City, but the overalled farmers did seem to strut proudly to the old, black wall phone whenever the call was for them.

MAUSTON

★ MA'S KITCHEN
Route 12 (west) (608) 847–4214
MON–FRI 6 AM–4:30 PM / CLOSED WEEKENDS

Ma's Kitchen is an old-fashioned greasy spoon run by a thoroughly delightful lady. The cooking at Ma's is minimal—well-done meat loaf, roast beef, and frozen fried chicken. But the atmosphere is charming, and Ma herself resembles Apple Annie. When we first saw her, she was wearing a white cook's hat placed at a rakish angle on her gray hair. It was not the high, puffy kind of hat, but one similar to what G.I.'s used to wear—flat and elongated. She was talking about black and tan hunting dogs with a very old man seated at the counter. The diner is filled with dog trophies, ribbons, and photographs. Ma would much rather talk about doggie obedience than cooking, and from the look of the assorted customers who trickle in, they don't come for the food either. Ma's is the gathering ground for Mauston chatterboxes. If local color is what you want, Ma's Kitchen is a great place for a cup of coffee.

If you insist on eating in Mauston—and don't like the laminated looks of nearby Jermoo's truckstop—try Ma's Swiss steak. A characterless piece of meat is put in the oven with decent tomatoes, green peppers, carrots, onions and peas and is slow-simmered. It's a pleasant dish, and Ma's proudest culinary effort.

Ma's is only a few yards from the Mauston railroad tracks, and we can't help but imagine that this tiny joint has been the gossip and gathering spot since the days streamlined locomotives used to be the flashy way to travel. The tracks are now the province of slow-moving freight trains, but at Ma's, not much seems to have changed.

MINERAL POINT

★★THE WALKER HOUSE

1 Water Street (608) 987-2000
MAY–OCT MON–FRI LUNCH & DINNER / SAT & SUN UNTIL 10 PM

The Walker House serves traditional Cornish food in a charmingly authentic setting. The perfectly maintained building is a lovely stone structure dating back to 1836. The town of Mineral Point is an old mining community where the lineage is still Cornish, and where the residents still enjoy the traditional favorites like pasties, figgyhobbin, and saffron cake. The Walker House is the only place we know of— except, perhaps, a miner's own dining table—to enjoy these traditional Cornish meals.

The pasty is a dish with humble beginnings. It was designed as a portable meal, to be taken down into the mines and heated at lunchtime on the end of the miner's shovel. Plates replace shovels at The Walker House, but everything else about the meat pie is the same. It is a mixture of steak, potatoes, onions, and chopped suet with an English pastry dough crust. It is hearty fare, especially if you order the "large pasty platter," on which you get two of the papery-crusted meat pies. Unlike the truly portable pasties served on Michigan's upper peninsula, the Walker House versions are served either topped with an odd but tasty chili sauce or, as we prefer, slit open and filled with extra butter and a little cream. Pasty platters come with hot, homemade bread and fresh-churned butter, salad, and a cup of English tea.

It is the Cornish desserts that make Walker House meals unique. A selection of our three favorites includes figgyhobbin—a rolled pastry dough filled with brown sugar and raisins, topped with whipped cream;

saffron cake—a loaf cake with raisins, currants, candied fruits, and yellow saffron spice, served with scalded milk and Damson plum preserves; and a traditional Cornish bread pudding topped with hot caramel sauce and ice cream.

The Walker House is a unique eating experience, and the building itself, as well as the town, is worth an inspection after dinner. If you want to try your own hand at making a Cornish pasty, the management provides recipes for you on the way out.

NORTH SHAWANO

★ L & L RANCH
Route 22 (715) 524–4595
ALWAYS OPEN

The L & L is a large truckstop in a small Wisconsin town. It serves the northbound gearjammers and doubles as Shawano's most popular restaurant. The heritage of the people in these parts is German, and the food at the L & L has a Bavarian flair. It is heavy on the all-you-can-eat style of service, and specializes in home-cooked daily specials like chicken and dumplings, roast chicken and dressing, and fish. The Thursday special is NOT all you can eat, but our waitress told us it was the local favorite nonetheless. It is pork hocks, sauerkraut, potato pancakes, and sausage.

We happened to come to the L & L on a Friday. Since all the fried smelts and flounder we want to eat is very little—especially when it is set out on a steam table under a heat lamp—we chose a fresh ham dinner instead. The ham was savory like new pork, and was served with vinegary sauerkraut and large, fried potato hunks. Our meal began with a strange but tasty split pea and carrot soup, and ended with a mealy strawberry shortcake.

What we liked more than the inexpensive hearty food at the L & L was the very casual tone of the place. There seemed to be a natural mingling of locals, truckers, and tourists like ourselves, with the feeling of an easy-going beer hall. You'll know the place from the outside by the immense plaster statue of a cow perched on the roof. The cow is wearing a plaid chef's hat, and lording over the entryway to the L & L.

OSSEO

★★★ THE NÖRSKE NOOK
7th and Harmony Streets (715) 597–3069
MON–SAT 5 AM–9:30 PM

The Nörske Nook is a coffee-shop café in the little Wisconsin community of Osseo, the kind of place you whiz past on the interstate, never dreaming that about a mile away are some of the world's best pies and cakes. The Nörske Nook is a completely casual place. Its rare treasures are spread out on newspapers across the counter. There is a selection of about six pies, arranged a little messily, but there's no mistaking their excellence. Not the whipped-up fancy-crested wonders that one sees in aspiring diners, they are modest in height, majestic in breadth, and topped with unmistakeably ripe fruits, or with pastry-light powder-sugar-dusted crusts, or with the lightest and most perfectly crisped meringues.

You are served your pie by blonde girls of Norwegian descent who cut each piece themselves with the kind of sweet generosity they might employ when offering a slice of mom's pie to a new boyfriend. The strawberry pie was almost pure sugared berries, barely held together within the thin crust. These were thick, fresh berries, still firm after cooking and naturally sweet. The sour cream raisin pie hardly fit on the pie plate. It was a mighty slice, but light and whipped up of Wisconsin's best dairy cream and plump raisins.

We asked Julie Johnson, our waitress, what else was served here. She pointed to several jars of saucer-sized cookies—oatmeal, date, chocolate chip, date bars, hermits, all made fresh by the Nook's cooks. What else? we asked. Honey buns, caramel rolls, and fresh apple turnovers every morning. And carrot cake—we got two slices to go. As for dinners, Julie told us, "We make pretty much American food. Except on Christmas. Then they go a little crazy and make *lutefiske* and *lefse*. It's poorman's food, but delicious."

So except for Christmas, The Nörske Nook remains a pie, cake and cookie stop, one of the best in the country. We ate the two pieces of carrot cake that night in our Minnesota motel room. They were unbelievably moist, spicy, redolent of finely shaved carrots. We dreamt about The Nörse Nook that night and occasionally still do—waking up very, very hungry.

SAUK CITY

★SWISTYLE DAIRY BAR
200 Phillips Avenue (608) 643–6332
DAILY 7:30 AM–10 PM

The Swistyle makes ice cream sodas as thick and rich as you would expect in Wisconsin, "the dairy state." It is a small sit-down, countered café where the menu is limited to ice cream, homemade doughnuts, or open-faced Wisconsin cheese sandwiches.

Locally produced Schoeps ice cream is used exclusively, and the counter lady told us as she blended the ingredients for our ice cream sodas that "We make 'em the old-fashioned way here—lots of cream." "Old-fashioned" at the Swistyle also means an ample amount of chocolate syrup is added to the cream at the bottom of the tall soda glass and stirred with a long spoon until it is well mixed before the seltzer and ice cream are added. The richly butterfatted ice cream creates a delicious soda, a heavyweight delicacy that is the pride of the Swistyle.

"Linda's doughnuts" were coming out of the oven as we sipped the sodas. They were small doughnuts, topped with carnival-colored sprinkles clinging to the warm glaze. Viola, our sturdy midwestern waitress, asked us if we wanted to try a few. The sodas were too powerfully rich to follow with doughnuts, so we opted instead for a cheese sandwich. The sandwiches are small, displayed in Saran Wrap on the counter "so that the cheese is eaten at room temperature, when it's best," Viola explained. Thin slices of rye are topped with beer kaese cheese, some with Wisconsin Cheddar. The Cheddar was bitingly strong, the result of a three-year aging process. The beer kaese was milder, with a slight undertaste of yeast. Viola explained that the Cheddar is always available, and that mapleton, Swiss, kimelkaese and several others are available in sandwiches on a rotating basis. There are small crocks of horseradish available as toppings, and an extra thick, icy buttermilk drink to order on the side.

The Swistyle sells cheese by bulk to take out or mail to your friends. The Dairy Bar is unusual because it is tourist-aimed, but still manages to seem homey and sell food that is personally prepared and inexpensive.

WESTBY

★★BORGENS CAFÉ AND BAKERY

109 S. Main Street (608) 634–3516
MON–SAT 6 AM–8:30 PM, SUN 6:30 AM–8 PM

Borgens is a clean and lively Norwegian café. There are Norwegian proverbs on the walls and festive-looking cut-out dolls in the window. The specialty is baking, a fact you notice the moment you walk into the place. On the right is a case filled with fresh loaves of bread, ten types of cookies, rolls, donuts, and *sandbakkelse* (small shells of thin shortbread). There is a help-yourself salad bar with a good-looking fruit and marshmallow ambrosia. The specialty of the house is Norwegian meatballs. These are mild, delicate and not nearly as sweet as the common variety of Scandinavian meatballs usually found warming over a can of Sterno. There is no evidence of tomato in their taste and when, in fact, we questioned the manager Jim Suhr about the dearth of ketchup on his tables, he said squarely, "If you threw ketchup on these meatballs, you'd ruin them."

The menu at Borgens isn't heavily ethnic, except during the winter when they go all out and make the traditional *lefse* and *lutefiske* specials. At other times of the year you can count on a good selection of roasts, distinctive meatballs, and a terrific array of baked cookies and desserts.

FAIRS AND FESTIVALS

ALMA CENTER
Strawberry Festival / LATE JUNE

ANTIGO
Maple Syrup and Pancake Festival / LAST SUNDAY IN MAY

EAGLE RIVER
Blueberry Festival / JULY

The Southwest

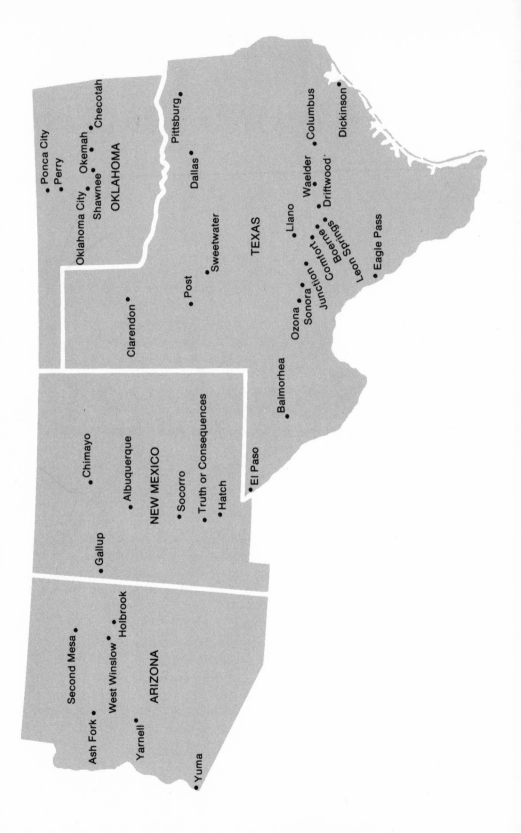

ARIZONA

ASH FORK

★★ THE ROUTE 66 CAFÉ
Route 66 W. of Ash Fork (602) 637–2298
MON–SAT 6 AM–10 PM, SUN 8 AM–8 PM

Ash Fork is a dusty, ghostly town. There are a few stores and a hotel undergoing renovation, a bus stop and a school. The Route 66 Café was the joint effort of a few local women who decided to turn this old café in this nearly forgotten town into a pleasant eatery, serving good food. We admire their efforts.

When we first visited the Route 66, one of the women was cleaning fresh beans on the back table—a good sign in arrid Arizona, where canned or frozen goods are more usual. Our meal came with fresh vegetables, a nice small salad with a heavy homemade Roquefort cheese dressing, and a side dish of cucumbers, cottage cheese and jello. Main courses are the standard offerings: pot roast, roast beef, burgers. They are simply cooked, made from good quality meat. The Route 66 specializes in Mexican food, offering red or green enchiladas, burritos, and tacos at reasonable prices. The nicest surprise of our meal was the homemade blackberry pie for dessert. The alternative was "red cantaloupe," which our waitress said was grown nearby, and was a favorite hot-weather way to end a meal.

Service at the Route 66 is a bit slow, since it also serves as the town bus stop. But the café is in an old building, full of character, and Ash Fork is a slow-paced town. It's a pleasant place to linger.

HOLBROOK

★ JOE AND AGGIE'S CAFÉ

Hopi Drive (602) 524–6540
TUES–SAT 10 AM–6 PM

Joe and Aggie's is a small storefront café in the middle of a town that makes its money on the trading of Indian crafts. It seems that every store window is arrayed with silver concho belts, turquoise bracelets, and earth-toned Navajo rugs. The streets are filled with white traders and Indians in traditional dress, or cotton shirts and blue jeans.

Joe and Aggie's is a popular place for the Indians who come off the reservation to sell their crafts. It is a good place to sit and talk, relaxed and sunlit.

The main annoyance here was a waitress who acted as if she had stayed out in the unrelenting desert sun too long. Questions on the menu's offerings were answered with her favorite word "huh?" and a vacant stare. We second-guessed our way through the menu. Here is what we found. The best item was a cheese crisp. It is a tortilla the size of a small pizza, topped with chili sauce and shredded jack cheese. It is a simple but effective combination of tastes and textures. We tried a "burro," a grandaddy to the more popular burrito. The ingredients were similar to the crisp but with the addition of a mild chopped meat filling, and a sprinkling of diced onions. Chili is allegedly Joe and Aggie's specialty. It seemed to be on every table in the place. It had a unique consistency, almost like egg drop soup but filled, instead of eggs, with ropy shreds of cheese. There were no beans, as is traditional in southwestern chili, but strangely enough, there was virtually no meat. The chili, at first, measured against standard brews, was a disappointment; but after half a bowl we started to appreciate the flavors of this strange blend.

We liked Joe and Aggie's for its unhurried ambiance and odd-ball cheese chili.

SECOND MESA

★★★HOPI CULTURAL CENTER RESTAURANT
Route 264 (At the Center of the Universe) (602) 734–2401
DAILY 7 AM–8 PM

The Hopi tribe calls their land "the center of the universe," a perspective that is easy to understand if you drive here through the primeval desert and up through the vibrant red clay rocks. There is no place in the country like this—an elemental land that looks like the first day of creation.

The Hopi Cultural Center is perched above this awesome vista. It is operated by the tribe as a showcase for Hopi craftsmen and cooks. The buildings are adobe and wood, and blend visually with the land. The restaurant is a spacious room decorated with displays of the best Hopi crafts—rugs, Kachina dolls, and jewelry.

The menu explains that food has always been sacred to the Hopi tribe. It is closely associated with their Kachina religious rituals, appreciated for its ceremonial value as well as sustenance. The *Tunosvongya* (bill of fare) lists the food according to the movement of the sun. Lunch is *Tawa'nasave* (when the sun reaches its zenith). Dinner is *Tap'kemi* (when the sun sets).

For *Tawa'nasave* be sure to try *Nokquivi,* a Hopi hominy stew served with a pocket of Indian fry bread filled with honey and a side order of baked chili peppers. The fry bread and honey comes with most lunch dishes. Here the breads are made the way they ought to be—individually, in very hot oil. The yeasty dough puffs up into a soft, chewy disc like a triple-size bialy.

Be sure to get a side order of piki bread, too. You may not like it, but this is the only restaurant we know where it is served. Made from slate-blue cornmeal, the piki bread is a strudel-thin spiral of flaky pastry, endless layers thick and so delicate it crumbles as you pick it up. It has a taste like corn-scented air, too fragile for any condiment.

The same Hopi blue cornmeal is used for breakfast pancakes. A favorite Hopi breakfast choice is piki bread and fresh canteloupe—a combination of subtle textures and tastes well suited to a meal "at the center of the universe."

There are also a number of non-Indian dishes on the menu, including ham steaks or short ribs with potatoes.

The restaurant's menu is decorated with "mudhead" Kachinas carrying baskets of food and clowning around. The mudhead, or *koyemsi,* is one of the only Kachinas who stoops down from his lofty role in the Hopi religion to communicate with humans, to make them laugh, and to provide them with food. A visit to the Hopi Cultural Center Restaurant, presided over by this knobby-headed Kachina, is a joyous experience not soon forgotten. Leave yourself half a day to imbibe the richly aesthetic culture of the ancient Hopi tribe.

WEST WINSLOW

★★ THE CASA BLANCA CAFÉ
Route 66 (1201 East Second Street) (602) 289–4191
MON–SAT 11 AM–9 PM

The Casa Blanca's customers are mostly local Indians who come from the reservation to trade. Ancient Navajo men with ribbon-tied gray braids, and young Indian families with modern clothing line the booths of this dimly lit café. The favorite song on the jukebox was "El Rancho Grande," played like a litany over and over, Freddy Fender's south-of-the-border yelps punctuating the native dialect spoken by the customers.

The food at Casa Blanca is Mexican rather then Indian. Prices are low, with a combination plates being the most popular item. If you are only able to order one item, make it the cheese and avocado crisp. Crisps are, by and large, well made all over the Southwest but at Casa Blanca they were covered by the best and sharpest cheese we sampled as well as spicy garlic and tomato-chunked avocado guacamole. Crisps may be ordered with either yellow corn or flour tortillas.

All dinners come with the airy pillows of dough known as Sopaipillas, and containers of honey are on each table for pouring into the center of these warm delights. There is also Menudo, a Mex-Indian tripe stew, and burritos, either chicken- or beef-filled.

While the Casa Blanca menu doesn't contain any dish that is not a tried and true standard, the food is excellently prepared. The native dress and striking faces of the Navajo clientele make a trip to this café an experience that goes beyond good food.

YARNELL

★★THE YARNELL SENIOR CITIZENS CHAT AND CHEW
Route 89 (602) 427–6347
WEEKDAYS: LUNCH

One gets to believe that the reason there are so many old folks in Yarnell is that it's easier to stay here and grow old gracefully than to risk your neck on the treacherous road out of town, Route 89. Whatever the reason, Yarnell is an octogenarians' paradise, and the Chat and Chew is where you'll find oldsters in the know coming for lunch every weekday.

Flora Phillips is the cook, although other senior citizens take over on her days off. She handwrites and posts the sometimes misspelled menu on the door of the YSCCC weekly. Meals are always a dollar, "except for the kids," Flora explained. "They have to pay $1.50." "Kids" are anyone under sixty.

We sat in the tiny storefront restaurant gazing through the crisp organdy curtains and at the ironed plaid tablecloths as Flora told us about the restaurant. "We use only fresh ingredients here. Nothing frozen or canned." She walked us into the kitchen and opened the oven to display a tray full of browning roast chicken, and a large pastry pan filled with a bubbling peach cobbler. Other ladies were peeling carrots, mixing the fresh greens for the salad, and grating cabbage for cole slaw. One was mixing the ingredients for a birthday cake—a regular event here.

The YSCCC menu is different every day. The week we were here it listed entrées of roast beef, baked fish, meat loaf, and meatballs in gravy, as well as the chicken dinner. There are always two vegetables, a salad, fresh-baked rolls or corn bread, and a variety of gravies. Desserts are made from different ladies' recipes every day.

"My friends who cook the days I'm off like to make muffins instead of hot rolls," Mrs. Phillips told us. "Today we have the cobbler. But it's Mrs. Harwell's birthday, so all lunch guests will be offered a piece of cake, too; and we sing Happy Birthday . . . loud, because she is hard of hearing."

The YSCCC is as charming as only a kitchen full of white-haired grannies could be. It is a lively, spirited place. Meals are served by teen-age girls who help out, and the seniors linger in the Arizona sunlight streaming in the windows until well after the 1:00 P.M. closing hour. Even if you're a "kid" under sixty, you'll probably be invited to join in the birthday celebrations and have a piece of cake.

YUMA

★★ OLD WESTERN BAR B QUE
2400 East 16th Street (Highway 95) (602) 783–2671
TUES–SAT 11 AM–8 PM / CLOSED MON / CLOSED AT 3 PM JULY AND AUGUST

The decor of the Old Western Bar B Que is as bleak as the desert that surrounds it. The inside of the café is painted a coral-pink, sparse except for two velvet paintings of "noble-looking Indians." The atmosphere is almost like an operating theater, immaculately clean, almost sterile, and so strongly air-conditioned that the shock of walking inside out of the 100 degree-plus Yuma heat is practically paralyzing.

The Old Western is famous for its Smokey Pig Platter. Oddly, it is also the cheapest thing on the menu. A Smokey Pig Platter is made up of the cut-off, slightly charred end tips of the ribs. The "brownies" taste like pure essence of bar b que; they have the wondrous ability to absorb maximum amounts of hickory smoke, and sauce. The Smokey Pig Platter comes like the other plate lunches on the menu with delicately shredded cole slaw, and bar b que-sauced pinto beans. Beer, Pepsi, and even ice water are served in iced glasses—a nice touch for a tiny restaurant with minimal luxuries.

All of the Old Western's bar b que is best accented by a wash of hot sauce made by the cook. It is a thin, amber sauce, slightly vinegary and moderately hot.

The Old Western Bar B Que is on the outskirts of town; not exactly "the wrong side of the tracks," but we did notice the customers looked tougher and more sun-weathered than in the business district. One man, a recently sprung ex-con, was lunching on Smokey Pig Platters with his parole officer. Two tables down a group of Yuma Indians were eating ribs. In the corner an old prospector was finishing his third Coors. Contrary to the hard-looking faces of the customers, the tone of the Old Western was completely unscary. We figure the harsh penetrating sunlight of the desert creates the opposite effect of a dark shadowy bar. Everyone is on his best behavior.

FAIRS AND FESTIVALS

BULLHEAD CITY
Wild Burro Bar B Que / 3RD WEEK IN MAY

CLARKSVILLE
Johnson County Peach Festival / LAST WEEKEND IN JUNE
Turtle races, bass fishing contests, and peaches

NEW MEXICO

ALBUQUERQUE

★STANDARD TRUCK PLAZA
1915 Menaul Boulevard, northeast (Intersection of Interstates 40 & 25)
(505) 247–9531
ALWAYS OPEN

The Standard Truck Plaza may look like a standard truck plaza, but the Mexican food served here is way above highway standards. It's not up to La Casita, but here at the sprawling Auto/Truck complex you will find authentic Mexican dishes freshly prepared 24 hours a day. This is a well-known stop for southwestern truckers, appreciated not only for its Mexican food, but for the reasonably priced and mostly home-cooked American dishes too. But let's skip the "Truckburgers" and T-bones and get to the chili.

At the Standard, chili is red or green. A bowl of red without beans is mild. A bowl of green without beans is made with green jalapeño peppers, and is therefore hot. But if you like it even hotter, get a bowl of "Special Green Chili Sauce." Mixed with either your red or green, the result is practically combustible. We were moaning and groaning our way through a bowl at the Standard counter one evening, and a gearjammer seated next to us inquired, "Too hot for you?"

"Naw," we said. "We can take it."

"Then it's not hot enough," he declared. "The only way to eat chili right is when it's so hot you can't stand it."

For those who do like hot food, we recommend the special sauce with any dish, from huevos rancheros in the morning to the top of the line New Mexican dinner—tacos, enchiladas, a tamale, refried beans, a lettuce and tomato salad, and green chili. Also available are enchilada plates, burrito plates and tacos.

For homesick southerners, and those unwilling to start the day with what the Standard menu too modestly calls "The Spicy Breakfast" of eggs and chili, there are also biscuits. A reliable Mississippian described them as "damn good biscuits. Not as good as back home, of course." Of course. Biscuits, like chili, are always better back home.

While having none of the magic and mystique of out-of-the-way chili parlors, the Standard Truck Plaza does very well serving good Mexican food to those who haven't the time or inclination to search for it in the back alleys of Albuquerque. And it is a life-saver when you're passing through at 4 A.M.

CHIMAYO

★★★★ RANCHO DE CHIMAYO
Route 76 (north) (505) 351–4444
TUE–SUN NOON–9 PM / CLOSED MON / CLOSED JAN

The Rancho de Chimayo is one of the loveliest Mexican restaurants in the state. It consists of three simple whitewashed rooms in Arturo Jaramillo's ranch, furnished with rough-hewn tables. The village of Chimayo is over 400 years old, situated in the green and temperate Upper Rio Grande Valley.

The food at the Rancho de Chimayo is traditional New Mexican, with a few additions dreamt up by Arturo with his native staff. We had his famous Chicken Chimayo—a parboiled and roasted chicken, covered with hot chili and grated cheese; and *carne adobada*—a large pork steak first soaked in a chili marinade, then baked in a chili sauce. Warning: both dishes are extremely hot. The chili at Rancho de Chimayo used to flavor both the bird and the chop is made from Chimayo chilies, known to southwestern chiliheads as some of the hottest and the best in the state.

Meals at Rancho de Chimayo always begin with sopaipillas, fried to feathery perfection, and served with honey. There are also freshly fried tortilla chips, perfect for dipping into guacamole, which is lightly garlicked and thick with ripe avocados. The Chicken Chimayo came with peas and a colorful tomato-flavored rice. The pork steak was served with a tomato and lettuce salad and a soothing side dish called posole, made from hominy.

Another way to try and put out the fire that Chimayo chilies start on the tongue is to try the special house drink, a Chimayo cocktail. This is a cooler made from tequila, apple cider, lemon, crème de cassis, and served with a slice of orange. It is a refresher for the taste buds, although one runs the risk of starting fires of a different sort.

In addition to the special house dishes, there is a full array of enchiladas, tacos, guacamole salads, and chilies. The Rancho's chili rellenos are unusual and worth ordering, especially for a late noon brunch. Instead of being the usual stuffed chili pods, here they are chopped chilies, melted cheese, and diced meat, stirred into an egg batter and fried like an omelette. They are served with rice and a salad.

Desserts are not usually a strong point on Mexican menus, but here they serve a simple and earthy-tasting *panocha,* a cinnamon and sugar flavored pudding, to which you can add honey for extra sweetener. There is also a *capirotada* (bread pudding), flavored with nuts, slivers of fruit, and cheese.

Service at Rancho de Chimayo is convivial, and it is a beautiful town in which to linger after a lunch or dinner. It was no surprise to learn that gourmets from all over the Southwest have been coming here for years to eat what many consider to be the best New Mexican food in the country.

GALLUP

★ GRANDMA'S DINER
1501 West 66 Avenue (Route 66, west) (505) 863–9689
MON–SAT 6:30 AM–9 PM

Gallup is a big trading town for Indian crafts, a fact unhappily reflected in the polarity of its restaurants. They are aimed at either money-bagged white traders or the very poor Indians. It is therefore very hard to get a decent meal.

Grandma's is a basic wood diner just west of town. It has squatty wood booths and a narrow counter. Most of its clientele seem to be traveling people and although the food here isn't terrific, it's less pretentious than the town's $10 steak houses, and more inviting than the bleak cafés. The only problem here is the waitress corps—a group of uncommunicative and unhelpful teenagers, who seem like they'd just as soon spend ten minutes wiping a glass as wait on a customer.

In spite of the waitresses, we managed to locate a menu and order some very good food. We sampled a hearty mutton stew. The chunks of lamb were chewy and intensely gamy, interspersed in the bowl with hominy corn and a thick spiced gravy. The stew came with a circle of Navajo fry bread—large and suitable for mopping up gravy. We also ordered an "Indian taco," which is a disc of the fry bread topped with meat, sauce, and cheese, then sprinkled with lettuce and tomato chunks. The doughy consistency of the bread makes this a much more filling dish than a Mexican taco, made on tortillas.

There is chorizo sausage on the menu—a spicy Iberian-tasting link, served with eggs for breakfast. Desserts were a bland selection of commercial pies.

Grandma's is not an especially pleasant place to eat, what with the inattentive service and roadside-diner ambiance. But the food is good; the mutton stew a special treat; and the Indian taco is itself a filling meal. The other nice thing about Grandma's is that it's on the way out of Gallup.

HATCH

★★ KEARNEY'S
302 East Hall Street (Route 85) (505) 267–9919
MON–SAT 5 AM–8 PM

We sat down and asked our waitress, "How's the chili here?" She paused for a breath, then bellowed, "IT'S THE BEST IN THE WEST!" Hatch, New Mexico, claims to be the chili capital of the state, and chili seems to be on everyone's mind in these parts. Half the cars in town sport bumper stickers advertising the annual chili festival, and when you pay your tab at Kearney's, you can purchase chili bolo ties, chili pencils, chili tie clips, and chili decals. If there's anything that comes close to loco weed in the way it drives people to extremes and eccentricities, it is the chili pepper, the state vegetable of New Mexico. The people of New Mexico are less prone to cook-offs and fiery contests like their two-fisted Texas neighbors. They're more apt to celebrate in a civilized manner. For example, by establishing organizations like the International Connoisseurs of Green and Red Chili in Las Cruces.

Kearney's is a perfect place to get a taste of Western chili and the mild mania it inspires. There are two basic varieties of chili made in the Southwest—Indian and cowboy chili. Indian style is stewlike with large hunks of meat and a laquered red color something like the sands near the Navajo reservation. Cowboy chili, as served at Kearney's, is more soupy, with finer-cubed meat, less primary in its reddish color. It is almost like a meat gravy. We were amazed to find the chili at Kearney's very mild. It is served with a side dish of jalapeño peppers, which may be spooned into the bowl to add heat. Kearney's also serves other Mexican-American dishes like enchiladas, burritos, burritos supreme, and a "famous taco basket."

This seems to be a meeting place for Hatch's chili aficionados. Their coffee cups are lined up on the wall for daily breakfasts of coffee and—no doubt—huevos rancheros (chili and eggs). We soon learned that our waitress' bellowing voice was attributable not to her pride in the chili, but to a hearing defect. Her conversations with the customers in this medium-sized café are as audible and as constant as the jukebox. "You can't bother me," she called out to one table of chili heads. "Experts have tried." She then brought around a birthday card for the customers to sign for ninety-two-year-old Mrs. Little. We signed it, figuring that even though we didn't know Mrs. Little, partaking of chili here made us part of the Kearney club, and of the community of Hatch, which calls itself "The Best Place This Side of Heaven."

SOCORRO

★★★★LA CASITA
519 Central Avenue (505) 835–0821
MON–FRI 11 AM–9 PM / SAT & SUN 11 AM–10 PM

We once spent an entire day at La Casita sampling its array of Mexican food. On the way out to the car, while we were bending over to get a roll of film, a pair of pants split down the seam. The pants had been loose-fitting when we left New York. It was time for a policy of roadfood moderation. The end of a full day of La Casita's sublime food seemed a particularly appropriate time for the new resolution—just as one might expect a man about to give up smoking to enjoy one last Havana cigar, or just as a sailor about to ship out will spend his last night on shore in a bawdy house. La Casita is Mexican food at its very best; the place to go if you are to have but one grand southwestern meal.

The cook here is Juanita Martinez, a sparrow-sized old lady who has been cooking since she was eleven years old. She loves to pamper the La Casita guests. Mamie Trujillo, La Casita's owner, loves to show off. Between Mamie's pride and Juanita's skills, diners at La Casita rarely leave without first thanking both of them for a memorable meal.

Everything starts from scratch. And the basic primal ingredient is the chili pepper pod. Mamie auditioned peppers from every part of the state before she was satisfied that Salem, New Mexico, grew the best. Juanita takes these unusually large pods and grinds them on coarse stone, creating the basis for her dark red chili. Corn is selected with the same care. Juanita has giant bags full, ready to grind for tortillas and posole—a popular corn and hominy side dish. The kernels can be bought by the pint to take home, or already kneaded into corn dough.

Mamie first invited us back into the kitchen to watch Juanita make sopaipillas. We noticed that the kitchen, like the dining area, was immaculately clean. Mamie showed us a letter written on the back of an A-plus health department rating certificate. The inspector told Mamie personally that La Casita was, in his opinion, "the cleanest restaurant in all of New Mexico."

But the cleanliness did not intoxicate us the way the sopaipillas did. It looks so *easy* the way Juanita does it. Small rectangles of dough are rolled paper thin under her dowel, then cut faster than the eye can follow into the proper shape. The shapes are then tossed into a kettle of hot oil where in seconds they puff up into cloud-light pillows of dough. These sopaipillas are eaten hot with honey. They are a standard item of southwestern menus. We have had none to compete in tender lightness with Juanita's.

Sopaipillas usually come like bread at the beginning of a meal. The La Casita Special consists of a rolled enchilada, a taco, a tamale, sopa de arroz (dry rice soup), frijoles refrito (refried beans), chili rellenos (a large bean- and cheese-stuffed hot pepper), a choice of red or green chili, a La Casita salad, and a beverage. Beer and wine are available.

Juanita laughed kindly at our overawed praise of her skills. "After forty years in the kitchen it is easy to know how to do things the right way," was her explanation.

TRUTH OR CONSEQUENCES

★THE DONUT SHOP
107 North Foch Street (Business 25) (505) 894–2408
MON–SAT 5:30 AM–4:30 PM / CLOSED SUN

One has to wonder what kind of town would choose to name itself
after Ralph Edwards' semisadistic game show. What kind of food might
be found in a town that seeks its identity with TV pies in the face and
public humiliation? Residents of the town tell you that the name was
changed to give the place an identity separate from the other arid
towns in the state. The ploy was successful, and most people know this
strange community more for its name than for its natural resource—the
nearby mineral baths.

To us, Truth or Consequences will be remembered for something
else: it serves the mildest chili in the West. This false-alarm chili, guaranteed to set no fires to the tongue, is the specialty of The Donut Shop.
It is brewed out of respect for the old people of the town, those who
come here for the climate and the mineral water, and who can be seen
gathered around chess boards in the sun across the street from The
Donut Shop.

The chili is just like regular Southwestern chili, but without the
peppers. There are no beans ("These people can't eat beans," the chili
cook sympathetically told us). Ground chuck meat is simmered with
cumin and the binding agent called masa harina. The finished product
is mild but tasty, like a hamburger soup.

The shop used to be part of the Spudnut chain, and the owner still
makes donuts from the potato flour recipe. These taste just a little
heavier than regular donuts, and are made fresh every morning. There
are good hash browns with breakfast, too.

We watched one old man after another cane his way across Foch
Street for a bowl of tame chili. We salute The Donut Shop for keeping
Truth or Consequences' natives healthy and chili-fortified long into
their golden years.

FAIRS AND FESTIVALS

HATCH
Hatch Valley Chili Festival / EARLY SEPTEMBER
Cook-off sponsored by International Connoisseurs of Green
and Red Chili

HILLSBORO
Apple Festival / EARLY SEPT

SAN ILDEFONSO PUEBLO; SANTA FE
Corn Dance / EARLY SEPTEMBER

OKLAHOMA

CHECOTAH

★PENNY'S COZY GRILL AND HOMEMADE TAMALES
Business 69
DAILY 7 AM–4 PM

It is traditional for western towns to crown a tamale king. Some are rumored to cruise the streets selling hot tamales from their Cadillacs; others sell them from carts or tiny storefronts. Penny is the Tamale Queen of Checotah. She sells her hot T's from a traveling wagon and from a tiny café. We recommend buying them from the wagon if it happens to cruise past you while you're in Checotah. The same tamales are sold in the café, but inside there is a temptation to order something else. Do not! Penny makes no-nonsense tamales, but we once made the mistake of branching out to a grilled "honey bun," an unhappy descent into floury indigestion.

Penny's Cozy Grill does have its charms. Aside from the honey buns and an untested beef stew, her menu is simply several ways to eat tamales and chili. A "three spread" is three tamales spread with chili; a "six spread" is six of the same, at a 50% higher price. Individual tamales are also sold without chili.

What is nice about Penny's is the ambiance—a powerful dose of small-town Oklahoma funk, watched over by Penny herself, a young blonde with Indian cheekbones who is a ringer for Mary Hartman's old friend Loretta Haggers. Her clientele is a small band of regulars. We were sitting at one of the two tables in the six-by-six room, when an old farmer in overalls came in, looked us over, sat at the counter and noted matter-of-factly, "They got the good seats." We offered the "geezer" his favorite seat back, and he gladly accepted. We ate a heartburn-bound three-spread with him, and decided that while Penny's is an authentic slice of Checotah life, her hot tamales just may be a little too hot and hoary for all but the most adventuresome travelers.

OKEMAH

★THE OKEMAH CAFETERIA
Route 27 (Broadway) (918) 623–0661
MON–FRI 2 AM–8 PM, SAT & SUN 2 AM–2 PM

The Okemah is worth a mention because it is a friendly place that serves decent meals at hours when all surrounding restaurants are closed. The specialty at The Okemah is chicken, served in every imaginable way, and using just about every part of the bird but the cackle. Platters of white meat, dark meat, legs, breasts, gizzards, livers, you-name-it are available, including homemade slabs of warm corn bread and French fries. There is a "poor-folks" special of gizzards, neckbones, and corn bread too.

Between 2 a.m. and 10 a.m. there is table service, but by 10:30 a.m. the steam table is set up, and the restaurant works cafeteria-style. Breakfasts are fresh doughnuts, powder-topped biscuits, and corn bread and eggs. The morning baked goods fare better than the cakes and pastries, which come off too dry and lacking in filling or frostings.

The Okemah is a large, noisy place which is comfortable to eat in and cordial to out-of-towners. This is an attitude that unfortunately isn't shared by the townies of this small burg who wile away the hours hot-rodding up and down Main Street cat-calling at unfamiliar faces, and throwing half-empty beer cans at moving targets called tourists. We pity the poor traveler who eats elsewhere than The Okemah. We suggest you notify your next-of-kin first. While not the best chicken in the state, this tiny café-cafeteria provides a safe harbor.

OKLAHOMA CITY

★THE RICKSHA DRIVE IN (UNCLE RALPH'S)
7301 Northeast Expressway (Route 35, north) (405) 478–1252
SUN–THURS 10 AM–1 AM, FRI & SAT 10 AM–2 AM

The Ricksha is a confusingly situated drive-in sharing a concrete truck parking lot with the Pro-Am Truck Terminal. People often pull into the Pro-Am looking for The Ricksha and vice-versa, but once inside The Ricksha there is no doubt you are at the home of the only oriental-cowboy bar b que pit in Oklahoma.

Long ago a pitmaster named Uncle Ralph started the original bar b que pit at this location. When he died six years later, someone got the bright idea to turn it into a Chinese restaurant. But the truckers who had been Uncle Ralph's supporters wouldn't let the ribs give way to chow mein, so The Ricksha adjusted its menu and now serves Chinese-style spareribs with jalapeño hot sauce. It is not likely that the Ricksha ribs would please a bar b que purist since they are fibrous and dry. They are served in trucker-sized portions and bathed with an insanely hot sauce that seems to be a pure blend of ketchup and cayenne pepper. The ribs, like the "jalapaño ham sandwich," come with cottony bread good for tamping down the low-grade burns on the tongue after a run-in with the fire-brew hot sauce.

There is an aura about The Ricksha which is perhaps even more appealing than the food. It is a hot, grimy, country-western mood that practically wails all the clichés associated with this genre: Heartbreak, Mom, The Open Road, Prison, Drinkin' and Fightin'. Our waitress, who used all her tips to keep the jukebox going, likes Saturday night the best. "That's when there's dancing, and drinking, and all the *good* stuff," she said. The weekends are for those Roadfooders braver than us. We like The Ricksha during the days when it is a sleepy, perhaps hung-over atmosphere with Dolly Parton playing softly on the jukebox, and plenty of room at the long wooden tables to eat your ribs. The benches and tables are there, according to the waitress, "Because it's harder to fling a bench around then a chair." Daytime is safe; in fact it's family time. Next table to us was a truck-driving man and wife with their four-old-year child. Mama was offering junior small pieces of bread dipped in hot sauce and jalapeño peppers. We assume by the time the child is old enough to steer his own semi, he will also be able to consume flaming torches like a fire-eater.

PERRY

★THE 89ER CONOCO GAS STATION RESTAURANT

Interstates 35 and 64 (405) 336–9207

ALWAYS OPEN

It is not likely The 89er will ever get a feature article in *Oklahoma Gourmet* magazine; but then it's unlikely there would ever be such a magazine. Oklahoma cuisine is best known around the country as the butt of Johnny Carson jokes, and while the food at The 89er is nothing to write home about, it is a notch above the charmless all-nighters that line the highway.

It is a plastic-looking restaurant, dressed up a bit by owner Ray Witt, who loves horses. Above the molded booths are horse pictures and horse paraphernalia to look at while you eat.

About the food Ray says bluntly, "If the menu says it's home cooked, it is." The best bets are the Mexican dishes. A crisp, deep-fried burrito platter comes with chili, a taco, and beans, and barely fits on a twelve-inch dinner plate. A taco plate comes with three tacos. Home-made chili is too bean-laden, but energetically spiced.

There is also freshly-breaded chicken, served with powdered potatoes and salad and homemade rolls, and a freshly prepared chicken-fried steak. "The rest of the stuff," Ray told us, "is trucked in and ready to go." Fair warning.

The best meals at The 89er are the ones that take full advantage of the on-premises bakery. Four biscuits with sausage gravy for break-fast are a good bet, as are fresh-baked honey buns. And there are Ray's special blueberry pancakes. We had two pieces of pineapple pie here one day. The crust was soggy, but the pineapple filling was chocked with real pineapple chunks, and the meringue was light and puffed with air. The milk shakes are not preblended, but rather made from separate ingredients, starting with hard-packed ice cream (55¢).

The 89er isn't worth a detour, but it's the best food on Oklahoma I–35, and it's always open.

PONCA CITY

★ THE SNACK SHACK

102 North Second Street (405) 762–4197
MON–SAT 7 AM–4 PM / CLOSED SUN

Ponca City is known to feminists as the site of the Pioneer Woman's Museum, featuring a statue dedicated to the women who trekked West. There are two restaurants practically next to each other on Second Street, both appropriately run by women. We prefer The Snack Shack, because while less hip and lacking the elevated consciousness of its neighbor, it serves good food in down-to-earth atmosphere. The other place has cleverly named sandwiches and long-outdated flower-child posters; The Snack Shack has fresh-grated hash browns, homemade corn bread, and first-class, Oklahoma-style blue-plate food.

The woman who runs The Snack Shack and does all the cooking looks like a blonde Loretta Lynn, a handsome country woman capable of beating a biscuit batter until the biscuits are ready to float into the air. We tried meat loaf with mashed potatoes and gravy, served with fresh rolls, vegetables, and a salad. We also had the Oklahoma "special" of corn bread, brown beans, and home-fried potatoes. This feast of starch was surprisingly varied in its tastes and textures, but still heavy for all but the sturdiest pioneer diners. We finished our meals with slices of apple and cherry pie.

The food here was good; the atmosphere was clean and basic; our fellow-eaters all looked like working people; and the woman boss looked like her bloodlines ran back to the days of the frontier.

SHAWNEE

★★ WIDE AWAKE CAFÉ

2202 North Kickapoo Street (405) 273–9689
DAILY 6 AM–9:30 PM

The Wide Awake is set down in the midst of an endless roadside development that looks like the home-siding manufacturers' hall of fame. The Café itself is an actual wood building, well kept and distinctive among its modernized neighbors. The food, like the building, is simple, down home, and made by hand.

Almost every morning there are beaten biscuits. They are the chewy kind, of medium consistency, with a hearty taste crying out for butter and honey, which is served alongside. A plate of these biscuits and a cup of coffee is a delicious kick-off for a drive to Texarkana, or a day at the construction site. Most of the morning people seem to be the pick-up and crew cab crowd; big healthy workers who appreciate the joys of a good biscuit.

The best bet for lunch is fried chicken. A platter includes pinto beans, real whipped potatoes, and homemade rolls which, for some reason, are not as good as the morning ones. They too come with honey, which we noticed was being used by other patrons as a dip for shreds of chicken. The other lunch choices are roast beef, a T-bone, and bar b qued ham.

The homemade lemon pie is a perfect way to finish off a honey-dipped chicken dinner, because it is extremely mild, with a lemony flavor and a flaky pastry crust.

The Wide Awake Café is clean; the service is friendly; there is no drinking on the premises. It's a good stop for a biscuit breakfast or a simple plate lunch.

FAIRS AND FESTIVALS

JAY
Huckleberry Festival / EARLY JULY
Free huckleberries and ice cream

MADILL
National Sand Bass Festival / MID–JUNE
Free fish fry

PAUL'S VALLEY
World Championship Watermelon Seed Spitting Contest
LATE JUNE

PORTER
Peach Festival / EARLY AUGUST

PRAGUE
Kolache Festival / EARLY MAY
Filled sweet rolls and coffee

RUSH SPRINGS
Watermelon Festival / EARLY AUGUST

SALT CREEK CANYON
Rattlesnake Round Up / EASTER
Bar b qued rattler

STILLWATER (OKLAHOMA STATE U.)
Cheese-Sausage Food Fair / LATE OCTOBER

STILWELL
Strawberry Festival / EARLY MAY
Free strawberries and ice cream

TEXAS

BALMORHEA

★★★★ RICK'S SPANISH INN
Route 290
MON–SAT 5 AM–9:30 PM / CLOSED SUN

There is no restaurant that says "Texas" as surely as Rick's. Balmorhea is a little dump of a town, with chickens running loose in the street, and sullen cowboys and Mexicans loafing around the gas station. Rick's is one of the two or three buildings in the town, a ramshackle, slightly foreboding place that looks like a tavern from the outside. But go on in and you will find easy-going Texas hospitality, great steaks, and Texas bar b que prepared by Rick Moon. Rick is the owner and pitmaster at the Inn, as well as pitmaster for local rodeos and celebrations. Before he was a cook and rodeo man, Rick worked in Stockton, at a meat market. Rick knows everything anybody could know about what to do with a piece of meat.

Rick's bar b que is smoked over wild mesquite wood, the traditional Texas choice. We couldn't guess at his secrets, but the product of his pit is fall-apart tender brisket, succulent and smoky. Not satisfied to place his prime meat on a crummy bun or serve it along with crackers, Rick also makes his own rolls from a cornmeal batter, and the result is a pocket-shaped roll that has its own tasty character in addition to being a perfect receptacle for the meat. The plate bar b que comes with dense corn bread on the side, pinto beans, onions, and jalapeño peppers.

"Kings don't eat better," Rick says about his famous steaks. From the hamburger, which is ground here and served on a homemade bun, to the "steak for 8," a colossus cut to order, Rick's meat comes in the proportions and quality demanded by professional cowboys, rodeo men, and ranchers. Sirloins are ordered by the person, and there are rib eyes and club steaks too. All come with baked or fried potatoes, fried corn bread, and double-cut Texas toast. Rick's also serves fresh-butchered sweetbreads breaded with cornmeal, and assorted breakfasts including a "Depression breakfast" of fried sow belly, eggs, corn bread, and milk gravy.

This array of first-class Texas food is served in an atmosphere that could exist only in a sleepy town by a Texas highway. Nobody just "drops in" to Rick's for a quick sandwich. Coming here brings out people's sociability, and in our case, the hospitality began as soon as the knife hit the brisket. Ten-gallon-hatted cowboys sauntered up, pegging us for dudes, and wondering where we came from. Once Rick and the boys saw we weren't fellow Texans, they made it their business to make us feel at home. One local rancher offered us a guided trip through the mountains; another, free tickets to a Sunday rodeo; an old-timer wanted to buy us drinks at a nearby cantina. Despite the odd and dusty "guest book" at the door of the Inn, it's obvious that tourism in Balmorhea isn't booming, and an unfamiliar face is a source of excitement for the crowd at Rick's.

The flavor of Rick's heavy smoked meat, and the warm cowboy hospitality of the Inn lingered with us to El Paso. We promised that Rick's would be a first stop on our return trip through Texas. And the next time around, we intend to corral six hungry cowboys and sit down in the Spanish Inn over a steak for eight and an evening of Lone Star beer and four-star feasting.

BOERNE

★★★ PO-PO CAFÉ

Interstate 10 (Welfare Exit, 7 miles west of Boerne) (512) 537–4399
TUES–SAT: DINNER / SUN 11 AM–9:30 PM

How good can a simple steak dinner be? Order one at Po-Po and find out. The steaks are blackened on the outside and seem to expand with natural juice as they are broiled, so that your first slice with the knife punctures a pocket of natural flavor. The juices run out, and one is tempted to gobble down the steak as quickly as possible. But relax. Po-Po deserves unhurried attention.

You may want to start your meal with a shrimp or oyster cocktail. There is no need to worry about freshness, because Po-Po has no freezers. The owners buy what they need, as they need it, with daily deliveries of seafood and vegetables. With that guarantee of freshness, you can feel free to order fried shrimp or oysters from the Texas Gulf as the main course, or a southern-fried chicken dinner. But this is the Hill Country, the culinary heart of Texas. And steak seems the ideal Po-Po dish.

Po-Po is crowded at dinner. It's popular with the locals, and has the flavor of a club. In fact, "The Club Po-Po" began as a beer joint back in 1947 catering to Boerne's largely German population. It hasn't moved from the original oak-shaded, cool, stone building, labeled by the blinking neon "EATS" sign. The interior is filled with hundreds of souvenir plates from around the world, and a viny indoor garden. It's a very comfortable, easy place to enjoy some of the best steaks to be had in Texas.

CLARENDON

★★★★ MRS. BROMLEY'S DINING ROOM

702 S. Carhart (806) 874–2186
WEDS–SAT & MON 11 AM–8:30 PM, SUN 11 AM–3 PM, CLOSED TUES

Mrs. Bromley's Dining Room consists of the dining and living rooms of a gracious old residential home. There are easy chairs and gentle upholstered couches set about, a few reading lamps and side tables, even some of Ruby Bromley's personal momentoes and bric-a-brac. Light filters into the dining rooms through high amber-tinted windows. Classical music plays quietly on a radio. The dining tables are covered with thick white cloths and soft napkins. It is all quite elegant.

After entering and selecting one of the dining tables, a waitress brings you juice or soup and a beverage. You are then free to help yourself to the food, which is set out on tables and in cooling compartments towards the rear of the main dining room.

There are always three or four homemade breads: corn bread, white bread, light rolls and small sticky buns are the usual offerings. There are seven kinds of salad, including guacamole, ambrosia, and a few slaws. There are innumerable vegetables and potatoes (always fresh), candied yams and creamed corn. The entrées include glazed ham, roast beef, fried chicken, pork chops, etc. For dessert there is peach cobbler or strawberry shortcake that you prepare yourself from a large shortcake and separate bowls of strawberries and whipped cream.

We could raid our thesaurus and find superlatives to describe Mrs. Bromley's food, but let us just say this: if we wanted to take a visitor to this country to a restaurant that serves the very best American food, we would come here. Mrs. Bromley is a great chef—not because of her inventiveness or imagination, but because each dish—from simple greens and mashed potatoes to the substantial ham and roast—is a perfect, classical rendering. It is beautiful, photogenic food, lovely to look at, better to eat.

And eat. You can keep going at Mrs. Bromley's from 11 in the morning to 8:30 at night. Our waitress on a recent visit offered us use of a bed upstairs if we wished to take a nap between portions of our marathon meal. Or you can take time out from the repast to have a chat with Mrs. Bromley herself. She moves from table to table during the day, encouraging return trips for another helping of ham or more dessert, and chatting with customers about how blessed she feels to have been running her dining room successfully for so long. "This is my piece of heaven here," she says, leading you back to the strawberries and whipped cream.

COLUMBUS

★★★ THE CITY CAFÉ
520 Walnut (Route 90) (713) 732–8009
MON–SAT 5 AM–8 PM / SUN 5 AM–2 PM

Whatever else you order at The City Café, get the rice. Nearby Eagle Lake is the center of Texas rice country, and rice at The City Café is a celebration, not a side dish. Margie Knippel, the cook (and co-owner, with her husband), boils the native rice with green peppers, celery, onions, tomatoes, and spices. The result is an ivory-white base, peppered festively with red and green, spiced to accent the pure flavor of the natural grain. We had the rice with the lunch special of German sausage, a thick, dark, and mightily spiced variety notable here in Texas for its *not* being smoked.

The food at The City Café is more German-accented than it is typically southwestern, a reminder of the German immigrants who settled here when Texas was an independent state. Even the chicken-fried steak we had here for lunch was closer to a delicate Wiener schnitzel in its zesty robust flavor than to the pedestrian chicken fries one anticipates at roadside cafés.

No lunch or dinner special at The City Café should end without one of Mrs. Hertha David's (Margie's mother) pies. We had the Dutch apple, laced with cinnamon and spiced apples, and with a delicious crispy crust—the result, Margie explained, of her mother's exclusive use of cast-iron pie pans.

Mrs. David also makes the breakfast rolls, served here every morning starting at 5 a.m. These pastries are not too large to prevent you from sampling two or three. We especially recommend the kolaches—light, braided dough sprinkled with cinnamon and filled in layers with almond paste. If you get here early enough, you will get a hot slice of the kolache, minutes from the oven. We can't think of a better way to start the day than watching a pat of butter melting into the cinnamon.

The City Café is a boisterous place, cavernous and filled with sociable Columbusites. The dining room is powerfully air-conditioned; but the kitchen in back must be well over 100 degrees. We first met Margie back there. She was neatly dressed, with her hair styled high on her head, beads of perspiration on her forehead from lording over the great pot of boiling rice. While we were there she took a break from her cooking to tell us that she was a lucky woman. A "second honeymoon" trip to Las Vegas had netted her husband $500 on the nickel slot machines.

Margie may be lucky. So is anyone who stops in The City Café for a meal.

COMFORT

★★★★ CYPRESS CREEK INN
just off Route 10 (512) 995–3977
TUES–SAT: LUNCH, DINNER / SUN: LUNCH

The facts and figures speak eloquently of the Cypress Creek Inn's greatness. We had two dinners here—Hill Country pan Sausage, pan-fried boneless trout, two salads, fresh mashed potatoes (two orders), a dish of corn pudding, a bowl of Harvard beets, hot just-baked rolls, two cups of coffee, a slice of pumpkin pie, and a large strawberry shortcake topped with a spoon of freshly whipped cream. The total bill for these two meals, each perfectly prepared from the freshest ingredients, was under five dollars.

Other entrées on the Cypress Creek menu the day we ate here were home-baked meat loaf, grilled fresh calves liver and onions, and creamed chicken on flaky biscuits. Steaks are available a la carte, either filet mignon, or a 12-ounce T-bone. Every day Charlotte Holmes prepares four or five entrées, all from scratch, all from her own recipes.

The Cypress Creek is as plain as a restaurant can be. There are chrome chairs and plastic tablecloths. The only decor is a lone "jackalope" head on the wall. "You can't eat atmosphere," declares Charlotte Holmes, and when great dinners can be had for well under $3, who needs atmosphere to make a great meal?

DALLAS

★★★★ TOLBERT'S TEXAS CHILI PARLOR
802 Main Street
MON–FRI 11 AM–2 PM, SAT 7 PM–1 AM

We're stretching the roadfood rule of easy accessibility by including this chili parlor in downtown Dallas, but no chronicle of real Texas cooking would be complete without it. The proprietor, Frank X. Tolbert, knows more about chili con carne than anyone, and this restaurant is the meeting place of a Dallas chapter of the Chili Appreciation Society International. The walls are graced with pictures of famous chili-eaters and displays of trophies won at the Championship Chili Cook-Off in Terlingua.

The chili is cooked by Frank X. Tolbert, Jr., about whom Frank, Sr., says "There is no one better." He uses choice chuck cut into cubes, then simmered in beer. To this he adds cilantro, comino, sandia peppers, a little garlic and a pinch of oregano. It is served in either a 12-ounce bowl or a cup. To go with it there are French fries, with the skin left on, black-eyed peas cooked with smoked bacon, or pinto beans made with smoked jowls. You can also get burritos or German hot dogs with Tolbert hot sauce. And for the adventurous diner there is "Son-of-a-Bitch Stew," a concoction of lesser-known and unappreciated parts of an unweaned calf. Tolbert calls this "the working cowhand's favorite."

Tolbert's is a casual, chatty place, frequented by that most passionate breed of food afficionado, the chilihead. Many have called it the only true chili parlor left in Texas.

DICKINSON

★★ HILLMAN'S SEAFOOD CAFÉ
Route 146 (just south of Route 517) (713) 339-1731
TUES–SUN 11 AM–10 PM / CLOSED MON

There are few places on Galveston Island that serve as bountiful a table of seafood as Hillman's. There are none that do it as cheaply, and in so beautiful a location. Outside are the grasslands, the mesquite trees, the windmills. Fishing boats are docked at the wharf. Inside, the restaurant manages to be at once low-ceilinged and airy, a cozy place to partake of the heady salt air blowing in over the bay.

Hillman's was once a small snack bar catering exclusively to the Dickinson Bayou fishermen in the 1950s. Grandma Hillman's husband was one of these men, "so hungry when they came in after a day," she said, "that pretty soon we added tables so they could sit down and have dinner. These men would rather fish than eat, but I'm a 'Louisanne' woman and my shrimp gumbo kept 'em coming back." Grandma's Cajun touch can be tasted not only in the dense filé gumbo, but in the New Orleans-style Italian olive salads with lemon dressing, and in the special cole slaw, seasoned with bay shrimp. "I use only bay shrimp here. They're smaller than those from the gulf," she explained, "but they have none of the iodine taste of the larger ones."

We tried an order of fried shrimp, double-dipped in seasoned cracker meal and milk. The coating gave each piece a crunchy-rich texture, but was mild and light enough to allow the shrimps' flavor to dominate. A dozen raw oysters on the half shell were large and freshly opened, intense with briny sea flavor, a perfect prelude to a red snapper filet, which was crustily breaded like the shrimp, but still tasted of the sea.

Hillman's today is a large, fairly noisy place, crowded on weekend nights. You can pull up by boat, just past April Fool Point and into the Dickinson Bayou, or by car on Route 146, between Texas City and Seabrook. You'll recognize the restaurant by the fishing boat "Grampa's Pride" that is now perched upon its roof. The boat was christened in 1922, when Grampa first started to fish in the Texas Gulf. All the seafood is still caught by Hillman fishermen, and Grandma Hillman can still be found almost any night at the large family table in the restaurant, expounding on the virtues of bay shrimp and the secrets of Louisiana gumbo.

DRIFTWOOD

★★★ THE SALT LICK
FM 150 (512) 858-4437
THURS–SUN: DINNER

The Salt Lick was slow to mature. There was a time when it lacked not only four walls, but rest rooms, as well. Thurman Roberts, The Salt Lick's creator, was heard to tell one distressed patron, "Lady, there's 600 acres out there. . . . Choose one!" Things have been toned down since the wild days of The Salt Lick, but it is still run by the odd couple of Thurman and Hisako Roberts, she a 4'11" Hawaiian, and he a rangy, full-bred Texan. He taught her the delights of bar b que, and she showed him how to cook gulf shrimp in tempura batter, and how to make green tea-flavored ice to clear the brisket-worn palate.

The Salt Lick is a famous place, famous enough for its neighbors in Driftwood and Dripping Springs to beg the Roberts to get a phone at the restaurant to keep the traveling gourmands from knocking at their ranch house doors day and night for directions. They are famous for their pit-cooked bar b que, served at long picnic tables. It is beef, spareribs, or sausage, or any combination thereof, along with potato salad, pinto beans, relish of onion and dill pickles, hot bread, and cole slaw. There are no menus; the offerings of the day are posted on butcher paper on the door. The only choices, other than bar b que, are desserts. This is difficult, because you have to choose between Thurman's pecan, mince meat and sweet potato pie, and Hisako's homemade ice creams. "There are people twenty years old who have never tasted real cream," she said. She puts an end to this deprivation by serving all the ice cream and banana splits with real whipped cream.

The bar b que itself is delicious—heavy prime cuts of meat cooked for eighteen hours over crushed pecan shells. This creates a unique aroma that will be of assistance in locating The Salt Lick when you get lost, as everyone does, trying to find it on FM 150 near Dripping Springs. The richness of the meat is gracefully complemented by Hisako's special slaw. "I use a light Japanese dressing, since the rest of the meal is heavy."

Groups of six or more are served "family style." The meat comes on large platters, along with bowls of the side dishes. The portions of everything when served this way are so prodigious, and the table looks so good when weighed down with them, that gluttonous roadfooders are known to come in parties of four and order family style anyway, paying for six, and getting too much of a good thing, which is exactly what they're after.

There is a new branch of The Salt Lick, in nearby Blanco, in a 100-year old courthouse. You can get beer in Blanco. Driftwood is dry. Either place is a real salt lick, which Thurman described to us as "a place that is wild and natural. A place sought by animals including men. Where they meet, like at a waterhole, there is a sort of peace. It is a friendly place with no pretensions, where there is something good and essential."

EAGLE PASS

★★ HOTEL EAGLE
Main Street (512) 773–2363
DAILY 6 AM–9 PM

Border towns are often characterized by lawlessness and a certain seedy aura, and although Eagle Pass has had its share of both, the Hotel Eagle, the only place in town, is a good place to eat and spend the night.

It is operated by Thurman and Hisako Roberts, who run the Salt Lick and Salt Lick Too, but the Eagle, unlike those brush country hideaways, is a landmark establishment with a long history.

It's not the kind of town you'd ever vacation in, nor is it worth a detour from Route 35. But if you find yourself here, try these items on the Hotel's menu. For breakfast, the best bet is *chilaquiles,* thin strips of fried crisp tortilla thrown into a sauce of fresh chopped tomatoes, onions, hot jalapeño peppers, melted cheese, and scrambled eggs. It is a fiery omelette that will prepare you for the trip south into Mexico. For those with slightly milder tastes, there are eggs with spicy chorizo sausage and ham and eggs, served with a center-cut bone still in the ham slab. Our favorite lunch at the Hotel Eagle is chicken *a la portuguesa*—chicken sautéed with chopped tomatoes, celery, onions, green olives, and jalapeño peppers. This mixture is put into a casserole, seasoned with pepper and comino, topped with grated cheese, and baked. The other best bet is *guisado,* a Mexican stew of beef, peppers, and vegetables. This is served with tortillas. The Eagle Pass also serves an assortment of steaks, a delicious jalapeño corn bread, and home-baked pecan pies. As Hisako Roberts told us, "The Hotel Eagle is not exactly the Beverly Wilshire or the Regency." But then what other hotels offer a "Special Tampiqueña Dinner" of strip steak, enchiladas, tamales, guacamole salad, tostadas, and refried beans from a recipe created by a Japanese Texan?

EL PASO

★★SMITTY'S
6219 Airport Road (915) (722–5876)
TUES–SAT 11 AM–10 PM / CLOSED SUN

We include Smitty's for those who travel by plane instead of auto. It is conveniently located near the El Paso airport and makes an ideal first stop if you have flown to Texas starved for genuine bar b que. It is close enough to the airport so that it is possible to call Smitty's as soon as you arrive, grab a cab, pick up your goodies and be back at the airport in time to catch your baggage as it comes down the ramp.

Smitty's sells bar b qued beef, ham, pork, and corned beef by the pound, regular or extra lean. With all but the corned beef we recommend *not* getting the meat extra lean, because if Smitty's has one fault, it is that the meat is too dry to begin with, and requires a thorough drenching with sauce to attain the right consistency. Lean only accentuates the problem.

There are other ways than Smitty's sauce (regular or extra hot) to accent the dense and chewy flavor of the meat. Jalapeño peppers are hot enough to sear the lips. A pint of German-style potato salad or pinto beans in bar b que sauce are available on the side.

At Smitty's you can eat in a large and noisy bar-dining room, or get the food to go at a speed that must have taken years of waiting on nervous airport-bound travelers to develop. If you are waiting, ticket in hand to catch a flight, calm your nerves with a glass of Lone Star beer, or the oddest brisket companion yet . . . a jug of "Magen-David" (sic) wine. If you are New York-bound, a glass of Mogen David and a bar b qued corned beef sandwich should set you up for the trip.

While it is not the best bar b que in the state, Smitty's is a traveler's friend, a sample for the visitor to Texas of the glorious eating ahead.

★★★★ THE TIGUA RESERVATION CAFETERIA
Almeda Avenue (915) 859–3916
SUMMER: DAILY 10 AM–6 PM / WINTER: DAILY 8 AM–5 PM

The Tigua Reservation looks nothing like those you see in vintage westerns. It is located in an urban neighborhood of El Paso, a part of town occupied mostly by Indians and a few Mexicans. The reservation is a concrete structure that serves both as a tourist attraction and a community meeting place for the small tribe of Tiguas. Outsiders are welcome, and there is a crafts store selling Tigua-made pottery, as well as displays of native Indian dancing and bread-baking, and best of all, a cafeteria run by Natalia Lopez.

Natalia is a full-blooded Tigua who is also the runner-up in the annual National Chili Cook-Off held at Terlingua, Texas. Tigua Indians in fact are among the staunchest competitors at this chili cook-off, but many, like the tribal Chief, José Sierra, make their "bowl of red" so hot that the judges refuse to even take a spoonful.

This silver-medal chili is the backbone of The Tigua Cafeteria fare. It comes either green or red, accompanied by a large round of adobe oven-baked bread. The red chili is the color of cinnabar, grainy thick, and hot enough to bring a moistness to the forehead. It was, without doubt, the best "Indian style" chili we have sampled, a seemingly simple blend of ground chili pods, cumin, coarsely cut beef, a bit of tomato base, "masa" for thickener, and a little sugar and salt. The red chili was so alive and layered in flavor that we have used it as the scale to match all comers against. The green chili is a more complex dish. It is made from mutton, coriander, green chili, and countless spices. It is also so blisteringly hot that it caused us to stop for fear of passing out half way through the bowl. It is a test by fire for non-Indians.

There are some excellent non-chili dishes to be had here. Try the *flautas,* named for their flutelike shape. They are dried, shredded beef wrapped with crisp tortillas and topped with sour cream. A *gordita* is a soft cornmeal pocket of dough stuffed with ground meat and shredded cheese and a dash of green chili sauce. Tripe and hominy stew is a bland-tasting dish by comparison to the other spicy choices. There is a magnificently constructed short-rib soup with small riblets simmering in the broth, quarter ears of corn-on-the-cob, and delicate, almost oriental-looking slices of squash.

Natalia is proud of her *capirotada* dessert. It is her secret Tigua recipe for what is closest to a bread pudding. The adobe-baked bread is toasted, layered with mild cheese, scattered with raisins, pecan meats, and soaked with a syrup made from cloves, cinnamon, and brown sugar. The whole dish is then put in the oven and allowed to slowly bake. The wonderful aroma of the baking *capirotadas* is matched only by the taste.

The Tigua Cafeteria is a delight. It is the best way we know of to eat the traditional dishes of this diminishing tribe, to talk with these native Americans on their own territory, and to admire their crafts on display and for sale.

★★TONY'S MEXICAN CAFÉ
706 North Piedras
ALWAYS OPEN

Tony's Mexican Café is the one beloved by El Paso cognescenti for two reasons. First, it is always open—a spicy salve available when the 3 a.m. craving for Mexican food hits, and just about everything else is closed. Second, it serves the best *cabrito* (roast baby kid) around, at prices that make it a virtual giveaway.

A five-course dinner at Tony's goes for under two dollars, and while the neighborhood might give some folks second thoughts, we never had any regrets. Tony's is a neighborhood bar. The patrons are Mexicans and gringos—anyone who is tired of the old enchilada-taco-tortilla rut and wants a change of pace. The *cabrito* dinner comes with guacamole salad and tostada chips. The meat is unbelievably tender, with a crisp skin. You can get a bowl of *menudo,* the traditional tripe and hominy stew popular all over the Southwest with Mexicans and Indians. It is rescued here from blandness by onions, black peppercorns, and ancho chilis.

The *tostadas de gallina* is another special dish at Tony's—rolled tortillas stuffed with chicken and green chili sauce. It's hot, so beware!

It's hard to say if Tony's food is really better than neighboring daylight cafés, or if gratefulness for the twenty-four-hour kitchen has influenced us to love it more. Paula Yardeni, the cook, told us, "We make everything fresh. All the ingredients are the best we can get." Any time of day, the *cabrito* is a special treat, worth a special trip to Tony's.

JUNCTION

★★ THE CACTUS BAR B Q
Main Street (915) 446–2478
MON–SAT 7 AM–6 PM, SUN 7 AM–4 PM

The Cactus Bar B Q is so primal a pit that it appears to be running itself. Tod Mills, an eight-year-old boy, and his older sister Irene were in attendance here, but the meats out in the pit seemed to have reached a state of cooking self-sufficiency.

A bar b que plate includes separate ingredients of brisket, cole slaw, beans, onions, and jalapeño peppers. Sauce—so basic an element in southern-style and Kansas City bar b que—is here replaced with simple meat drippings. The brisket is first-quality Texas meat, flavored only with its own juices that have been coaxed from it by long hours over the smoking wood. One quickly learns that with this pure brisket the application of sauce would be like pouring ketchup onto a choice T-bone. If you want extra tang, bite into the onion slice. For hotness, chew on a jalapeño. Cole slaw provides a touch of sweet, and beans, moisture.

Like the bar b que it serves, The Cactus is a basic place. There is a pit, a "feed pen," and a small shack next to the pit, from which Irene can keep an eye on the meat and the hot links outside. It is a very lazy and relaxed place. You eat at a picnic table out in the sun. The brisket, smoked over cedar, is juicy and only mildly spiced with woody flavor. Tod and Irene sat with us while we ate, and as eight-year-old Tod spent the entire time trying to slice a slippery onion, Irene was loquacious in a pleasant and breezy Texas way.

LEON SPRINGS

★★ THE SETTLEMENT INN
off Interstate 10 (512) 698–2580
MON–THURS 5 PM–9 PM / FRI, SAT & SUN 11 AM–9 PM

The Settlement Inn is a perfectly preserved rock and wood structure originally built in 1849 as a general store. Added onto the store was a post office, a stable, and a hotel, all of which operated in the wild and wooly days of early Texas. The building has survived gunslingers, pony express hijinks, and the sands of time, and has been revived today to serve as a lunch or dinner stop for passers-by and those who want to take a quick drive out of modernized Houston into more primitive Texas countryside.

Ina Ringuette is the cook and pitmistress, and an enthusiastic man named Steve Spence is in charge of renovations and preservation of the small group of buildings.

You can eat outside on a rustic terrace with bleached wood posts and sagebrush outcroppings, or in a quaint inner room looking out across the brush onto the facade of the hotel, which Steve is now restoring. Service is good, and although this is not a "wipe the grease from the bar b que on your jeans" place, it is relatively informal and easygoing.

The most copious bar b que plate consists of beef brisket, sausage, and ribs. The ribs of beef served separately come with beans, rolls and potato salad. The meats are served with a mild sauce, a blend of ketchup, Worcestershire sauce, chopped onions, horseradish, and vinegar. The meat has been cooked for thirty-six hours over hickory, turning the huge slabs a pitch-dark color.

Lunch sandwiches come with 5¢ dishes of hot peppers, and with potato salad. There are also steaks from a small filet on up to a thirty-two-ounce giant. The pies served at The Settlement Inn are delicate fruit creations, made in the summer from local peaches and in the winter with juicy Texas pecans. The pie is high-priced, but it's a sweet way to clear your senses after the smoky aromatics of the bar b que.

LLANO

★★★★ ABBY'S KITCHEN

1206 Bessemer, Highway 16 (915) 247–5318
WED: DINNER / THURS–SAT: LUNCH, DINNER / CLOSED SUN–TUES

Abby's has everything—stereo tape, portable TV, and room for twenty-one diners. These creature comforts and some of the best Mexican food in the Texas Hills can be had for $2 to $3 in Abby's mobile home. Abby is a Texas firecracker who can't keep from cooking. She was cook at the Fireside and Starlight Restaurants in Buchanan Dam for twenty-six years. "I quit cooking for two years," she said. "Then my husband bought this mobile home. So there it was, just standing still: I said I'll start cooking Mexican food, to take out only. Finally I ripped a wall down and I put in two tables, and I could sit eight. Now it's twenty-one, and that's it!"

Although Abby has expanded and modernized to her present twenty-one-seat establishment, no one could accuse her of showboating. Even the purist roadfooder has got to find Abby's—for all its amplified splendor—to be one of the funkiest places to eat a meal north of the Rio Bravos. At lunch you are likely to enjoy your enchiladas to the sound of Abby's favorite soap operas on TV. For dinner music, there are eight-track tapes of Willie Nelson.

Everything here starts from scratch. Abby grinds peppers for her hot sauce and makes tortillas from corn flour. She rolls her own tamales. Meals are simple. "Abby's special" is a guacamole salad, a taco, an enchilada, a tamale, rice, and refried beans. A lesser dinner consists of enchiladas, a tamale, rice, and beans. There are also *chalupas* (tortillas with beans, cheese, and lettuce), nachos (tortilla crisps with cheese), and Abby's tamales.

Abby's is an easy place to drive by. There is only a small sign outside the trailer to let you know it's a restaurant. It's a clean place, and it is unique. We know of no other combination of authentic food and mobile-homespun atmosphere that so perfectly captures the spirit of Tex-Mex roadfood.

★★ INMAN'S KITCHEN

1006 Berry Street (915) 247–5257
JAN–OCT: MON–SAT 7 AM–8 PM / CLOSED SUN / NOV–DEC: DAILY
7 AM–8 PM

If it moves, Texans are likely to catch it and bar b que it, so smoked turkey ought not to be a big surprise in the Lone Star State. In fact, turkeys are often found roasting slowly over a pit in Texas' Hill Country, right along with the beef, goat, and occasional rattlesnake. Inman's Kitchen not only serves smoked turkeys; it happens to be the self-proclaimed "Home of the Turkey Sausage."

So we detoured off of our southern route along Interstate 10 to Llano, to visit this strange sausage's home. It is an old house, purposely quaint on the inside with checked tablecloths, sawdust on the floors, and tractor seats around the tables instead of chairs. The menu is burned into old wood boards hung on the wall, and there is a wood stove in the dining room where patrons help themselves to pinto beans and bar b que sauce.

This stove with the beans and sauce happens to be Inman's ingenious solution to the basic culinary problem inherent in the smoking of a turkey. Smoking generally dries out meat, and turkey, any way you cook it, has a propensity toward dryness. The smoked turkey platter is dry until one follows one's natural inclination toward gluttony and piles on the free beans and sauce, and eats the turkey with alternate spoonfuls of Inman's homemade chow-chow. Thus eaten, smoked turkey is a deliciously different meal.

Inman's also serves beef and smoked ham plates, all with slaw, pickles, pinto beans, onions, and homemade bread. Sandwiches and sausage meat can be ordered to go. But before we left with our pound of turkey sausage, we had a large slice of delicious, heavily-spiced hot apple pie a la mode.

Back at our motel room, we tried to analyze the taste of the turkey sausage and the smoked drumstick we had also taken out. But a six pack of Lone Star later, we were wishing for a pint of Inman's chow-chow or a quart of sauce to help us in our tasting. Turkey sausage as made at Inman's seems to dry out even more away from Llano. But eaten in its home, with plenty of sauce, beans and chow-chow, it is a unique Texas treat.

OZONA

★★THE HIGHWAY CAFÉ
Route 290 (915) 392–2722
TUES–SUN 6:15 AM–9:30 PM / CLOSED MON

The Highway has an exterior that closely resembles a black tiled bathroom. It is constructed from the same four-by-four squares that are so common in johns all over the country. At The Highway they are not merely decorative, but manage to keep the air-conditioning in and create an oasis of coolness on the hottest desert day.

Within the walls of this tiled shelter some respectable home-cooked meals are served at prices often under $2.

One of the most popular, especially with the local cowboys, is "calf fries." These are served with cream gravy and are considered a delicacy. They are smaller versions of the dish called "mountain oysters." We passed on the calf fries, selecting a less "painful" meal of lamb stew with pinto beans. The lamb was not a young animal, but was nonetheless tender and juicy. Grilled pork chops with peaches is a popular Highway Café dish: thick chops spiced with clove-studded peaches that are grilled quickly under the broiler. Calf brains, sweetbreads, and a variety of other organ meats attest to the economical nature of the ranchers and restaurateurs in this part of Texas. The dishes come with potatoes O'Brien (cubed spuds spiced with bits of green and red sweet peppers), or rice with giblet gravy.

There is a small Mexican menu at The Highway. The cost of nachitos, guacamole, or enchiladas with green chili is hardly over a dollar. They are economy meals by comparison to the American dinners, but come unaccompanied by corn bread and dessert.

Desserts are a selection of handsome pies, fruit puddings, and the Highway's specialty, a vanilla wafer pudding.

Because of the super-strong air-conditioning, The Highway attracts practically the whole town of Ozona at noon. The café is large enough to fit the good-sized crowd, but small enough to easily observe the interaction of Western town life. The cast of characters are sheriffs and their deputies, local beauticians on their lunch hour, and the ubiquitous, straw-hatted cowpokes who taciturnly eat calf fries and wafer pie.

PITTSBURG

★POTTER'S HOT LINKS
136 Marshall Street (214) 856-7746
MON–SAT 9:30 AM–6 PM, SUN (TAKE-OUT ONLY) NOON–2 PM

In his definitive study of Texas food, *A Bowl of Red,* Frank X. Tolbert reports that the Pittsburg Hot Link was invented in the nineteenth century by a man named Charley Hasselback. Pittsburg is now the "Hot Links Capital of Texas," and the only town we know where you can sample the descendants of Mr. Hasselback's original link. They are served in an eating hall called Potter's Hot Links, an immense space that resembles a garage in which heavy machinery is repaired. The walls are raw brick, there are long plank tables and benches, and the whole cavernous room is cooled by a fan near the front that is as large as a B-36 propeller.

You walk to the back of the great room and order the number of links you wish. They are the size of small hot dogs, served on trays covered with wax paper along with a few saltines. A "meal" of links would consist of anywhere from six to a dozen. You take your tray back to a space at one of the tables, buy a soda from a machine against the wall, and dig in. These are very oily links, moderately spiced, and only slightly smoky-tasting. They are a sausage-lover's delight, but if you prefer your meat lean or dry, you'd best skip the links at Potter's.

Quite aside from its links, Potter's is an essential roadfood landmark for its historical value and deeply imbedded character. The thermometer outside read 105° the day we stopped in. It was ten degrees warmer inside, in spite of the fan, and the air was laced with hot link smoke. The place was as lazy and laid-back as only an ancient Texas link parlor can be. Outside, a small brigade of old-timers sat in the shade, the black men fanning themselves with Martin Luther King Jr. fans, offering a wry commentary on the lazy pace of Pittsburg life. Some of them might even have remembered Charley Hasselback and his original hot link.

POST

★JACKSON'S CAFETERIA
214 N. Broadway (806) 495–2970
MON–SUN 5 AM–10 PM

Throughout our meal at Jackson's Cafeteria there was a man sitting at a nearby table delivering a monologue that seemed to touch on most subjects in the *Encyclopaedia Britannica*. He was shaped like a bowling ball with a marble for a head. There was a tiny cowboy hat perched on top of the marble. Most of the patrons of Jackson's wore cowboy hats, although all but this easily tolerated town "nut" were the tall, silent Texas type. Post, Texas, is at the bottom of the panhandle—cowboy-oilman country, known more for the Post Sanitarium than for its cuisine. But the western types who frequent Jackson's do all right here. The food is the best for miles around.

The highlight of the cafeteria line is the salad area. The guacamole salad, made with chili peppers, bits of tomato and diced onion, is a stand-out. There are jello salads, green salads, cucumber and onion salads, and salads studded with tiny marshmallows. The main courses here are good, too. We sampled the fried chicken and bar b que. Neither was inspired, but both had a "down home" taste that satisfied. For the various salads and vegetables, the cafeteria line offers a wide assortment of relishes and hot peppers to spice things up. Only the pies at Jackson's were disappointing—heavy and without any of the deft or subtle touches that make the salads here worth a stop.

SONORA

★★★ THE COMMERCIAL RESTAURANT
Glassok and Plum Streets (915) 387–9928
TUES–SUN 10:30 AM–3 PM, 5 PM–9:30 PM / CLOSED MON

The Commercial Restaurant is situated in the heart of Sonora's Mexican district. The houses that surround it are small stucco dwellings. A few dogs sleep lazily in front of the aqua and bright yellow doors, and there is little activity in the streets at noon when the sun becomes glaringly direct. At this time the local population is seated at plain brown tables inside The Commercial, eating platters of enchiladas and dipping tostada chips into guacamole.

The Commercial has been on this same corner for thirty-five years, founded by the Lopez family and now co-run by their cousins, the Cervantes. Everything from the hot sauce to the stuffing for the chili rellenos is made from scratch here, and anyone entering through the front door can't help but notice the large pot on the kitchen stove where the triple-X hot peppers and a rainbow of spices boil for hours until the perfect hot sauce is brewed.

Start your meal with super-natchos. They are tortilla chips topped with refried beans, grated cheese, avocado, hot sauce, and a strip of pepper. If you can manage the challenge, The Commercial Special Dinner is a terrific bargain. It is a sampler of all things made at The Commercial and includes an enchilada, a taco, a chili relleno (a large cheese-stuffed pepper), chili con queso (cheese chili), guacamole, refried beans, and Mexican rice.

While The Commercial is a Mexican restaurant run by Mexicans in a solidly Mexican district, there is no sense of awkwardness for the "gringo" traveler who wishes to eat here. At lunch, non-Mexican cattlemen and cowboys fill many of the booths and English is spoken as fluently as Spanish. The "3 beers to a customer" sign on the wall attests to the respectability of the Cervantes restaurant.

SWEETWATER

★★★ ALLEN'S FAMILY-STYLE MEALS
1301 E. Broadway (915) 235–2060
TUES–SUN 11 AM–2:30 PM

Mrs. Allen has been famous around Sweetwater for her fried chicken since World War II. It's served family-style, at tables set for eight or ten people. When you walk in, Mrs. Allen or one of her helpers directs you to a table that is about to begin, or is in the beginning stages of the meal. The food keeps coming, so you eat as much as you want, as long as you want. The only problem is that there are so many dishes, you spend as much time passing and receiving food as eating it.

The entrées are always fried chicken and a beef dish. We advise you skip the lackluster brisket or roast beef and concentrate on the chicken. You can see it being breaded and fried in the open kitchen at the back of the restaurant. It comes to your table hot and crispy, with a mildly nutty taste with lots of character. Galaxies of side dishes circle the table: cabbage slaw, squash flavored with honey, macaroni salad, pea salad, boiled potatoes and butter, green beans, corn niblets, beets, rolls and butter. Your ice tea is replenished throughout the meal.

When your table starts looking tired, a peach cobbler appears. It is ridiculously rich—especially when you're satiated at this stage of the meal—but it shouldn't be passed by. It's a compote, chocked with crispy bits of crust throughout, as sugary-sweet a dessert as we've ever tasted.

WAELDER

★★★★ MILLER'S
Miller's Grocery Store, Main Street (Highway 90) (512) 665–3221
MON–SAT 8 AM–6 PM / CLOSED SUN

There is no place more richly steeped in bar b que mystique than Miller's. It is the ideal Texas smoke pit and hot link parlor, located in the back of a grocery store, in what is a virtual ghost town.

Park your car on the empty street, walk up the stairs to the raised sidewalk, under the tin awnings, still perforated in spots with bullet holes, and enter the dimly lit grocery. Business is so slow here that Mr. Miller turns on lights only in those parts of the store where you need to look. We asked about the bar b que, and Mr. Miller pointed us to a wooden door in back. We moved through the dusty dark aisles and peered through the small window in the door. A black man was sitting at a wood picnic bench in a back storage room. On a piece of butcher paper in front of him on the table were two hot links and a pile of brisket, drenched in sauce. The walls of the small room were lined with soap boxes and bags of feed. It was illuminated with two bare bulbs hanging from the ceiling.

The man hardly looked up from his food as we entered the room. It was as if he was in a meditative state; the bar b que and hot links set before him were his mantra. We moved quietly to the small "office" at the side of the room. There was the ancient pit, and there was Thomas Fields, the pitmaster, sitting silently in the near-darkness.

Fields selected two hot links from among the dozens strung up above the smoking mesquite, and cut us a pound of beef. The links and beef were put on butcher paper with a half-stack of saltines. We bought a soda from the machine at the wall, and carried our butcher paper full of meat to one of the two picnic tables. We noticed that Mr. Fields now stood in the doorway of his small room, half-hidden in the shadows, watching us eat.

Each table has a long, pointed knife on a chain for cutting into the links, and there is a roll of paper towels tacked onto a pillar, for wiping your hands. This is sleeves-up eating, and so we dropped a little hot sauce onto the meat and dug into the most tender bar b qued brisket we have ever tasted. It was falling apart from its hours over the smoking wood, moist with its own juices, and demanding only the lightest application of sauce. The links burst open with slight pressure from the sharp knife. They were greasy, spiced, and so sharply hot that our taste buds were limp after finishing them. The meal was one to be eaten slowly. By the time we finished, we felt saturated with the smoke and atmosphere of this quiet Texas link parlor.

"You like your links?" The question came from the man we had first seen at the other table, who had finished his meal about the same time we did. We enthusiastically tried to tell him and Fields how wonderful it was, how perfect. They listened patiently to our neophyte enthusiasm.

As we were ready to leave, two old ladies in flower print dresses and Sunday bonnets, neither of the women over five feet tall, walked through the door and marched over to the large figure of Thomas Fields. "Let's see your pit," they commanded. "We came from Houston for what we heard was the best bar b que in Texas. Is it?" Fields opened the cast-iron door to the brisket and hot links with a knowing smile.

FAIRS AND FESTIVALS

BRAZOSPORT
Rotary Shrimp Boil / LATE MAY

CASTROVILLE
Five-ton Prime Beef Bar B Que / AUGUST

GALVESTON
Shrimp Festival / LATE APRIL

GILMER
Yamboree / LAST WEEK IN OCT

LOCKHART
National Cornbread Cooking Contest / MID-MAY

LULING
Watermelon Thump / LATE JUNE

NEW BRAUNFELS
Wurstfest / EARLY NOV

SAN MARCOS
Chilympiad / MID-SEPT

TERLINGUA
World Championship Chili Cook-Off / OCT OR NOV

The West

CALIFORNIA

ALTADENA

★★ROBBIE'S RIB CAGE

1926 North Lake (213) 798–8001
TUES–THURS 11 AM–10 PM / FRI & SAT UNTIL–MIDNIGHT
SUN 3 PM–8:30 PM / CLOSED MON & MONTH OF AUGUST

North of Los Angeles, beyond Pasadena, almost on the outskirts of Southern California civilization is Robbie's Rib Cage. It is a prefab plastic bar b que shack that serves the best soul smoke on the West Coast. It is a well-known stop for truckers—black and white—who call their orders ahead and have their ribs and hot links waiting for the run out of "Shakey City." "All kinds of people come here," Robbie told us. "From all walks of life: ministers, tourists, locals, truckers, students. We make the bar b que like we're expecting guests for supper."

Robbie's is a family operation. He smokes the meats and prepares the sauce. Bobbie, his wife, makes the cole slaw, molasses beans, and sweet potato pies; and daughters Pat, Pam, and Sharon work the counter. Robbie's is friendly, with a few umbrella'd tables outside for eating on the spot, although a good portion of the business is takeout.

The specialty is of course ribs—slow-cooked over hickory wood, and almost falling off the bone with tenderness. Robbie's sauce is mild, and a little ketchupy—but hardly necessary on the already juicy meats. There is also brisket, chicken, sliced pork, and hot links—all served on platters with baked beans and slaw. Bobbie's sweet potato pie is thick and sweet; perhaps a little too rich after a full bar b que dinner.

There are other "hickory pits" in the Los Angeles area, but none that produce such authentic soul bar b que as Robbie's. The Rib Cage is closed during August, so Robbie, Bobbie, and the kids can take their vacation.

AUBURN

★★ CAFÉ DELICIAS
1591 Lincoln Way (916) 885–2050
WED–MON 11:30 AM–9 PM / CLOSED TUES

Auburn is gold rush country—Sutter and Yuba City to the west, Eldorado Forest to the east, and tiny towns all around with names like You Bet, Rough and Ready, Smartville, and Rescue. In the old and historic section of Auburn is the Café Delicias, a deliciously unhokey and inexpensive Mexican restaurant. There are a few concessions toward decor here—a black hat trimmed with gold, some wall hangings. But the tables are simple wood and there are only twelve of them. The result is a plain and intimate place to enjoy first-class Mexican meals for under $3.

A good policy of the Delicias is to offer everything on the menu either as a main course, or as a side dish. Whatever else you choose, be sure to get the expertly prepared chili rellenos—peppers stuffed with cheese, tasting faintly of egg, with enough of the chili seeds left inside the pod to keep it hot. There are also homemade tamales, big soft-rolled burritos, enchiladas, and tacos—full dinners of any for about $3.00. The specialty of the house here is steak *chicana,* a sliced sirloin cooked in a tomato, onion, and green pepper sauce. We found this disappointing, the combination of flavors ill-directed, and the meat without character. It was like an aspiring Swiss steak. The traditional Mexican dishes were perfect, and cheaper. All dinners come with beans, rice, tostadas, and a green salad. Beer can be ordered on the side.

CASTROVILLE

★ THE GIANT ARTICHOKE
2 Locations
3100 Stephens Creek Boulevard, San Jose (408) 244–7240
FRI–SAT 11 AM–11 PM, SUN–THURS 11 AM–9 PM

Merritt Street & Highway 1, Castroville (408) 633–3204
DAILY 8 AM–8 PM

We are not prone to recommending gimmick restaurants, and except for the sleek Steak 'n' Shakes of the Midwest and Bob Sykes's Bar b ques around Birmingham, neither are we fond of chain operations. But in the case of the two Giant Artichokes, we make an exception.

In general their menus are typical and boring: burgers, dogs, fried seafood. But as the name of the places suggests, and as the greenish decor and leafy appearance of the booths further hint, artichokes are a specialty of the house. And where we come from, a good cheap artichoke is hard to find.

The menu lists an envigorating artichoke soup, French fried artichoke hearts, oily and delicious marinated hearts, a tossed salad with artichokes, and a boiled artichoke (which would be better off had it been steamed). There is artichoke cake for dessert with a peculiar taste for which one might easily acquire a liking after a few pieces.

Castroville proclaims itself to be the Artichoke Capital of the World, and its restaurant sprouts a large statue of an artichoke out in front. The Giant Artichoke in San José is garlanded with artichoke pictures around the top.

CORONA DEL MAR

★★ THE ORANGE INN
7400 East Coast Highway (Route 101) (714) 644–5411
DAILY 9 AM–6 PM

The customers' good looks inside The Orange Inn are more blinding than the Southern California sun they just stepped out of. The Inn is a juice bar that makes health shakes and nourishing sandwiches for the surfers and bikini'd bunnies who laze on the white sands of the beach across the road. It is hard to imagine these people dressed in anything but surf-and-sun attire; hard to imagine they have been anything but 100 percent healthy every sunshiny minute of their lives. We thought they might be advertisements for the products sold at The Orange Inn. They were the "after." And we—with our brunette hair, pale skin, and overabundance of clothing—felt like "before."

The Inn was one of the original health restaurants on the coast, dating back to the mid-1930s, when health food meant unpleasant things like blackstrap molasses and dried prunes. Nowadays, health food at The Orange Inn means seductively delicious creations like fresh date milk shakes, sesame candies, and fresh-baked breads and carrot cakes. It's hard to imagine how a steady diet of this stuff produces the sleek, sunstreaked figures lined up at The Orange Inn counter. We're certain if there were an Orange Inn around the corner from us, the steady diet of cakes and milk shakes would put on far too much ballast for us to ever venture in the surf over our heads.

The menu at The Orange Inn is limited, as is seating. There are some tables outside—none inside—but most customers brownbag the food and walk back to the beach. The one thing you shouldn't miss here is a milk shake. Date, fig, raspberry, carob, guava, and papaya are a few of the varieties offered. All use the best organic fruits and are whipped up when ordered. Sandwiches are served on whole wheat bread with crisp bean sprouts as a garnish. The choices are things like avocado with cheese and cucumber, tuna and avocado, or organic peanut butter with strawberry jam.

Desserts are rich but not sugary, since they are sweetened with honey and coconut. Trays of Saran-Wrapped banana cake and apricot brownies are lined up alongside pecan tarts and date nut squares.

The Orange Inn is a lovely white building with oranges painted on the outside walls. The managers are broad-grinned Californians whose favorite expressions are still "oh wow" and "far out." While one of them bragged to us how no meats or eggs are ever served here, a sleek gray cat, perched on a counter nearby, rubbed a wet paw over its whiskers and purred, contented like the sun people of Corona del Mar with his life of coconut milk and organic tuna.

CRESCENT CITY

★★ THE HARBOR VIEW GROTTO
Citizen's Dock and Highway 101 (707) 464–3815
WED–MON NOON–10 PM / CLOSED TUES & OCTOBER 1–MID–NOV

The Harbor View Grotto is perched on stilts over the Crescent Harbor and affords a beautiful view of the fishing fleets and private boats that cruise this northern port. The town itself has a lighthouse accessible only at low tide that is an oceanophile's delight, housing ships' clocks, compasses, logs, and illustrations of famous shipwrecks.

The menu at The Harbor View is extensive, ranging from filet of sole lunches to full-scale Pacific lobster dinners. Lunches are mostly deep-fried fish like scallops, oysters, prawns, or fish and chips. There is a large oyster stew and offerings of crab and shrimp Louie. Lunch is served from noon to 2 p.m.

If the lunch menu is simple, dinner is a fish lover's extravaganza, with everything that swims available, for prices mostly between $4 and $6. One of our favorites is the fresh oyster hangtown fry—a mixture of oysters and scrambled eggs, slightly mild-tasting, but a tactile adventure for the taste buds. We also tried a good grilled red snapper, but missed the razor clams and Chinook salmon, both out of season. There are plenty of chowders, fresh oyster cocktails, stews, salads and Louies, as well as an assortment of steaks for those who aren't inspired by the menu's nautical offerings. The oceanic tone of The Harbor View makes it an ideal place to sample the sea's bounty, as you watch the fishing boats come and go on the misty ocean off the North California coast.

EL CENTRO

★★EL SOMBRERO
841 Main Street (at North Ninth) (714) 352–9188
DAILY 6 AM–10 PM

El Centro is not only the oldest city in the Imperial Valley, it claims to be the most air-conditioned. El Sombrero, a fixture in this town long before the invention of air-conditioning, is the Valley's oldest Mexican restaurant. There is nothing quaint or antiquated about it today. It is well-air-conditioned, and decorated in "velvetoid" Mexican paintings, with molded Day-Glo chairs and Naugahyde booths.

The food and service here is absolutely authentic. Our waitress could barely understand English, and the other help here was taking its mid-afternoon siesta, so we struggled through our order; and spent the fifteen minutes waiting for it trying to shoo away a bee that had flown into the restaurant to escape the heat. The first dish we sampled, an avocado dip, made us suspect that somehow our waitress had interpreted our broken Spanish as a request for extra salt. Or perhaps the dish is designed to go with tequila. In any case, it was too salty. The chorizo burrito was perfectly seasoned—highly spiced by the inclusion of crumbled chorizo sausage and hot sauce. We also sampled the *machaca* with eggs, a shredded beef dish similar to but spicier than Cuban *ropa viejo*. The menu was extremely varied, including the usual combination plates, as well as menudo (a tripe stew), a delicious-looking chili rellenos, "Special Enchiladas Rancheros" with sour cream, side dishes of buttered flour or corn tortillas, full breakfasts of eggs rancheros or chorizo sausage, and an assortment of American steaks and pork chops as well.

The customers are a mixture of Mexicans and local businesspeople, who seem to linger for a long time in the cool air. El Sombrero is an unpretentious place, with a full and inexpensive Mexican menu. If you're driving along Route 8 on Sunday, and don't have time to stop for the generally slow service, call 355–9188 or 352–0534. That's "call for tacos day," when you buy 'em by the dozen to take out.

MOUNTAIN VIEW

★★★ EL CALDERON
699 Calderon (415) 967–9986
MON–SAT 11 AM–2 PM, 5 PM–8:45 PM / CLOSED SUN

We have no standard with which to compare the El Salvadoran food served here, so whether it is authentic or not, peasant or city, ritzy or every day we cannot say. We can say that for a very low price, you can come to El Calderon and enjoy some of the most palatable and finely prepared ethnic food outside the San Francisco city limits. El Calderon is not much more than a storefront—ten tables, a red rug, demure atmosphere, candles at night.

Although there is evidence of chili pepper in the foods of El Salvador, the food is mild compared to Mexican seasonings. Sauces play a big part. There is a hot sauce to add, for those who want their *pollo encevellavo* to taste more fiery, but we preferred the unadulterated subtleties of the buttery onion taste of the chicken, lurking under a mild tomato sauce. This was the most expensive dish on the El Calderon menu, with salad, rice, refried beans and tortillas. We also tried the *yucca con chicheronas,* a cubed pork dish made with yucca root, sautéed in a garlic lemon sauce. The root is potatolike, but stringier, and with a louder flavor—perfect for mopping up the extra sauce. This dish came with a side order of pickled cabbage and a spiced tomato.

Our dinners were preceded by *caldo deres,* a beef stock soup enriched with a colorful mixture of cabbage, corn, zucchini, carrots, and chioti—the latter a very tender cucumberlike vegetable balanced between sweet and pungent. We also tried a *papusa el sal*— normally a lunch "sandwich"—made from two tortillas wrapped around slices of pork, melted cheese, and some refried beans to form a tightly closed package. It is lightly fried, and comes hot with a side dish of pickled cabbage, which our enthusiastic (non-Salvadoran) waiter explained should be put inside the *papusa* as a relish.

Our only regret at El Calderon was that we ate too much to try also the sliced beef tongue in cream sauce and their well-known dish of plantains (coarser bananas) fried and served in a sweetened cream sauce. It's a place well worth coming back to, especially as a break from the wall-to-wall perfection of San Francisco city food. It is no *less* here, but different: informal, family-run (Angela and Robert Lopez), with the feel of a neighborhood. In fact, you may think you are lost on your way here—699 Calderon is a small shopping area in a mostly residential district. It's a quick drive from San Francisco, and a perfect stop on a trip along the coast.

OAKLAND

★ CHRIS' HOT DOGS
4366 Broadway (415) 652–9538
MON–SAT 9 AM–MIDNIGHT, SUN 10 AM–MIDNIGHT

There are fewer hot dogs sold at Oakland A home games than at any other ball park in the country. Fans in the know are waiting until they get outside to enjoy their dogs at Chris'. The hot dog is a much maligned food. Other than super patriots and kids, it has few supporters among American gourmets. People who will take a stand in favor of the best hamburger, or the best pizza, or the best hot fudge sundae will just curl their lip at the mention of frankfurters. And why not? Under close federal scrutiny, the average American hot dog has come out of the closet to reveal its true character: usually a mélange of unwanted poultry parts and "filler."

Chris' is a good place to restore your faith. Since the stand was opened in the 1930s, it has been serving hand-packed and hand-twisted hot dogs—ones that taste like real meat, with identifiable flavors of garlic, onion, and pepper. The original 1930s stand is out back; wieners are now served from a modern blue and white building by Constance "Chris" Foster, wife of the late Chris. She claims that Chris' is the favorite Oakland eatery for both Clint Eastwood and Frankie Laine. With endorsements like that, who could doubt Chris' excellence?

PASADENA

★BEADLE'S CAFETERIA
850 East Colorado Boulevard (213) 796–3618
DAILY 11 AM–7:30 PM

Beadle's is not for those who seek adventure in dining. It is a modern cafeteria in the center of the Pasadena shopping area, just a hop off the Colorado Freeway. It is a laboratory-clean environment, frequented by the Pasadena polyester set. Southern California is the home of "fast foods," and we include Beadle's for its stubborn refusal to go the way of every other inexpensive fast-foodery. There is no exotic food here. But what is served is all prepared right here in the Beadle kitchens, from rich potato and split pea soups to carrot cake and strawberry pie.

There is something delightful about cafeterias: all that food; so much to choose from; no funny looks from the waiter when you take four pats of butter or two desserts. Beadle's boasts an especially nice cafeteria line. It begins with cloth napkin-wrapped silverware, proceeds past a beautiful array of salads, then to the soups. These are all freshly made, and our potato soup was chunky with irregular hunks of potato floating in the creamy brew. Halibut and prime rib are always on the menu; and while the fish did look carefully prepared, the heat lamp is simply unbecoming to fish, so we chose the meat, rare, which is exactly how we got it. It was sliced that way off the roast, with no beet juice added to make it red (i.e., rare) and no tenderizer used to make it chewable. It was a perfect piece of meat. It came with freshly mashed potatoes and hot rolls. For dessert we selected German chocolate cake and carrot cake—both baked that morning, and still moist. There's nothing esoteric about Beadle's. It's just good food, like they've been serving here for over thirty years.

SAN JOSE

★THE GIANT ARTICHOKE—SEE CASTROVILLE

SAN JUAN CAPISTRANO

★★MAC'S COFFEE BREAK
34157 Coastal Highway 101 (714) 496–9270
DAILY 6 AM–4 PM

Mac's served one of the best breakfasts we ate in the West. If all the food here were as good as that meal, we might move to the sunny shores of San Juan Capistrano just to take advantage of the bonanza. But, alas, lunches fall short, and dinners even shorter. So we remain East.

The restaurant itself is an off-handedly artsy coffee shop. From the outside it looks truckdriverish, with a giant coffee cup and the name Mac. Inside it is random-seeming in its assortment of mismatched tables and chairs. Coors beer lamps and Marimekko prints hang on the walls. The customers are a weird assortment of bronzed surfers and surferettes, local truckers and salesmen, and what look like CIA types from nearby San Clemente.

The breakfast menu is presented quickly by waitresses who seem at least half a beat faster than the usual Southern California tempo. By all means order the orange juice. Served in a tall glass, it is the pulp and juice freshly extracted from native oranges using a Flash Gordon-like juicer. The banana-nut pancakes were spectacularly good. They were fragrant with mashed bananas in the batter and chunks of diced pecans and sliced bananas hidden among the cakes. French toast was made with sourdough bread and sprinkled with powdered sugar. The guacamole and mushroom omelette our health-food-fancying friend ordered was a sublime mixture of tastes.

We returned to Mac's for a disappointing lunch. The menu listed avocado and bacon sandwiches or tuna on a homemade muffin. There were heartier but run-of-the-mill meat platters too. We tried the French dip, the West's version of hot roast beef au jus, and found the meat to be almost tasteless, a far cry from our fondly remembered breakfast.

There are a few tables outside Mac's on an open courtyard favored by the sun. Inside, nature is present in the fluffy ferns that grace the walls next to the beer signs. Mac's is unique. It combines roadside-truckstop hospitality with a healthy sunshine-tinged menu: the best of both worlds—at breakfast.

TEHACHAPI

★KELCY'S CAFÉ
110 West Tehachapi Boulevard (Route 58) (805) 822–4207
DAILY 6 AM–9 PM

We include Kelcy's by default. It is surrounded by miles of desert and bad food. Tehachapi itself is interesting, especially to railroad buffs who know it for the 360-degree curved track where the train's caboose actually passes the engine. For railroadmen on a break, or the generally curious, Kelcy's is the spot for lunch.

The waitresses are older ladies who are most friendly to travelers and railroadmen alike. They recommend the hamburgers, a safe bet here and far more reasonable than the menu's expensive steaks. Good-looking omelettes are served with oniony hash browns and toast. Avoid the hot roast beef—gray and gristle-streaked, and accompanied by two pieces of cotton loaf bread and instant mashed potatoes swimming in equally spurious gravy.

The coffee is decent, as are the homemade pies. The lemon pie in particular was impressive with a high, airy egg-white topping and a tart citrus flavor.

Stick to the simple things on the menu, and a palatable meal is yours at Kelcy's. The beef or fried steaks are a bad idea; but an even worse bet is to try and find edible food anywhere else in Tehachapi.

FAIRS AND FESTIVALS

DINUBA
National Raisin Festival / LAST WEEK IN SEPTEMBER

HOLTVILLE
Carrot Festival / MID-MARCH

INDIO
National Date Festival / MID-FEBRUARY
    To celebrate the date harvest; camel & ostrich races

KLAMATH
Salmon Festival / LAST SUNDAY IN AUGUST
    Salmon Bar B Que, logging contests, Indian dances

PISMO BEACH
Clam Festival / LATE FEBRUARY OR EARLY MARCH
Clamming contests, chowder cook-off

REDDING
Strawberry Festival / LATE MAY

WALNUT CREEK
Walnut Festival / LATE SEPTEMBER

COLORADO

BRUSH

★★★ DROVERS RESTAURANT
the Livestock Exchange (½ mile east of Brush on Route 34)
(303) 842–5115
MON–SAT: 5:30 AM–8 PM / CLOSED SUN

The Livestock Exchange in Brush is the home turf of Ron Ball, the World Champion Auctioneer. It is a complex of buildings that includes the holding and selling pens for heifers and bulls, a photographic studio that specializes in airbrushed romantic portraits of famous or up-and-coming auctioneers, and a western saddle and clothing store with the nicest boots and attire this side of Nudie's of Hollywood. The place that the buyers and auctioneers all go after selling cattle and buying boots is Drovers Restaurant, also on the premises.

Thursday and Friday are the big auction days at the Exchange. Waitress June Stoops will warn you to eat here on those days only if you like crowds. "They all pile in here for steak, and we serve it any way they want; but they all seem to want the same—medium rare T-bone." The steaks are bought from Monfort of Colorado, a beef company that is famous for the quality of its meat. On Thursday or Friday nights, the smell of sizzling T-bones is almost overwhelming, and the customers with fancy boots, western-cut suits, and small cattle whips epitomize the cowboy flavor of the real West.

While steaks are the staple of the Drovers' menu, desserts are its flights of fancy. The waitresses could hardly recall all the countless varieties of pie produced by the hefty kitchen cooks. June tried to count the varieties by hand, but soon ran out of fingers. "There's cherry cream with egg white topping, peanut butterscotch, hot deep-dish apple, raisin cream, sour raisin cream, coconut, lemon cream, lemon-lime cream . . ."

The steaks and pies are enough to fill up practically anyone, but if your appetite is insatiable, or if you like the white-walled simplicity of this café and its colorful patrons so much you want to linger, try a bowl of good heavy soup, made fresh daily. The varieties are almost as numerous as the pies. A short selection would include beef with homemade noodles, chicken with rice, bean, chili, hamburger soup made with ground sirloin, barley, lentil, etc.

Drovers is our favorite steak place in Colorado. It gives you a feel for the beef-centered life in these parts better than anywhere else except perhaps a rodeo. And if that's what you like, Brush is one of the rodeo centers of the state, too.

DENVER

★ THE TOMAHAWK TRUCK STOP
Route 76 (east) (303) 659–0810
ALWAYS OPEN

The Tomahawk is a hard-to-miss truckstop on the interstate that bypasses Denver. There are other members of The Tomahawk chain in the West, but this particular truckstop is a favorite of the western truckers who haul cattle to the East. There is a special section for these bullshippers, a wire cagelike structure within the dining room called the "Gearbox." It looks directly out into the truck lot, affording these highway cowboys a full view of their favorite scenery—their trucks.

Nontruckers sit at booths or a counter but they get the same menu as the gearjammers, right down to the "Tomahawk coffee," which allows two free refills. The menu is diverse. In addition to beef, there is an item referred to as "The Best Ham Dinner You Ever Ate" and a spaghetti and meatball platter. We passed up the best ham dinner we ever ate and ordered instead an eight-ounce cowboy steak, with baked potato, Texas toast, and salad. The meat was flavorful, and tough enough to give the teeth a good workout. We also ordered the spaghetti dinner, with pasta so mushy it had been pressed into a doughy pancake under the weight of the meatballs.

Dinners can be had with your choice of homemade soup (try the first-rate beef barley) and warm but cottony buns. The salad is a small bowl of wilted greens, so the option of sliced tomatoes is a good alternative. Dinners come with coffee but no dessert. The specialty of The Tomahawk is a gross fantasy known as deep-dish apple pie with rum butter sauce. We ordered this extravaganza, and it took a full twenty minutes to prepare. Our waitress kept nervously reporting back to us on its progress. What finally arrived was a large cereal bowl full of stewed apples, heavy on the cinnamon, with a ridiculous little pinhead of a biscuit perched on top. If you like twelve-ounce bowls of stewed apples, it is worth the wait. But if pie is your preference, forget it, because this tiny biscuit is unbreakable with a fork, and any pie that requires a steak knife hardly seems worth the effort.

In the tradition of truckstops everywhere, breakfast is served round the clock, accompanied by powerful, road-worthy coffee.

GRAND JUNCTION

★★★OLD MEXICO FOODS
755 North Avenue (Eighth Street) (303) 243–1556
DAILY 11 AM–9 PM

For some reason, Mexican food thrives in Colorado primarily as a "takeout" business. There are few Mexican restaurants, but many places with two or three small tables and a takeout window. Old Mexico is one of the best.

A sign over the cash register announces, "If you have to wait more than fifteen minutes for your meal, it's free." Usually such signs are a warning that the food is already cooked and ready to reheat, or that you'll get it half-raw. Not at Old Mexico. At our last meal there we saw the cook personally come out of the kitchen to explain to us that the lettuce leaf placed over our cheese crisp was there "just to keep the foil from the cheese, so it doesn't stick." We were instructed to discard the lettuce when we were ready to eat the crisp.

There is a full range of crisps at Old Mexico—variations of the tortilla. There is a dessert crisp—a tortilla dusted with powdered sugar. There are various tostadas covered with green chili, bean chili, cheese and avocado, and cheese only. There are combination plates of chili, taco, enchilada, and refried beans. The Mexicali plate is a large salad with lettuce, tomatoes, guacamole, turkey slices, cottage cheese, pineapple chunks, orange slices, and tostada crisps. Sopaipillas are a little too heavy. The tostadas make a better side dish. Lunch specials feature chilis and occasionally a luscious sour-cream green chili enchilada. An interesting change for dessert is Mexican chocolate, a semisweet hot drink that cuts through the coldest Colorado weather.

IDAHO SPRINGS

★★★ THE VALLEY CAFÉ
Miner Street
WED–MON 7 AM–2 PM, 5 PM–9 PM / CLOSED TUES

"Rocky Mountain" trout appears on menus all over the country with the same evocative powers as "Kansas City" sirloin and "Maine" lobster. If you want to go right to the source, try The Valley Café— known to citizens of Idaho Springs as "The Trout Café" for its pure and simple devotion to the fish that made the Rockies famous in great restaurants all over the world. The further away one gets from the source, the more of an expensive delicacy this fish is. Here at The Valley Café, the freshest trout from Colorado Springs are served on Formica tables, with paper napkins, and you sit under giant taxidermined specimens on the wall. The trout is simply pan-fried in butter, and flavored lightly with salt and flakes of parsley. There is no taste in the world more suggestive of mountain streams and clear high-altitude air, and the unspoiled wilderness. Only if these trout were cooked on a stick over an open fire could they taste more like the great outdoors.

The Valley Café is hardly more than an expanded coffee shop. It has a lovely old-fashioned atmosphere, with a fading cabbage rose wallpaper and old wooden booths. The waitresses are older ladies, calm and efficient, who have been serving trout at the café for years. Unlike other trout restaurants in town, there is no atmosphere trumped up here to upstage what The Valley knows is its best feature, fresh trout. The dinners come with either a baked potato or freshly made potato salad, and a vegetable. Desserts are nice-looking homemade pies, and there are breakfast specials of French pancakes, rolled around locally put-up strawberry preserves, or Swedish pancakes (a little thicker than the French, and more buttery) served with apple sauce.

PUEBLO

★★ LA MEXICANA

321 West Northern Avenue (303) 545-1161
MON–SAT 9 AM–6 PM / CLOSED SUN

La Mexicana has some of the best Mexican food north of New Mexico; certainly the best pastries. Shells, turtles, crescents, or bullhorns—all are names for Manuel Ramirez' sweet glazed pastries baked here every morning. "I try to make them as fluffy as I can," Manuel told us. "Most pastries, American pastries, are doughy, and thick. You can't eat but one or two. Mine are light, and just semisweet." They are like a sopapailla, only crispier, and with the honey glazed onto the top. They are, in fact, so light that it is hard to imagine filling up on them, as difficult as they are to stop eating.

Beyond the pastries, Manuel makes tacos and burritos Indian style. That is, he uses shredded rather than ground meat. "I've got to do it different than anybody else. My people, and the anglos here, like the taste of real meat, and they like it hot." The meat used is like shredded pot roast—intensely flavorful in its own right, then intensified when Manuel pours on the green chili. The burrito is the large, soft, rolled variety; the taco comes with meat, chili, tomato slices, and onions. Also available by the piece are enchiladas and tamales, or for those who have difficulty choosing, there is the combination plate, which includes a taco, a tostada, a tamale, a burrito, refried beans, rice, and a cup of chili.

La Mexicana is a very small restaurant—barely bigger than the bakery. Most of the business is takeout, but there are two or three small tables. It is an especially nice place to dine early in the morning, when Manuel's pastries perfume the air with the thick smell of corn and sweet honey. It is in the old part of town, next to the steel mill. And best of all for roadfooders, it is only two blocks from Exit 36 of I-25.

RIFLE

★ AUDREY'S BAKERY CAFÉ

Fourth Street & Railroad Avenue (303) 625-3163
DAILY 6 AM–10 PM

At six in the morning, the high-altitude town of Rifle flocks to Audrey's for western-style breakfasts and lots of local gossip. Every table in the little storefront café is buzzing with cowboys and Rifle tradesmen socializing to beat the band. Despite the "Help Wanted" sign in the window, service was fast. A waitress appeared with super-sonic speed as soon as we claimed a seat. She was back equally fast with the food. A check must be requested, since the cardinal sin at Audrey's is for a waitress to hint that a meal is finished. After all, a customer might be in the middle of his best story.

Everybody gets doughnuts for breakfast. They are dense, sweet, and irregularly formed. Even customers who ordered the ham and egg breakfasts got doughnuts on the side. We splurged on a Colorado steak and eggs which came with what could easily have been a nice-sized dinner steak and three eggs. The luxury breakfast is eggs and two pork chops—a cowboy-sized meal, unfortunately at oilman prices.

At dinner time, Colorado beef seemed to be the theme of the menu. Regulars clued us in to the roast leg of pork with apple sauce that is served a few times a week. It sounded like a good change from the 100 percent beef diet that characterizes this high-altitude country.

We lingered over our meals and several cups of good, strong coffee. We couldn't help but notice the odd style of hat sported by many of the patrons. Colorado "ten gallons" are sharply creased down the center, then pressed flat and apparently stomped on or run over with a steamroller. It seems to be a popular fashion to have a hat that looks well-worn or worn out.

After casually hanging out for what seemed at least an hour, we asked the waitress for a check. "Why are you rushing off? You just got here," she said. Audrey's is a social center in Rifle. If you want to be pegged as anything other than a greenhorn, come prepared with some good long-winded yarns to spin over coffee.

FAIRS AND FESTIVALS

GLENWOOD SPRINGS
Strawberry Days Festival & Rodeo / LATE JUNE

GRAND LAKE
Buffalo Bar B Que / MID-JULY

GRAND JUNCTION
Peach Festival / LATE AUGUST

IDAHO SPRINGS
Sowbelly and Bean Festival / AUGUST—1ST WEEK

ROCKY FORD
Watermelon Festival / LAST WEEK IN AUGUST

IDAHO

KOOSKIA

★★SYRINGA CAFÉ
Route 12 (16 miles east of Kooskia) (208) 926–8890
DAILY 6 AM–10 PM

In 1805, Lewis and Clark came down from the mountains into the White Pine forests of what is now Idaho. They were starving and frozen and, like travelers today who leave Missoula, Montana, heading west, the explorers would probably have eaten shoeleather. There is just no food around here, which is why the Syringa is remarkable. In a wilderness without competition for miles around, the Syringa goes to the trouble of baking eight different kinds of pie every day, of brewing homemade soups, of baking Sunday dinners with homemade noodles or special Syringa stuffing for the pork chops. It is not at all unusual for truckers who are traveling Route 90 to detour at Missoula in order to make a stop at Syringa, then rejoin the interstate at Spokane. We recommend that roadfooders follow their example.

Sunday really is the best day to be at Syringa. That's when the dinners are things like baked ham with apricot glaze, stuffed pork chops with dressing and mushroom gravy, and baked chicken with homemade noodles. During the week, the regular menu features dinners of "chicken supreme in curry sauce," pork chops, a "Cordon Bleu plate" (veal, ham, and Swiss cheese), and an assortment of steaks and large dinner sandwiches. All dinners come with soup (homemade), potato, salad, and wine. None of this food is likely to make an urban gourmet want to move to Kooskia, but what we have sampled was prepared from fresh ingredients, and seasoned with an experienced touch.

In line with the international flavor of the dinner menu, breakfasts include Spanish omelettes with jalapeño peppers as well as three-egg omelettes with toast and hash browns or hotcakes. We've never had the hotcakes, being partial to potatoes while in Idaho. The last time we were eating breakfast at the Syringa, two drivers sitting across from us were eating eggs with baked potatoes on the side, an appropriate complement to any meal in the state whose name is synonymous with spuds.

The syringa is the state flower.

LEWISTON

★STOCK YARDS CAFÉ
2615 Seventh Avenue North (208) 743-9795
MON–SAT 6 AM–5 PM / CLOSED SUN

You can't beat the Stock Yards for atmosphere. It really is in a stockyards building, surrounded by the aroma of livestock on the hoof. As you dine, you'll hear cattle down at the other end of the building being branded for out of state shipment, and cattlemen in the restaurant discussing feed prices and government regulations.

Peter Flynn is a local cattle buyer who selects the meat for the café. He takes a particularly juicy-looking cow to the federal butchering center and has it ground into hamburger, which is served here. Oddly enough, the Stock Yards serves no big freshcut steaks. What they get from their cow is turned into Swiss steaks, liver and onions, and hamburger steaks with every sort of topping you could imagine—bar b que sauce, mushroom soup, natural gravy—take your pick. The hamburger steaks come with any sauce you choose and include instant mashed potatoes or a freshly made potato salad.

In truth, the Stock Yards Café is one place where the hamburger steak actually did taste more like a ground-up steak than an overgrown hamburger. Maybe it was just the cows' pictures on the wall, but our burger really did seem fit for that patron of the pretentious hamburger, the Earl of Salisbury.

The cow products are good, but the veal patties and the fried chicken are frozen, so beware.

For full appreciation of the Stock Yards Café, come on Saturday or one of the Mondays during the fall when the big sales are held. The small café is packed with buyers and sellers, and although service is frenzied (most men go behind the counter and help themselves), it is a real taste of a smalltown livestock market. Other times, the Stock

Yards serves as a slightly out-of-town eatery for the citizens of Lewiston. It's just a short drive across the Clearwater River, across from the Idaho Highway Department building.

POCATELLO

★★HARRIS' BAR B CUE
427 North Fourth Street (208) 232–4715
TUES–SUN 11 AM–3 AM, CLOSED MON

We caught wind of Harris' Bar B Cue by noticing that more than a few Pocatello business establishments had his calendar on the wall, and that even the gas station had a Harris calendar rather than a nudie over the tool bench. Harris' Bar B Cue is in a part of town that, while not disreputable, could not rightfully be called uptown Pocatello. It is directly across from the Salvation Army, and while we flirted with the idea of finding an old trunk and taking Polaroids to send back to Judy Garland-fan friends ("Born in a trunk in Pocatello . . ."), the lure of hickory smoke brought us into Harris' without so much as a peek into the trunks across the street.

Mr. Harris runs a most reputable bar b que. "People of all the states come in here," he told us. "A man from Germany was here. People of all races enjoy my food." Indeed, the customers here at lunchtime were a motley group, all eating the day's lunch special of pighearts and pinto beans at the tables watched over by Mr. Harris' portraits of Dr. King, the Kennedys, and himself. He explained to us that every day he makes bar b qued ribs, chicken, and beef, and that there are soul specials, too. The entrées include an alternating assortment of various pig parts, as well as hot links, meat loaf, stuffed peppers, and Mr. Harris' own invention, a soul slumgullion stew—made, we guess, from leftover hearts, maws, chitlins, and plenty of his bar b que sauce. He makes no pies, except during the holidays.

The ribs, whose sweet odor had lured us here, were not yet ready, so we chose two lunch specials—greens and neckbones, and pighearts and pinto beans. The neckbones were the better of the two—highly peppered and tasting of sage and chicken stock, served with heady, almost chewy greens. The pigheart came in a Brunswick stewlike consistency, and seemed undercooked. The meat was chewy, but yielded almost no flavor.

Harris told us that sometimes he makes a special hog maw salad, which is one regular customer's favorite. What is served at Harris' seems to depend on Mr. Harris' moods, and in our limited experience the quality seems variable. For an adventuresome eater, this Pocatello café makes for an enjoyable soul stop in southeastern Idaho.

ROSE LAKE

★ MANON'S CAFÉ
Exit 34 off Route 90 (208) 682–2217
WED–MON 8 AM–8 PM / CLOSED TUES

Manon's is a woodsy, cabinlike building, surrounded by nothing but trees. Inside it is all wood, with heavy wooden tables, and lots of windows for patrons to look out at the evergreens. There are picnic tables outside, or a small counter and about ten tables inside. In cool weather, the fireplace is kept going. There is some western art on the walls, and the general ambiance here is a friendly, rustic, northwestern one.

What these people like to eat is meat. There are inexpensive sirloins and club steaks all the way up to a pound-plus tenderloin as well as a full array of burger choices. Steak dinners come with the works, including homemade soup. There was a leather-faced old cowboy next to us who had never heard of minestrone, but ordered it as a side dish to his hot beef sandwich. He approached it cautiously, but by mid-bowl was exclaiming "What good soup! What good soup!" between spoonfuls. We concur with his judgment, having found it filled with good-quality vegetables and made with a rich beef stock. Our sirloin was a good piece of meat; though a little thin, and a little overcooked over too low a flame, it was still juicy. We also sampled a bowl of "Mexican hot chili" which was rich and meaty, but neither Mexican-tasting nor hot. A side order of sautéed mushrooms was perfect—buttery but not greasy, the fresh mushrooms retaining a good fibrous snap without being in the least bit rubbery. The homemade cheesecake was a dry disappointment. But if the food is only fair, the setting is lovely and the people are friendly. Manon's makes a good short stop on a lonely stretch of highway.

FAIRS AND FESTIVALS

RIGGINS
Annual Riggins Bar B Que / AUGUST 31
Raft races, C&W, huge bar b que

SHELLY
Spud Day / MID-SEPTEMBER
Free baked potatoes for all

MONTANA

BILLINGS

★BAIR'S CAFÉ
1309 First Avenue (406) 252–9829
ALWAYS OPEN

Bair's has long been a favorite stopping-off place for truckers along I-94, the northernmost cross-country superhighway. In the ice-age winters that hit Billings, you'll be able to spot it among the other businesses on First Avenue by the clouds of steam and smoke from the exhaust of idling trucks that surround the tiny café. Closer you'll see the large sign on the roof, and the cutout bear on the sidewalk, beckoning you to enter and get warm.

If you've come for breakfast, you're in luck. Every morning Bair's has large trays of freshly made cinnamon rolls—yeasty spice-and-sugar beauties that are a perfect bracer against the below-zero temperatures outside. As you eat your cinnamon roll, you'll probably get a good sniff of the pies baking in the oven for the lunch specials. The choices vary, but there are at least two varieties baked every day. We have tried the pumpkin and peanut butter pies, both baked in a thick, flavorful crust.

Lunches at Bair's are standard stuff, notable mostly for their low price tag. This buys a cup of soup, bar b qued ribs or Swiss steak, instant potatoes, vegetables, dessert, and coffee.

Bair's was being remodeled and renovated the last time we were there. It used to have the weathered charm of a long-familiar outfitting station for the icy north. There is a small truckers' store next to the café where basic supplies are sold for further travels into the wilderness.

BOULDER

★★ FRAN'S CAFÉ
124 Main Street (406) 225–3382
DAILY 5 AM–7 PM

"The way I make these baked apples," Christina Smith said as she pulled a tray of twelve from the oven, "is the way I remember my mother making them. Butter and just the right amount of cinnamon make them good." The apples sizzled as they cooled, and we thought that if there were a café like Fran's every fifty or hundred miles along the interstates, we could travel forever. We had just finished two of Christina's freshly baked pasties—tender hunks of pot roast, potatoes, onions, minced celery and seasonings all wrapped in her flaky pie crust. They had been covered with a gravy made from the roast's drippings, were accompanied by tart cole slaw, and followed by two servings of sweet raisin-flavored bread pudding.

Fran has been gone for a long time, and Christina has been operating this café since before we were old enough to drive. Every day she makes something special. "Tomorrow I'll make corned beef and cabbage. They love that here. Especially in the cool weather. Or chicken casserole. Or my meat loaf with bacon. Or beef stew . . ." Christina continued her list of specialities, arriving finally at pies—apple, cherry, blueberry. "Nothing special," she said. "Most people like these baked apples better. I make them every day." Christina knows her customers, and gives them the kind of food they've been coming to Fran's for since it was converted from a service station back in 1945.

Fran's is set back slightly from the road, but if you keep an eye out for the O-Z Motel (with which Fran's is not affiliated), you'll see the minuscule twenty-five-person café. It's the best food for miles around.

DILLON

★★SKEET'S CAFÉ

Interstate 15 (East Bannack & South Montana Streets) (406) 683–9964
ALWAYS OPEN

According to our Montana friend Bruce, Skeet's serves "the best café food I've ever tasted." We approached Skeet's cautiously, aware that Bruce has been known to consume an entire Nick's Special in Boulder, Colorado, in hopes of winning himself a Nick's T-shirt. (A Nick's Special is about six pounds of eggs, potatoes, and toast. Bruce thought that the shirt you win is the one that the waitress is wearing. He was disappointed and not a little sick when he got his T-shirt from a box in back.) Anyway, he is known for his iron gut and a propensity for places with cute waitresses and lots of potatoes, preferably both.

The dish he recommended was the veal dinner. It is two huge breaded cutlets—undoctored, tender slices of decent veal, nicely breaded in seasoned meal and fried until the breading begins to puff up from the meat. The meat comes with vegetable soup and real potatoes on the side.

The pies are the usual assortment of fruit and cream and although they are so good, Bruce says, that Skeet's won't sell them to go, for fear other café owners will resell them, we found the sour cream raisin too thick, and the apple too sweet. They were good, and fresh, and some of the best in the state, but they do not belong in the Cake and Pie Hall of Fame. They are, in fact, the kind of overwhelmingly rich concoctions you'd expect a guy who can eat six pounds of potatoes to recommend.

Skeet's has two rooms, one a dining room open during meal hours, and the other a counter-and-booth room, which is open all the time. The kitchen is between the two. Skeet is seldom around. "He doesn't have to work," the waitress said. "We've made him rich." Skeet's really is a first-rate roadside café, light on the grease, easy on the pocketbook, with a good assortment of home-cooked food.

GARDINER

★THE PIT STOP CAFÉ

Third Street (406) 848–9992
MON–SAT 6 AM–9 PM / CLOSED SUN

The Pit Stop Café is at the northern entrance to Yellowstone Park, and is located near other eating places that are far more expensive and elaborately decorated. While we might pull into a fancy joint for a grand-scale meal, the Pit Stop is the best bet in this area for a snack.

The Café is a simple Formica-furnished room with a distinctive lack of atmosphere.

Follow the lead of the straw-hatted cowboys at the counter and order the beef bar b que. "The meat here is local raised," our grinning waitress told us as she set a platter of good-looking beef in front of us. She slid a jar of home-brew hot sauce down the counter. She then continued to flirt with the best-looking ranch hand at the counter.

The beef was juicy and flavorful, yet chewy as Westerners seem to prefer. The hot sauce was thick-grained and chili-peppered, made by someone who understood the mystical marriage of bar b que to sauce.

Gardiner Street is only about thirty yards long, and the Pit Stop an easy place to locate.

LIVINGSTON

★★MURRAY HOTEL CAFÉ

West Park & Second Street (406) 222–1350
DAILY 6 AM–9 PM

Livingston is on the eastern side of the Bozeman Pass, which used to divide hostile Indian plains (to the east) from the mining boom towns (to the west). The Indians have been subdued, and the mining towns have mostly turned to dust, but Livingston remains the hellzapoppin tourist center of Montana. Travelers should come equipped with full wallets, and prepare to leave with empty stomachs. Fishermen and part-time resident Peter Fonda are the only ones who really make out well here. The former can catch plenty of their own fresh-water fish. Fonda, it is rumored, has all his food flown in.

For the rest of us, there is the Murray Hotel Café. Every day there is a lunch special which includes all the porcine favorites of Montanans

—pork tips, roast pork, pork chops, pork tenderloin and sweet and sour pork. The entrées come with real potatoes that have been mashed to a smooth consistency with lots of butter and cream, vegetables and a salad. Aside from pork the Murray offers more expensive steaks and a full salad bar which includes not only lettuce and its usual companions, but jello molds, macaroni and potato salad, carrot and raisin salad, and three-bean salad.

The food at the Murray Hotel Café isn't memorable, but it does stand out in contrast to the town's other eating places. One of Livingston's fancier restaurants is notorious for serving a dish called "Newburg Oriental," a seafood conglomeration that surely originated in a Taiwanese cat food factory.

FAIRS AND FESTIVALS

LIVINGSTON
National Trout Derby / AUGUST

RED LODGE
Pea Festival / LATE JUNE
Pea-shelling contests

NEVADA

ELKO

★★BASQUE RESTAURANT
246 Silver Street in the Star Hotel (702) 738–9925
DAILY: DINNER

There is a Basque restaurant in Elko whose menu offers such unlikely "Basque" dishes as frozen shrimp and spaghetti for $8 per person. The only Basque element seems to be that the food is served family style. But at *this* Basque Restaurant, the food is authentic; so authentic, in fact, that it might be too exotic for some tastes.

The restaurant has been in Elko since 1909 and is now run by

Joseph Sarasva, a charming man "from the old country," who maintains the best traditions of Basque dining. There are tables enough here for eighty-five patrons, and better food by far than anywhere else in Elko. Of course, you might need a winch to lift you out of your seat at the end of the meal. Basque cuisine is not dainty.

Soups start the meal, and although the owner brusquely described the ingredients as "hog meat," the blend was a flavorful mixture of pork, beans, and vermicelli. Then come the stews: pigs feet and tripe with cabbage; paella with spicy sausage and mussels. The sausages used are *chorizo* and *morillas,* both garlicky and fatty rich. Both mix well with the sliced potatoes that come as a side dish. The menu changes daily, and for the fixed price you get what the kitchen decides to cook. On other days the stews might be codfish and eggs, tripe, or hearts.

Traditionally, Basques are not dessert eaters, so no dessert, not even cheese, is served afterwards. There is of course the tasty Picon Punch, sweet but potent, served here in lieu of pie or cake. We recommend the Basque Restaurant as the least expensive and most jovial eatery in Elko.

RENO

★★THE BASQUE RESTAURANT
235 Lake Street in the Santa Fe Hotel (702) 323–1891
DAILY: DINNER

Reno, like its big sister Las Vegas, is a town overrun with gamblers, newlyweds, and newly divorced. It is hard to find a snip of reality in these round-the-clock towns, harder still to find home cooking. But the Basque fills the bill on both counts, and that's why it's our favorite in this "biggest little city in the world."

The customers are mostly local families who come to sit in groups of ten or twenty at long Formica tables. There is no menu. You are greeted, and the waitress brings on the food for the fixed price of about $5, including wine.

Basque food is a cross between French and Spanish, and since traditionally the Basques have been shepherds, meat is the central theme. The meals start with vegetable soup, thick with potatoes and leeks and seasoned with garlic. Next comes a bowl of mutton-simmered pinto beans and a green salad with a mild French dressing. Basque cuisine is hearty, and a stew follows the salad in order to whet your appetite for a subsequent main course. The stews here alternate between four classic offerings: oxtail, tripe, lamb, or beef tongue. All except for the cream-based lamb are simmered in a garlic-zinged tomato base. The main dish is a steak, except Thursday nights when pork chops are served. The steak is thick-sliced and smoky tasting—the way it must be when enjoyed by the outdoor-living Basques, roasted over an open fire.

After dinner Monterrey cheese is offered along with Picon Punch, the Basque drink of quinine, brandy, and soda.

WINNEMUCCA

★★★ MARTIN HOTEL
Railroad & Melarkey Streets (702) 623-3197
MON–SAT: DINNER / CLOSED SUN

A friend of ours once said he would never set foot inside a restaurant that operated on the "Here's what you get" principle. These are the places that offer, for a low price, a limited selection from among a "bottomless" salad bowl, a "groaning" bread board, a carafe of wine, a hunk of meat tenderized into submission, and perhaps a piece of allegedly famous cheesecake. The Martin Hotel in Winnemucca is a wonderful exception to the dreary predictability of "Here's what you get" style of eating. It is, in the Basque tradition, a family-style dining room, where you pay a fixed price and get the meal of the day, your only choices being how much to eat, and whether you want to begin your meal (or end it) with the addition of the Basque drink Picon Punch. It is a powerhouse drink, and we recommend saving it for after the meal, to be leisurely sipped on a full stomach.

"They hardly have room for the punch after," chef John Liberto told us. "There's never any dessert. This is down-to-earth eating. Cakes and pies don't fit." A down-to-earth dinner at the Martin Hotel begins with soup—split pea, navy bean, or when we ate here, lentil. It was served, like the rest of the dinner, in large bowls, passed among the strangers who sit together at the weathered Formica tables. ("The tops wore out long ago," Liberto told us, "from the weight of the platters.") Also on the table are long, crusty French breads and butter. The first pieces of this bread were sliced off by more demure diners. But as soon as a native-looking Basque reached a loaf and tore off a piece with his hands, all followed in this informal manner. Along with the soup came the wine, replenished as needed throughout the meal.

After the soup, there was a salad, a nice leafy break before the waitresses brought on the heavy artillery. This was the pinto beans and the stews. The stews were a tripe and a *baccala*. The tripe was in a highly seasoned garlic tomato sauce, with enough parsley to lend the dish a fresh chlorophyll-tasting counterpart to the garlic. The *baccala* was a dried cod fish dish that had been simmered in garlic sauce, and then lightly flavored with tomatoes. The pinto beans were handy, like the French bread, for mopping up the stews' sauces.

At this point, the main course arrived. It was a one-pound sirloin steak, plain-looking by comparison to everything that had come before, and anticlimactic. We could easily have done without it, but the regular Martin eaters, who had been more discreet through the earlier courses, dug into their steaks as if the two stews, beans, soup, bread, and wine had actually given them an appetite.

By the time we were finished with the steak it was nearly 8 p.m., and dinner was over. We tried the Picon Punch, which was a strangely bittersweet mixture that on top of everything else we had consumed did serve as a kind of lightener—for the head, if not the stomach.

★ THE STAR BROILER

Bridge Street & Winnemucca Boulevard (702) 623–2892
ALWAYS OPEN

In the surrealistic land of silicone bosoms and one-armed bandits rests The Star Broiler. Like a desert oasis, this "eat drink play" establishment lures the hungry and thirsty with a smorgasbord of decent food at low prices. The hope is, of course, that diners will lose double their meal money on the roulette wheels or keno tables conveniently provided by the management.

The daily buffets here are calculated to be as fantastic in scope as the rest of the Midas Touch-ambiance in this strange land. The manager describes the Star's cuisine as being "part Italian, part Chinese, with other parts Xanthippe, Yukon, Zouave, Lyonnaise, Welch, Juvenile, and Gambler." While we can't claim expertise in evaluating Zouave or Gambler cuisine, we tried enough seemingly American food here to get a fair idea.

The typical lunch and dinner offerings include roast turkey, bar b qued codfish (a weird-tasting concoction, perhaps Xanthippe in origin?), baked salmon, sweet and sour fish puffs, fried oysters, fried chicken, and a large choice of mixed salads, most with gloppy dressing. The fried chicken and roasted turkey were by far the best, still managing to have a juicy inside and a crisp skin under the heat lamps. The fish puffs tasted like sour-sauced poker chips, and the oysters like salty-crusted dice.

Desserts were an unexciting assortment of puddings and jellos, best avoided unless you are a fan of Juvenile cuisine.

Dinners and lunches are inexpensive. If you can resist the keno tables, the meal you have here will be a bargain if not a culinary fiesta.

FAIRS AND FESTIVALS

ELKO

National Basque Festival / EARLY JULY
Chorizo sausage, wine, and brandy

OREGON

CAPE KIWANDA

★★ THE HUNGRY HARBOR RESTAURANT

At Cape Kiwanda, N. of Pacific City, Or. (503) 965–6245
MON–FRI 11:30 AM–8 PM, SAT & SUN 7 AM–9 PM

The Hungry Harbor is a homey place with a picture window overlooking the ocean. The decor is a bit self-consciously "old-timey," with ye olde-fashioned wallpaper and a few antique-style items scattered about, but we were happy to learn that these artifacts were left by previous owners. The current management dismisses the décor as unimportant. What they are concerned with at Hungry Harbor is made-from-scratch food, from soup to dessert.

Soup is a specialty of the house. There is always a thick, cream-style clam chowder and one soup du jour. We have encountered an old-fashioned bean soup, thick with ground meat, beans, onion bits and celery, flavored slightly with molasses. They are known here, too, for a pea soup made with carrots and egg whites. "Sometimes I make my soup too thick," the cook told us. "I get carried away and make it more like a stew, with lots of meat."

Soup is followed by a good green salad and your main course, which is seafood. There is fresh salmon steak in season; also fried oysters, ling cod or fish and chips and, if you want, clam fritters on the side.

Dessert is a choice of cobblers—peach, apple, cherry—served in a bowl and customarily topped with ice cream.

Full dinners, which include all of the above-mentioned courses, are well under $5, and include warm, homemade muffins.

PORTLAND

★★★ DAN AND LOUIS' OYSTER BAR
208 Southwest Ankeny Street (503) 227–5906
DAILY 11 AM–1 AM

Louis Wachsmuth was the founder of this wonderful old oyster bar, and centered his cooking around the Yaquina Bay oysters that his father claimed squatters rights to when he was shipwrecked near the oyster beds in 1881. Louis started with a stand-up oyster bar in the days at the turn of the century when oysters were as popular as hamburgers are today. Louis would stand behind the bar, cigar in his mouth, and shuck oysters for local fishermen and friends. One cold day he had the idea to throw a few handfuls of the succulent oysters into a milk stew with butter and serve it to the frostbitten oystermen who came here to get out of the cold. The stew was such a success that Louis started to add tables and chairs and now, sixty years later, the Oyster Bar still exists, serving Louis' famous stew.

Dan and Louis' place is beautiful. The oyster bar itself is a boat's hull called the Star of Oregon—highly lacquered and perfectly preserved right down to the gleaming portholes along the side. The whole interior of the Oyster Bar is made of nautical wood, very old and weathered, with brass fittings; lanterns are hung from the ceiling.

The menu is small and oyster-shaped. The inside lists the limited offerings and informs patrons that the oysters are still from the original fruitful beds that gave Louis his Yaquina oysters—noteworthy for their unique salty tang.

Yaquina oyster stew is available with chopped oysters or cocktail-sized whole oysters. It is possible to get it with double oysters; and if you like oysters, the Yaquina variety are so extraordinary, you might want to order triples. There is also a shrimp stew, and a Louis-invented Garibaldi crab stew, both based on the original oyster stew recipe.

For the raw oyster lover, the oyster cocktail comes on the half shell with red sauce, and it is in this raw form that the salt tang of Yaquina Bay beauties is best savored. Slightly more expensive is the crab cocktail, mounds of pink and white crabmeat pulled from Oregon's icy waters and served with red sauce or Thousand Island dressing.

Despite its local fame, Dan and Louis' has maintained a simple, conservatively priced menu. It is the perfect setting for old-salt oyster-men and sight-seeing tourists to convene and savor the Yaquina Bay bounty.

ROSEBURG

★★THE HILLS TIMBER GRILL
732 Southeast Cass (503) 672–5631
ALWAYS OPEN

The Hills is a tiny café located in a partially abandoned hotel. Cook Marion Campbell couldn't recall a time when the people of Roseburg didn't come to The Hills to eat salmon yearling in season.

Salmon yearling is a young fish, the size of a small trout. To pre-serve the delicate and juicy flavor of the red salmon meat, the fish is quickly grilled. A salmon yearling dinner comes with with soup, salad, baked potato, vegetables and desert.

The Hills specializes in Oregon dishes. One soup served before dinner is cream of mushroom, the mushrooms from nearby growers. Potatoes are an Oregon staple, best appreciated in their simplest form —baked and slathered with butter.

Desserts also rely on local products. The Hills is well known in this area for their great blackberry pies. We found the crust to be a little heavy, but the berries were so ripe and delicious that no sugar or spices could have possibly improved their taste.

For those who don't like salmon, The Hills also cuts beef steaks to order. Our waitress told us that most customers stick to a twelve-ounce cut but that the kitchen is willing to give the patron what he wants. She cited as an example a trucker who singlehandedly ate a 36-ounce steak a few years back.

The Hills is a pleasant, small restaurant, always open, and conven-iently located near the interstate. Salmon, not uncommon on Oregon restaurant menus, is usually a slice of a large whole fish. Salmon yearling is harder to find, and we thought well prepared at this unpretentious grill.

SPRINGFIELD

★★ THE PIT
Eighth and Olive Streets (503) 344–5467
MON–SAT 7 AM–8 PM / CLOSED SUN

If you are a purist of the bar b que pit, please skip this roadfood entry. If, on the other hand, you have catholic and forgiving sensibilities, and a craving for the unique taste of hickory-scented meat, by all means come to The Pit. What they do here is to throw hickory chips into their ovens and, we suspect, sprinkle the meats with "liquid smoke." We have tried these tricks at home in desperate attempts to duplicate the elusive flavor that permeates meat when it is slowly cooked over real hickory or mesquite wood. They don't really work, but the bastardized product helps to tamp down the desire. At The Pit you get a dinner of spare ribs, bar b qued chicken, ham, beef, or sliced pork —all scented with hickory—along with a salad, a hickory-baked potato, and fresh homemade bread. Lunch sandwiches come on good bread which is dense enough to absorb the juices from the meat without disintegrating like ordinary white bread.

The Pit really does try hard. In addition to bar b que, they offer Texas hot chili, without beans. It has all the proper ingredients, a good measure of hotness, but none of the mystique of the product sold in the Southwest. If you are here for lunch and not a full dinner, we highly recommend a side order of the hickory-cooked potato, which has developed a chewy skin and a fluffy inside. Also recommended are the fresh-baked pies, especially the peach and rhubarb—both are delicious.

If you are not expecting mystically great bar b que, a meal at the Pit will leave you satisfied.

FAIRS AND FESTIVALS

ASTORIA
Astoria Regatta and Fish Festival   /   LATE AUGUST

BANDON
Cranberry Festival and Bar B Que   /   MID-SEPTEMBER

KLAMATH FALLS
Klamath Basin Potato Festival / MID-OCTOBER

LEBANON
Lebanon Strawberry Festival / LATE MAY
The world's largest strawberry shortcake is made

LINCOLN CITY
Indian Style Salmon Bake / MID-SEPTEMBER
Open pit salmon bar b que

McMINNVILLE
Turkey Bar B Que / EARLY JULY

YACHATS
Silversmelt fry / 2ND SAT IN JULY

UTAH

CEDAR CITY

★★★ HUGHES CAFÉ
Main Street (801) 586–6371
MON–THURS 6 AM–10 PM / FRI & SAT 6 AM–11 PM / CLOSED SUN

Hughes Café is the best roadfood restaurant in Utah. It is a clean, well-run café with a powerful concern for the mental as well as gastronomical well-being of its customers. There is a sign on every table that requests "No playing of the jukebox between 12 and 2 or 6 and 8." During these hours, Hughes plays soothing dinner music as an aid to digestion. But the most pleasant aspect of the Hughes service is the waitresses. They are older ladies who are very much concerned with making patrons happy, which means not only attentive service, but almost motherly coaxing of nonregular patrons to sample Hughes' specialties.

Our waitress recommended we try the meat pie, so we began our meal with two cups of thick chicken and noodle soup, then proceeded to a meat pie and a roast pork dinner. The meat pie was filled with spicy pot-roast-like chunks of meat, a few peas, carrots, celery and spices, and the crust was tender enough to fall apart with the first touch of a fork. The roast pork dinner was comparatively bland and underseasoned, served with drab vegetables. The meat pie, made here every day, is definitely the Hughes' best meal.

We were happy to hear our waitress tell us that no meal is complete without a slice of pie, so we tried one pumpkin and one banana cream. The pumpkin was strong-tasting, dense, and slightly undersweetened. The banana was sublime, with at least as much real mashed banana as cream filling. It was sweet with its own natural flavor, gilded only slightly by a light meringue top. Since coffee in Utah is generally terrible (as frowned-on as tobacco by the Mormons), we finished the meal with two cups of hot cider, which was cinnamon-flavored and tasted of good, sweet apples. Our waitress was pleased that we had enjoyed our meal, and very politely thanked us for coming.

MONUMENT VALLEY

★MONUMENT VALLEY SEVENTH DAY ADVENTIST HOSPITAL CAFETERIA
just off Highway 163 (behind Rock Door Canyon) (801) 727–3241
DAILY: BREAKFAST, LUNCH, DINNER

The unearthly vistas of the Monument Valley landscape conjure up visions of John Ford's western films. This is known as John Ford country in Hollywood. Traveling here even today you see familiar faces, members of the same Navajo tribe who called Ford "Tatani Nez" (Tall Soldier). They are still here, and although the land is now more overrun with tourists than with the cavalry, it is still an overwhelming vista. It has a spooky otherworldliness—certainly not the kind of place you'd expect to find a comfortable café and a good meal.

In Ford's westerns, the cowboys ate pan-fried steaks that overhung the edges of the two-foot skillet. But in Monument Valley today, the closest you'll come to a cowboy steak is a moderate-sized slice of wham at the all-vegetarian cafeteria in the Seventh Day Adventist Hospital. The cafeteria is really a fine place to stop before or after a visit to the Valley north and west of Mexican Hat. It is in a tiny hospital with only a few beds, serving both the native residents of Monument Valley and tourists who stay too long in the sun.

"When you've had one of my Navajo tacos," says Laura Moore, "you've had a meal!" It may be one of the cheapest meals in the Southwest, and one of the most unusual in this meat-crazed part of the country. Laura Moore runs the Hospital Cafeteria for patients and travelers, with an eye on the pocketbook and a way with that most difficult of cuisines—health food. The taco is a disc of freshly made Navajo fry bread, topped with a vegetarian chili of pinto beans, soy protein cubes, mild spices, onions, lettuce, tomatoes, and cheese. Other choices on the menu were entrées of nut meat loaf, cottage cheese loaf, or a maritime patty. The maritime patty was apparently some sort of artificial fish substance, so we passed it up and sampled the nut meat loaf instead. It came in a small slice, and was so dense that it had to be eaten in tiny increments, morsel by morsel. There was also a chef's salad, with wham replacing ham and turkey, and good-quality cheeses and fresh greens. There are good desserts—freshly made fruit cobblers and cakes sliced into demure squares.

The view from the small hospital cafeteria is of a Rock Door Canyon mesa, and although the food is often too self-consciously healthful in its whamism and maritime patties, there is nothing hospital-like about it. Laura Moore is a delightful person, and a visit to the cafeteria here is an inexpensive and peculiar meal in the midst of an awesome land.

RICHFIELD

★★ LITTLE WONDER CAFÉ
101 Main Street (801) 896–4428
MON–SAT 6:30 AM–4 PM / CLOSED SUN

When we first sat down in the Little Wonder Café we heard the waitress scolding Deon Torgeson, her boss, about his pies. "They fall apart, Deon. We can't hardly cut the boysenberry because by the time we get it onto the plate, the crust is all broken. It looks terrible!"

"Don't worry," Deon said. "Send the complaints to me." The waitress came to take our order and told us that the special of the day was meat pie with potatoes, vegetable, and soup. We ordered two specials and two pieces of the maligned boysenberry pie. The soup was what she explained as "old-fashioned Navy bean." That is, it was white beans in a tomato base. It was very thick, with small flecks of onion floating with the tender beans in the tomato stock. The meat pie was filled with large, shredded pieces of pot roast, and the potatoes alongside had absorbed much of the natural gravy, as had the carrots. It was a juicy and highly seasoned pie. The mashed potatoes were grainy and thick, covered with the same gravy used in the pie. Alongside this hearty meal came a good bakery hard roll and butter.

The pies came, just as the waitress' complaint had anticipated, broken up on the plate. They had begun as double-crusted pies, but by the time they got to us, the slices resembled deep-dish. We didn't complain. The crust had fallen apart only because it was so light, one of the flakiest we have ever seen, too flaky to hold together, but delicious when spooned up with the tiny, tart boysenberries. The coffee that came with the pies was strong and freshly brewed.

The Little Wonder is, in fact, a little wonder, notable for its seasoned, savory food in a land of prissy underflavoring. Utah's roadside cuisine tends to be either tasteless or franchised, often both. The Little Wonder is a serious-minded place—no jukebox, no smoking, no drinking. It's not open on Sundays. That is Deon Torgeson's day of rest. As for the other six days, Deon says about his cooking, "It's not easy. Everything here comes from hard work."

SALINA

★MOM'S CAFÉ
10 East Main Street (801) 529–3921
DAILY 5 AM–10 PM

The best thing about Mom's are the beautiful Western murals painted on the walls of buildings across the street. They are like workers' project art from the depression, fading visions of stylized Indians and cowboys and the Utah desert.

Inside Mom's we saw a half-dozen look-alike blonde teen-agers, and nary a "Mom" in sight. When Mom's away, the blondies play, and so order-taking and serving was inept and punctuated with blushes, giggles, and goofing around.

Why include Mom's? There *were* telltale hints of a caring hand in the kitchen. Between the blonde brigade's antics, we noted that hamburgers here are shaped from ground meat when ordered. According to the menu, the steak served here is grown, slaughtered, and aged in Salina. There are fresh trout dinners (so the menu says) and hot turkey with cream gravy and homemade dressing.

Unfortunately, except for the hamburgers, none of this was available when we stopped in Mom's. After much ado with the serving staff about nothing, we ordered a couple of burgers and a piece of pie and a doughnut to go. The burgers were first-rate; the pie, a creamy coconut, was acceptable; the doughnut had an annoying greasy film over its surface. It was not a memorable culinary experience. But the pickings in this part of the country are slim. Next time around, we'll peek in the kitchen first. If Mom is there and the staff is on good behavior, we'd give it another try.

SPANISH FORK

★MOUNTAIN VIEW CAFÉ
985 North Main (801) 798–6451
DAILY 5 AM–11:30 PM

Utah encourages the roadfooder to start counting his blessings. In this land of awesome beauty, good food seems as rare as a Mormon tavern. But there are some real blessings, like the scones at the Mountain View Café, deep fried and served with lots of butter and honey. You can get either a small scone or a "large," which is easily the largest scone we have ever seen. It looks like an entire loaf of white fruitcake, or perhaps John Wayne's English muffin. The scones at the Mountain View are served from about 5 AM until 7 PM, as a breakfast in themselves or as an accompaniment to the otherwise lackluster menu.

The teen-aged chef at Mountain View tried to convince us that he made the best steaks south of Salt Lake, describing the juicy well-marbled qualities of his "Spencer steak," that cut from God-knows-where on the cow. We opted instead for the high-priced dinner, the "T-bone," which reminded us of our youthful visits to Tad's $1.19 Steak House, where everyone else seemed to be enjoying their steaks, and we got the ones that were all gristle. The other folks who had pulled off the highway seemed to be enjoying their T-bones and Spencers, and while ours wasn't all gristle, we suspected that it might have been half hockey puck. Dessert was better—a freshly baked boysenberry pie, not too sweet, and a good chocolate cream. The chef told us he also made a terrific Swiss steak and an "Acey Special," his invention—a cheese-topped chicken-fried steak. Next time we stop in the Mountain View, we'll stick to the scones.

FAIRS AND FESTIVALS

BRIGHAM CITY
    Peach Day Celebration   /   1ST WEEKEND AFTER LABOR DAY

WASHINGTON

CHEHALIS

★★★ MARY McCRANK'S DINNER HOUSE
2923 Jackson Highway (206) 748–3662
WED–SAT 11 AM–2 PM, 5 PM–8:30 PM / SUN 12:30 PM–5 PM
CLOSED MON & TUES

Mary McCrank has lived in this home by the road for over forty years, and has been serving what she calls "wholesome family food" for all that time. She allows others to help prepare the meals "because I am trying to back down, to enjoy the rest of my years." Mary may be taking it easy, but the food she prepares bears no signs of slacking off. It is basic American cuisine, simply prepared, the kind of food that depends not on fancy flourishes or exotic preparation, but on a cook's fundamental skills.

Our dinner at Mary McCrank's began with a choice of chicken soup or chilled apricot nectar. We chose the soup, which was a thick parsleyed stock, filled with shreds of chicken, with some of the chicken fat skimmed off, but enough left in to make it rich. There are always four choices on the dinner menu. We passed up the pan-fried chicken and Swiss steak and chose chicken fricassee and grilled rainbow trout. Both came with a lettuce and tomato salad, freshly mashed potatoes, and garden green beans. The dumpling with the chicken was a masterpiece. It was aerated and light, yet rich tasting, soaked in the cream fricassee sauce. The trout was perfectly crisped, lightly seasoned with pepper and the butter and corn meal in which it had been fried, requiring just a slight squeeze from the lemon wedge to attain perfection.

Dessert was a choice of pies or ice cream, and of course we chose the pie. Mary is famous for it. A large wedge of sour cream raisin pie was fluffy, sweet, and almost whipped into a high cloud of plump raisins and cream. The chocolate angel food cake was lighter—a felicitous combination of cocoa flavor and angel food moistness.

Eating at Mary McCrank's reminded us of a visit to a mythical Irish nanny's house. The smells of the kitchen are tantalizing when you first enter. The dining room is decorated with Mary's antique plates. And her flower-frilled menu offers an Irish blessing for all those who dine here: "May God hold you in the palm of His hand."

DUVALL

★★THE SILVER SPOON CAFÉ
Main Street (Route 203) (206) 788–2734
TUES–THURS 7 AM–8:30 PM, FRI–SUN 7 AM–9:30 PM, CLOSED MON

Although Seattle is only twenty miles away, Duvall is a rustic farming community with no echoes of big city life. The Silver Spoon is a renovated grange hall circa 1900 on the only big street in town—Main Street.

The Silver Spoon has been revamped by an artsy crowd who put in stained-glass windows, multitudes of hanging plants and macramé, and staffed the place with long-skirted neo-peasant waitresses.

The prime virtue of the "Spoon" is their use of fresh vegetables, eggs, and fruits all bought from local farmers. Even cider served here is milled just a few miles away. The fresh eggs usually wind up as omelettes. They are filled with native mushrooms, grated cheeses, and various vegetables. There is a selection on the menu called "A Truckers Breakfast" consisting of three eggs, three strips of bacon, and three pancakes. The dish is well made considering its humble strivings, but it is unlikely that you will find a trucker here eating one. All the gear-jammers are at the greasy spoon down the road.

Sandwiches reflect the California influence. Avocado and bean sprouts is a favorite. Bacon, lettuce, and tomato is served in ample portions on a dill-seeded bun. Try a half pound of grilled mushrooms on the side.

Dinners are different every night. The menus rotate, offering vegetarian food one night, chicken dishes the next, French cooking the night after, and so on. The one common denominator is the use of all local products.

The Silver Spoon might be a little too self-consciously hip for some tastes. The patrons are mostly in their twenties, modishly attired in clothes found mostly on college campuses. There is a country-western band playing some weekends, but unfortunately it isn't the real McCoy; only whitenecks dressed up in their blue-collar best.

MARYSVILLE

★ THE VILLAGE CAFÉ

Ash and Third Streets (206) 659-2305
MON–THURS 5:45 AM–MIDNIGHT / FRI & SAT 5:45 AM–2 AM
SUN 5:45 AM–9 PM

The Village Café was founded forty years ago, which by Washington standards is a long time. It began as a small pie shop and sandwich stand, and today has grown to the point where the menu boasts "The original pie place making fresh pies daily since June 1937." Although it trades on its reputation, a sign announces "For pie and coffee only, sit at the counter." One look at the Formica surroundings and routine lunch menu, and we decided to take our chances with a couple of the sixteen varieties of pie at the counter.

We tried chocolate cream and banana cream, and although the meringues were a spectacular five inches high, and the crust was fresh and still flaky, both pies suffered from mass production and culinary complacency. They were good pies, but there was no bouquet, no hint of an inspired pie maker in the kitchen.

The Village has mastered the trick of turning out good pies at the expense of great ones. As in the doughnut world, "home style" here becomes a code word not for homemade, but for mass-produced. The Village does a good job of mass production. We recommend it for a pie and coffee stop, or for a hamburger in the sunny but too-sanitary Meringue Room Annex.

PORT ANGELES

★ CILE AND WALT'S CAFÉ
117 North Oak Street (206) 457-3511
MON–SAT 7 AM–4:30 PM / CLOSED SUN

Cile is most proud of an article her son clipped out of *Road and Track* magazine. It was written by a sports car driver, en route to Vancouver on a test run of a fancy new machine. He stopped at Cile and Walt's to give the high-powered sports car and himself a breather, ate a piece of Cile's wild blackberry pie, and wound up spending half of his sports car review extolling the pie!

Sweet-toothed gourmands that we are, we rushed through our soup and sandwiches to get to dessert. The pie was everything the test driver had claimed—intensely sweet blackberries enveloped between two light pie crusts, brought to perfection with a scoop of vanilla ice cream.

If only the rest of the food served at Cile and Walt's were as good. . . . It is a soup and sandwich place only. The barley soup was well-stocked with beef and barley pearls, but the chicken noodle was completely anonymous. The meat loaf sandwich was as plain as such a thing can be, as was the roast beef. Both came with a molded jello salad on the side.

When blackberries are out of season, Cile makes a pecan pie, which her son claims is "almost as good."

SOUTH MOUNT VERNON

★★ CRANE'S RESTAURANT
Old Highway 99 (206) 424-8334
ALWAYS OPEN

Crane's is a truckstop café that occupies a semicircular-shaped airplane hangar in the farm country of Washington. While the outside looks vintage World War II, the interior retains an early 1950s cast: brown linoleum floors, lots of stainless steel, and a jukebox with classic country-western hits.

Except for a few preformed and prefab items, Crane's makes a good selection of modest foods. All turkeys are roasted fresh and the smell of slowly roasting poultry is often in the air. The chicken-fried steak, an ordinarily plebeian dish, attains character at Crane's. The steak meat is cut daily, and the batter that it is dipped into is thickly-egged and filled with spiced bread crumbs.

"I come twenty miles outta my way for a bowl of clam chowder," truckdriver Herb Wittenberg told us. "And I'm from New England, where I can get it all the time." We ordered a bowl and at once understood this gearjammer's detour. The soup is chocked full of Washington State clams, with small pieces of celery and potatoes simmered in the cream-based stock. Crane's serves a great oyster stew, the oysters for which are caught fifteen miles away, in local oystering beds.

The desserts are half fresh, and half commercial. The best selection isn't listed on the menu. Deep-dish apple pie is so well known by the regular patrons that Crane's feels it unnecessary to offer it in writing. The pie is brought to the table in a deep china bowl. It is filled with native apples and awash with a butter rum sauce. The crust is rich and break-apart light.

Crane's is one of the few truckstop cafés in this area that prides itself on producing simple fare that uses the local harvests from the fields and the sea.

ZILLAH

★★ EL RANCHITO
First Avenue (509) 829–5880
DAILY 8 AM–7 PM

El Ranchito is a very authentic Mexican café that caters mostly to the Mexican laborers who work in the Yakima Valley harvesting fruit. It is part-restaurant, part-general store, and part-tortilla factory. There are canned goods and Mexican tabloids for sale, and from the back of the room there is a thick smell of tortilla flour.

A row of old school chairs is available for seating, but these seem better-suited to fourth-graders than adult taco eaters' rear ends. Most customers get their food to go, and eat in their cars or on the back bed of a pickup truck. El Ranchito is a busy place, serving the laborers, locals, and gringos from Seattle and Spokane who know it as a bargain in genuine south of the border food.

The food is dispensed by stout older women. Most is sold by the piece: tacos deluxe, burritos, enchiladas. A combination plate consists of tacos, enchiladas, and refried beans. All this food has a real Mexican taste—hot, greasy, lavish with cayenne and chili peppers. This is the way Mexicans like it. It is *not* like what you get at a taco stand in L.A. There is also a selection of Mexican pastries, from flan to chongitos, which go well with the rest of the meal. But remember that this is fruit country, and there are fresh fruit stands everywhere to sell you a perfect chaser to the hot and heavy food.

A word of warning for bacteriaphobes: this food is not untouched by human hands; nor is El Ranchito particularly clean and sanitary-looking by American standards. As we said, it's authentic south of the border food, in authentic surroundings.

FAIRS AND FESTIVALS

BALLARD
Seafood Festival / MID-SEPT

HARRAH
Sugar Beet Festival / MID-SEPT

ISSAQUAH
Salmon Days / EARLY OCT

LA CONNER
World Smelt Derby / EARLY FEB
"World's Ugliest Smelt" contest

LAKE CITY
Salmon Bar B Que / EARLY AUG

LONG BEACH
Cranberry Festival / MID-SEPT

MARYSVILLE
Strawberry Festival / MID-JUNE

OCEAN SHORES
Great International Clam Prix / SPRING

ODESSA
Deutches Festival / LATE SEPT

PATEROS
Apple Pie Jamboree / LATE JULY

TEKOA
Slippery Gulch Bar B Que / JULY 4

WYOMING

CODY

★★ THE IRMA GRILL
1192 Sheridan Avenue (307) 587-2121
MON–SAT 6:30 AM–10 PM / CLOSED SUN

The Irma Grill is the dining room in the original hotel built by Buffalo Bill Cody in 1902. Named for Cody's youngest daughter, The Irma has survived and flourished over the years, retaining its elegant western charm, and serving good food at modest prices. The dining room is decorated in the ballroom-baroque style popular in the turn-of-the-century West. There is a huge cherrywood rococo bar, a gift of Queen Victoria to Buffalo Bill.

Hot, full-course lunches at The Irma seldom cost more than $3. A typical selection starts with a bowl of thick split pea soup with ham, and follows with grilled pork sausage and beans or pork shoulder with celery dressing. Luncheons are served with hot rolls, good mashed potatoes, whole kernel corn, and a banana pudding for dessert. There is a less expensive lunch "for merchants." The only difference between this and the regular meals is the entree, which is always meat loaf.

For dinner the popular meal is heavy-cut prime rib, or any one of a selection of twenty dinners ranging from stewed spring chicken with homemade noodles up to expensive T-bones and sirloins. We loved the Wyoming turkey roasted with celery-flecked stuffing, served with cranberries. Dinner vegetables are peas, carrots, and potatoes. All dinners come with soup or marinated herring, rolls, tossed salad, and apricot cobbler for dessert.

The Irma Grill is one of the last bargains in the West, with genuinely charming artifacts of the past and an adjoining hotel restored to the way it was when it first opened in 1902. For the last seventy years the Irma has been the meeting place for Wyoming's wool growers, stockmen, and oilmen, who gather at the cherrywood bar or in the elaborate dining room. From the Victorian washbowls in the hotel rooms to the homemade noodles on the dinner plates, history stands still at The Irma.

HUDSON

★★ SVILAR'S
Highway 287 (307) 332-4516
MON–SAT: DINNER / CLOSED SUN

Svilar's has been in the five-building town of Hudson for fifty years. It is where the wealthy wheat farmers and horse breeders eat on weekends, catching up on friends and making deals over dinner. Just because the wealthy gentry eat here doesn't mean that the prices are high; in fact, the menu and atmosphere inside is as simple as a cowboy's speech. Dishes are listed simply as "chicken," "beef," or "shrimp." The only modifier is the price. Steak is expensive, as it is throughout the West. Chicken and shrimp are less. But the main course is only half the story at Svilar's. The side dishes consist of hot homemade bread served with honey and butter, a full sideboard of relishes and salads, and hot plates of homemade sarma, ravioli, and fried potatoes. Sarma is a Croatian dish of pickled cabbage stuffed with seasoned rice. It is rich and highly spiced, and lends the otherwise straightforward food at Svilar's a nice ethnic twist.

On Friday and Saturday nights the ladies from Riverton (the next town) and the few who live in tiny Hudson put on their stoles and best dresses and step out with their husbands to Svilar's to dance. The music is Lawrence Welkish, and some might find the two-stepping couples corny, but Svilar's is a warm, friendly gathering spot where the country atmosphere complements the good food.

LUSK

★SOUTH SIDE CAFÉ
junction of Routes 85 & 20 (307) 334-2941
ALWAYS OPEN

The South Side is a no-frills truckstop in cowboy country. What you read on the menu is exactly what you get, and some of the food, especially the steaks, and the "homemade" selections, is very good.

We had the thick and creamy potato soup and a cup of chili. We got both in the smallest available sizes, which would have been almost any other restaurant's "large." One main course was a rib steak—a beautiful cut of meat, cooked rare, juicy and cowboy-style chewy. It was served with a plain green salad, a chunk potato salad, and good hot rolls. Our other choice was the chicken-fried steak dinner, thickly breaded meat sided by suspiciously flaky-tasting mashed potatoes and a nice cottage cheese salad. The menu announces that "all desserts are extra," so we looked to the pie list and found that pies are homemade, and cost less if you have had dinner. Our lemon cream was underflavored but fresh; and the apple was firm and fruity, but with too thick a crust.

As at most truckstops, breakfasts are a specialty here, the top of the line being an eight-ounce round steak, two eggs, toast, and coffee. The menu says "hash browns are not included in the breakfast orders" which is just as well, since we saw them being poured out of a long-frozen bag.

Lusk is the home of the annual August Rawhide Pageant, an appropriately tough thing to celebrate in this tactiturn town. The service here, although not long on hospitality, was courteous.

ROCK SPRINGS

★★★SWEET'S CAFÉ
Route 2 (5½ miles west of town, near Husky Stop) Flaming Gorge
Exit off Interstate 80 (307) 362–3125
WED–SAT 6 PM–10 PM / CLOSED SUN–TUES

There seems to be a consensus in western Wyoming that Sweet's makes the best ribs in the state. Redneck ranchhands and newly arrived post-hippy cowboys "doing a gig on the range" unanimously sang the praises of Mrs. Sweet's Café. One bearded, booted dude, who looked like he was doing a report on the Wyoming Narc squad for *Rolling Stone,* recommended Sweet's but warned us to carry a can of Mace if we went after dark. We followed his advice, and kept a nervous finger on the trigger of our voluntary swoon reflex, ready to faint at the first sign of intimidation. The honky-tonk frame building in the middle of a few acres of house trailers did not look inviting from the outside, but once we entered and saw Mrs. Sweet and daughters Margot and Patty, and felt the warmth of their pit-cooked ribs and hospitality, we felt a little foolish for having believed the dope-induced paranoia of our counterculture friend. Sweet's is a friendly place, and the best food stop on Route 80 in Wyoming.

Mrs. Sweet has been in business here for twenty-six years, just about the time it takes to perfect a recipe for bar b que. "People think I'm from the South," she told us in what sounded like a sugary southern drawl. "I've never been South. But a Mississippi man taught me about the pit, that's for sure." There is a small house in the back of her café where she performs the rituals of cooking the meat and preparing the sauce in solitary glory. Even her daughters, who help out in the café, do not go back to the pit with her. "I do that alone," she says simply and irrevocably.

The Sweet's *prix fixe* gets you a slab of ribs, uninteresting vegetables, hot biscuits, and honey. You can eat here in the small café—where there is a jukebox for entertainment and room for about twenty-five people—or take out your dinner to eat in the car while gazing at the trailer-strewn landscape. There are also dinners of beef or chicken, but we recommend the ribs. They are what has made Sweet's famous.

Mrs. Sweet's sauce—milder, she says, than the Mississippi original —is not soon forgotten. Slather it on the ribs and you have an eating experience that is as much tactile as it is gustatory, intense enough to convince you that your fingertips have miraculously grown taste buds. It is mandatory to wear jeans or bring a roll of paper towels, because you will finish a Sweet's meal with hickory-flavored rib drippings and sauce up to your elbows. These ribs are exhilarating to eat—a battle between irresistible flavor and insatiable appetite. Whether you conquer the ribs or they you, Sweet's will long linger in your memory as an eating adventure unequaled anywhere in Wyoming.

WORLAND

★★THE RAM'S HORN
629 Big Horn, Routes 16 & 20 (307) 347–9958
OPEN 24 HOURS EXCEPT SUN 9 PM–4:30 AM

The Ram's Horn is a medium-size café on the main street of town that concentrates on simple, cheap food for its primarily local clientele. There are a few western pictures on the wall, and a portrait of the Wyoming Ram, but it's basically a simple counter-booth-table Formica eatery with atmosphere provided by a country-western jukebox. The menu is a no-nonsense affair, starting at the top with the cheapest dishes (braised sirloin tips with egg noodles, meat loaf and brown gravy, baked beans with a strip of bacon) through the medium price range (roast leg of pork and dressing, two center cut pork chops on toast, breaded veal sweetbreads on toast) to the luxury dinners of Ram's Horn Special Steak, three spring lamb chops with mint jelly and a rib steak. There are about twenty-five items altogether, including "fresh frozen" scallops and fried shrimp.

These prices are for entire dinners, including soup, vegetable or salad, bread and butter, potatoes, dessert, and coffee. We chose the grilled country sausage and apple sauce and the sweetbreads. The meal began with a thick navy bean soup, and the main courses arrived with real roughly cut French fries, and mashed potatoes with telltale flecks of real potato skin. The "bread and butter" turned out to be good bakery hard rolls. The sweetbreads were alarmingly rich—too much so in their breaded and fried state; but the country sausage was first-rate and fresh-tasting. The freshly baked raisin pie for dessert was loaded with raisins cooked to the point where they had broken open with flavor. Other choices of pie included cherry, apple, pineapple cream and chocolate, as well as several homemade puddings.

Our waitress was kept busy throughout the meal running next door to the bar, fetching customers' drinks—a peculiar Wyoming custom, having bars and restaurants next to each other, but not intermingling. She told us between trips next door that the Ram's Horn, in addition to paying special attention to its fresh meats (no portion control, except for the fish) bakes blueberry and cherry muffins for Sunday dinners.

For those interested more in New West atmosphere than in good, cheap food, there is the Washakie Hotel down the street where our waitress said she goes for dress-up dinner and cocktails. There is also a big sugar plant in town, with occasional tours; but we prefer our sweets in the form of Ram's Horn raisin pie, served around the clock, all week.

INDEX

ABOUT THE AUTHORS

JANE STERN was born and raised in New York City. MICHAEL STERN grew up in Winnetka, Illinois. Jane's mother collected clocks and played the piano and left the cooking to chefs in restaurants all over Manhattan. Michael's mother educated his taste buds with a heritage of family recipes at the home dinner table. They combined their culinary backgrounds with limitless appetites and set out across the country searching for *Roadfood*.

The Sterns are enthusiastic travelers of America's highways and back roads. When Jane was writing *Trucker: A Portrait of the Last American Cowboy*, Michael shared the sleeper bunk in the semi and took photographs. They have produced and written television documentaries and are co-authors of a number of screenplays. While they argue relentlessly about the comparative virtues of bar b qued pork and bar b qued beef, they share a love for John Ford movies, English bulldogs and luxuries they can't afford.

SEE THE OTHER WONDERFUL SIDE OF AMERICA!

AMAZING AMERICA

Here's another fine excuse to stray from the straight and narrow highway! In AMAZING AMERICA, Jane and Michael Stern describe over 600 little-known American attractions, including the world's only Frog University, a house in Massachusetts made entirely of paper, Uncle Sam's grave, a tour and feast at the Culinary Institute of America, the Edsel Museum, and the resting place of Elvis Presley's solid gold Cadillac. Over 50 black-and-white photographs complement the text. For wily wanderers or readers with lively imaginations, AMAZING AMERICA is the next best thing to traveler's checks—it's a trip in itself!

A Random House/ David Obst Book
$6.95